Atheism, Fundamentalism and the Protestant Reformation

This study of new atheism and religious fundamentalism advances two provocative – and surprising – arguments. Fraser argues that atheism and Protestant fundamentalism in Britain and America share a common historical origin in the English Reformation, and the crisis of authority inaugurated by the Reformers. This common origin generated two presuppositions crucial for both movements: a literalist understanding of Scripture, and a disruptive understanding of divine activity in nature. Through an analysis of contemporary new atheist and Protestant fundamentalist texts, Fraser shows that these presuppositions continue to structure both groups, and support a range of shared biblical, scientific, and theological beliefs. Their common origin and intellectual structure ensures that new atheism and Protestant fundamentalism – while on the surface irreconcilably opposed – share a secret sympathy with one another, yet one which leaves them unstable, inconsistent, and unsustainable.

Rev. Dr. Liam Jerrold Fraser is Church of Scotland Campus Minister at the University of Edinburgh.

Atheism, Fundamentalism and the Protestant Reformation

Uncovering the Secret Sympathy

LIAM JERROLD FRASER

University of Edinburgh

CAMBRIDGE
UNIVERSITY PRESS

CAMBRIDGE
UNIVERSITY PRESS

University Printing House, Cambridge CB2 8BS, United Kingdom

One Liberty Plaza, 20th Floor, New York, NY 10006, USA

477 Williamstown Road, Port Melbourne, VIC 3207, Australia

314–321, 3rd Floor, Plot 3, Splendor Forum, Jasola District Centre, New Delhi – 110025, India

79 Anson Road, #06–04/06, Singapore 079906

Cambridge University Press is part of the University of Cambridge.

It furthers the University's mission by disseminating knowledge in the pursuit of education, learning, and research at the highest international levels of excellence.

www.cambridge.org
Information on this title: www.cambridge.org/9781108427982
DOI: 10.1017/9781108552141

© Liam Jerrold Fraser 2018

First published 2018

Printed and bound in Great Britain by Clays Ltd, Elcograf S.p.A.

A catalogue record for this publication is available from the British Library.

Library of Congress Cataloging-in-Publication Data
NAMES: Fraser, Liam Jerrold, 1986- author.
TITLE: Atheism, fundamentalism and the Protestant Reformation : uncovering the secret sympathy / Liam Jerrold Fraser, University of Edinburgh.
DESCRIPTION: 1 [edition]. | New York : Cambridge University Press, 2018. | Includes bibliographical references and index.
IDENTIFIERS: LCCN 2018006514 | ISBN 9781108448611 (pbk.)
SUBJECTS: LCSH: Reformation. | Christianity and atheism. | Fundamentalism.
CLASSIFICATION: LCC BR305.3 .F73 2018 | DDC 270.6–dc23
LC record available at https://lccn.loc.gov/2018006514

ISBN 978-1-108-42798-2 Hardback

For Yvonne, Jerrold, Samantha, Theodore and Sebastian
amatus sum ergo sum

Contents

Acknowledgements

While researching and writing this work, I have been frequently reminded of the many debts I owe.

First and foremost, I wish to thank Nicholas Adams, David Fergusson, Iain Torrance and Graham Ward. Nick saw the originality and utility of this project when it was still in its genesis, and he provided invaluable comments on a number of early drafts. To David I owe two debts. First, he offered a number of helpful comments towards the later stages of the project that saved me from unnecessary errors. Second, David has been a great supporter ever since my undergraduate days, and it is to him that I owe many of the opportunities I have been privileged to enjoy. I am also grateful to Iain and Graham for taking the time to read my work and for their comments on an earlier instantiation of this book.

I also wish to thank the many other University of Edinburgh staff who, in different ways, played a role in this work's development. In particular, I wish to thank Zenon Bańkowski, Simon Podmore, Paul Nimmo and Sara Parvis.

This project was made possible by a generous Arts and Humanities Research Council award, which augmented my slender Church of Scotland stipend, and enabled my family and me to live comfortably during the course of my research. For the provision of these public funds I express my sincere gratitude.

For their support for this book, and for editorial and technical guidance during its production, I also wish to express my gratitude to Cambridge University Press, and especially to Beatrice Rehl and Margaret Puskar-Pasewicz.

My final note of thanks is to my family, and in particular to my wife Samantha, for all their love, care and support over the years. The path of research can be a lonely one, and Samantha had to suffer many evenings without her husband. This work stands as a testament to her forbearance.

Liam Jerrold Fraser
Holy Week 2017

Introduction

This is a story about Protestantism. It is a story about the attempt to find a new foundation for the Christian faith apart from the authority and tradition of the Roman Catholic Church, and the instabilities and contradictions that arose from it. The thesis of this work is that these tensions and contradictions gave rise – in the fullness of time – to two opposing, yet related, forms of thought: Protestant fundamentalism and new atheism.

This work began as an attempt to determine whether comparisons between fundamentalism and new atheism were cogent. Investigation revealed that these comparisons, far from being superficial, arose from deep similarities in structure between the two groups. Yet investigation also revealed that these similarities rest upon two shared presuppositions, presuppositions whose intellectual and social genealogy stretches back to the Reformation in England. In order to provide a complete answer to the question of the relation of fundamentalism to new atheism, then, it became necessary to integrate analysis of their contemporary structure with a genealogy of the presuppositions that gave rise to it. The two related questions that this work attempts to answer, therefore, are these: first, what common historical and theological root do new atheist and Protestant fundamentalist thought come from, and, second, how does this common root, and the presuppositions that arise from it, structure their thought? In answering these questions, the following argument will be advanced: that new atheist and Protestant fundamentalist thought is structured by the presupposition of a literal, univocal and perspicuous Scripture, and the presupposition that divine activity disrupts and substitutes for natural causation, beliefs that have arisen from a common historical root.

A number of commentators have made comparisons between new atheism and fundamentalism. Armstrong, Beattie, de Botton, Vernon, Cunningham, Robertson and Eagleton, *inter alia*, have all noted resemblances between the two groups.[1] Nevertheless, the existing literature on the subject of new atheism and fundamentalism suffers from three related failures. First, the majority of these remarks are made in polemical and popular works directed to attacking the social and intellectual standing of new atheism. For this reason, comparisons with fundamentalism could be rejected outright as being little more than insults. This failing is joined by a second, the occasional nature of the existing literature. Most of these comparisons are made in passing, and when more detail is given, it is generally not supported with sustained argument. These problems are compounded by a third factor, the serious neglect of atheism as a subject for theological investigation. Although the profile of atheism in the public life of Britain and America is greater than ever, and the publishing opportunities available for atheist and anti-atheist writers unparalleled, the majority of academic engagements with atheism are in the form of polemical works written by academic theologians.[2] This has two unfortunate consequences. First, it represents a failure of academic theology to fully address a serious social, political and intellectual challenge to the Church and the Christian faith, as polemical works are not suitable for the detail and depth of analysis necessary to critique the origins, structure and arguments of new atheism. As Hyman notes, the lack of serious research into the origins and structure of atheism mean that its nature and true significance are apt to be misunderstood.[3] The polemical nature of the existing theological engagement with atheism leads, second, to the impression that atheism is merely a 'popular' subject, and beneath the

---

[1] Alain De Botton, *Religion for Atheists* (London: Hamish Hamilton, 2012), 12; Mark Vernon, *After Atheism* (London: Palgrave Macmillan, 2007), 4, 7, 55–6; David Bentley Hart, *Atheist Delusions* (New Haven: Yale University Press, 2009), 4, 231–2; David Robertson, *The Dawkins Letters* (Ross-shire: Christian Focus, 2010), 78–83; Karen Armstrong, *The Case for God* (London: Vintage Books, 2010), 290; Terry Eagleton, *God, Faith, and Revolution* (New Haven: Yale University Press, 2009), 53; Conor Cunningham, *Darwin's Pious Idea* (Grand Rapids: William B. Eerdmans, 2010), xi; Tina Beattie, *The New Atheists* (London: Darton, Longman and Todd, 2007), 4; Stephen LeDrew, *The Evolution of Atheism* (Oxford: Oxford University Press, 2016), 2.

[2] E.g. Alister McGrath and Joanna Collicutt McGrath, *The Dawkins Delusion?* (London: SPCK, 2007); Keith Ward, *Why There Almost Certainly Is a God* (Oxford: Lion Books, 2008); John F. Haught, *God and the New Atheism* (Louisville: Westminster John Knox Press, 2008). Also see John Hughes ed., *The Unknown God* (Eugene: Cascade Books, 2013).

[3] Gavin Hyman, *A Short History of Atheism* (London: I. B. Tauris, 2010), ix–x.

attention of serious theologians. This is doubly unfortunate, for not only does it further stigmatise theological investigation of a prevalent intellectual, political and pastoral issue, but, as the present work shall reveal, prohibits investigation of the serious tensions and contradictions within Protestant theology which gave, and continue to give rise, to atheism.

There are, however, exceptions to this judgement. Michael Buckley's *At the Origins of Modern Atheism* began the contemporary academic study of atheism, arguing that atheism, contrary to popular opinion, did not arise from an independent, non-Christian source, but from within Christianity itself, and the natural-theological arguments advanced by the Church to defend its core doctrines.[4] The thesis of a theological origin for atheism was continued by Alan Kors in *Atheism in France 1650–1729: The Orthodox Sources of Disbelief,* which demonstrated how intra-ecclesial debates concerning natural theology and philosophy generated arguments later used by atheists.[5] A similar story was told by Turner, who in *Without God, Without Creed* charted the way in which American Christianity became assimilated to secular forms of thought, and became alienated from its own distinctive beliefs and patterns of reasoning.[6] Drawing upon the dependence thesis concerning the theological origins of atheism, yet focusing upon the doctrine of God, Gavin Hyman has recently advanced the argument that changes in late medieval theology laid the foundations for atheism by endangering God's transcendence, and re-conceptualising God's being as merely the highest among other beings.[7] Reduced to an object within the universe, it was then easy for science to reject God's existence. This 'modern' conception of God is passing away, however, and Hyman foresees a corresponding change in the nature of Western atheism. Another recent academic work that has engaged seriously with atheism, while also making connections between it and fundamentalism, is Conor Cunningham's *Darwin's Pious Idea.* Cunningham's work uncovers the agreement between ultra-Darwinists and creationists on the anti-religious import of evolution, yet argues that their shared conception of evolution is faulty, and that a correct conception of evolution by natural selection is compatible with faith.

---

[4] Michael J. Buckley, *At the Origins of Modern Atheism* (New Haven: Yale University Press, 1987).

[5] Alan C. Kors, *Atheism in France 1650–1729* (Princeton: Princeton University Press, 1990).

[6] James Turner, *Without God, Without Creed* (Baltimore: Johns Hopkins University Press, 1985).

[7] Hyman, *Short History*, 47–80.

In the last few years, two other works exploring the theological implications of unbelief have also appeared. Although not an academic work –
and hence not explicitly addressing the existing literature – Nick Spencer's
Atheists: The Origin of the Species offered a partial history of the development of British atheism from the late seventeenth century to the twentieth, and offers a number of important insights that parallel my own
conclusions.[8] Dominic Erdozain's *The Soul of Doubt* is similar to the
works listed previously in arguing for a religious origin for atheism, yet
traces this origin less to specific ideas than the inculcation of *conscience*
among European thinkers, a development that led increasing numbers of
educated people to question biblical morality, and reject the faith.[9]

The present work draws upon this earlier research by defending the
argument that atheism in Britain and America had a theological origin,
yet differs from it by proceeding with an alternative methodology, and a
different estimation of the factors involved. First, one feature of all of
these works is the relative absence of discussion concerning the importance of biblical hermeneutics. The overwhelming emphasis is on natural
theology and science, which, while of the upmost importance, cannot
fully be separated from the scriptural interpretations they were tasked
with explicating and protecting. This oversight is related to a second issue,
the relative absence of discussion concerning the Reformation and its
aftermath. While Turner undertakes discussion of Reformed theology,
its focus is more upon New England puritanism than the salient theological changes that made puritanism possible. Turner's work also suffers
from a certain diffuseness, as his – relatively short – history attempts to
outline *every* reason for American unbelief. The third difference between
this and earlier works comes in the relation of history to our contemporary context. All of the foregoing works, with the exception of Hyman's
introductory text, focus on either history or the contemporary debate, so
that the insights from one area of enquiry are not brought to bear upon
the other.

This work remedies these oversights in a number of ways. First, it
focuses on both biblical hermeneutics *and* science and natural theology,
and stresses their interrelatedness. Second, it pushes back the origins of
British and American atheism to the English Reformation. Third, it relates
the historical to the contemporary, stressing the continuities between

---

[8] Nick Spencer, *Atheists: The Origin of the Species* (London: Bloomsbury Continuum,
2014).
[9] Dominic Erdozain, *The Soul of Doubt* (Oxford: Oxford University Press, 2015).

contemporary atheism and its theological origins. The fourth – and greatest – contrast with earlier works, however, is that I argue that the same biblical and natural-theological problems that generated atheism *also* gave rise to Protestant fundamentalism, and that this common heritage gives rise to a similar intellectual structure in both groups. Central to this is the identification of two presuppositions foundational to both Protestant fundamentalism and new atheism in Britain and America: a literal, univocal, and perspicuous understanding of Scripture, and a disruptive and substitutionary account of divine activity in nature.

The method that structures this work, and makes such an extensive analysis possible, is adapted from R. G. Collingwood, and may be characterised as textual, genealogical and analytic.[10] This method minimises three potential difficulties in carrying out a work of this kind. The first potential difficulty is historical. A historical account of the origins of atheism and Protestant fundamentalism in Britain and America would require a multi-volume work, leaving little room for critical engagement with their contemporary forms. The present work does not attempt to provide a history of the origins of atheism and fundamentalism in Britain and America, but only a genealogy of two key presuppositions that structure them, and which played an important part in their genesis. It is not argued that these presuppositions exhaust all the causal factors that contributed to the development of atheism and fundamentalism. As we shall see, a wide range of intellectual and social factors were implicated. Rather, it is argued that these presuppositions played a particularly important role in their development, and continue to play an important intellectual function in their contemporary forms. Historical discussion is undertaken only to explain the origin or development of these presuppositions, or to show their effect in different time periods. The latter is of equal importance to the former, for I argue that these presuppositions have been unstable throughout history, and continually give rise to their own negation. Furthermore, the strategies used to stabilise them are equally unstable, or inadvertently contradict the presuppositions they are employed to protect.

Even when qualifications are stated, however, the genealogical approach used in this work may prove unsatisfactory to some, a dissatisfaction aroused by the wide timescale that is surveyed. Yet as Brad Gregory has recently argued, if historical investigation is confined to the

[10] See Robert G. Collingwood, *An Essay on Metaphysics* (Oxford: Clarendon Press, 1969).

life of one individual or one narrow timeframe then analysis of intellectual development and long-term trends becomes impossible. We are then robbed of important historical insights that can illuminate the present.[11] To echo Peter Harrison, while there are many ways of doing history, to the extent that they are governed by reasonable arguments and sound evidence they are worthy of our attention and serious engagement.[12]

The second difficulty that a genealogical method avoids is that of decontextualisation in the study of atheism. This approach is advanced against two groups. First are those such as Peter Gay and contemporary new atheist writers, who argue for the origins of atheism in science or secular philosophy, and who trace its history back to eighteenth-century France.[13] Second, it is advanced against writers such as David Berman and James Thrower who attempt to provide isolated histories of atheism, as if there has always been an anti-Christian tradition running independently of Christian tradition, and that the beliefs of Greek philosophers and seventeenth-century English peasants could be brought under a single category.[14] These assumptions can distort the questions we ask and the investigations we undertake, leading us to overlook national contexts, and the dominance of religion even in a reputedly religionless Enlightenment.[15]

The danger of decontextualisation is related to a third potential problem that the method adopted in this work minimises: the danger of conflating historical contingency with logical necessity. This potential difficulty has two aspects. First, in tracing the genealogy of the two presuppositions that form the primary basis of new atheist and Protestant fundamentalist thought, it is not argued that atheism or fundamentalism follow *necessarily* from Protestantism. Rather, it is argued that, under a range of contingent social, political and intellectual conditions, certain presuppositions established between the Reformation and Restoration came to play an important role in atheist and fundamentalist thought.

[11] Brad S. Gregory, The *Unintended Reformation* (Cambridge, Mass.: Belknap Press of Harvard University Press, 2012), 3–5.
[12] Peter Harrison, *The Territories of Science and Religion* (Chicago and London: Chicago University Press, 2015), 185.
[13] E.g. Peter Gay, *The Enlightenment: An Interpretation*, 2 vols. (New York: Knopf, 1966–1969).
[14] James Thrower, *Western Atheism* (Amherst: Prometheus Books, 2000); David Berman, *A History of Atheism in Britain* (London: Crook Helm, 1988).
[15] Cf. B. W. Young, *Religion and Enlightenment in Eighteenth-Century England* (Oxford: Clarendon Press, 1998), 1–2.

The second aspect of this potential difficulty relates to the 'Protestant Reformation' referred to in this work's title. The genealogical method adopted in this work does not pretend that all forms of Protestantism from the Reformation to the present day are structured by a literal, univocal and perspicuous understanding of Scripture, or a disruptive and substitutionary understanding of divine activity. All that is argued is that these presuppositions were present within a significant section of Protestant thought in Britain and America, and that, at various times, they held popular sway. Protestantism, in this regard, is wider than professional Protestant theology and encompasses a range of popular beliefs and practices. Just as the Lord left a remnant in Israel during the days of Elijah that did not bend the knee to Baal, so there has always been a remnant – sometimes greater, sometimes weaker – that refused to give these presuppositions the honour others thought due to them.

While the method adopted in this work minimises a number of potential difficulties, there remains the question of how to define atheism and fundamentalism themselves, and the related question of which texts to examine. We can find an avenue into this question by considering Stephen Bullivant's views in the *Oxford Handbook on Atheism*. As Bullivant says, 'The precise definition of atheism is both a vexed and vexatious question' and 'Atheism simply possesses no single, objective, definition.'[16] In spite of these observations, Bullivant comes to adopt a working definition of atheism as the absence of belief in God or gods, as well as ruling out other conceptions that would posit a dependence of atheism upon religion:

Certainly, there is some truth to this claim ... But the fact that prevailing theisms condition the focus and expression of certain kinds of atheism, does not mean that either they or atheism in general have no wider referent.[17]

Bullivant's views stand in contrast to those of Buckley:

Atheism is essentially parasitic ... atheism depends upon theism for its vocabulary, for its meaning, and for the hypothesis it rejects.[18]

We have here two different conceptions of atheism: the simple absence of belief in God or gods, or a parasitic movement that is dependent upon the religion it rejects. It is instructive to recall that these competing conceptions are advanced by a sociologist and an historian respectively. If we

[16] Stephen Bullivant, 'Defining "Atheism"', in *The Oxford Handbook of Atheism*, ed. Stephen Bullivant and Michael Ruse (Oxford: Oxford University Press, 2013), 11, 12.
[17] Bullivant, 'Defining "Atheism"', 18.   [18] Buckley, *Origins*, 15.

bracket historical considerations, and look only at the current intellectual and social manifestations of atheism, Bullivant's definition is plausible. Atheists have their own physical and online communities, their own particular worldview, and they engage in a range of social practices that mark them out from others. In this sense, they are as substantial and 'positive' as any other group. Yet when one comes to ask *why* they hold the beliefs they do, looking not only to their current social form but examining their historical origins, one very quickly comes to realise that Buckley's dependence thesis is more plausible. As we shall see, at every turn, atheism and anti-Christian thought in Britain and America have been dependent for their motivation, methods, arguments, vocabulary, categories and social and political form upon the Christianity they reject. In spite of this, Bullivant's definition is helpful when we turn to the present-day context, for it encourages us not to seek a theological explanation for atheist or anti-Christian beliefs too readily. For that reason, I attempt to assess atheist arguments on their own terms, paying close attention to the self-understanding of the texts surveyed.

While this work advances a dependence model of atheism in general, there remains a more specific issue regarding the definition of *new* atheism. In spite of the wide use of the phrase, and the multitude of works seeking to defend or attack it, Zenk has urged scholars to refrain from use of the term:

By using the label 'New Atheism', several individuals are subsumed under one unifying concept, thereby implying a uniform phenomenon ... there is simply no programme or manifesto of 'New Atheism' and there is no all-embracing organization, in which all, or even most, of the so-labelled persons are united.[19]

Zenk's approach to atheism is similar to Bullivant's, yet takes a negative form. Like Bullivant, Zenk is concerned to find a positive definition for atheism, yet, failing to find such a definition, he urges scholars to refrain from using a term that suggests that such a definition exists. Yet the existence of a spate of popular anti-Christian texts, written in English since the early years of the new millennium, is a fact, as is the labelling of these texts as 'new atheist'. While Zenk claims to find 'more differences than similarities' in these texts, as we shall see, the textual evidence to the contrary is so great that it is difficult to see how Zenk can hold this view.[20]

---

[19] Thomas Zenk, 'New Atheism', in *The Oxford Handbook of Atheism*, ed. Stephen Bullivant and Michael Ruse (Oxford: Oxford University Press, 2013), 255.
[20] Zenk, 'New Atheism', 255.

Nevertheless, Zenk presents a helpful warning for scholars not to see connections where there are none. In particular, he reminds us that not all new atheist writers claim to be atheists. For the purposes of this work, however, this observation is not particularly important. First, the results of the genealogical method adopted in this work make it clear that British and American atheism – as a historically contingent and theologically dependent phenomenon – possess a fluid nature, sometimes resembling an extreme form of Protestantism while at other times resembling something that stands over and against Protestantism, and, indeed, Christianity itself. This is not a failing of scholarship, but the scholarly recognition of what is a complex social and intellectual phenomenon. Second, I do not seek to address the issue of whether new atheist texts are truly 'atheist' or not, but only whether the range of texts called 'new atheist' have similarities with Protestant fundamentalist texts, and, if so, why this is the case. For this reason, the selection of texts is not dependent upon them meeting a certain definition of 'atheist' but upon the far more modest criterion of being popular anti-Christian works written in English since the millennium. The only addendum to this criterion is that occasional reference will be made to earlier texts by new atheist authors such as Richard Dawkins, or, less commonly, other texts that have been particularly influential on new atheist writers. Such works can help illuminate the current phenomenon of new atheism.

Analogous difficulties, however, attend the definition of 'fundamentalist'. Recent decades have witnessed a great expansion in the quantity of literature on fundamentalism, and a corresponding increase in the range of phenomena labelled as such. This trend reached its climax in *The Fundamentalism Project* of Martin Marty and Scott Appleby, which examined fundamentalism as a global phenomenon, encompassing a range of diverse religions, practices and beliefs.[21] The use of the word 'fundamentalist' is, however, deeply problematic, as there is no agreement on its definition.[22] As Partridge and Ruthven note, in practice, it is sometimes little more than a term of abuse, used by culturally dominant groups within Western society to label other groups they view as socially

---

[21] Martin E. Marty and R. Scott Appleby, eds., *The Fundamentalism Project* (Chicago: Chicago University Press, 1993–1995).

[22] Kathleen C. Boone, *The Bible Tells Them So* (Albany: State University of New York, 1989), 7–8.

undesirable.[23] It is a 'receptacle for socially undesirable qualities,' an 'intolerant epithet for those we regard as intolerant ... a label that immediately delegitimates'.[24] The difficulties are particularly great when the term is used to describe communities and social phenomena very different from the conservative evangelical culture in which it originated. While factors such as exclusivity, foundationalism and antipathy to the core narratives of other groups serve as useful criteria for the application of the term, it is better to speak of *fundamentalisms* rather than *fundamentalism*, and any researcher must be attentive to the particular historical and social context of the phenomena they are studying.[25]

The current work navigates these difficulties in two ways. First, it examines the form of fundamentalism that gave its name to all others: conservative Protestantism. Importantly, the use of the word 'fundamentalist' was first used by members of this group to describe their own beliefs and was not meant pejoratively. For this reason, it is a *native* term, and not imposed upon the material in an arbitrary manner. Second, this study deploys the term in a very specific way. There are two methods that one might adopt when investigating the relation between Protestant fundamentalist and new atheist thought. The most common would be to begin with a set of criteria for 'fundamentalism', and then compare each form of thought with it to discern whether they are, or are not, 'fundamentalist'. Alternatively, one might compare new atheist and Protestant fundamentalist texts, and consider their similarities. It is the latter method that is adopted in this work. In doing so, much of the difficulty in defining and limiting the term 'fundamentalism' is avoided, and the discussion is given a textual specificity that militates against abstraction and generality.

Nevertheless, while the term 'fundamentalist' is native to conservative Protestantism, there are many different kinds of conservative Protestantism, and reference to every work by conservative Protestants would be unfeasible. For this reason, the majority of Protestant fundamentalist texts examined are from the Reformed tradition, including those strands

---

[23] Christopher H. Partridge, 'Introduction' in *Fundamentalisms* (Carlisle: Paternoster, 2001), xiv; Malise Ruthven, *Fundamentalism: The Search for Meaning* (Oxford: Oxford University Press, 2004), 6–7.

[24] Sara Savage, 'A Psychology of Fundamentalism', in *Fundamentalism: Church and Society*, edited by Martyn Percy and Ian Jones (London: SPCK, 2002), 31; Mark Juergensmeyer, 'The Debate over Hindutva', *Religion* 26, no. 2 (1996): 130.

[25] Harriet A. Harris 'How Helpful is the Term "Fundamentalist"?', in *Fundamentalisms*, ed. Christopher H. Partridge (Carlisle: Paternoster, 2001), 14–16; Partridge, 'Introduction', xvi.

of the Baptist tradition that have been most influenced by Reformed theology. In this way, Pentecostal texts – which may also conceivably be called 'fundamentalist' – have not been examined. Even with this limitation, however, the range of possible texts for examination would still be too great. For the purposes of this work, therefore, investigation has been limited to English-language works produced since the late 1960s – when the seminal *Genesis Flood* was produced – with particular attention directed towards texts that oppose evolution. The reason for a focus upon evolution is threefold. First, it is the issue of evolution around which fundamentalist opposition to contemporary social and intellectual norms has crystallised. Second, it is upon the issue of evolution that the similarities and differences between new atheists and Protestant fundamentalists become most clear. Third, it is the debate between atheists and fundamentalists over the issue of evolution that has received most attention from commentators. A focus upon this issue therefore allows engagement with an existing corpus of literature.

Focus upon Protestant fundamentalist texts that oppose evolution, however, raises two further issues that require comment. First, it might be objected that the focus of this work should not be upon Protestant fundamentalism but *six-day creationism*. While understandable, this argument is misguided for historical, logical and social reasons. Historically, six-day creationism does not have an independent genealogy from Protestant fundamentalism. For a work employing a genealogical method, this is a decisive consideration. The argument also fails on logical grounds. Six-day creationism is unintelligible without a belief in scriptural inerrancy and a preference for a literal, univocal and perspicuous understanding of the biblical text. It is dependent upon such Protestant fundamentalist beliefs for its existence. Lastly, the argument fails for social reasons. Creationists do not form a separate community from other Protestant fundamentalists. There are not, for example, special six-day creationist churches that only preach on six-day creationist themes. The illusion that six-day creationism is a separate intellectual and social phenomenon is created by the existence of Protestant fundamentalist ministries established to demonstrate the scientific accuracy of a literal reading of Genesis 1–3. Notwithstanding, there is a second issue concerning the choice of anti-evolutionary works. Occasional reference is made in what follows to the work of intelligent design theorist Philip E. Johnson. While there are important differences between six-day creationism and intelligent design theory, the more conservative and philosophical of intelligent design theorists – like Johnson – share almost exactly the same philosophy of science as six-day creationists do, and there is now an increasing cross-pollination occurring between the two, with creationists adopting many arguments that first arose with Johnson. Occasional reference to intelligent design theory can therefore be used to illuminate certain features of Protestant fundamentalist thought.

With these methodological considerations complete, we turn now to the structure of the following work. It is divided into five chapters, with Chapters 1–3 tracing the genealogy and historic effects of the key presuppositions of new atheist and Protestant fundamentalist thought. Chapters 4 and 5 then examine the way in which these presuppositions continue to structure each form of thought, and the problems that attend them.

Chapter 1 examines how the English Reformation and its aftermath generated presuppositions and oppositions that gave rise to the first anti-Christian forms of thought in British history. By assaulting the authority and tradition of the Roman Catholic Church with the principles *of sola scriptura* and *sola fide*, the reformers set in motion a crisis of authority, a dialectic within Protestant thought that would see the polemical weaponry wielded by Protestants against their theological adversaries being used, in turn, to undermine the position of the Church of England. This crisis of authority resulted in a proliferation of heterodox and anti-Christian sects during the Civil War. The Restoration Church, seeking to inhibit the caustic effects of *sola scriptura* and *sola fide*, adopted a robust literalism, yet one grounded in reason rather than theological tradition. This strategy reached its apogee in the philosophy of John Locke, who manifested and furthered the philosophical and theological trends of his time. Unfortunately, this strategy backfired, giving rise to the first freethinkers, who, looking to Scripture alone, and adopting the new robust literalism, questioned the authority of Scripture. The growth of freethought was temporarily averted, however, by the promotion of natural theology, which wed theology to the burgeoning sciences, and made a disruptive and substitutionary understanding of divine activity in nature a vital component of cosmology, physics and biology. Yet this had the effect of making divine activity one cause among others, so that the customary distinction between primary and secondary causation – and the related notion of general concurrence – became largely redundant in relation to the question of origins, as well as certain aspects of preservation. At the end of these developments, the presuppositions foundational to new atheist and Protestant fundamentalist had crystallised: a literal, univocal and perspicuous understanding of Scripture, and a belief that divine activity in nature substituted for or disrupted natural causation.

Chapter 2 charts the way in which these presuppositions were placed under increasing strain in late eighteenth- and nineteenth-century British society, before inverting themselves and coming to be held negatively, thereby giving rise to anti-Christian and atheist forms of thought. The rise of evangelicalism brought large numbers of poor, uneducated Britons into the practice of unaided Bible reading for the first time, with the majority joining nonconformist churches. Yet, having rejected theological tradition to a greater extent than Anglicans, nonconformists lacked the theological apparatus needed to harmonise apparent inaccuracies and contradictions within Scripture. When such contradictions and inaccuracies were found, the result was sometimes the abandonment of faith, and the adoption of a militant atheism that mirrored the literalism and anti-Establishment ideology of the dissenting denominations. Whereas natural theology had previously provided an alternative justification for faith, the discoveries of geology and biology, added to existing forms of literalism, did irreparable damage to the hermeneutical and natural-theological synthesis established at the Restoration, thereby claiming an increasing number of middle- and upper-class Anglicans for agnosticism and atheism. While these groups may have lost their faith, however, they retained many of its presuppositions regarding Scripture, divine activity, and the capacity of science to help or harm faith, presuppositions that would be later be transmitted to new atheist thought.

Chapter 3 turns to the genealogy of Protestant fundamentalism, and how the presuppositions of a literal, univocal and perspicuous Scripture and the disruptive and substitutionary nature of divine activity were given new emphases through the adoption of Scottish Common Sense philosophy by American theologians. While the philosophy of Thomas Reid arose as a reaction against the development of Locke's philosophy by David Hume, Reid actually *strengthened* the connection between knowledge with immediate consciousness, thereby reinforcing a tendency already found within Locke. This gave rise to an inductive method in theology and the sciences known as 'Baconianism', which rejected hypotheses and theories in the construction of knowledge. When radicalised by war and unprecedented social upheaval, this ideology would enable large numbers of Americans to view evolution and biblical criticism as unscientific, irrational and socially pernicious. These developments resulted in a breach between conservative evangelicals and contemporary thought, thereby laying the foundations for contemporary Protestant fundamentalism.

Chapter 4 brings us to the present day and uncovers the secret sympathy that exists between new atheist and Protestant fundamentalist thought. While, at first sight, it appears that these forms of thought are utterly unrelated, analysis reveals that they share the same intellectual and social structure, one that arises from their inheritance of the presuppositions of a literal, univocal and perspicuous Scripture, and the belief that divine activity in nature disrupts and substitutes for natural causation. These presuppositions give rise to a common conception of Scripture and biblical hermeneutics, the belief that evolution disproves faith, the rejection of postmodernity and a dismissive attitude towards non-fundamentalist Christians. These beliefs, and the presuppositions that ground them, arise from each group's shared theological and historical roots in Protestantism, a Protestantism that, in the face of scientific advances and social change, has now broken apart into two opposing forms, opposing forms that, paradoxically, share the same structure, and are mutually reinforcing.

Chapter 5 completes the work and argues that the presuppositions that structure new atheist and Protestant fundamentalist thought are intrinsically unstable. The beliefs and strategies used to stabilise them, moreover, contradict their foundational presuppositions, rendering each form of thought self-contradictory. The chapter concludes with a recapitulation of the genealogy of Chapters 1–3, and its integration with the analysis of Chapter 4.

In course of advancing its primary argument, this work reaches a number of important conclusions regarding atheism, fundamentalism and the structure of Protestant thought in Britain and America, conclusions that call for new kinds of theological and historical enquiry. First, it will be demonstrated that, while lacking detail, popular comparisons between new atheists and Protestant fundamentalists are cogent. Second, it will be shown that atheism in Britain and America grew out of problems within Protestantism. This discovery undermines a range of academic and new atheist authors who see no such connection, or who vehemently deny any historical dependence of atheism upon Christianity. Third, it will be shown that Protestant fundamentalism was itself a response to the same train of problems that gave rise to atheism. Fourth, it will be shown that new atheism is not an areligious movement but an atheological one, which finds it necessary to engage in the task of theology in order to reject the existence of God and the truth of the Christian faith. Fifth, this study casts doubt on the self-understanding of both Protestant fundamentalism and new atheism. It shows that Protestant fundamentalism is not properly biblical, nor new atheism scientific, and that both are heavily indebted to presuppositions that neither can properly justify, and which render both self-contradictory.

In addition to these substantive contributions to scholarship, the diagnosis of problems and tensions within Protestant – and in particular Reformed – theology in Britain and America makes the study programmatic, and provides a basis for future academic study. First, it highlights a number of areas which ecclesiastical historians should examine further in order to understand the genesis of atheism. Second, it raises awareness of areas of Protestant theology that stand in need of repair by systematic theologians, especially when these continue to inform contemporary thought. The need for such work is pressing, and it is the hope of this work that, if nothing else, further research will be carried out to diagnose and repair the theological problems that engender atheism, and which continue to structure much of the Church's practice and proclamation.

With these introductory remarks complete, we begin our story.

I

The Unfinished Reformation

This chapter examines the development of two presuppositions that would come to structure new atheist and Protestant fundamentalist thought and the role they played in generating the first anti-Christian writings in British history: a literal, univocal and perspicuous understanding of Scripture and the belief that divine activity disrupts, and substitutes for, natural causation.

In order to undermine the authority of the Roman Catholic Church, the Reformers established a series of oppositions between Scripture and Church, literal and non-literal readings of Scripture's text and personal and institutional faith. Yet these oppositions set in train a crisis of authority, a dialectic within Protestant thought that would see the polemical weaponry wielded by Protestants against Roman Catholics being used, in turn, to undermine the position of the Church of England. The political and theological weapons forged – often in haste – to defend against this assault gave rise, in turn, to yet more attacks. By attending to the tensions present within English Protestantism, and the hermeneutical and natural-theological strategies adopted to overcome them, we can understand why many came to abandon the faith of their ancestors, and why English Protestantism could only preserve itself in this first phase by adopting principles contrary to the spirit of the Reformation that founded it.

There are two potential misunderstandings that are necessary to address before we begin. First, throughout this chapter, we do wrong if we attempt to discern, at each juncture, whether or not a specific claim or argument is 'really' atheistic. Apart from the danger of anachronism, this is to miss the true significance of the developments surveyed. For the true significance of these developments is that beliefs, contrasts and lines of reasoning which, under certain conditions, are Christian and theological, come, under changed conditions, to be atheistic and anti-theological. This method of analysis is supple enough to accommodate the continuities and discontinuities between Protestantism and atheism, and patient enough to trace the complex genealogy that converted arguments against the Roman Catholic Church into arguments against Christianity itself. Second, it is not argued that the causes of atheism arising from the Reformation were purely intellectual, and can be reduced to the two presuppositions we are investigating. Rather, it is argued that a series of intellectual, political and social changes ushered in by the English Reformation gave rise to the two presuppositions we are examining, and that these presuppositions played an important role in the genesis of anti-Christian thought. This is particularly important for the second of our presuppositions. It is not argued that the Reformation, in itself, changed theological understandings of divine agency in any decisive way. Rather, the social and political instability created by Reformation, and conflict between competing Christian and anti-Christian groups, gave rise to an apologetic use of science, and a correspondingly close identification between divine activity and natural causation that would, in time, provide the intellectual conditions for atheism.

REFORMATION TO REVOLUTION

It is sometimes difficult for us to understand that texts have not always been read in the way that we now read them. When we read a text, we typically read it in its plain sense, each word referring to distinct ideas or objects and nothing else. This has not, however, always been the case. The medieval world understood words and their significance in a very different way. This conception of language played a definitive role in the religious life of the time, and it is only by uncovering something of this intellectual world – now lost to us – that we can understand why the Reformers and their immediate successors adopted the hermeneutical strategies they did.

The medieval world was a world of objects, words and ideas, related to each other by sympathies of appearance, sound and function. Animals, flowers, insects and trees represented moral attributes, divine lessons and medicinal cures. Gold was not simply a metal but a cipher for the divine, the incorruptibility of soul and the perfected character. All transitory things exceeded their particularity and participated in a wider reference of meaning. Objects functioned as signs, and signs signifying objects could, through spiritual insight, come to signify not only their primary reference but other things in sympathy to that reference.

Such an approach towards meaning informed everything from popular bestiaries to biblical hermeneutics. In the study of the Bible, it found expression in the four senses of Scripture: the literal, the allegorical, the moral (or tropological) and the anagogical. These senses were summarised in a rhyme of John Cassian:

> The letter shows us what God and our fathers did;
> The allegory shows us where our faith is hid;
> The moral meaning gives us rules for daily life;
> The anagogy shows us where we end our strife.[1]

The literal sense, while holding prominence as the only sense that could determine doctrine, was nevertheless balanced by a number of other senses. The purpose of the moral and anagogic senses was to present meanings that were relevant to the needs, concerns and hopes of the present day, while the allegorical sense united the disparate texts of Scripture in a wider sympathy. Words symbolised things, and things signified divine truths.[2] Noah's flood symbolised baptism; the Ark, the Church of Christ; the snake in the wilderness, the Cross; the parable of the fig tree, the fate of faith without works. It should not be thought, however, that the allegory of medieval exegesis was an interpretive free-for-all. On the surface, the multitude of spiritual and allegorical readings might appear to be divergent or opposed. Yet this was only the natural impression of the natural man. If these readings were directed towards demonstrating the presence of Jesus Christ in the text, they were taken to be convergent and edifying, differing voices within the polyphony of the sacred Word. To discern this convergent, spiritual and Christocentric unity beyond the literal sense was to be converted to Jesus Christ himself; to have one's eyes opened, and one's mind illuminated, as the disciples on the Emmaus road.[3] In such an interpretive framework, passages that seemed contrary to common sense or conventional morality could be

---

[1] Cited in Steven E. Ozment, *The Age of Reform 1250–1550* (New Haven and London: Yale University Press, 1980), 66.

[2] Christopher Ocker, 'Scholastic Interpretation of the Bible', in *A History of Biblical Interpretation*, vol. II, eds. Alan J. Hauser and Duane Frederick Watson (Grand Rapids: William B. Eerdmans, 2009), 263–5.

[3] Henri de Lubac, *Medieval Exegesis*, vol. I, trans. M. Sebanc (Grand Rapids: William B. Eerdmans, 1998), 16–17, 31–2; Henri de Lubac, *Medieval Exegesis*, vol. III, trans. E. M. Macierowski (Grand Rapids, MI: William B. Eerdmans, 1999), 124–5.

harmonised by spiritualising their meaning within the ultimate meaning of Christ's Incarnation, Atonement, Resurrection and Ascension, thereby escaping contradiction or moral opprobrium.

This hermeneutical procedure was paralleled by an approach towards potentially conflicting authorities. The dicta of Aristotle, Scripture and the Fathers and Doctors of the Church would be stated, clarified and harmonised, thus repairing a potential rent in the great chain of meaning. The assumed unity of authorities meant that Scripture could not be isolated from the views of Popes, Councils, Church Fathers or ancient philosophers, and this had an effect on the manner in which Scripture was transmitted and presented. The Bible, as we know it today, was alien to the great majority of medieval people, and was transmitted only in excerpts during the Mass, or surrounded by a great cloud of interpretation and tradition in the *Glossa Ordinaria*.[4] To read Scripture, therefore, was to read it alongside the great Christian thinkers of the past, and to hear it was to hear it embedded in the sacraments and offices of a Church that held the keys to the Kingdom of Heaven.

This relative harmony between Church and Scripture, and literal and non-literal readings of Scripture's text, came under increasing strain in the late middle ages. The hermeneutical procedures used to harmonise texts and authorities were first undermined by Nominalist philosophy, which typically related words not to things but to ideas. This had the effect of doing damage to the capacity of words to signify more than one thing, and of objects to signify other objects, ideas and moral lessons.[5] This development was accompanied by a growing questioning of the function of authorities in intellectual life. Commentators began to supplement their treatment of a text with personal statements of blame or praise, pointing to a new sense of equanimity between the judgment of commentators and authoritative figures.[6] This new critical attitude towards authorities and texts developed into humanism, a literary and philological movement that was accompanied by a new desire to 'look behind' the glosses of previous generations and go *ad fontes*, back to the textual sources themselves in

[4] Cf. Peter Harrison, *The Bible, Protestantism, and the Rise of Natural Science* (Cambridge: Cambridge University Press, 1998), 93.

[5] Michael Allen Gillespie, *The Theological Origins of Modernity* (Chicago: University of Chicago Press, 2008), 19–43.

[6] Gillian R. Evans, *Problems of Authority in the Reformation Debates* (Cambridge: Cambridge University Press, 1992), 82–3.

their unadorned truth.[7] These literary and philological changes had theo-logical consequences. While there is ongoing debate in the literature concerning the nature and timing of the 'reformation breakthrough' of justification by faith, it is now generally recognised that Luther's change of heart only came after many years of intellectual development. While soteriology was a vital component in Luther's development, this must be balanced by new methods of interpretation that he developed through his lectures on the Psalms.[8] The students who girded themselves to brave the early-morning cold of Wittenberg may have expected a traditional expli-cation of the Psalms from their new doctor of divinity. Yet they were met not with a host of authorities but a naked text, with wide, white margins, making it possible for students to write their own glosses on the text. The excitement and intense spirituality of this new engagement with God's promises in the Scriptures appear throughout Luther's early works and are epitomised in his outburst during his later controversy with Erasmus, 'Let's blow up the tropes and glosses of men and simply accept the words of God!'[9] As Harrison puts matters:

By extricating the original biblical text from what had become its natural setting – a thousand-old tradition of gloss and commentary – Luther not only made possible novel ways of reading scripture, but also to the first step in distinguishing the authority of scripture from the tradition of the Church.[10]

This innovation marked an important juncture in the development of the Reformation principle of *sola scriptura*.

Matters in Wittenberg and the German Lands soon deteriorated, how-ever, and what began as the mere possibility of opposition between Scripture and the Church soon became a new social and political reality, making the choice between one or the other a live dilemma for many Europeans. In the polemical exchanges that followed the Wittenberg reformation, the Reformers alleged that the Church was distorting the meaning of scriptural passages to secure its authority, a strategy strengthened by the limitations it imposed on lay Bible reading.[11] Whatever the truth of these allegations, in the absence of the Roman

---

[7] Erika Rummel, 'The Renaissance Humanists', in *A History of Biblical Interpretation*, vol. II, eds. Allen J. Hauser and Duane Frederick Watson (Grand Rapids: William B. Eerdmans, 2009), 280–1, 294.

[8] See, e.g., Alister McGrath, *The Intellectual Origins of the European Reformation* (London: Blackwell, 2004), 159–66.

[9] Cited in Evans, *Problems of Authority*, 84–5.   [10] Harrison, *Protestantism*, 93.

[11] Evans, *Problems of Authority*, 75–6.

Catholic Church, which had witnessed to the authority of Scripture, and had supplied normative interpretations of biblical texts, the Reformers had to find new criteria to prove the authority of Scripture, and new hermeneutical procedures for producing their own authoritative readings of its text. John Calvin, for example, rejected the notion that Scripture's authority depended on the judgment of the Church, and he sought to ground its authority upon a variety of other factors.[12] Arguments for the veracity of Scripture, present in patristic and medieval works, were now employed for the new function of justifying the independence of Scripture from the authority of the Church. Among the factors appealed to were the admirable arrangement of Scripture's contents, the power of its truth, the witness of the martyrs, the internal harmony of the Gospel accounts, the miracles accompanying the calling of the apostles and the simplicity of its text.[13] It was the last of these criteria that was vital, for if the biblical text were not sufficiently simple, authority would come to reside once more in a specialist class of clerical interpreters. Luther and Calvin, following trends within humanism, attempted to avert this possibility through a new emphasis upon the literal sense, and the supposed perspicuity of Scripture. Perspicuity was crucial to Luther's programme, for, without it, biblical authority would be meaningless, and the need for the tradition and Magisterium of the Roman Catholic Church would remain. The perspicuity of Scripture was so great for Luther that he argued that even a heathen could determine its meaning, a line of reasoning that, as we shall see, would have unforeseen consequences.[14] The perspicuity of Scripture was closely linked with a new emphasis upon the literal sense, and a reconfiguration of its relation to the three non-literal senses. Calvin saw much of the spiritual interpretation of patristic and medieval exegesis as an expression of human pride, and a cover for disobeying the clear and univocal teaching of the Holy Spirit.[15] His emphasis was upon the clarity and simplicity of Scripture's teaching, with an accompanying

---

[12] John Calvin, *Institutes of the Christian Religion*, trans. Henry Beveridge (Peabody: Hendrickson, 2008), I.7.1.

[13] Calvin, *Institutes*, I.8.1–I.8.13.

[14] Mark D. Thompson, 'Biblical Interpretation in the Works of Martin Luther', in *A History of Biblical Interpretation*, vol. II, eds. Allen J. Hauser and Duane Frederick Watson (Grand Rapids: William B. Eerdmans, 2009), 303–4.

[15] R. Ward Holder, *John Calvin and the Grounding of Interpretation* (Leiden: Brill, 2006), 128–9.

dislike for strained or tortuous readings.[16] This meant that a correct reading of Scripture became identified with its plain, or literal sense, which was taken to be the sense intended by the author.[17] The Reformers did not, however, intend the abandonment of all non-literal exegesis. Both Luther and Calvin retained typology, and elements of the older spiritual tradition that saw Christ as the ultimate sense of Scripture, particularly in Old Testament passages where the literal sense would seem to make no reference to him.[18] Yet what *was* new was the collapse of these figurative and typological senses into the literal, and the association of the Roman Catholic exegetical tradition with arbitrary speculation, and the subversion of the plain sense of Scripture.[19] While, in the short term, these bibliological and hermeneutical changes created a plausible superstructure to support the new faith, they would, in the long term, have unforeseen, and devastating consequences. Scripture's self-authentication through miracles and internal harmony, the reduction of the fourfold sense into the literal and a belief that Scripture's sense was open to all – including the nonreligious – created new oppositions between Church and Scripture, and literal and non-literal interpretations of Scripture's text. While these oppositions justified the Reformation and undermining the Roman Catholic Church, they would, in turn, come to undermine Protestantism itself.

These oppositions were accompanied by another, which developed from Luther's reconceptualisation of the medieval *ordo salutis*. Luther's objection to the soteriological model of the medieval Church was not primarily intellectual but pastoral and existential.[20] In monastic life as an observant Augustinian, Luther was unable to attain certainty through the penitential cycle that his contrition and faith were genuine, and he felt terrorised by a God whose righteousness was turned towards unrepentant

[16] David C. Steinmetz, 'John Calvin as an Interpreter of the Bible', in *Calvin and the Bible*, ed. Donald K. McKim (Cambridge: Cambridge University Press, 2006), 285; Holder, *Grounding of Interpretation*, 131.
[17] Barbara Pitkin, 'John Calvin and the Interpretation of the Bible', in *A History of Biblical Interpretation*, vol. II, eds. Allen J. Hauser and Duane Frederick Watson (Grand Rapids: William B. Eerdmans, 2009), 354 and 356.
[18] See, e.g., Thompson, 'Martin Luther', 308–9; Martin Luther, 'Preface to the Old Testament' and 'How Christians Should Regard Moses', in *Martin Luther's Basic Theological Writings*, ed. Timothy F. Lull (Minneapolis: Fortress Press, 1989), 118–34, 135–48; Calvin, *Institutes*, I.13.10, II.9.1.
[19] Harrison, *Protestantism*, 113–15.
[20] Heiko A. Oberman, *Luther: Man between God and the Devil* (New Haven and London: Yale University Press, 1988), 151.

sinners.[21] As a priest, he had also witnessed the abuses to which the penitential cycle was subject to, as, in practice, individuals were often taught to believe that their actions could induce God's favour.[22]

Luther overturned this *ordo salutis* in favour of the primacy of the Word.[23] The Word is located in the commandments and promises of Scripture, which are proclaimed to the individual.[24] The commandants of the law drive us to despair of ourselves, so that we do not trust in ourselves but in God.[25] The faith that justifies is thus not a new, inner work of the individual, but a response of trust to the promises of God.[26] The faith and trust of the individual in the promises of God results in a mystical union with the Person of Christ, something that cannot be effected by works.[27] Just as husband and wife cling to one another and are one flesh, all that belongs to Christ is imputed to us.[28] Thus we are righteous, even as we remain sinners, *simul iustus et peccator*.[29] The status of the individual as simultaneously both righteous and sinful undermined a penitential cycle whose purpose was the ordering of the transition from sinfulness into righteousness.[30] Moreover, as justification was brought about by the union of Christ with the human heart effected by the Word, the Church lost its monopoly on the means of grace. This idea – which would come to be known as *sola fide* – created the potential for a new opposition between personal and institutional faith, an opposition that would have a destabilising influence upon the Reformation churches.[31]

It would be over a decade before the Reformation came to affect Henry VIII's ecclesiastical policy, yet the foundations of English Protestantism had already been laid by William Tyndale. After failing to receive patronage for a translation of the New Testament, Tyndale had left England to work on the continent. It was at Worms in 1526 that the first edition of his translation of the New Testament was published, and copies of the work began to be smuggled into England soon after. In addition to

[21] Bernard M. G. Reardon, *Religious Thought in the Reformation* (London: Longman, 1995), 46.
[22] Reardon, *Religious Thought*, 61.
[23] Oswald Bayer, 'Martin Luther', in *The Reformation Theologians*, ed. Carter Lindberg (Oxford: Blackwell, 2002), 52.
[24] Martin Luther, 'The Freedom of a Christian', in *Martin Luther's Basic Theological Writings*, ed. Timothy F. Lull (Minneapolis: Fortress Press, 1989), 600.
[25] Luther, 'Freedom', 600–601.
[26] Euan K. Cameron, *The European Reformation* (Oxford: Clarendon Press, 1991), 119.
[27] Luther, 'Freedom', 598.   [28] Luther, 'Freedom', 601.   [29] Luther, 'Freedom', 598.
[30] Cameron, *Reformation*, 132.   [31] Cameron, *Reformation*, 111.

arguing for vernacular translations, Tyndale, following Luther, accused the Roman Catholic Church of locking up the true meaning of Scripture in allegory, for 'The Scripture hath but one sense, which is the literal sense. And the literal sense is the root and ground of all.' While not denying that Scripture sometimes uses images and metaphors to convey meaning, 'that which the proverbs, similitude, riddle or allegory signifieth, is ever the literal sense'.[32] Even where non-literal readings are admitted, then, they are *univocal*, possessed of *one* meaning. The controversy generated by Tyndale's translation, and his popularisation of Lutheran views, prompted England's Lord Chancellor, Thomas More, to begin a series of attacks upon him, beginning with *A Dialogue Concerning Heresies*. Following Augustine and Roman Catholic tradition, More argued that 'the fayth of the chyrche is the worke of god as well as the scrypture, and therefore as well to be byleaved. And that the fayth and the scrypture well vnderstandin be neuer contrary.'[33] The Holy Spirit resides in the Church, so that the Church cannot err. How would we know that the Scriptures were divine if not for its testimony?[34] Scripture itself tells us that some are appointed to teach and others to learn, for the mysteries of the faith are 'a thyng yet requyreth good helpe and long tyme and an hole mynde gyuen gretely thereto'.[35] If scholars spend years of their lives working over a few verses of Scripture:

Then far more vnable must he nedys be, that boldely wyll vpon the fyrst redyng bycase he knowth the wordys, take vpon hym therfore to teche other men the sentence with parell of his owne soule and other mennys to, by the bryngynge men into madde wayes, setys, and heresyes.[36]

According to More, Scripture is such that a poor and lowly man, with the aid of the Fathers and the Church, may tred its waters without fear, while a proud and haughty man will charge in and be drowned.[37] More warns that Tyndale's efforts will result in the uneducated treating Scripture as they might treat a ballad of Robin Hood, altering and distorting it to suit their vulgar purposes, so that that all honour and reverence for it will be lost.[38]

---

[32] William Tyndale, *The Obediéce of a Christen Man* (Norwood: Walter J. Johnson, 1977), Section CXXX.

[33] Thomas More, *Complete Works of St Thomas More*, vol. VI, eds. Thomas M. C. Lawler, Germain Marc'hadour and Richard Marius (New Haven: Yale University Press, 1981), 153.

[34] More, *Complete Works*, vol. VI, 179–81.   [35] More, *Complete Works*, vol. VI, 334.

[36] More, *Complete Works*, vol. VI, 335.   [37] More, *Complete Works*, vol. VI, 152.

[38] More, *Complete Works*, vol. VI, 152.

Tyndale responded to More by arguing that the canon of Scripture is not secured by the authority of the Church but by the miracles accompanying its texts and the teaching of their authors, as well as the assent of all the Christian world.[39] Far from preserving and guaranteeing the truth of Scripture, the Roman Catholic Church, aided by the pagan philosophy of Aristotle, has distorted it with glosses and allegorical readings so that no one can understand it.[40] If taught the fundamental truths of the faith, Scripture is plain and easy to understand.[41] It is Holy Scripture, and not the Church, that mediates saving truth to the Christian. Tyndale can claim this because of his new understanding of faith, adopted from Luther. Tyndale distinguishes *historical* from *feeling* faith. The former is faith based on the testimony of others, while the latter is that which is taught by God himself through the immediate action of the Spirit. Only feeling faith is true faith, for 'If I have none other fealynge in my faith then because a man so saith, then is my faith faithlesse and fruitlesse.'[42] Feeling faith is a living awareness of God's love through acceptance of the promises of God in Scripture, when our sins are forgiven, and we are born again. It is this faith, and not the teaching or sacraments of the Roman Catholic Church, that is the basis of Christ's true Church, and it is only this true Church that is infallible.[43] God has, from time immemorial, preserved this Church from error, first by teaching the Patriarchs directly from his own mouth, and then, as society developed in complexity, by giving the people Scriptures, which exhaust all that he would teach us concerning salvation.[44] The Roman Catholic Church, however, by ignoring the Scriptures and the need for living faith, has become a fortress of superstition and unbelief.[45]

More had a keen appreciation of the basis of Tyndale's theology, and responded in his *Confutation of Tyndale's Answer* with an attack upon the certainty that Tyndale believed he had found in Scripture, and in the experience of saving faith. Against the trustworthiness of the biblical text, More cites the errors of writers, scribes and printers, while against the supposed clarity of Scripture – the basis for the Reformers' promotion of vernacular translations – More reasserts the difficulty of many of its

---

[39] William Tyndale, *An Answere Vnto Sir Thomas Mores Dialoge*, eds. Anne M. O'Donnell and Jared Wicks (Washington, DC: Catholic University of America Press, 2000), 135–137.

[40] E.g., Tyndale, *An Answere*, 10, 25, 49, 139.   [41] Cf. Tyndale, *An Answere*, 96.

[42] Tyndale, *An Answere*, 48–52.   [43] Tyndale, *An Answere*, 28–9.

[44] Tyndale, *An Answere*, 24–8.   [45] Tyndale, *An Answere*, 69–70.

passages.[46] More also posed two unanswerable questions to Tyndale: how does Tyndale *know* that Scripture alone suffices for one's salvation, and contains all necessary elements of the faith? Does it tell us so? And if Scripture *could* be shown to contain all necessary truths, does Scripture also tell us whether Tyndale has accurately understood them?[47] In this way, More sought to demonstrate that, apart from the tradition and authority of the Church, there can be no religious certainty, for Scripture is *never* self-authenticating, and *never* self-interpreting.

We have not dwelt on the exchange of Tyndale and More to illustrate the early reception of Reformation in England but for two less obvious reasons. First, we see in this exchange the conflict brought about by the new Protestant oppositions between Church and Scripture, literal and non-literal, and personal and institutional faith. Yet second, and more importantly, we see in More and Tyndale – rather unexpectedly – the arguments against the authority of Scripture and the Church that would, within a hundred years, come to be advanced by the enemies of the Church of England and orthodox Christianity, enemies who accepted the Protestant oppositions between Church and Scripture, literal and non-literal, and individual and institution, yet used them against the Protestant faith itself.

Before that time, however, the new understanding of Scripture and personal conversion promoted by Tyndale began to gain supporters, among them Thomas Cranmer. While Cranmer, like Erasmus, had taken Scripture seriously prior to his conversion, it was not until he had been convinced of justification by faith alone that he appreciated the need for a new understanding of the Church and its sacramental practice.[48] It would now be Scripture in its plain and literal sense, and not the Church, that would mediate God's saving grace.[49] Although the Crown would persecute those who expressed the new faith openly, it was not long before Henry VIII's personal circumstances favoured the promotion of the evangelical party, and a partial implementation of its goals. Chief among his reforms was the placing of a vernacular Bible in every parish church in the land, so that the people themselves could read or hear, in their own

---

[46] Thomas More, *Complete Works of St Thomas More*, vol. VIII, eds. Louis A. Schister, Richard Marius and James P. Lusardi (New Haven: Yale University Press, 1973), 335, 331, 337.

[47] More, *Complete Works*, vol. VIII, 158, 337.

[48] Diarmaid MacCulloch, *Thomas Cranmer* (New Haven: Yale University Press, 1996), 32–3, 209–11.

[49] McCulloch, *Cranmer*, 114.

tongue, the justifying righteousness of Christ, and reject the penitential cycle of the Roman Catholic Church as unscriptural and superstitious. The justification for this innovation was Scripture's supposed clarity, a clarity that came from the intention of their authors and not the interpretive traditions of the Church. As Cranmer framed it in his preface to the second edition of the Great Bible:

The apostles and prophets wrote their books so that their special intent and purpose might be understanded (*sic*) and perceived by every reader.[50]

The personal caprice that ushered in these reforms, however, soon made further progress impossible, and Henry's ecclesiastical policies changed repeatedly throughout his reign. The uncertainty, frustration and hope of this time gave rise to the new phenomenon of lay conventicles, sometimes drawing on regional Lollard traditions.[51] Men and women would gather, often at night, to hear the reading of Scripture, pray together and discuss the religious questions of the day. Although such conventicles were not explicitly separatist, they were implicitly so, as they took place outside the services of the Church of England, and some were soon infiltrated by anti-Trinitarian and Baptist beliefs.[52] In addition to conventicles, the responses of parishioners to the new vernacular translations varied. While some warmed to the new faith, in London in particular, there were alarming incidents. Parishioners would cite the Bible to embarrass or harangue their priests, even disputing with them over theological matters for sport.[53] Such incidents greatly concerned Henry and his advisors, and laws were brought in to control dissent. Towards the end of his reign, this resulted in attempts to curb the lay Bible reading he had first promoted. The reading of Scripture was limited to the nobility and to those who would not be impertinent enough to challenge Henry's Reformation by references to Scripture.[54]

The death of Henry and the accession of Mary saw the establishment of a pattern that would be repeated time and again, as the repression of dissenting views was followed by growing radicalism. Mary wasted little time in restoring Catholicism and using the full force of the state against Protestantism. Hundreds of Protestant clergy and laymen were forced to

---

[50] Quoted in Harrison, *Protestantism*, 114.
[51] Joseph W. Martin, *Religious Radicals in Tudor England* (London: Hambleden Press, 1989), 18–24.
[52] Martin, *Religious Radicals*, 30.   [53] Martin, *Religious Radials*, 72.
[54] Martin, *Religious Radicals*, 71–2.

flee to the continent, forming conventicles wherever they settled. These exiled Protestant communities launched a flurry of polemical attacks against the restored Roman Catholic establishment in England, and these attacks saw the beginning of a new strain of English anti-clerical literature, such as William Turner's *The Huntyng and Fyndyng Out of the Romish Foxe*. Such works would provide a precedent for attacking the English Episcopacy and its teaching at a later time.[55]

The accession of Elizabeth brought the restoration of Protestantism, but her reign was accompanied by a new phenomenon: the spectre of atheism. What was unusual about this threat, however, was that, in spite of dozens of anti-atheist works appearing from the mid-sixteenth century onwards, no contemporary atheist texts had been published, and there had been no public avowals of atheism.[56] The panic over atheism culminated in a wide-ranging investigation into Christopher Marlowe and his associates, with the state gathering intelligence on a supposed network of atheists, sceptics and scoffers occupying the upper ranks of society. While this episode could be taken as an early example of atheism, atheism at this time did not have the narrower meaning it has today, and could cover a multitude of sins, such as an immoral lifestyle or the denial of providence, as well as an explicit disavowal of the existence of God.[57] As we shall see, we miss the significance of the changes taking place in English intellectual life if we attach too much importance to these occasional instances of apparent atheism. Developments of far greater significance for the future of atheism would make such examples look trivial.

Whatever the nature of the sixteenth century atheism scare, the development that posed the greatest danger to Elizabeth and the reconstituted Church of England was not atheism but sectarian division. The carefully-managed Elizabethan settlement satisfied almost no one, and the re-established Protestant Church of England faced opposition from both extreme Protestants and the remaining Roman Catholic community.[58] It is at this time that the principle of *sola scriptura*, and the contrast between scriptural and Church authority upon which the Church of England was founded, began to undermine the Church's authority, with dissidents

---

[55] William Turner, *The Huntyng and Fyndyng Out of the Romish Foxe* (Bonn, 1843); cf. Reventlow, *Authority*, 109–10.

[56] See Michael Hunter, 'The Problem of "Atheism" in Early Modern England', *Transactions of the Royal Historical Society* 35 (1985): 137–8.

[57] Hunter, 'Problem of "Atheism"', 138–40.

[58] Peter White 'The Via Media in the Early Stuart Church', in *Reformation to Revolution*, ed. Margo Todd (London: Routledge, 1995), 80–1.

making use of Scripture to challenge the supposedly unscriptural practices of the Church. The extreme Protestant party was frustrated by the retaining of 'unscriptural' vestments, choirs and crosses in the established church as well as the 'popish liturgy' of the Book of Common Prayer. This dissent arose due to different understandings of *sola scriptura*. The hierarchy of the established church understood it as a *negative* rule, meaning that only practices which Scripture condemned should be proscribed, while the extreme Protestant party, known from this time as 'puritans', read Scripture as a positive rule, meaning that practices that were not explicitly approved by Scripture could have no place within the Church.[59] The result was that conventicles continued to grow, becoming more separatist as the century drew to a close.[60] For now, however, nothing more could be done. The Church maintained control through civil magistrates and church courts, enforcing the *status quo* through law. The moderate divinity of the time is exemplified in Thomas Hooker, whose *Laws of Ecclesiastical Polity* would come to influence the unique position of the Anglican Church. Against the more extreme puritans who, due to their emphasis upon unmediated Scripture reading, believed that they no longer required the tradition and theological apparatus of the Church to arrive at truth, Hooker stressed the need for careful discursive enquiry, enquiry that should be structured by theological tradition and scholastic categories, and which, like all human efforts, was liable to error, and required periodic revision.[61] For Hooker, the unaided Bible reading of puritans was the beginning of the end for the Church, for when one is alone with one's Bible, enwrapped in a purely personal relation to Christ, one can believe the Spirit to condone almost anything, and what begins as earnest piety ends in antinomianism, or worse.[62]

Yet Hooker's defence of elements of older Roman Catholic theology and practice was problematic. His use of scholastic method, and his plea for the Church to be allowed to direct the reading of Scripture, provided useful polemical material for the Roman Catholic enemies of the Church of England. The English Jesuit Edward Knott seized upon Hooker's plea for guided Bible reading, arguing in his *Mercy and Truth, or Charity Mayntayned* for the necessity of the Roman Catholic Church's

---

[59] Reventlow, *Authority*, 116.   [60] Martin, *Religious Radicals*, 37.
[61] Egil Grislis, 'The Hermeneutical Problem in Hooker', in *Studies in Richard Hooker*, ed. W. Speed Hill (Cleveland: Case Western Reserve University, 1971), 174–5, 179.
[62] Grislis, 'Hermeneutical Problem', 196.

teaching office.[63] A reply came from the ex-Catholic William Chillingworth, in a work that, more than any other, laid the foundations for the strange convergence of Anglican and freethinking thought in the next generation, *The Religion of Protestants*.

Chillingworth argued in this work that the authority of the Roman Catholic Church was preserved by two abuses of Scripture. The first was forcing individuals to surrender their judgement over whether or not Roman Catholic doctrine is justified by Scripture.[64] The second was that, when Scripture was allowed to speak, its words were bound with a spurious tradition of interpretation. In this, the Roman Catholic Church contradicts itself, for it cannot assert Scripture to be normative while denying this normativity with hermeneutical and theological traditions that are contrary to Scripture and reason alike.[65] Either Scripture is sovereign or it is not. In the absence of shared doctrine, the only criterion available that can secure the authority of Scripture, and can form the basis for unity amongst Christians and the conversion of atheists, is *reason*.[66] It is reason that witnesses to Scripture's truth, and reason that discloses its meaning. Chillingworth asserts that whoever considers 'the Divine matter, the excellent precepts, the glorious premises contained in it, may be confirmed in their faith of the Scripture's divine authority.' This unity is possible because Scripture's meaning is, in its essentials, clear and open to all, and those things that are not clear no one is required to believe.[67] If Roman Catholics reply that Protestants have no way of knowing whether their interpretations of these texts are correct, it must be remembered that those who heard Christ and his apostles had no guarantee as to whether their interpretations of this teaching were correct either. *No one* can claim the gift of infallible interpretation, whether Catholic or Protestant.[68] What we *can* agree on, however, is that Scripture is normatively binding on all Christians, a belief that gives rise to Chillingworth's infamous boast, 'The BIBLE, I say, the BIBLE only, is the religion of Protestants!'[69]

Chillingworth's thought confirms the view that, in the absence of doctrinal agreement between Protestants and Catholics, reason slowly

[63] Edward Knott, *Mercy and Truth, or Charity Mayntayned* (Saint-Omer, 1634).
[64] William Chillingworth, *The Religion of Protestants a Sure Way to Salvation* (London: Henry G. Bohn, 1846), 92.
[65] Chillingworth, *Religion of Protestants*, 92–3.
[66] Chillingworth, *Religion of Protestants*, 107, 151.
[67] Chillingworth, *Religion of Protestants*, 93, 129.
[68] Chillingworth, *Religion of Protestants*, 148.
[69] Chillingworth, *Religion of Protestants*, 463.

became the sole surviving criterion for ascertaining religious truth.[70] In Chillingworth, we see all of the ideas that will be most generative for the coming generation: the rejection of tradition, with the Bible as the sole basis of religious truth; the verification of the canon and content of Scripture by reason; the necessity for free enquiry of Scripture's contents; necessary truths as clear and accessible to all; and the impossibility of infallible interpretation. Hooker foresaw the danger facing English Protestantism, and he attempted to integrate Scripture, reason and tradition to produce common criteria for establishing doctrine. Yet his appeal owed more to Catholicism than the intellectual heritage of Tyndale, for whom a theological framework for the reading of Scripture was deemed unnecessary. In such a context, the principles of *sola scriptura* and *sola fide*, forged by the Reformers, would soon turn upon the Church of England itself. Everything More feared was about to come true.

THE CIVIL WAR

The logical consequences of *sola scriptura* and *sola fide*, and the attacks upon Scripture and Church authority advanced by Protestants and Roman Catholics, had, until this point, been averted by the controlling power of the Crown. When individuals and groups tried to popularise radical ideas, or introduce religious reforms, they were met with censorship, imprisonment and exile.[71] With the dawn of the Civil War, however, this quickly changed. The chaos of war permitted the growth of a multitude of theological parties, and necessitated a new strategy for securing religious certainty. This would see a new limitation upon the principles *sola scriptura* and *sola fide*, and increased emphasis upon the literal, univocal and perspicuous meaning of Scripture's text.

It is commonly assumed that, prior to the Enlightenment, Europe was a continent of pious, God-fearing people. Yet recent studies have shown how occurrences of blasphemy and outright unbelief were not uncommon in medieval Europe, including England itself.[72] For this reason, it is doubtful whether England had ever been a nation of earnest Christians.[73] The majority of medieval people had only the rudiments of the faith, and

---

[70] Richard H. Popkin, *The History of Scepticism from Erasmus to Spinoza* (Berkeley: University of California Press, 1979), 4.

[71] Cf. Gregory, *Unintended Reformation*, 369–370.

[72] See John Arnold, *Belief and Unbelief in Medieval Europe* (London: Hodder Arnold, 2005), 216–230.

[73] Collinson, *Protestants*, 190–2.

would not have conceived of their religion as a series of propositions to be believed but a series of practices to be undertaken. Because the Mass and the other sacraments of the Church were always the same, no matter the priest administering them, there was little reason for groups to set up conventicles wholly separate from the Church. Yet, at the Reformation, the very concept of religion changed. A new emphasis upon the Word and the preached sermon meant that there were now two differentiating factors between clergy. First, the *content* of the sermon varied with the opinions and prejudices of the speaker. Second, the *manner* in which they preached varied, being either engaging or dull, scholarly or 'homely'. While the parish system, and the relative isolation of communities, kept the majority tied to their local church, there was, then, the logical possibility that individuals might harken to another preacher closer to their own doctrinal position, or who engaged them in a special way. An emphasis on the Word also had implications for the congregation, who now, as individuals, were called upon to give their assent to a host of doctrines. Protestant thought required every person to understand that their personal salvation depended upon faith alone, without recourse to works or the sacramental machinery of the Church.[74] Each person had to be taught to understand the Scriptures, and to search for God's will therein. The result was that poor, uneducated people were, for the first time, asked to confirm the preaching of their priests, and the teaching of the new Protestant Church of England.

Yet disquieting news was emerging. When, in the first decade of the seventeenth century, Josias Nicholls of Kent introduced a system of catechesis for his four hundred parishioners prior to communion, he found that scarcely one in ten were familiar with the basic tenets of the Protestant faith, and that the religion of the majority consisted in 'meaning well' and not hurting others, experiences shared by many other divines. The situation in parishes without clergy can be supposed to have been much worse, absenteeism and the crippling poverty of many livings leaving significant parts of the country without the ordinances of religion.[75] While clerics often preached to near empty churches, the alehouses were always full, with many Easter communicants stumbling in drunk to fulfil their religious duty, before stumbling off again to resume their drinking.[76] While religious ignorance and indifference may have been the state of many, within fifty years of the Reformation in England,

---

[74] Cf. Ozment, *Age of Reform*, 437–8.   [75] Collinson, *Protestants*, 199–202.
[76] Collinsion, *Protestants*, 203–7, 212–14.

there was already sporadic mockery of Scripture, as people, for the first time, read and heard the book that was the supposed basis of all true religion. As Hobbes put it, 'Every man, nay, every boy and wench, that could read English thought they spoke with God Almighty.'[77] Familiarity with the Lord soon bred contempt. Some thought it ludicrous that God would punish our ancestors with death for stealing an apple, others mocking the notion that a single man such as Samson could demolish Dagon's entire temple.[78] With the new emphasis upon Scripture and its literal interpretation, cut free from tradition and the liturgy, it was harder to reinterpret difficult or seemingly irrational passages through allegory. Bibles were publically mocked as being unworthy of the glory of God, being filled as they were with immoral, ludicrous stories, and replete with inconsistencies and obscurities that made it a waste of time for anyone to read them. This contempt even led to Bibles being burned.[79] Whereas, under Roman Catholicism, Bibles were relatively scarce, and the focus of religion was sacramental, now, in a Protestant age, Bibles were readily available, and religion was largely propositional. Anyone who could read could form their own judgement on matters of doctrine, and draw a group of like-minded people to himself. The breakdown of order during the Civil War made it easier for such persons to popularise their views, and originality and heterodoxy was one way of pulling a crowd.[80] For the first time, people had a degree of freedom in deciding what to believe, and what preacher, if any, they would listen to.

It was not only lay Bible reading, however, that led to the rejection of orthodoxy during the Civil War. Another source of irreligion was the principle of *sola fide*. We have seen in Tyndale the potential of inward piety to annul the necessity of an institutional church and its sacraments. For a time, this impulse, directed against the Roman Catholic Church, was generative for the Protestant faith. Yet the chaos of the Civil War allowed individuals to follow the latent anti-institutionalisation of this piety towards the rejection of the Church of England, the Bible and the priesthood. This exaggerated personal faith was a composite of rationalism and mysticism. While these two streams would soon part, at this stage, they converged to negate orthodox Christianity, castigating it for

[77] Cited in David S. Katz, *God's Last Words* (New Haven and London: Yale University Press, 2004), 40.
[78] Christopher Hill, *The English Bible and the Seventeenth-Century Revolution* (London: Allen Lane, 1993), 225.
[79] Hill, *English Bible*, 232–3.   [80] Hill, *English Bible*, 19.

its superstitious attachment to 'externals' like ritual, Scripture and the sacraments.[81] This may at first seem paradoxical, yet it arose from the subjective structure of the new Protestant faith. Because Christ and the Spirit could, by a possibility already implicit within *sola fide*, come to be located solely within the individual, it implied that authority also resided in individual people, who were free to believe and follow wherever the Spirit led them, without recourse to any conventional theological framework.[82]

The most disturbing manifestation of an emphasis upon *sola fide* was the emergence of poor, itinerant preachers holding extreme heterodox views, travelling the lanes and open countryside of England, preaching to inns and villages, soldiers and farmworkers.[83] The term of approbation applied to such persons was 'ranters', who found a ready audience among the uneducated poor, who, in many cases, were already alienated from religion, especially in those areas of the country where the Church of England had only a nominal presence. The ranters frequently subscribed to an extreme antinomianism, holding any external law or written Scripture as apostasy from the Spirit, and sin as a fable invented by priests.[84] In their place they taught an immanent spiritual presence in nature and the human heart. This mysticism led to two apparently contradictory, yet united, positions. On the one hand, it could issue in a deep nature-orientated spirituality, where God could be found in all things, making Word and Sacrament redundant as sources of grace. Yet, on the other hand, this mystical tendency could result in outright materialism, God becoming indistinguishable from the ordinary material objects that populate the world.[85] If the term were not anachronistic, one might say that this was one of the first real examples of atheism in England.

We miss the true significance of these developments, however, if we only notice in them the presence of apparently atheistic claims. Their

---

[81] Cf. Reventlow, *Authority*, 166; Steven E. Ozment, *Mysticism and Dissent* (New Haven: Yale University Press, 1973), 8; A. L. Martin, *The World of the Ranters* (London: Lawrence & Wishart, 1970), 13.

[82] Cf. J. G. A. Pocock, 'Within the Margins: The Definition of Orthodoxy', in *The Margins of Orthodoxy*, ed. Roger D. Lund (Cambridge: Cambridge University Press, 1993), 41.

[83] Christopher Hill, *Some Intellectual Consequences of the English Revolution* (London: Weidenfeld & Nicholson, 1980), 76–7.

[84] Cf. J. F. McGregor, 'Seekers and Ranters', in *Radical Religion in the English Revolution*, eds. J. F. McGregor and Barry Reay (Oxford: Oxford University Press, 1984), 129–34.

[85] Martin, *Ranters*, 73–4.

importance does not lie in the specific atheistic *content* of the claims made, but what they tell us about the *theological context* they arose from. In pushing *sola fide* to one of its logical conclusions, the ranters were not deploying categories that were alien to the Protestantism of their time, but developing tendencies latent within it. The true significance of these examples of materialism and atheism lie in what they tell us about the theological strategies employed by the Protestant Church of England, and the future developments they hint at.

Such heterodoxy, of course, did not constitute the majority of English belief at the time. Yet it existed nevertheless, and without the apparatus of the state behind them, clergy – of whatever political or church position – could do nothing save preach and write, quoting Scripture and the Fathers against men and women who were quite capable of citing Scripture back at them, or questioning the authority of Bible to settle anything at all. While the Reformers had attempted to inhibit the destructive effects of *sola scriptura* by appeal to a literally-interpreted Bible, normative for all Christians, they had not considered the effects of opening the interpretation of Scripture to poor, uneducated people who, given the opportunity, would sometimes reject Scripture completely for an inner spirituality already implicit within *sola fide*, or hearken to preachers who rejected the theological framework of the established church. *Sola scriptura* and *sola fide* fulfilled their function well when they animated sober and educated people with a stake in the existing order, yet quickly came into contradiction with each other, and issued in every form of madness, when they animated those that did not share those privileges.[86] If the Church of England was to preserve itself, a new mechanism had to be found to inhibit the principles that had established it.

RESTORATION AND RESTRAINT

Since the Reformation, England had been a country where the Bible had authority to settle arguments. Yet the Civil War had shown how illusory this authority was, dependent as it was upon the machinery of church and state to decide upon, and enforce, what the Bible said. The citing of Scripture by every sect and party to support contrary positions had produced a disorientating effect on the national consciousness, and had

[86] Christopher Hill, 'Irreligion in the "Puritan" Revolution', in *Radical Religion in the English Revolution*, eds. J. F. McGregor and B. Reay (Oxford: Oxford University Press, 1984), 198–201.

shown the necessity of discovering common criteria that could secure agreement on questions of religion.[87] The Restoration Church, wishing to regain its former position through comprehension of as many parties as possible, and realising the need for something more than bare Scripture to defend orthodoxy, turned to the faculty that Chillingworth had earlier identified as the guarantor of revelation: *reason*. It would be reason, in addition to Scripture, that would provide the religious certainty England so desperately needed. Reason would yield a plain and unglossed reading of Scripture that was less exclusive and confessional, allowing for a degree of reasonable latitude in readings of its text. Reason would insulate the religious life of the nation from the dangerous extremes of Protestant enthusiasm on the one hand and Roman Catholicism on the other, rejecting both subjective revelation and Church tradition as authoritative guides to religious questions. Unfortunately, reason would show itself to be not only on the side of the Establishment but also of its enemies, and, by adopting this approach, the Anglican Church pursued a course of action that would result in short-term victory, but long-term strategic defeat.

Those clergy who first championed reason were known as *latitude men*, or *latitudinarians*.[88] Chief among them was John Tillotson, Archbishop of Canterbury. For Tillotson, Scripture's verification as revelation is made by reason alone, a faculty possessed by all.[89] Nothing should be received as revelation without good evidence, for faith is not a subjective, existential phenomenon, but a simple act of ratiocination. As Tillotson puts it, 'all Assent is grounded upon Evidence, and the strongest and clearest evidence always carries it.'[90] Reason performs two functions for Tillotson. First, it prevents individuals from holding up private revelation as authoritative, and encourages others to test its truth, thereby discouraging religious enthusiasm. Second, reason challenges the authority of the Roman Catholic Church, for if evidence alone carries the day, no one can hold authority over another's beliefs without giving reasons. No one should be forced to endorse a religion without being convinced that it is the *true* religion, and we should be suspicious of any person or church that shields their doctrines from investigation. Scripture gives the

[87] Christopher Hill, 'Freethinking and Libertinism: The Legacy of the English Revolution', in *The Margins of Orthodoxy*, ed. Roger D. Lund (Cambridge: Cambridge University Press, 1993), 63.

[88] Cf. Simon Patrick, *A Brief Account of the New Sect of Latitude-Men* (London, 1662).

[89] John Tillotson, *A Sermon Preached at White-Hall* (London, 1679), 6–13.

[90] Tillotson, *A Sermon*, 13.

individual freedom of conscience, and no Pope or council may usurp it.[91] In a brief remark prescient of future developments, Tillotson even claims that we have proof against transubstantiation by virtue of our sense knowledge.[92] We see here, apparently undeterred by the Civil War, the popular Protestant belief in perspicuity and the self-interpretation of Scripture. If individuals are afforded freedom of conscience and access to Scripture, they will naturally become moderate Protestants, for the substantials of religion, with a little gentle guidance, are so clearly presented there as to be obvious and self-evident to all. Needless to say, the correct interpretation of Scripture for Tillotson is the literal, rejecting the 'over-laboured and far-fetched' allegorical glosses of the past.[93]

Yet this positive account of freedom of conscience and personal interpretation is held in tension with a series of warnings over the necessity of submitting, in the majority of cases, to the teaching of the Church. Tillotson adopts what appears to the modern reader as a strange *non sequitur*: since God has given us the privilege of private judgment in matters of religion, we ought to submit to the spiritual rulers and guardians that God has appointed.[94] Indeed, while a measure of reason has been given to all, many lack the capacity to engage in theological investigation, and such people should submit to the judgement of those whose theological and biblical training makes them experts.[95] Even if we do not understand mysteries of the faith such the Trinity, it is rational to have implicit faith in all that Scripture reveals, even if we do not fully understand it.[96] Likewise, it is not unreasonable to believe in mysteries that are incomprehensible to reason.[97] Tellingly, Tillotson suggests that such submission is necessary, because the only alternative is schism, and insurmountable religious conflict.[98]

We see a number of unusual conjunctions in the thought of Tillotson. The essentials of the faith are clear and open to all, yet some of these essentials are mysteries not fully revealed in Scripture; all are given reason to discern the truth of revelation and doctrine, yet everyone must submit to their priest. The theology of Tillotson stands with feet in two different

---

[91] Tillotson, *A Sermon*, 17–41.
[92] Tillotson, *A Sermon*, 14–15. The same argument forms the opening salvo of Hume's 'On Miracles'.
[93] Cited in Sullivan, *Deist Controversy*, 62.   [94] Tillotson, *A Sermon*, 39.
[95] Tillotson, *A Sermon*, 18.
[96] John Tillotson, *A Sermon Concerning the Unity of the Divine Nature and the Blessed Trinity* (London, 1693), 17–18.
[97] Tillotson, *Divine Nature and the Blessed Trinity*, 22–3.   [98] Tillotson, *A Sermon*, 39.

worlds. The first is in the noonday sun of Protestantism, with its mistrust of authority and rejection of unscriptural doctrines and practices. The second, however, stands in the twilight shadow of Catholicism, where there are truths beyond our comprehension, truths that require the mediation of the Church if they are to be understood at all.

Ideas that are opposed to each other in this way may be held, for a time, in personal union. Yet, as the tensions between them become stronger, people will seek to collapse the tension by electing for one of the conflicting poles.[99] An argument from authority was not effective in a Church founded upon the principle that Scripture alone should determine doctrine, and if Protestantism was to be stabilised, a new understanding of biblical hermeneutics had to be found. The change came in the work of the man who, more than any other, was to influence the structure of English Protestantism for the next hundred years: John Locke.

Locke was part of the latitudinarian circle that included Tillotson amongst its members, and is most famous today for his *Essay Concerning Human Understanding*, which is usually read as a purely philosophical text. Yet this was not how it was read during his lifetime. In denying the presence of innate ideas in the mind, Locke was accused of undermining Christianity, Calvinism holding that the human mind had been given a degree of natural knowledge concerning God.[100] It was a common complaint that Locke's declarations of orthodoxy simply did not follow from his ideas, but were at best wishful thinking or, even worse, purposefully deceptive, a fig-leaf for the insidious, atheistic nature of his thought.[101] In reality, Locke's faith was sincere, if unorthodox. Yet his critics were correct in viewing his philosophy as holding a polemical intent. The essay was a result of Locke's attempt to find religious certainty after the disorientating effects of Reformation and revolution.[102] Like his latitudinarian contemporaries, his intention was to limit the destructive tendencies of *sola fide* and *sola scriptura*, and his method for accomplishing this was empiricism, and an accompanying philosophy of language.

The basis of knowledge – and hence certainty – for Locke is experience. Experience is composed of the sensations we receive from our senses – from which we derive simple ideas – and reflection, which observes the

[99] Sullivan, *Deist Controversy*, 248.
[100] Allan P. F. Sell, *John Locke and the Eighteenth-Century Divines* (Cardiff: University of Wales Press, 1997), 16–61; cf. Calvin, *Institutes*, I.3.
[101] E.g. Sell, *John Locke*, 20.
[102] Cf. Roger Woolhouse, 'Locke's Theory of Knowledge', in *The Cambridge Companion to Locke*, ed. V. C. Chappell (Cambridge: Cambridge University Press, 1994), 166.

operations of the mind, and combines simple ideas to form complex ideas. Sensation and reflection are thus the two 'Fountains of knowledge' from which we should draw our ideas.[103] The objects of knowledge for Locke are, importantly, not objects themselves, but our *ideas* of these objects, a distinction that will later prove decisive for the development of Protestant fundamentalism.[104] As the objects of knowledge are ideas, is it vital that these ideas are clear and distinct rather than obscure and confused. Yet our attempt to make our ideas clear and distinct is hindered by tradition, Church authority, and obscurantist scholarship, which affect both our association of ideas and the language we use to express them. From an early age, we are taught to associate many unworthy or confusing ideas with the idea of God, or are taught that authority, or even infallibility, reside in certain persons or institutions.[105] When challenged on this association, we are understandably reluctant to give up the positions of a lifetime.[106] The reasoning capacities of those raised in Roman Catholic or radical Protestant homes are therefore severely diminished by their biased upbringings, and we struggle, often in vain, to free them from their errors.[107] Yet even if we are privileged enough to be raised as true Protestants, *language itself* has been corrupted by centuries of submission to the arbitrary dicta of those accorded authority. Many words currently in use do not stand for any clear and distinct idea at all, but have been introduced by philosophical and religious sects as masks to disguise their own ignorance.[108] They use such 'learned Gibberish' to confuse laymen, and to justify their own authority and dominion as learned interpreters of a specialised language.[109] Part of this obscurantism is the wilful equivocation of words, an equivocation that, for Locke, is 'plain cheat and abuse, when I make them stand sometimes for one thing, and sometimes for another'. The words of a text such as Scripture, which are perfectly plain to any man, are contorted by the learned divine, who 'makes the Words signifie either nothing at all, or what he pleases'.[110] Locke's response is to encourage his readers not to be bound by tradition or human authority, but to be bound by evidence and truth alone, and to demand clarity of thought and language, one word standing for one object alone.[111] If the authority of others was a sufficient guarantee of

---

[103] John Locke, *An Essay Concerning Human Understanding*, ed. Peter H. Nidditch (Oxford: Clarendon Press, 1979), 104–9.
[104] Cf. Locke, *Essay*, 499.   [105] Locke, *Essay*, 394–401.   [106] Locke, *Essay*, 499.
[107] Locke, *Essay*, 713.   [108] Locke, *Essay*, 490–1.   [109] Locke, *Essay*, 497.
[110] Locke, *Essay*, 496.   [111] Locke, *Essay*, 690, 698.

truth then 'Men have Reason to be Heathens in *Japan*, Mahametans in *Turkey*, Papists in *Spain*, Protestants in *England* and Lutherans in *Sweden*'[112]

Despite locating the sources of knowledge in sensation and reflection, Locke nevertheless preserves an important and unique role for revelation. In reason, God communicates to us that portion of the truth that lies within our natural capacities. Revelation, on the other hand, is natural reason enlarged by a new set of discoveries communicated directly by God, and verified through the testimony and proofs accompanying it.[113] As a result, faith, as it was for Tillotson, is an assent of the mind to evidence, and while *genuine* revelation cannot be doubted, we can doubt whether something is, *in fact*, a revelation.[114] One might suppose that this would lead Locke to examine Scripture to determine which of its teachings are true or spurious revelation. Yet he accepts the Bible in its entirety as the Word of God, appealing to the same proofs as Tyndale and the Reformers: the miracles accompanying the teaching of Christ and his apostles.[115] Locke nevertheless maintains a distinction between the existence of God – which is *according* to reason – and other truths of revelation – such as resurrection – that are *above* reason.[116] This distinction would prove generative for future freethought. Locke's belief that the existence of God was according to reason, and could be determined through experience and deduction, would also have an important influence on the growth of natural theology in Britain and America, and would contribute to an understanding of divine activity as that which disrupts and substitutes for natural causation.

While Locke accepted the authority of Scripture and the importance of natural-theological arguments, he directed critical attention towards systems of theology and confessional statements. In the anonymous *The Reasonableness of Christianity* and its following *Vindications,* Locke set out to determine what Christians should believe regarding justification. His substantive conclusions regarding soteriology need not detain us, but his views on biblical hermeneutics, and the tensions and contradictions present within them, are important for understanding the development of Protestant freethought from the 1690s. Central to Locke's thought is a reluctance to cite, or be guided by, religious authorities, desiring instead to go *ad fontes*, back to the source of faith as Luther and the

---

[112] Locke, *Essay*, 657.   [113] Locke, *Essay*, 698.   [114] Locke, *Essay*, 687, 667, 705.
[115] Locke, *Essay*, 704–5.   [116] Locke, *Essay*, 687.

Reformers did.[117] Yet while Luther and Calvin preserved a theological superstructure with which to interpret Scripture and present its teaching, Locke took *sola scriptura* to its next logical step by abandoning confessional documents and Church tradition as aids to interpretation. This was due to Locke's belief that the conflict that had devastated England during the Civil War was due to the abuse of religious authority, which compelled assent to arbitrary human confessions and systems of doctrine rather than the simple faith revealed in Scripture. With Chillingworth, Locke believed that the Bible alone was a sure way to truth.[118] As Leslie Stephen put it, in turning to the Biblical text, Locke 'resolved simply to use his eyes to see what was before him ... The meaning seemed to him so plain that he could not understand how any one could have missed it.'[119] For Locke, all that one should do is comprehend the 'plain direct meaning of the words and phrases' as they would have been used by the speakers, and not 'according to the Notions, that each one has been brought up in'. Scripture speaks to us not in the words of wise men, but 'in the plainest and most vulgar dialect that may be', so that 'children, women and the common people' may understand them.[120] Most systems of theology act '[a]s if there were no way into the Church, but through the Academy or Lyceum', and one might as well 'talk *Arabick* to a poor day labourer, as the Notions and Language that the Books and Disputes of Religion are filled with'.[121] Scripture tells us that Christ preached to the poor, and therefore the true gospel must be one intelligible by the poor.[122] It is this democratic and lay spirit in Locke that lies at the heart of what he believes the 'reasonableness' of the faith consists in, placing him within a long Protestant tradition of lay Bible reading, advocating the literal sense to thwart the authority of the clergy.[123] No one can draw up a list of fundamentals for anyone else, because Scripture as *a whole* must be believed, and – echoing Tillotson – we are not bound to believe something we do not understand, or have not

---

[117] John C. Higgens-Biddle, introduction to *The Reasonableness of Christianity*, by John Locke (Oxford: Clarendon Press, 1999), xix; Victor Nuovo, introduction to *Vindications of the Reasonableness of Christianity*, by John Locke (Oxford: Clarendon Press, 2012), xxvi.

[118] Locke, *Vindications*, 134, 174.

[119] Leslie Stephen, *History of English Thought in the Eighteenth Century*, vol. I (London: Harbinger, 1962), 79.

[120] Locke, *Reasonableness*, 6.   [121] Locke, *Reasonableness*, 170.

[122] Locke, *Reasonableness*, 169–71.   [123] Locke, *Reasonableness*, xx–xxi.

been convinced of ourselves.[124] Yet Locke goes further than Tillotson, arguing that we cannot be asked to give assent to mysteries we cannot comprehend, for no man can give his assent to something unless he has a clear conception of what he is giving assent to, an argument that Locke used to defend himself against those that demanded from him an explicit declaration of faith in the Trinity.[125] Anyone who attempts to legislate for the beliefs of others usurps the authority of Christ, wishing to become Christ's vice-regent or pope, an authority rivalling God himself.[126] While Scripture itself is infallible, then, Locke agrees with Chillingworth that there can be no infallible guide or interpreter of it.[127]

The mistrust of authority, the necessity of personal engagement with questions of faith, and the rejection of human credenda in favour of the unadulterated Word of God, all mark Locke out as a quintessentially Protestant philosopher, one who systematised the epistemology of the dominant Protestant party of his time, keeping both Roman Catholicism and enthusiasm at bay by the twin swords of Scripture and reason. Yet what is new, apart from the rejection of clerical authority still present in Tillotson, is Locke's belief, contrary to the latitudinarians, that while we must believe all genuine revelation, revelation is not *true* knowledge, for it can never match the certainty of experience. This means that if a conflict were to occur between the two, we must question whether the revelation in question is genuine.[128] The reason for this difference was that, while holding to the importance of reason over confessional positions, the latitudinarians held to traditional scholastic presuppositions regarding the nature of faith and evidence. Following Aristotle, they believed that the degree of certainty possible, and hence the evidence necessary, varied from object to object. In mathematics, where the objects of enquiry are *a priori*, a high degree of certainty is possible, and therefore a high degree of evidence is necessary. On the other hand, in theological matters, where certainty is much harder to obtain, and the objects of enquiry – God and the means of salvation – are remote from our immediate experience, *moral* certainty, based on a balance of probabilities, is all that can be expected, and such moral certainty is a form of knowledge.[129] Locke's

[124] Locke, *Vindications*, 78, 174–7.
[125] J. T. Moore, 'Locke's Analysis of Language', *Journal of the History of Ideas* 37 (1976): 712.
[126] Locke, *Vindications*, 175.   [127] Moore, 'Language', 712–3.
[128] Locke, *Essay*, 692–3.
[129] Robert E. Brown, 'Edwards, Locke and the Bible', *Journal of Religion* 79, no. 3 (1999): 365; M. Jamie Ferreira, 'Locke's "Constructive Skepticism" – A Reappraisal', *Journal of the History of Philosophy* 24, no. 2 (1986): 216–21.

empirical philosophy rejected these distinctions, and established a methodology that achieved the homogeneity of evidential standards across all objects of investigation, removing Christianity from a specialised tradition of interpretation.[130] In doing so, he carried the Protestant mistrust of authority to its next logical step, questioning the traditional – scholastic – notion that different objects require different forms of investigation. Why should we accept that some beliefs warrant less evidence, or that a text should be interpreted in a unique way, simply because the Church says so? How do we know the truth of the matter unless we look for ourselves? Due to residual cultural reverence for the Bible, however, Locke failed to direct this methodology towards Scripture itself. Yet in jettisoning the traditional preservation of theological subjects from the evidential standards applied to other fields, and dismissing the confessional and theological superstructure of the Reformation, Locke wedded the traditional Protestant emphasis upon the literal sense with methodological assumptions that would see the authority of Scripture assailed by a wave of men who were unwilling to submit to the authority of the Church of England. The measures advanced by Locke and the latitudinarians to inhibit the adverse effects of *sola scriptura* and *sola fide* went too far, and would soon bring about their own negation.

FREETHOUGHT IN A PROTESTANT KEY

Locke's philosophy would dominate English religious thought, directly or indirectly, until the late eighteenth century.[131] His empirical philosophy, and his evidential approach towards faith, both manifested and furthered the spirit of the age, filling the intellectual void left by the slow demise of scholasticism.[132] The trajectory of *sola scriptura* and *sola fide,* altered by Locke and the latitudinarians to inhibit their radical potential, moved inexorably towards the point where the authority of the individual to determine the meaning of Scripture and the fundamentals of the faith for themselves, free from tradition and Church control, became a viable possibility for the first time. Yet the spirit of the age was countered by an Established Church whose Articles affirmed the right of the Church to determine doctrine in matters of religious controversy and laws which barred substantial sections of the population from holding public office

---

[130] Sullivan, *Deist Controversy*, 53–4; cf. Locke, *Essay*, 720, where Locke places the study of God within the same discipline as the physical sciences, a necessary prerequisite for the future proliferation of natural-theological methods.

[131] Young, *Religion and Enlightenment*, 1–2.   [132] Sullivan, *Deist Controversy*, 243–4.

due to their failure to conform to its teaching and authority. It was this political and religious oppression, reasserted at the Restoration, and continued after the accession of William and Mary, that would bring about the first sustained assault of anti-orthodox opinion upon the Church of England, setting in motion a dialectic of religious and political radicalism that would eventually bear fruit in the infidel movements of the nineteenth century.

This event has come to be known as the *deist controversy*, yet the term 'deist' was not a technical term at this time, and was little more than an insult. Moreover, a number of the writers in question – for example Toland – do not even fit our modern understanding of what a deist is. For this reason, the term 'freethinker' is more appropriate, as this was a native term, used by Anthony Collins to describe those who opposed the political and religious establishment of the day on the grounds of reason.[133]

Terms of art, however, are secondary to the difficulties interpreters face when seeking to understand the motivations of the actors involved. In our day, a common distinction is made between theology and politics. This logical distinction is reinforced by institutional differences, with churches and divinity schools engaging in theological discourse, and parliaments engaging in debate over social and economic issues. This distinction was not present in the seventeenth and eighteenth centuries. Theological positions entailed political positions and vice versa. Indeed, we can make this statement stronger: theological arguments were the intellectual expression and vehicle of political movements, what political movements became when they entered into the realm of thought. While the existing literature on this period is plentiful, the difficulties in accurately mapping the unity of religion and politics in the Protestant settlement of the period generally leads commentators to overstate either the political or religious elements in the controversy, or isolate the controversy from the wider development of Protestant thought in England. Frei, for example, has produced a very useful account of the hermeneutics adopted in England at this time, but is less interested in the political and historical reasons for their adoption.[134] Champion, on the other hand, emphasises the political factors that led to attacks upon the Establishment, but, like Frei, does not particularly seek out the origins of the

---

[133] Cf. Margaret C. Jacobs, *The Newtonians and the English Revolution 1689–1720* (Hassocks: Harvester Press, 1976), 202.
[134] Frei, *Eclipse*.

controversy.[135] While Reventlow corrects Frei and Champion in placing freethought within a wider historical context of Protestant theology, his exposition ends rather abruptly at the 1740s, with only a few brief observations about the legacy of this period for the nineteenth and twentieth centuries.[136] By adopting the hermeneutical analysis of Frei, the political contextualisation of Champion, and the interest in origins present in Reventlow, the dialectic between the Church of England and its freethinking opponents can be understood in its full complexity, and its relevance for the future properly articulated.

That a serious dispute over the status and interpretation of Scripture could have arisen in England in the last decade of the seventeenth century was only possible due to the adoption, by each side, of an empiricist epistemology and philosophy of language, exemplified in the thought of Locke.[137] As we have seen, this philosophy attempted to stabilise the Protestant principles of *sola scriptura* and *sola fide*, and achieve a new basis for religion upon a literal, univocal and perspicuous understanding of the self-authenticating biblical text. The freethought controversy should not be seen, then, as an attack by proto-secularists or atheists upon the Christian faith, but a controversy generated by tensions *within* Protestantism: between a moderate reformation guided by the theologically trained clergy of the Church of England and a radical reformation led by the desire for religious freedom and the reasoned judgement of the individual interpreter.[138] Both positions had precedent within English Protestantism, and the spirit of empiricism only heightened the ambiguity of the Reformation legacy. While the freethinkers shared a great deal with future secularists and atheists – such as anti-clericalism and an emphasis on reason and evidence – it would be wrong, as some do, to view their claims of upholding Protestantism as a ploy to conceal their true intent.[139] An approach towards Scripture, while substantively the same in two historical periods, can nevertheless have a very different meaning depending on what question it is an answer to, and there is a serious danger, when considering freethought, of seeing atheism where it was simply not present. Rather than some form of 'atheist tradition' originating in Britain or elsewhere, the evidence suggests that freethinking was the

[135] J. A. I. Champion, *The Pillars of Priestcraft Shaken* (Cambridge: Cambridge University Press, 1992).
[136] Reventlow, *Authority*.   [137] Sullivan, *Deist Controversy*, 243–4.
[138] Cf. Young, *Religion and Enlightenment*, 5–6.
[139] See, e.g., Berman, *History of Atheism*, 70–88.

outcome of simply reading the Bible with some of the popular presuppositions of the day.[140] Considering that many freethinkers held orthodox
Christian views in addition to heterodox and anti-Christian beliefs, we
make better sense of their motivations and intentions if we see their anti-
clericalism and interest in reason as one possible Protestant response to
the intellectual and political legacy of Reformation, rather than part of an
anti-Christian tradition which has an independent, non-theological
origin.[141]

The areas in which the empirical attitude exemplified in Locke made its
greatest impact upon the defenders of orthodoxy and their freethinking
adversaries was in philosophy of language, logic and forensic approaches
towards scripture. We have noted how, prior to the Reformation, the
words of Scripture supported a range of literal and non-literal readings,
which were not seen to be in competition with each other in any decisive
way. Yet the Reformation irrevocably changed the way Scripture was
read, a legacy that, as Frei argues, was preserved even by those who
rejected the confessional dicta of the Reformers and their successors:

Not very much of Protestant orthodoxy passed over into rationalist religious
thought, but this one thing surely did: the antitraditionalism in scriptural interpretation of the one bolstered the antiauthoritarianism of the other ... Moreover,
the remnants of orthodox belief joined with rationalist interpretation to combat
any understanding of scripture claiming to rest on the direct influence of the Holy
Spirit on the reader, in lieu of settling for its plain meaning ... the eighteenth
century was the period of the direct reading of the 'plain' text, the common
ground among all the different hermeneutical schools.[142]

The direct reading of the plain text entailed that the interpretation of
Scripture should follow the same methods of interpretation as any other
text. To make any sense at all, the words of Scripture must have a
univocal meaning, each word referring to a specific object or event.[143]
This had two effects. First, it meant that the complementarity of literal
and non-literal readings was dealt a greater blow than it had received at
the Reformation.[144] Second, the reference of the words of Scripture to
objects and events meant that if those events had not, in fact, occurred,
then the words were simply *false*. The outcome of this new understanding

---

[140] R. K. Webb, 'The Emergence of Rational Dissent', in *Enlightenment and Religion*, ed.
Knud Haakonssen (Cambridge: Cambridge University Press, 1996), 16.
[141] See Joseph Waligore, 'The Piety of the English Deists', *Intellectual History Review* 22,
no. 2 (2012): 181–97.
[142] Frei, *Eclipse*, 55.   [143] Frei, *Eclipse*, 56, 82–3.
[144] Cf. Sullivan, *Deist Controversy*, 249–50; Reventlow, *Authority*, 370.

of language and its reference was that the scriptural narrative now required justification in light of *evidence*. The concept of 'fact' – a term originating within English common law, and signifying the judicially determined outcome of adversarial debate – came to dominate the approach of both apologists and their critics.[145] Early works such as Tillotson's *The Rule of Faith*, Gilbert Burnet's *Rational Method for Proving the Truth of the Christian Faith* and Edward Stillingfleet's *Origines Sacrae* all employed legal approaches to determine the honesty and reliability of the disciples and gospel writers as witnesses to the Resurrection.[146] Even later thinkers explicitly opposed to Locke, such as John Edwards, adopted this approach towards the New Testament.[147] The result of this trend was that the foundations of Scripture's supposed self-authentication – its internal harmony, the fulfilment of prophecy, and the miracles accompanying the teaching of Christ and the apostles – would come under increasing scrutiny.

These developments in philosophy of language and epistemology were not sufficient, in and of themselves, however, to turn increasing numbers against Christianity and the established Church. At this time, the Church was an organ of the state, and the state claimed its authority from its promotion and protection of orthodox, Trinitarian Christianity, as preserved and interpreted by the bishops of the Church of England. To attack Christianity was to attack the state, and to attack the state was to attack its religious foundation.[148] While arguments against the divinity of Christ may strike modern readers as religious arguments *simpliciter*, to a late seventeenth century reader, they had direct political import. To deny the Trinity was to deny the divinity of Christ, and to deny the divinity of Christ was to deny his mediatorship between God and humanity, a mediatorship continued by Christ's vicars, the Anglican clergy.[149] Likewise, to deny the authority of the Old Testament was to deny the possibility of using the Levitical priesthood as an analogical justification for the hierarchy of the established church.[150] The new philosophy, which strengthened the Reformation principle of the perspicuity of Scripture,

---

[145] Barbara J. Shapiro, *A Culture of Fact* (Ithaca: Cornell University Press, 2000), 170–1.
[146] John Tillotson, *The Rule of Faith* (London, 1666), 85, 102, 118; Gilbert Burnet, *Rational Method for Proving the Truth of the Christian Faith* (London, 1875), 27–8; Edward Stillingfleet, *Origines Sacrae* (Oxford: 1815), 255–75.
[147] Shapiro, *Culture of Fact*, 174.
[148] J. C. D. Clark, *English Society 1688–1832* (Cambridge: Cambridge University Press, 1985), 277–8.
[149] Pocock, 'Within the Margins', 48.   [150] Reventlow, *Authority*, 143–6.

called into question in a new way the legitimacy of the Church of England, a church that claimed in its Articles to have the capacity to settle religious controversies by its own authority.[151] If the words of Scripture were univocal, and should be interpreted like any other text, then if my personal interpretation of Scripture were to differ from the Church's, what right could a priest have to tell me I was wrong? And if I were denied public office, excluded from the universities, and subject to fines and imprisonment for voicing my opinions, what choice would I have but to attack the state as well as the bishops? This assertion of personal conscience coincided with the rising power of the High Church party. This development created an additional political aspect to the controversy. Freethinkers such as Toland, Collins and Tindal were all Whig propagandists, working to eject the Tories and their High Church brethren from political office through their writings.[152] It was this political logic that gave impetus to the new philosophy, a logic that, as we shall see, would continue to inform anti-orthodox thought in Britain until the close of the nineteenth century.[153] While something of an overstatement, then, one might say that there were strong *political* reasons for the development of freethought in England.[154]

The convergence of Lockean epistemology and political radicalism found its first great expression in the figure of John Toland, sometime ministry candidate of the Church of Scotland. Toland moved Locke's epistemology to its next logical step, against Locke's own views given in the *Reasonableness of Christianity*.[155] In that work, Locke had argued that Scripture must be accepted *in toto*, whether it is understood or not. Toland adopts Locke's epistemology almost wholesale, with its disdain for theological authorities, and the desire to derive doctrine solely from Scripture, which should be read as any other text.[156] What is different, however, is his willingness to use reason not simply to verify that Scripture is revelation, but to attack the idea that revelation should be accepted contrary to reason, the idea – still present in Locke – that some revelations

---

[151] Article XX of the Thirty-Nine Articles.   [152] Reventlow, *Authority*, 328–9.
[153] Champion, *Priestcraft*, 10–11.   [154] Reventlow, *Authority*, 329.
[155] Toland was not a slavish Lockean, and he had an important rationalist streak in his thought. Nevertheless, the basis of his thought was Lockean, and his innovations represented natural developments of Lockean themes. See Ian Leask, 'Personation and Immanent Undermining: On Toland's Appearing Lockean', *British Journal for the History of Philosophy*, 18, no. 2 (2010): 231–56.
[156] John Toland, *Christianity not Mysterious* (Dublin: Lilliput Press, 1997), 21–30, 8–12, 44.

can be *above* reason.[157] To believe something *contrary* to reason simply because it is found in Scripture is to give license to every absurdity.[158] Moreover, to claim that any doctrine is above reason, and hence 'mysterious', is to play into the hands of priests, who use mysteries to introduce absurdities into the faith, and usurp power for themselves, an argument that Toland advanced against the ambitions of the High Church party.[159] A mystery is something perfectly intelligible in itself, but veiled by the deception of others.[160] To those detractors who worry that such views could play into the hands of atheists, Toland explicitly places himself within the line of the Reformers, arguing that he can no more be blamed for encouraging religious doubt than Luther, Calvin and Zwingli can, for they too opposed the prevailing religious authorities of their day.[161]

Toland's star reached an early apogee in *Christianity not Mysterious*, before beginning a slow decline into obscurity. The mantle of freethought was soon taken up, however, by Anthony Collins.[162] Like Toland, Collins also adopted Locke's epistemology, yet took its implications much further.[163] The continuing rise of the High Church party, which opposed both dissenters and their latitudinarian sympathisers within the Church of England, raised the possibility of a reversal of legal toleration for nonconformists. During the Sacheverell Affair, rioting broke out against nonconformists in London after the impeachment of Henry Sacheverell, who had preached an incendiary sermon against dissent. It was the rising threat of persecution from High Anglicans that led Collins to attack the very basis of the Church of England's authority.[164] In *Priestcraft in Perfection*, Collins marshalled older puritan arguments against the popish trappings of the Church of England to push for a new *rationalist* agenda. The Twentieth Article of the Thirty-Nine Articles States:

---

[157] Toland, *Mysterious*, 17.   [158] Toland, *Mysterious*, 35.

[159] E.g. Toland, *Mysterious*, 10–11, 33–4, 92–8; Reventlow, *Authority*, 328–9; Jeffrey R. Wigelsworth, *Deism in Enlightenment England* (Manchester: Manchester University Press, 2009), 125.

[160] Toland, *Mysterious*, 56.   [161] Toland, *Mysterious*, 99–100.

[162] There is debate over the nature of Collin's thought and, in particular, whether he disbelieved in God's existence. While outright atheism does not capture Collins' thought correctly, there is no doubt that his beliefs extended far beyond a 'low-church' position. cf. Berman, *History of Atheism*, 70–88 and James O'Higgins, *Anthony Collins: The Man and His Work* (The Hague: Martinus Nijhoff, 1970).

[163] Frei, *Eclipse*, 74–77; Reventlow, *Authority*, 354.   [164] Wigelsworth, *Deism*, 113.

The Church hath power to decree rites or ceremonies and authority in controversies of faith; and yet it is not lawful for the Church to ordain anything contrary to God's word written.

Collins begins by noting that if authority is the basis of the Church's power, then there should have been no Reformation, for the Roman Catholic Church also claims such authority for itself, and he expresses surprise that the English Reformers should have promulgated such an article. Collins concludes that the article is, in fact, a forgery, inserted at a later date contrary to the spirit of the Reformation, an assertion he then attempts to substantiate through a discussion of the textual history of the Articles.[165] While we need not detain ourselves with the cogency of his argument, its import is important, for Collins uses the uncertainty surrounding the textual history of the Articles to launch an attack upon his *real* target: *any* authority that seeks to govern the interpretation of Scripture. As Collins puts it:

If Priests are capable of venturing to forge an Article of Religion, and Mankind are so stupid as to let them have success how can we receive Books of bulk (such as the *Fathers* and *Councils*) that have gone thro their hands, and lay any stress or dependence on their Authority?[166]

If any sensitive reader should worry that 'Books of bulk' might include Holy Scripture, Collins is quick to soothe their concerns, claiming that he would obviously not include it within his critique, and even ends his treatise with Chillingworth's boast that the Bible alone is the religion of Protestants.[167] If some may have missed the full import of Collins' argument, however, he soon followed with a far more wide-ranging attack upon the established church. In his *Discourse of Free-Thinking*, Collins illustrates the contradictions present in the Anglican settlement by contrasting the 'Confession of Eye-sight Faith' held by the subjects of a hypothetical land, with the instruction of their leaders to ignore what they see, and instead believe a host of absurdities, telling then that such things are not *contrary* to eyesight but *above* it.[168] Drawing on the 'true Christian and Protestant (and by consequence great Free-Thinker)' Chillingworth and the 'Head' of all English freethought Tillotson, Collins pushes their arguments for the authenticating and regulative function of reason in relation to Scripture to their logical conclusion, urging his

---

[165] Anthony Collins, *Priestcraft in Perfection* (London: B. Bragg, 1770), 3–9, 11–21.
[166] Collins, *Priestcraft*, 46.   [167] Collins, *Priestcraft*, 47.
[168] Anthony Collins, *A Discourse of Free-Thinking* (London, 1713), 15–18.

readers to search Scripture and consider religious questions with an open mind, unprejudiced by the theological systems of corrupt priests.[169] It speaks volumes about the legacy of Reformation in England that such a plea, however unpopular, was nevertheless a logical option given the presuppositions established by the Reformers and developed by their successors. The ambiguity between Protestant zeal for the primacy of Scripture and heterodox rationalism becomes even more prominent with Collins' assertion that personal freethought in relation to Scripture is now vital due to the doubt created over the biblical text itself by new methods of textual and philological study by specialist clergy. Collins presents this as another example of their falsifying impulse, and their wish to demean the standing of Scripture to further their own religious ambitions.[170] The irony is not far beneath the surface: the clergy themselves have already cast doubt on the authority of Scripture and traditional doctrine, and the people should therefore possess the same right.

The ambivalence of the age, however, meant that doubts over the accuracy of the biblical text, and the necessity for a fresh appraisal of the foundations of faith, could give rise to both an anti-Christian writer such Collins as well as pro-Christian figures. William Whiston, successor to Newton at Cambridge, was aware of growing criticism of Scripture, and reached the conclusion that the Church of England was in danger of becoming an easy target for its enemies because of its possession and promotion of a biblical text that disproved its own doctrines. He sought to do something to remedy this problem. The result was an *Essay Towards Restoring the True Text of the Old Testament*.[171] Prior to the Reformation, apparently conflicting texts could be harmonised through allegory, a method that also lay at the basis of the so-called *internal proofs* of the faith: prophecies contained in the Old Testament, and fulfilled in the New. Yet a literal, univocal and perspicuous reading of Scripture meant that words, if they meant anything at all, could only refer to *one* object. This led Whiston to believe that the prophecies of the Old Testament could not reasonably be said to refer to events and persons in the New Testament at all, as, read literally, they seemed to refer to very different objects. The resulting danger was that there were no prophecies concerning Christ and his Church in the Old Testament, and that the New

[169] Collins, *Free-Thinking*, 34, 171, 45–6, 75, 109–10.
[170] Collins, *Free-Thinking*, 85, 87, 90.
[171] William Whiston, *Essay Towards Restoring the True Text of the Old Testament* (London, 1772).

Testament writers – who quoted the Hebrew Scriptures in support of their faith – were delusional enthusiasts. Whiston notes in his *Essay* that the differences between the citations of the New Testament and the texts in the Old to which they refer have led interpreters to torture and strain Scripture through the use of allegory.[172] Yet this method of allegorisation is a 'weak and enthusiastick sort of Reasoning', one of the 'most ill-grounded, and most pernicious things that ever was admitted by the later Ages of Christianity'.[173] Whiston calls on scholars to accept that their efforts have failed, and that the Old and New Testaments, as they currently stand, are irreconcilable, a scandal that invites the ridicule of infidels and Jews alike. Such a situation would be bad enough in any church, but is particularly serious for Protestants, for Protestants base their *entire religion* upon Scripture.[174] Rather than blaming priests for this state of affairs like Collins, Whiston blames Jewish rabbis, who, due to their hatred of Christianity, count 'Lying for God' to be a virtue. They purposefully altered the Old Testament in the early centuries of the Church, and, in particular, those passages which support Jesus's Messiahship.[175] The majority of Whiston's work is taken up with the reconstruction of the Old Testament text supposedly possessed by Christ and the Apostles, based largely upon the Hebrew texts of the Samaritans.[176] The result is that texts such as Matthew 1:22–23, which reference Isaiah 7:14, now succeed, the reference to King Ahaz being 'corrected' to allow for a literal fulfilment of prophecy in Christ.

Whiston combined superb learning with eccentricity bordering on delusion, and Collins did not miss the opportunity to turn Whiston's reconstruction to his own mischievous ends. Collins begins his *Discourse of the Grounds and Reasons of the Christian Religion* by noting:

Christianity is founded on Judaism, and the New Testament on the Old; and JESUS is the Person said in the New Testament to be promised in the Old, under the Character of the MESSIAS of the Jews, who, as such only, claims the Obedience and Submission of the World.[177]

If the prophecies are valid, Christianity is 'invincibly established', fulfilled prophecy being far more secure than proofs based on authority, or the trustworthiness of witnesses to miracles.[178] If the prophecies are not

[172] Whiston, *True Text*, 281.   [173] Whiston, *True Text*, 92.
[174] Whiston, *True Text*, 281–3.   [175] Whiston, *True Text*, 220–9.
[176] Whiston, *True Text*, 149–50.
[177] Anthony Collins, *Grounds and Reasons of the Christian Religion* (London, 1737), 1.
[178] Collins, *Grounds and Reasons*, 24.

valid, however, then Christianity and, more specifically, the Messiahship of Christ, have no foundation.[179] Collins agrees with Whiston that many of the Old Testament prophecies appear to be couched in literal terms, yet also notes the way in which Christ and the writers of the New Testament appear to interpret them in a non-literal way.[180] For this reason, he wonders what rules Christ and the early Church used to interpret Old Testament prophecy, noting that modern interpreters seem unable to supply such rules. Collins expresses his delight, therefore, at having recently came across the work of 'the learned Surenhusius', Professor of the Hebrew Tongue at the 'illustrious school of Amsterdam', who – during a felicitous conference with a group of Jewish doctors – was given the precise rules by which Christ and the apostles cited and applied Old Testament texts. Among the most productive rules for relating Old Testament prophecy to the New Testament are:

- Changing the letters
- Adding some letters and taking away others
- Adding other words to those that are there, in order to make the sense clear, and to accommodate it to the subject
- Changing the order of the words
- Changing the order of the words and adding other words
- Changing the order of words, adding words and retrenching words, 'which is a Method often used by Paul'[181]

The import of Collins' irony is clear: if allegorical interpretation is 'weak and enthusiastick' then Christ and his apostles were the weakest and most enthusiastic of all. This, of course, leaves Whiston's original aim of reconstructing the Old Testament as a remaining option. Yet Collins argues forcefully that it is absurd to suggest that the Old Testament is as corrupt as Whiston claims, but that, if it is, people are entirely justified in rejecting Christianity altogether, rather than spending their lives hoping for a lost book that cannot be found.[182] Whiston is therefore left with two impossible options: accept an allegorical reading of Scripture that uses irrational principles to produce arbitrary meanings, or accept that the prophecies fail, that Scripture is errant, and that Christianity is a lie.

Collins was answered by a great number of writers, among the most respected being Edward Chandler, future Bishop of Durham. Chandler

---

[179] Collins, *Grounds and Reasons*, 26–8.　　[180] Collins, *Grounds and Reasons*, 35, 5–12.
[181] Collins, *Grounds and Reasons*, 53–4.　　[182] Collins, *Grounds and Reasons*, 92–102.

generally opts for the first of Collin's horns, and tries to retrieve something of an allegorical reading of the Old Testament prophecies. Yet what is telling is how circumscribed and stilted this reading has become. Chandler begins by *diminishing* the traditional importance of prophecy for the Christian faith, placing more emphasis on the moral virtue of the faith, and the miracles accompanying it, and arguing that the citation of Old Testament prophecies by the early church was less a matter of proof than of situating Jesus within a wider context of Jewish thinking.[183] He notes the difficulties in properly understanding the prophecies, which are no longer chronologically ordered, and couched in an ancient language framed by an alien understanding of the world.[184] Nevertheless, Chandler *does* accord a role for allegorical interpretation, yet one in keeping with the philosophy of the age. Prophecy, according to Chandler, is a language of its own, one which uses 'metaphorical words'.[185] Metaphorical words are those which

Give a secondary, figurative, borrowed sense, being translated from the things which they originally express'd, to others, with which, they have some resemblance. And use having establish'd the meaning of these, they are as ready understood, as simple words, and give the true literal sense, of him that speaks or writes.[186]

The combination of the old and the new here is telling. Chandler, trained within an Anglican Church which had traditionally schooled its clergy in scholastic thought and the Fathers, *wants* to accord a place for allegory, but can only do so by reducing it to the status of a foreign language which, once understood, functions in the same way as the 'simple words' of everyday English. As Reventlow argues, with this, allegory becomes as univocal as the literal sense.[187] Chandler's ultimate justification for according a role to allegory is even more curious: *because* Christ is a prophet, his citation of Old Testament texts in support of his person *cannot* be wrong.[188] This deductive method, favoured also by Stillingfleet, and premised as it is upon the witness of the Church, stands in marked contrast to the inductive method favoured by Collins, who is

---

[183] Edward Chandler, *A Defence of Christianity from the Prophecies of the Old Testament* (London, 1725), i–x.
[184] Chandler, *Defence*, xi–xv.   [185] Chandler, *Defence*, xiv–v.
[186] Chandler, *Defence*, 196.
[187] Reventlow, *Authority*, 370. This was also Newton's approach to prophecy, cf. Katz, *Last Words*, 112–14.
[188] Chandler, *Defence*, 397, 399.

quite prepared to examine the evidence afresh and ask himself whether Christ is, in fact, who he claims to be.[189]

Given the spirit of the age, there was little churchmen could do to refute freethinkers, sharing as they did the same evidential standards and hermeneutical principles as their opponents, and their professed orthodoxy frequently running contrary to their own presuppositions.[190] What could a Protestant bishop really say in response to Matthew Tindal, when he argued that the Church of England was an affront to the Reformers' belief that the authority of Scripture and its correct interpretation were taught by the Holy Spirit alone? How could one say that Scripture was *both* authoritative, requiring implicit faith, *and* call in reason to verify this authority? What was the legal enforcement of orthodoxy and the oversight of priests but the imposition of a new Roman tyranny, and the setting up of a Pope in every parish?[191] In this way, freethinkers did not challenge the Protestant establishment by being deist or secularist or atheist, but by being more *Protestant* than the Protestants, playing on tensions present within the early English enlightenment.[192] They realised, better than their adversaries, that the principles of *sola scriptura* and *sola fide*, forged by the Reformers against the Roman Catholic Church and stabilised by Locke and the latitudinarians, favoured their own position more than the Church of England's. If Scripture could be read as any other text, and did not require a theological framework for its interpretation, anyone could read and form their own opinion of it. In taking seriously the supposed self-authentication of Scripture, and testing it through literal exegesis, Collins and his freethinking contemporaries were simply taking the presuppositions of the Reformation to one of their logical conclusions.

Whatever the logical strength of such arguments, however, the works of the freethinkers were in vain. Freethought was not, in the end, overcome by argument, but by the weight of the state, and the inability of the cultured freethinkers to promote their views amongst the working classes.[193] It would be for the disaffected men of another generation to make good on these failings, and bring freethought to a popular audience.

---

[189] Cf. Stillingfleet, *Origines Sacrae*, 71–3.
[190] Reventlow, *Authority*, 239, 294; Sullivan, *Deist Controversy*, 245–50; Frei, *Eclipse*, 77.
[191] Matthew Tindal, *Christianity as Old as the Creation* (London, 1730), 193, 302, 307.
[192] Young, *Religion and Enlightenment*, 5–6.
[193] Cf. Stephen, *English Thought*, 229; Hill, *English Bible*, 430.

RE-NARRATING NATURE

It may be thought that changes in the reading of Scripture would have consequences for theology alone. Yet the medieval chain of meaning that united Scripture to nature and allowed natural objects to symbolise divine truths ensured that the crisis of authority ushered in by the Reformation would have consequences not only for the things of God but for the things of nature. Central to these changes was the development of the second key presupposition that this work examines: that God's activity in nature is disruptive and substitutionary.

The connection between this presupposition and the Reformation may, at first, appear obscure, yet such an intellectual and social dependence existed. Intellectually, literalism and the doctrinal primacy of Scripture ensured that nature would no longer be read primarily as an allegory of divine truth but as a system of causal relations. This facilitated a reading of Genesis 1–3 that prompted an identification of God's creative and preserving activity with direct, unmediated, supernatural power. Socially, the fragmentation of English life into a variety of competing sects and parties – both Christian and anti-Christian – necessitated a new means for securing a base level of religious agreement. These outcomes of Reformation contributed to the development of natural philosophy, where there arose a new desire to uncover natural causes for phenomena, and produce a universal and univocal description of reality. This coalescence would increasingly associate divine activity with direct, unmediated force, and had two effects. First, divine activity became ontologically distinct – yet functionally equivalent – with natural causes in a range of natural-philosophical models. Second, it pitted divine agency against natural causation, and led to a decline in the distinction between primary and secondary causation. The association of divine activity with immediate, disruptive force integrated theology and science into a single hermeneutical and natural-theological synthesis, where a literal reading of Genesis guided natural philosophy, and natural philosophy justified a literal interpretation of Genesis. This met the social, intellectual and apologetic needs of the age, yet created a precedent for thinking about God's activity in creation that would prove disastrous when its intellectual cogency was questioned by the scientific advances of the nineteenth century.

The first issue bearing upon the development of a disruptive and substitutionary conception of divine activity was changes in biblical hermeneutics introduced by the Reformers. In a development charted by Harrison, the Reformers' rejection of allegorical glosses and their desire to determine the original meaning and intention of the Bible's words had a corresponding effect upon the natural world. If previously natural phenomena were part of a sophisticated system of analogy, sympathy and semblance where nature's primary function was to teach divine truths that supplemented Scripture, the new doctrinal primacy of Scripture and the turn towards literalism broke the ability of natural objects to function in this way. Just as the words of Scripture meant one thing rather than many things, so too did natural objects come to signify one thing and not another. Animals and flowers, insects and trees, minerals and metals were what they were and nothing else, a change in meaning that was part of the same process that led to iconoclasm, where religious imagery lost its power to connect believers with transcendent realities, and became nothing more than idols. The evacuation of meaning from nature cleared the world of thousands of years of significance, leaving space for new descriptions of nature based on causal relations.[194]

The turn to literalism, and the evacuation of meaning from nature, also led to significant changes in the interpretation of Genesis and its relation to models of divine activity. Patristic and medieval hermeneutics had permitted exegetes, at times, to give allegorical and spiritual readings of the opening chapters of Genesis.[195] This hermeneutic dovetailed with the distinction between primary and secondary causation, given its most famous formulation by Aquinas.[196] Between them, these hermeneutical and theological beliefs allowed for the possibility of God's creative and preserving activity being mediated through natural causes over great swathes of time. While the concept of primary and secondary causation was still present in Calvin, we nevertheless witness in his thought a new ambivalence between the order and regularity of the created order and the direct intervention of divine activity at each moment to preserve creation from dissolution, evidence of an occasionalism that will come to the fore at a later point.[197] More significant than any change in conceptions of divine activity, however, was a new emphasis upon perspicuity and the literal sense, used by the Reformers to undermine the tradition and magisterium of the Roman Catholic Church. First, an emphasis upon the literal sense and the perspicuity of Scripture made allegorical readings

---

[194] See, in particular, Harrison, *Protestantism*, 194–205.
[195] See Harrison, *Protestantism*, 126–8.
[196] See, e.g., Thomas Aquinas, *Summa Theologiae*, vol. I (California: NovAntiqua, 2008), I.62.3; Thomas Aquinas, *Summa Theologiae*, vol. II (California: NovAntiqua, 2010), I.74.2, I.103.6.
[197] S. E. Schreiner, *The Theater of His Glory* (Durham: Labyrinth Press, 1991).

of Genesis 1–3 far more difficult to maintain. Second, because a literal reading of Genesis 1–3 gives no indication of the mediation of divine power through secondary natural causes, the adoption of such literal readings impinged upon dual causation models of divine activity. Genesis 1–3 was to be interpreted literally, and this meant that God created instantaneously in six twenty-four hour time periods. As John Donne argued:

I forebear this [allegorical] interpretation; the rather because we are utterly dis-provided of any history of the World's Creation, except we defend and maintain this Book of *Moses* to be historical, and therefore literally to be interpreted.[198]

Scripture's sense was clear, and the needs of the age demanded that it be taken as literal, historical fact.

The second issue bearing upon the development of a disruptive and substitutionary conception of divine activity was the religious and social conflict brought about by the Reformation. The freethinking controversy had shown how reason could pull away from its ordained role as verifier of revelation to become autonomous, and undermine the Christianity it was charged with protecting. Yet if *revealed* religion had become prob-lematic, there remained the possibility of using reason to establish the basic truths of *natural* religion. In this effort, the new sciences – recently given official approval by the granting of a charter to the Royal Society – would prove invaluable, for if God's direct activity could be shown to be a fundamental element in the creation and preservation of the world, freethinkers could be persuaded of their folly, and come to accept God's creative, preserving, and providential control of nature. The growing popularity of natural-theological assumptions and methods also arose from ecclesiastical conflict. Conflict between Catholics and Protestants precipitated the eclipse of traditional accounts of God's interaction with creation, as natural philosophers sought objective, empirical methods of determining this activity that were not subject to the doubts of confes-sional disputation.[199] In this context, there arose the impression that natural philosophy could be a better guarantor for the existence of God

---

[198] John Donne, *Essayes in Divinity* (Oxford: Clarendon Press, 1952), 18.

[199] Gregory, *Unintended Reformation*, 40–41. Gunton has suggested that the eclipse of traditional understandings of divine activity arose from a failure of the Reformers and their successors to anticipate and integrate the growing sciences into their theological systems, with the result that natural-theological accounts of creation and preservation came to supplant those offered by dogmaticians. See Colin Gunton, *The Triune Creator* (Edinburgh: Edinburgh University Press, 1998), 125–30, 153–6.

and the fundamental doctrines of creation, preservation, and providence than the Church itself.

These intellectual and social changes provided important catalysts for the third factor bearing upon the growth of a disruptive and substitutionary understanding of divine activity: the development of natural philosophy. Natural philosophy instantiated and promoted two new tendencies. The first was a desire not to be led by authorities but by the senses, and the teaching of nature alone. This saw the rejection of scholasticism, and a new ideological commitment to experimentation and enquiry into natural causes. The second was the attempt to find a universal and univocal language for describing reality. This process saw the search for a universal language that was analogous to mathematics.[200] We see both developments in the rhetoric behind the establishment of the Royal Society, represented by Sprat's *History of the Royal Society of London*. Sprat rejects any form of natural philosophy founded on tradition, and condemns the cloistered approach of earlier scholastic writers, who blindly followed ancient authorities. In its place, Sprat enjoins his readers to adopt the experimental method, which seeks to uncover the natural causes of natural effects.[201] Freed from tradition, authority, and national differences, natural philosophers are then able to make a 'universal, constant, and impartial survey of the whole Creation'.[202] Central to this effort is the need for a plain and universal language. Sprat – foreshadowing Locke – rails against the lack of clarity found in many existing works of natural philosophy, and lays the blame for this in ambiguous forms of speech:

of all the Studies of men, nothing may be sooner obtain'd, than this vicious abundance of Phrase, this trick of Metaphors, this volubility of Tongue, which makes so great a noise in the World.

In order to remedy this vicious abundance of phrase, Sprat recounts the actions taken by the members of the Royal Society:

They have exacted from all their members, a close, naked, natural way of speaking; positive expressions; clear senses; a native easiness: bringing all things as near the Mathematical plainness, as they can: and preferring the language of Artizans, Countrymen, and Merchants, before that, of Wits, or Scholars.[203]

---

[200] Amos Funkenstein, *Theology and the Scientific Imagination* (Princeton: Princeton University Press, 1986), 28–31.

[201] See, e.g., Thomas Sprat, *The History of the Royal Society of London* (London, 1667), 15–22, 100–11.

[202] Sprat, *Royal Society*, 124.   [203] Sprat, *Royal Society*, 112, 113.

Due to the commitment of English natural philosophers to the experimental method, and to a plain and rational language, Sprat makes a direct comparison between the methods of the Royal Society and the Church of England, which can both claim to be products of Reformation:

They both may lay equal claim to the word Reformation; the one having compass'd it in Religion, the other purposing it in Philosophy. They both have taken a like cours to bring this about; each of them passing by the corrupt Copies, and referring themselves to the perfect Originals for their instruction; the one to the Scripture, the other to the large Volume of the Creatures.[204]

Just as the Church makes a rational search of the Scriptures to discern the Word of God, so does the natural philosopher make a rational search of nature to uncover its secrets. Yet the desire to ground knowledge empirically, to develop a univocal and universal scientific language and to draw comparisons between the methods of theology and those of natural philosophy would, when wed to contemporary hermeneutics, have serious consequences for prevailing conceptions of divine activity. First, investigation into natural causes weakened the attractiveness of dual causation models, for if an effect could be explained naturally there was less explanatory need to make reference to God. The decline in importance of dual causation led to an increasing desire to determine what was natural and what was supernatural, what was of nature and what was of God. This tendency was strengthened by literal readings of Genesis, which seemed to suggest that creation was unmediated, and the product of direct divine activity. The result of this was that divine activity came to be viewed as being, at least in principle, opposed to natural causation, *disrupting* it whenever it entered into creation. Second, the desire of natural philosophers to produce a description of reality centred on causes led them to enlist divine activity as a form of supernatural cause, especially in contexts where their knowledge was incomplete. This meant that divine activity *substituted* for natural causes within natural-philosophical models, most commonly those touching upon creation and preservation. Due to these changes, descriptions of God's activity were no longer limited to Christian doctrine, but became a component of natural philosophy. When added to the social, political, and apologetic needs already recounted, a disruptive and substitutionary understanding of divine activity began to form.

---

[204] Sprat, *Royal Society*, 375.

We can illustrate this development, and chart its consequences, by examining the system of Isaac Newton. Newton had a lifelong interest in theology and biblical prophecy, and wrote the Principia with an eye to its apologetic potential, which he thought necessary to combat the perceived atheistic tendencies of Cartesian physics.[205] Yet Newton's God was not the Trinitarian God of Christian orthodoxy. Newton's unitarian God lacked an immanent relational essence, and exercised his power and attributes only in his *forceful* relations with creation. In this way, 'Lord' became a relative term, with God's existence and attributes being identified with his ability to control matter.[206] For Newton, motion was not inherent in bodies but was imposed from without by the external, immaterial force of God. The space within which matter was moved and attracted was the medium by which God's power operated.[207] This meant that natural philosophy – and particularly physics – could study the work and activity of God in creation, and could provide evidence of his existence and providential oversight. Yet in conceiving of God's immanent presence and activity in terms of physics, Newton made God's activity functionally equivalent to physical force.[208] Theology was reduced to natural theology, and knowledge of God's being to his observable direction and command over matter.[209] This conception of divine activity would have serious consequences for future thought.

Newton's system was intentionally dense and enigmatic, and it would take a host of lesser figures to transmit and popularise it. Robert Boyle, mindful of increasing dangers to the Christian faith, left a legacy in his will for the creation of a lectureship of eight annual sermons directed against the enemies of religion. The inaugural lecturer, Richard Bentley, with the encouragement of Newton himself, was the first to use the new physics for apologetic purposes. Bentley took the older design arguments of writers like John Ray and combined them with the new Newtonian physics. In his sixth and seventh Boyle sermons, Bentley used a range of philosophical and physical arguments to prove that the revolutions of the planets, the motion of matter, and the system of the universe could not have existed eternally without a divine lawgiver.[210] In the seventh

---

[205] Simon Oliver, *Philosophy, God and Motion* (London and New York: Routledge, 2005), 156–7.
[206] Buckley, *Origins*, 135–7.
[207] Isaac Newton, *Opticks*, 2nd ed. (London, 1718), 31st Querey, 372–3.
[208] Funkenstein, *Scientific Imagination*, 25.   [209] Oliver, *God and Motion*, 159–61.
[210] Richard Bentley, *Eight Sermons Preach'd at the Honourable Robert Boyle's Lecture* (Cambridge: Cornelius Crownfield, 1724), 226–92.

sermon, Bentley used Newtonian accounts of gravitation to argue that gravitation could not be inherent in matter, but existed by the direct 'energy and impression' of the Deity.[211] To these Newtonian arguments, Bentley added more traditional design arguments, moving from the beauty and order of the world to the existence of a wise and all-powerful Creator.[212] In making use of physical, cosmological, and design arguments to prove the direct creation and governance of nature by God, Bentley's apologetics both expressed and furthered the presuppositions of the age, advancing a disruptive and substitutionary understanding of God's activity in two ways. First, his physical arguments, based on Newton's *Principia*, conceived of divine activity as being exercised directly over matter to produce gravitation, as well as making occasional interventions to maintain planetrary movement. Second, the design argument, reasoning from effects to ultimate cause, conceived of divine activity as a supernatural cause, which substituted for natural causes. Both lines of natural-theological argument used by Bentley, and emulated by others, either directly or indirectly viewed God's activity as being a substitution for what would otherwise be a natural cause, and, in this way, integrated God's actions into natural-philosophical and apologetic models.

After the success of Bentley's Boyle sermons, natural theologians began to draw upon an ever-increasing range of disciplines and data to confute the error of sceptics. Thus, the citizens of eighteenth-century England were treated to such weighty proofs for the existence of the Deity as *soil* and *water* theology. All creation came to be enlisted for the defence of its Creator. Such projects, while fanciful, do not diminish the vital political and intellectual function of natural theology during this period and thereafter. Natural theology helped to harmonise the positions of competing theological parties in a way that did not materialise in a French context, where there was a pronounced dichotomy between egalitarian irreligion and hegemonic Catholicism.[213] The evidence of God's activity in nature was something which men and women of every theological party could accept. Moreover, it was politically useful. The Newtonian

---

[211]   281. As Haughen points out, however, this use of Newton's physics was not necessarily Newton's own; a salutary example of the apologetic misuse of science. See Kristine L. Haughen, *Richard Bentley: Poetry and Enlightenment* (Cambridge, MA: Harvard University Press, 2011), 102.

[212]   Bentley, *Eight Sermons*, 293–342.

[213]   John Hedley Brooke, *Science and Religion: Some Historical Perspectives* (Cambridge: Cambridge University Press, 1991), 200.

worldview, with its emphasis on inert bodies moved by sovereign force and following foreseeable laws, harmonised with the desire of the latitudinarian party to preserve first the Restoration and, later, the political settlement of the glorious revolution: a benign constitutional monarch operating according to the rule of law.[214] Intellectually and socially, the unity of natural philosophy and theology was beneficial to both the Church of England and the aspiring natural philosophers who comprised the newly founded Royal Society. On the one hand, the spectre of materialism made natural philosophers worry over their social and political position, and led them to stress the piety and theological utility of the new science. On the other hand, Newtonian physics and natural theology provided the Church with a ready reply to those who argued that reason and religion were opposed. Natural theology took over scholasticism's function as a means of harmonising the potentially competing authorities of revelation and reason, and restored order and meaning to nature.[215] Natural objects came to symbolise both the causal relations studied by natural philosophy and the attributes of the deity taught by the Church. The books of nature and Scripture, once united in the medieval mind through a great chain of analogy and allegory, found a new unity in natural theology, and a conception of divine activity that made it one cause among others. All creation witnessed once more to the power and wisdom of Almighty God.[216]

Yet the harmonisation achieved by natural theology was limited and temporary, the product of a convergence of theological, political, and social factors that would soon pass. The use of science for religious ends was largely contingent upon the personal piety of scientists, and the utility of aligning the interests of science with those of the Church and its clergy. For those thinkers who had less stake in the existing order, other understandings of nature were already possible. Long before d'Holbach and Diderot, Toland was presenting a materialist model of motion that denied the need for a divine Lord and lawgiver. In his *Letters to Serena*, Toland argued that 'all the Matter in Nature, every Part and Parcel of it, has bin ever in motion, and can never be otherwise' and 'Matter can no more he conceiv'd without Motion than without Extension, and that the one is as inseparable from it as the other.'[217] With characteristic irony, Toland

---

[214] Jacobs, *Newtonians*, 187–200. Of course, as Brooke points out, such science could be used for alternative political ends. See Brooke, *Science and Religion*, 158–9.

[215] Sullivan, *Deist Controversy*, 242–3.   [216] Harrison, *Protestantism*, 193, 203.

[217] John Toland, *Letters to Serena* (London: Bernard Lintot, 1704), 167, 168.

claimed that a self-moving and self-governing universe only strengthened the cause of religion against atheists, yet few were fooled.[218] Toland's argument undermined the central proposition of Newtonian physico-theology, that God's existence, creation, and continuing providenital oversight could be demonstrated by scientific investigation of its physical effects. Toland's argument did not go unanswered, however, and was serious enough for Samuel Clarke to refute in his Boyle Lectures.[219] Yet this dialectic of claim and counter-claim – a positive account of the agency of God in the natural world followed by a negative rebuttal – would gradually come to undermine the plausibility of the faith, natural theology increasingly testifying to its own weakness through a continual process of intellectual retreat.[220] As Collins jested, no one had cause to doubt the existence of God in England until the Boyle Lecturers set out to prove it.[221]

This dialectic, however damaging in itself, was exacerbated by the new nexus of theology and science with the literal, univocal, and perspicuous conception of Scripture that we have examined. While the unity of Scripture and nature – a rich and versatile feature of the medieval mind – provided for a wealth of interpretation, the new literalism, amplified by empiricism and a conception of divine activity as that which disrupts and substitutes for natural causation, led to an understanding of the relation between nature and Scripture that was univocal, and capable of one meaning only. Theological description was not distinct from, yet complimentary with, physical descriptions of reality, but was collapsed with it into a single homogenous category of 'knowledge', the methods and evidential standards of science being applied to Scripture and *vice versa*. The language of Scripture and the language of science became coterminous and convergent, and this langauge was perspicuous, universal, and univocal.[222] In this new understanding, Scripture recorded, in clear and unambiguous terms, the creation of the earth and all life in six days, a presentation of scientific fact. Moses was no longer an actor within the divine drama, but an historian and natural philosopher, diligently recording scientific data imparted to him by God.[223] This convergence

[218] Toland, *Serena*, 234–7.
[219] Samuel Clarke, *A Demonstration of the Being and Attributes of God* (Cambridge: Cambridge University Press, 1998), 19.
[220] See generally Buckley, *Origins*. cf. Jacobs, *Newtonians*, 171–2.
[221] Cited in John Hedley Brooke and Geoffrey Cantor, *Reconstructing Nature: The Engagement of Science and Religion* (Edinburgh: T&T Clark, 1998), 198.
[222] Funkenstein, *Scientific Imagination*, 28–31.   [223] Harrison, *Protestantism*, 122.

of language and methodology meant that much of science came to be directed by a literal reading of Genesis 1–3, while scientists and apologists increasingly sought to confirm the credibility of this literal reading against its detractors through recourse to the latest mathematics, astronomy, geology and biology. Newton himself used speculations concerning the earth's orbit to harmonise the days of Genesis 1 with contemporary knowledge, while Whiston's *A New Theory of the Earth* utilised exhaustive exegesis, astrological prediction and mathematical rigour to calculate that the Flood occurred due to a passing comet on the 27th November in the 1700th year of creation.[224] This approach reached its highest – or lowest – point in the work of Bishop Ussher, whose chronological calculations glossed the pages of many copies of the King James Bible, achieving semi-canonical status in their own right.

It is easy to mock such efforts as eccentricities, yet they fulfilled important functions, helping to unify Protestant Christianity and the new sciences into a comprehensive vision of scientific and theological truth. History would reveal, however, that it was precisely this unity that would lead to conflict. Empiricism, and its corresponding hermeneutic of a literal, univocal, and perspicuous Scripture, collapsed religion and science into a single homogenous category, revelation being nothing more than philosophical and scientific knowledge imparted to humanity without investigation. When investigation did occur, it was assumed, quite reasonably, that this would confirm revealed truth. Yet what if this did not happen? If the Bible should *only* be read literally and univocally, and presents accounts of the natural world which contradict the results of science, then one *must* be wrong. Just as physics, geology, and mathematics could be used to prove the truth of Genesis, so the new nexus of science and theology could be used to refute it. While the Church entered the eighteenth century strengthened by the new science, within one hundred and fifty years, the dialectic we have seen throughout this chapter – the unforeseen consequences of attacks upon Roman Catholicism giving rise to restatements of Protestantism, which in turn give rise to new attacks – would rebound once again on the Church, and the tree of English Protestantism would yield strange and bitter fruit.

This chapter has traced the hermeneutical and natural-theological presuppositions that facilitated the genesis of the first anti-Christian thought in Britain, presuppositions that would, in time, come to structure

---

[224] Reventlow, *Authority*, 340.

both new atheism and Protestant fundamentalist thought. Two presuppositions were identified, and their development charted: a literal, univocal, and perspicuous reading of Scripture and a disruptive and substitutionary understanding of divine activity. That the English Reformation and its consequences could have led to the first flowering of anti-Christian thought is surprising, and is not widely considered in the existing literature. In order to overcome the authority of the Roman Catholic Church, the Reformers advanced the principles of *sola scriptura* and *sola fide*. The first principle undermined Roman Catholic tradition by positing the self-authenticating nature of Scripture and a literal and perspicuous reading of its text, while the second principle undermined the Church's sacramental function by teaching the direct, saving presence of Christ in the heart of the individual. Yet in the absence of government control and Church guidance, these principles led to contempt for Scripture, and an immanent understanding of God's Spirit that led to anarchic antinomianism. In response, the Restoration Church emphasised reason to limit the scope of *sola scriptura* and *sola fide*, confining revelation to Scripture and its literal, univocal, and perspicuous sense alone, an approach that found systematic treatment in the work of John Locke. Yet this rejuvenated literalism, allied to empiricist philosophy, led some to question whether Scripture was revelation at all, impugning its textual history and internal proofs, and questioning the right of clergy to give authoritative interpretations of texts that were capable of being read and assessed by all. In response to the threat of freethought, the social and religious conflict engendered by the Reformation, and the growth of natural philosophy, English divines and natural philosophers championed natural theology, and a disruptive and substitutionary understanding of divine activity. This development – made possible by new literal readings of Genesis 1–3 – helped to harmonise revelation and reason, unifying these potentially conflicting authorities into a greater whole. This was at the cost, however, of undermining traditional understandings of dual causation, and the inclusion of God's activity within models of natural-philosophical description. Divine activity became ontologically distinct – yet functionally equivalent – with natural causes. For a time, this hermeneutical and natural-theological synthesis served the Church well. Yet the constellation of social and philosophical factors that gave rise to this convergence of interests between science and religion would dissipate in the slums and laboratories of industrial England, where the Reformation would finally come of age.

2

Things Fall Apart

This chapter examines the transmission and popular effect of the hermeneutical and natural theological presuppositions established during the Reformation and Restoration. We shall see how a literal, univocal and perspicuous understanding of Scripture, and the belief that divine activity disrupts and substitutes for natural causation, contributed to both plebeian atheism and middle-class loss of faith. This was not, of course, the intention of the high principles that lay behind these presuppositions, and, for a time, they brought great benefits to the Protestant churches. Biblical literalism helped to immunise against the persistent threat of Roman Catholicism, while disposing of radical readings by Protestant enthusiasts. When wedded to natural theology, literalism marshalled the new sciences to the defence and promotion of Scripture and the Established Church. Yet while the new hermeneutic checked a number of inadvertent effects of *sola fide*, it did so by strengthening the principle of *sola scriptura*. This led to the decline of Reformed confessional theology among nonconformists, a tradition that had previously helped to ameliorate scriptural contradictions, and variance between Scripture and known fact. This, in addition to the political and social marginalisation of nonconformists, led to a dialectic within popular Protestantism between conservative evangelicalism and plebeian atheism, which mirrored each other in surprising ways. As long as the middle classes remained committed to the faith, however, there was little hope of atheism gaining ground. The change came when the natural theological framework, begun by Newton and Bentley, and brought to its culmination in Paley, was challenged by advances in geology and evolutionary theory, which questioned literal readings of Genesis, and the design theory that supported them. Due to the absence in many churches of theological traditions that could adapt to non-literal readings, this gave rise to both proto-fundamentalism and a loss of religious faith. These changes resulted in an unprecedented separation between Christian theology and science, yet not without many individuals retaining the belief that Genesis' sense was literal, univocal and perspicuous and that divine activity and natural causation were mutually exclusive. With the support of the respectable classes, unbelief was sheared of its political radicalism, and atheism was on its way to a new respectability.

In charting how the biblical and natural theological framework established at the Restoration gave rise to atheism and anti-Christian thought, we do wrong if we fall into four errors. The first is to mistake the scope of the argument presented here. It is not argued that the genesis of irreligion and atheism is due solely to the two intellectual factors we are examining. A range of social, political and intellectual causes were operative. Rather, what is argued is that these presuppositions played a leading role in the genesis of irreligion and atheism. The second error is to see atheism as either a purely intellectual or a purely social phenomenon. While it is legitimate – and indeed essential – for the purpose of analysis to take each intellectual and social factor in turn, atheist thought arises both from concrete social practices and cultures and is, in turn, instantiated within them. One cannot understand atheism by focussing on only one of these aspects. The third potential error is to see this relationship as a purely causal one. While such a causal account is necessary, we do better if we see atheist thought as the instrument and intellectual weapon of a particular culture and form of life, and the preservation and furtherance of that culture and form of life as the ultimate end of atheist thought. It is only by attending to this dynamic and dialectical relationship between thought and practice that the genesis of atheist thought will disclose itself to us. The fourth and final error is to see atheism as a phenomenon that came into being fully formed at some period of the recent past. Rather, under certain social, political, theological and philosophical conditions, the biblical and natural theological presuppositions we are examining took on a new atheistic function, serving ends very different from those intended by their Protestant originators. The following chapter aims to be attentive to this dynamic and dialectical process of intellectual and social change, thereby throwing into relief the complex theological origins of atheism.

DISSENTERS AND EVANGELICALS

The origins of nineteenth-century unbelief must be sought in the transmission and development of Locke's biblical hermeneutics within dissenting and Methodist churches from the end of the seventeenth century to the middle of the eighteenth. While this philosophy was conceived as a defence of Protestant theology and hermeneutics, the popular effect of a literal, univocal and perspicuous Scripture was the gradual neglect of Calvinist theology and confessional statements, and an increasing emphasis upon personal conviction of Bible truths. These developments laid the foundation for a great reversal in popular piety in later decades

The Restoration, and the anxieties of the Cavalier Parliament, ushered in a raft of measures to enforce uniformity within the Church of England, and restore ecclesial and political order after the chaos of the Civil War. These measures, beginning with the Act of Uniformity of 1662, became known as the Clarendon Code, and were designed to limit the civil rights of those who dissented from the Church of England. The Act of Uniformity required all clergy ordained during the Civil War to submit to episcopal re-ordination, as well as requiring the compulsory use of the Book of Common Prayer. We have already seen how puritans rejected many elements of the 'popish liturgy' of the Prayer Book. Yet the decision of over two thousand clergy to leave the Church of England was due to more than mere externals. The Great Ejection was also a result of the rejection, by a significant minority of clergy, of the ecclesiology and political theology of the Church of England. The Book of Common Prayer presupposed an organic and hierarchical unity of Church and state, with the King and Bishops at its head, and the people of England as its incorporated members.[1] The Church declared itself to possess the authority to settle religious disputes, and to regulate rites and ceremonies not contrary to the Word of God. Opposed to this conception of the Church were Presbyterians, Independents and Baptists, who rejected episcopal government and wished to return to a purely scriptural polity. The political instability and religious pluralism of the time demanded stabilising measures, and, in this context, the decision to enforce religious conformity through legal sanction made political sense. Yet these political aims, and the theological claims that enforced them, would have grave, unintended

---

[1] See A. M. C. Waterman, 'The Nexus between Theology and Political Doctrine', in *Enlightenment and Religion*, ed. Knud Haakonssen (Cambridge: Cambridge University Press, 1996), 193–218.

effects, which would secure division between Anglicans and nonconformists, and, more seriously, create the theological and political conditions for atheism.

Excluded from public office and the universities, dissenters soon began construction of an independent education system. An emphasis upon Scripture, rather than Church authority and theological tradition, gave the dissenting educational system unique features not shared by its Anglican equivalent. Dissenting academies favoured natural science and modern languages over classics, and were early champions of the empirical philosophy and political theory of John Locke.[2] As we have seen, Locke's thought favoured unguided Bible reading unencumbered by theological tradition, allowing the Word of God to speak for itself. From the Restoration until the early eighteenth century, dissenters retained a reputation for orthodoxy not always shared by their Anglican cousins. Yet, as the spirit of Locke and empiricism began to make its impact more deeply felt, the Calvinist theology that had been the foundation of dissenting life began to give way.[3] Works such as Samuel Clarke's *Scripture Doctrine of the Trinity* (1712) – which presented a new interpretation of the doctrine of the Trinity through a re-evaluation of the biblical data – resonated with the dissenting clergy, who felt that private interpretation of Scripture should take precedence over confessional statements, which were viewed by a growing number to be an odious remnant of Roman Catholicism. During the Salter's Hall Controversy of 1719, a small majority of dissenting clergy refused to assent to the inclusion of sections from the Westminster Shorter Catechism as a preface to advice they were asked to provide, preferring to use scriptural texts alone. At the time, such actions might be perceived as championing the supremacy of scriptural teaching over arbitrary human formulations, and completing the religious changes begun by the Reformers. Yet, within two generations, the largely Presbyterian group that refused to assent to the Catechism would move off into greater heterodoxy, eventually becoming Socinian and Unitarian in their theology. The abandonment of orthodox Trinitarian theology was not, as is sometimes supposed, due primarily to external Enlightenment pressure, then, but arose from the unguided reading of Scripture.

---

[2] Jeremy Goring, 'The Break-Up of the Old Dissent', in *The English Presbyterians*, ed. C. Gordon Bolam (London: George Allan and Unwin, 1968), 191; Roger Thomas, 'Presbyterians in Transition', in *The English Presbyterians*, ed. C. Gordon Bolam (London: George Allan and Unwin, 1968), 140; Young, *Religion and Enlightenment*, 7–9.

[3] Thomas, 'Transition', 146.

In contrast, the Independents – who retained greater use of confessional statements – would remain largely orthodox.[4]

The dissenting denominations – especially the Presbyterians – continued to decline as the century progressed. Yet an event of great importance would soon reverse their fortunes, taking their biblical hermeneutic and popularising it among unprecedented numbers of working people. The evangelical revival began with the innovative preaching of George Whitefield and John Wesley, and quickly spread throughout England. The new piety found particular support in those areas where political deference to the establishment was weak, or where the Church of England had only a nominal presence due to changes in population, such as the North.[5] The result was that its primary constituency was drawn from the skilled working and lower middle classes, as well as the dwindling dissenting population.[6] While it is notoriously difficult to locate the essence of evangelical Christianity, Bebbington's four criteria of conversionism, activism, Biblicism and crucicentrism provide a good working definition.[7] Although the evangelical revival had strong antecedents in puritan theology and popular piety, it has sometimes been seen as a quasi-irrational, affective response to the growing emphasis upon reason in mid-Enlightenment England.[8] Yet far from being opposed to Enlightenment, the primary factor for the genesis and growth of evangelical piety and preaching was the empirical spirit of the age, and, more precisely, the philosophy of John Locke. Bebbington argues that it is Locke's *Essay* – which appeared in nine separate English editions and four collected editions between 1727 and 1760 – that provided the greatest impetus for the revival.[9] Locke's philosophy was 'habitual' among evangelicals throughout the eighteenth century and beyond, who conceived of their faith in inductive terms, stressing 'experimental piety' over doctrine, and championing deep affective conviction of one's

[4] J. Goring, introduction to *The English Presbyterians*, ed. C. Gordon Bolam (London: George Allan and Unwin, 1968), 26–7.
[5] David W. Bebbington, *Evangelicalism in Modern Britain* (London and New York: Routledge, 2005), 27; George M. Ditchfield, *The Evangelical Revival* (London: University College London Press, 1998), 64.
[6] Ditchfield, *Evangelical Revival*, 65; E. Gordon Rupp, *Religion in England 1688–1791* (Oxford: Clarendon Press, 1986), 445.
[7] Bebbington, *Evangelicalism*, 1–19.
[8] Phyllis Mack, *Heart Religion in the British Enlightenment* (Cambridge: Cambridge University Press, 2008), 295; Bebbington, *Evangelicalism*, 34–5.
[9] Bebbington, *Evangelicalism*, 74.

salvation by Christ.[10] While the theology of Wesley was balanced, with a strong preference for the Church Fathers, he nevertheless summarised his devotion to the primacy of Scripture by identifying himself as '*homo unius libris*', and evangelical piety in general, like Locke's empiricism, had a strong anti-metaphysical and anti-traditional complexion.[11]

Evangelicalism would come to exert a profound effect upon British culture, and affected the course of popular Christianity in two important ways. First, the experiential and deeply personal complexion of evangelical Christianity, which called upon the individual to submit themselves totally to Christ, led to a changed understanding of what it was to be a Christian, particularly among nonconformists. A Christian came to be seen less as someone who engaged in churchgoing than as someone who had personal conviction of the truth of the Gospel, and had surrendered their heart and mind to Christ. This high standard of religiosity created a novel opportunity for unbelief, for the evangelical temper of the age encouraged those who could not meet its high standards to doubt the sincerity of their conversion. Questions and hesitations that, at an earlier time, might have been laid aside as trivial or unimportant, now assumed ultimate significance, and conscience demanded that sober individuals who could not satisfy themselves of their full conversion should separate themselves from the faithful.[12] Second, an emphasis upon the individual, and their personal assent to the faith, further weakened the place of doctrine, for individuals were no longer asked to give intellectual assent to a system of beliefs, nor to the authority of the Church, but to surrender their heart to the promises of God made in Scripture. This had three implications for the Bible and its interpretation. First, the diminution in importance of doctrinal systems raised the standing of the Bible to new heights. While there were a range of views among evangelical clergy on the subject of inspiration and inerrancy, the popular view, as we shall see, was less subtle, and, in practice, viewed the Bible as akin to truth itself, without admixture of error.[13] Second, while the loss of confidence in confessions and systems amplified the importance of Scripture, this rejection

---

[10] Bebbington, *Evangelicalism*, 57; Donald Davie, *Dissentient Voice* (Notre Dame: University of Notre Dame Press, 1982), 25–6.

[11] John Walsh, 'Methodism at the End of the Eighteenth Century', in *A History of the Methodist Church in Great Britain*, vol. I, ed. Rupert E. Davies and E. Gordon Rupp (London: Epworth Press, 1965), 297–8.

[12] Timothy Larsen, *Crisis of Doubt* (Oxford: Oxford University Press, 2006), 10–13.

[13] Bebbington, *Evangelicalism*, 86–7.

made Scripture's position precarious.[14] As long as the Bible was situated within a wider body of sacred doctrine, its canonicity was justified
by a theological tradition that accorded it supreme authority.[15] When
this was gone, the authority of Scripture had to be grounded in other
ways, and this came to be sought, in the first instance, in its internal
consistency, and, second, its harmony with current knowledge. As was
seen in Chapter 1, these changes first began with the Reformers' need
to secure the self-authenticating authority of Scripture. Yet this self-
authentication was balanced by a confessional superstructure that
accomplished many of the same functions as Roman Catholic tradition.
These changes meant that, third, the prestige and authority of Scripture
came to be conditional upon something *other* than Christ and the
Church's witness of faith, leaving Scripture vulnerable. The Lockean
spirit of the age, coupled with the relative lack of education among
Methodists and their ministers, led to a strong preference for literal and
perspicuous understandings of Scripture. This made internal consistency harder to achieve, and left faith vulnerable to the advances of the
natural sciences. For as long as no one sought to investigate and
display the inner contradictions of Scripture, and the natural sciences
remained underdeveloped, literal interpretations of Scripture divorced
from theological tradition caused no serious harm, and allowed the
Bible to be easily appropriated by all. Yet the presuppositions and
interpretive culture that facilitated the rapid popularisation of evangelical Bible reading would, with the vicissitudes of a new industrial
culture, facilitate the first popular anti-Christian movements, who, in
their infidelity, mirrored the presuppositions and practices of their
evangelical cousins.

THE GATHERING OF INFIDELS

The Victorian 'crisis of faith' is a familiar topic of nineteenth-century
British history. In the majority of works, it is commonly treated as a
largely middle-class phenomenon. Thoughtful, introspective Victorians,
abreast of the latest developments in modern thought, begin to doubt the

---

[14] Willis B. Glover, *Evangelical Nonconformists and Higher Criticism in the Nineteenth
Century* (London: Independent Press, 1954), 17.

[15] See Feyerabend for the argument that traditions ground Scripture and not vice versa. Paul
K. Feyerabend, 'Classical Empiricism', in *The Methodological Heritage of Newton*, ed.
Robert E. Butts and John W. Davis (Oxford: Basil Blackwell, 1970), 150–70.

truth of the faith they were raised in as children, and eventually the rest of society follows suit. While there was undoubtedly a middle- and upper-class tradition of unbelief, typified by the ideas and personalities later associated with the *Westminster Review*, this familiar narrative can give rise to what has been called 'middle class myopia', and frequently over-looks a much older, *plebeian* tradition of unbelief.[16] This is unfortunate, as plebeian unbelief sheds great light upon the scriptural and hermeneut-ical foundations of the unbelief of *all* classes in nineteenth-century Britain. This section will overcome this oversight by tracing the development of this form of unbelief, locating its origins in political radicalism, and the hermeneutical practices popularised by Methodist and nonconformist churches, who, in their frequent rejection of theological tradition, lacked the resources to overcome textual contradictions and variance between Scripture and known fact. Terminology for non-Christian groups during the late eighteenth and nineteenth centuries was not fixed, and a wide variety of terms was used. For the sake of consistency, this section will use 'infidel' and 'freethinker' – with their related adjectives – interchangeably, to denote individuals and groups opposed to the Christian faith. 'Unbelief' will be used to denote the absence or loss of faith. 'Secularist' and 'atheist' will be reserved for individuals and groups explicitly aligning themselves with secular or atheist thought.

The freethinkers of the eighteenth century failed to seriously challenge the Anglican establishment due to their inability to enlist popular support for their cause. Their arguments, too refined and specialised to have mass appeal, were launched upon a nation that was still overwhelmingly rural and agricultural, locked into patterns of life that supported the retention of traditional beliefs and practices, and which favoured obedience to parson and squire. Yet the growth in industry from the second half of the eighteenth century saw the gradual dissolution of this world, as thousands moved from the settled pattern of rural life to the cities. The social dislocation affected by this movement was unprecedented, and seriously undermined loyalty to the prevailing Church-State alliance, which drew its legitimacy from social relations that were beginning to disappear. Yet, as important as this social context was, the movement

[16] Adrian Desmond, 'Artisan Resistance and Evolution in Britain, 1819–1848', *Osiris* 3 (1987): 79; Susan Budd, 'The Loss of Faith: Reasons for Unbelief among Members of the Secular Movement in England 1850–1950', *Past and Present* 36 (1967): 125; Larsen, *Crisis of Doubt*, 245–50. For an introduction to the *Westminster Review*, see G. L. Nesbitt, *Benthamite Reviewing: The First Twelve Years of the Westminster Review* (New York: Columbia University Press, 1934).

from a rural to an urban society was not sufficient, in and of itself, to give rise to the first organised anti-Christian movements. The decisive factor was that which had so exercised the freethinkers of an earlier time: *politics*. In a time when government played little direct role in the lives of ordinary people, it was the Church of England that best represented the authority of the state to the average person.[17] The priest was not only a religious figure, but also a political one. Just as the Church-State alliance had previously threatened the freedom of conscience of dissenters, and had raised the prospect of a new High Church popery, so the Church of England would now come to be seen as the guarantor of an oppressive and corrupt establishment, and the preserver of a social system which exploited the majority for the benefit of the few.

The impetus for the growth of organised anti-Christian thought in Britain did not come from home, however, but from events across the Channel. The outbreak of the French Revolution provoked both celebration and deep alarm across Britain. If revolution had broken out in a country so heavily dominated by Church and nobility, then there was a chance that Britain could follow in its wake. This fear proved to be justified, as popular societies were formed in towns and cities across the country, with the intention of creating a united front to force reform upon Parliament. As war with France became ever more likely, the government became increasingly alarmed at the growth of such societies, and appointed a Parliamentary Committee of Secrecy to investigate and halt popular unrest. Their fears were not wholly unfounded. The leading popular society – the London Corresponding Society – had affiliates across the country, had toyed with the idea of arming the people, and was implicated in an assault upon George III's carriage.[18] Other societies sent delegates to the Jacobin club in Paris, and raised money to send winter boots to the Revolutionary Army.[19] A National Convention was assembled in Edinburgh. In haste, the government reacted to these developments with the full force of the law, the Bow Street Police breaking up the London Corresponding Society during a debate on what the society would do in the event of a French invasion. The government also facilitated the formation of the Association for the Preservation of Liberty and

---

[17] Clark, *English Society*, 277–8.
[18] Clive Emsley, *British Society and the French Wars 1793–1815* (London: Macmillan, 1979), 47–8.
[19] Edward Royle and James Walvin, *English Radicals and Reformers 1760–1848* (Brighton: Harvester Press, 1982), 57–9.

Property, an organised mob of patriotic commoners and landowners, who intimidated and attacked those with pro-Revolutionary sentiments. While such repression helped to break up political resistance, it further polarised attitudes, and inadvertently radicalised some working people. While there was initially little explicit anti-Christian sentiment among the popular societies, a marked change occurred as time wore on. French anti-Christian thought, which had gained much of its impetus from earlier English freethought, began to be disseminated along with French revolutionary politics, and started to exert an influence on working-class attitudes. Anti-clericalism – always a feature of urban working-class life – was now strengthened into outright hostility against the faith. Christians were side-lined within the London societies, and drinking sessions resounded with the toast 'May the last King be strangled with the bowels of the last Priest!'[20] Repression cemented the close connection in the minds of some working people between civil and religious tyranny, and anti-Christian intellectual radicalism became closely related with political radicalism.[21] Thanks to economic inequality and state violence, the rarefied, intellectual freethought of the eighteenth century began to take root into popular soil.

The man who epitomises these trends, and who came to have the greatest impact on the growth of anti-Christian thought in the nineteenth century, was Thomas Paine. Paine spoke to the half-educated sections of society ready for change, and nurtured the incipient unity of religious and political radicalism.[22] His contribution to nineteenth-century unbelief began with the political tract *Rights of Man*, which sought to defend the legitimacy of the French Revolution. In this work, Paine diagnosed the corruption of government as emanating from its close association with religion. Government usurps power for itself through its claim to divine right, so that there is not simply 'the state' but 'Church and state'.[23] The result is that 'a sort of mule-animal, capable only of destroying, and not of breeding up, is produced, called *the Church established by law*'.[24] Through their mutual validation, Church and state preserve a social and

[20] Cf. William H. Reid, *The Rise and Dissolution of the Infidel Societies of the Metropolis* (London, 1800), 5–9, 15–16; Harold Perkin, *The Origins of Modern English Society 1780–1880* (London: Routledge, 1969), 207–8.

[21] Clark, *English Society*, 277–8.

[22] Edward Royle, *Victorian Infidels* (Manchester: Manchester University Press, 1974), 27–8.

[23] Thomas Paine, *Rights of Man* (London: J. S. Jordan, 1791), 49.

[24] Paine, *Rights of Man*, 74–5.

political order that is corrupt, and contemptuous of the natural rights of its citizens. *Rights of Man* proved to be popular, and was followed by *The Age of Reason*, written in two parts in Paris after Paine was appointed to the National Convention. This work continues the criticism of Church and state developed in *Rights of Man*, and represents an emphatic rejection of Christianity and the need for established churches, for, as Paine protested, 'My own mind is my own church'.[25] According to Paine, the churches do not rule through temporal power alone, but through their supposed possession of revealed truth in the Bible. While, in and of themselves, many narratives of the Bible are inoffensive, if untrue, when wed to a corrupt regime, they take on a sinister significance that must be challenged.[26] Paine sets about undermining the authority of Scripture using four lines of attack, drawn heavily from earlier freethought. First, traditional interpretations of biblical narratives are disrupted by removing them from their ecclesial setting and placing them alongside pagan myth, casting doubt on their exclusivism.[27] Second, respect for the text is subverted by taking the pervasive literalism of the age to its irreverent conclusion. Genesis is likened to a seedy backstreet sideshow, where God the magician stoops to the level of a cheap conjurer, pulling light from darkness, and land from sea, in a narrative that has days and nights without a sun, and as much scientific value as the *Arabian Nights*, yet without their entertainment value.[28] The story of Jonah and the whale is so ludicrous that its only explanation is that of a Gentile satire on the pretensions and irrationalities of Jewish religion, inserted surreptitiously at some remote time.[29] The representation of God by a dove in the New Testament is barbaric and beneath his dignity, as is any representation of God in animal form.[30] The temptation of Christ, meanwhile, is met with impish incomprehension that the Saviour did not discover America when he was led up a high mountain to observe all the kingdoms of the earth, although Paine muses whether Christ's sight was limited to those nations with a monarchical system of government.[31] Paine's lack of understanding of genre, symbolism and allegory was noted and ridiculed by some of his contemporaries. Yet his literalism was not unfounded, for it found correlates within the contemporary Church.[32] Where his literalism

---

[25] Thomas Paine, *Age of Reason*, Part I (Paris: 1794), 3.   [26] Cf. Paine, *Reason I*, 71–2.
[27] E.g. Paine, *Reason I*, 13–16.
[28] Thomas Paine, *Age of Reason*, Part II (London, 1799), 9, 91–2 unnumbered note.
[29] Paine, *Reason II*, 55.   [30] Paine, *Reason II*, 90.   [31] Paine, *Reason I*, 110.
[32] Royle, *Infidels*, 28.

differed from his Christian contemporaries, however, was in its function, which, like earlier freethinkers, was used to break apart the biblical canon by denying the possibility of prophecy. Old testament 'prophecies', like the virgin in the time of Ahaz, were never intended to refer to future events, and it is only the ignorance of the Church that mistook them for anything else.[33] In summarising the history of prophetic interpretation, Paine concludes that 'Every phrase and circumstance is marked with the barbarous hand of superstitious torture, and forced into meanings it was impossible they could have.'[34] More serious than Paine's literalism, however, was his third line of attack, which threw doubt on the authorship of the biblical canon. Universal truths, such as Euclid's geometry, do not rely on the testimony of Euclid to guarantee their truth. Not so with the books of Scripture. These depend upon the testimony of witnesses, and the identity of these witnesses is therefore of paramount importance in ascertaining their trustworthiness. Paine engages in textual criticism to show that Moses could not have authored the Pentateuch, that the major prophets have more than one author, and that the four evangelists are unidentifiable.[35] The result is that we do not know who testifies to revelation, and their testimony fails.

It is perhaps Paine's fourth strategy against Scripture, however, that would be most generative for future unbelief: the argument from science. Over and above the textual and exegetical difficulties with Scripture looms the logical impossibility of revelation, and a corresponding preference for the certainties of empirical observation. Paine defines revelation as knowledge that we are incapable of discovering for ourselves, communicated immediately from God to an *individual*.[36] The moment one attempts to communicate this knowledge to another, one's testimony ceases to be revelation for two reasons. First – and echoing Locke – we must only believe what we have seen and experienced for ourselves. Yet, second, and moving beyond Locke, Paine emphasises the local and changeable nature of language, which is incapable of serving as a means of expressing immutable and universal truth.[37] For this reason, the Bible cannot be called the Word of God, as eternal truths are univocal and unambiguous, while the language of the Bible is open to countless interpretations, and heir to all the difficulties of translation.[38] While the book of Scripture fails to convey eternal truths, Paine knows of a book that

---

[33] Paine, *Reason II*, 49–50.   [34] Paine, *Reason II*, 38.   [35] Paine, *Reason II*, 9–58.
[36] Paine, *Reason I*, 22–3, 5–7.   [37] Paine, *Reason I*, 45, 47.   [38] Paine, *Reason I*, 31–2.

does reveal such truths: *the book of nature.*[39] 'It is an ever existing original, which every man can read. It cannot be forged; it cannot be counterfeited; it cannot be lost; it cannot be altered; it cannot be suppressed'.[40] Science, which discloses the teaching of this immutable book, therefore assumes quasi-divine attributes, penetrating the depths of existence to comprehend eternal, universal truths.[41] This universal and self-evident method calls Christian revelation into question, and, aware of this fact, the Church calls science and the study of nature irreligion, and persecutes great scientists such as Galileo.[42] In its place, it encourages the study of tradition and dead languages as ends in themselves, failing to see that language only has truth to the extent that it signifies *things.*[43] Science is *true* theology, while theology so-called is literally the study of nothing. It has no data, no verifiable authorities, and fails to demonstrate anything.[44] Summarising the Christian religion is an easy, if scathing activity:

Too absurd for belief, too impossible to convince, and too inconsistent for practice, it renders the heart torpid, or produces only atheists and fanatics.[45]

We have dwelt on Paine for some time, because while his personal beliefs halted at deism, his thought eloquently reproduces the presuppositions and methods of earlier freethinkers, presuppositions and methods that he would transmit to nineteenth-century infidels: the close connection of political and religious radicalism, the pre-eminence of literal readings of Scripture, the adoption of textual criticism as the primary weapon against Christianity, and a belief in the quasi-divine status of science and reason. We also find in his thought a suggestion that will prove strangely prescient: that the Protestant Christianity of his age would, if followed consistently and passionately, produce only atheists, or fanatics.

While famous in his day, Paine's legacy soon fell into abeyance, and it would be twenty years before his thought made itself felt again. During that time, war with France, and the necessity of preserving public order during the economic collapse following victory, brought even greater oppression. As before, such legal and political oppression brought short-term gains, but long-term strategic loss. Government oppression culminated in the deaths of fifteen people, and four to seven hundred injuries during a cavalry charge on a radical gathering at St Peter's Field Manchester in August 1819, an event known to history as the Peterloo

[39] Paine, *Reason I*, 45.   [40] Paine, *Reason I*, 47.   [41] Paine, *Reason I*, 56–7.
[42] Paine, *Reason I*, 70, 75, 71.   [43] Paine, *Reason I*, 70–1, 65–6.
[44] Paine, *Reason I*, 55; Paine, *Reason II*, 90.   [45] Paine, *Reason II*, 89.

Massacre. As a poignant symbol of the unity of Church and state, the Riot Act that day was read by an Anglican clergyman, acting in his role as a civil magistrate. One of the scheduled speakers at the rally was radical publisher Richard Carlisle. In reaction to government oppression, Carlisle soon began the popularisation of Paine's views by issuing his works in cheap editions, for which he was rewarded with prosecution for blasphemy, blasphemous libel, and sedition. Far from putting an end to Paine's legacy, however, this ill-conceived prosecution greatly strengthened it. Carlisle took the opportunity afforded by his defence to read *The Age of Reason* verbatim into the court records, which led to its inadvertent publication in the case reports, selling 10,000 copies in cheap two penny prints. Even if some of the traditional calculations for his print sales – 200,000 for *Rights of Man* – are exaggerated, there can be no doubt that Paine's reception among the working class was unprecedented.[46]

The Carlisle prosecution came during the years of 'fixed bayonets and despotic laws', running from the Regency to the Great Chartist Meeting on Kennington Common. As Desmond argues, these years would be crucial for the development of popular unbelief.[47] From 1800 to 1831, almost all the population of the proceeding century died, and were replaced by city-dwellers who did not belong to the traditional nexus of social and religious duties that underpinned the alliance of Church and state.[48] The population grew by ten million between 1800 and 1851, and most of the growth was in the irreligious cities.[49] For the first time, there was a literate working-class readership eager for radical literature, and open to the idea that the Established Church was among the greatest hindrances to social equality, and the dignity of working people. The most seminal movement of the period was the socialism of Robert Owen, which attracted the men – for these were overwhelmingly masculine movements – who would form the backbone of atheist and secular movements for decades to come. Although Owen's ventures ended in failure, they inspired the creation of periodicals such as William Chilton and Charles Southwell's explicitly atheist *The Oracle of Reason*, and George Holyoake's *Reasoner*, the latter of which was influential in the development of secularism as an ideology. While such enterprises were usually short lived and plagued with problems, the heterogeneity and

---

[46] Royle and Walvin, *English Radicals*, 54.   [47] Desmond, 'Artisan Resistance', 80.
[48] Clark, *English Society*, 373.
[49] Owen Chadwick, *The Victorian Church*, Part I (London: A&C Black, 1966), 325.

disorganisation of popular infidelity was ameliorated somewhat by the formation, in 1866, of the National Secular Society under Charles Bradlaugh, which brought a collection of smaller secular and anti-Christian societies under one banner. We need not detain ourselves with the tangled histories of these organisations and periodicals, yet one question concerning their activities is highly relevant for this study: just *who* was persuaded by such ideas, and *why* were significant numbers of people willing not only to abandon the beliefs of their neighbours, but to adopt beliefs diametrically opposed to them, risking imprisonment, personal ruin, and social approbation?

One might assume that such individuals were already irreligious, or were members of churches – such as the Unitarians – which were already heterodox. While there were some – such as Charles Southwell – that came from irreligious backgrounds, the great majority of converts to secular and infidel societies came, unsurprisingly, from Christian households. The biographical information available for membership of secular and infidel groups is not great, yet it reveals consistent trends. While Royle warns against drawing conclusions from biographies and membership information, the trends they suggest are amply supported by other evidence, and Royle himself adopts conclusions similar to those that will follow.[50] There are two striking features of the available data. First, one might expect recruitment to secular and infidel groups to be proportional to church membership, with the Church of England, constituting over 50 per cent of all churchgoing in 1851, being the largest denomination represented.[51] Yet this is not what the data shows. On the contrary, Anglicans are notable by their relative absence. Which churches, then, formed the largest constituency for secular societies? None other those churches whose pattern of piety and biblical interpretation we have already had cause to consider: Methodists and nonconformists.[52] It is *these* groups, in many ways the vanguard of Protestant conservatism and bibliolatry, that seem to have produced *the most* converts to secularism and infidelity, in numbers totally disproportionate to their size.

This paradox requires explanation. Two factors appear to have been significant. The first is the *class* of person that was typically involved in

---

[50] Cf. Edward Royle, *Radicals, Secularists and Republicans* (Manchester: Manchester University Press, 1980), 126–36, 167–70.

[51] See Owen Chadwick, *The Victorian Church*, Part II (London: SCM Press, 1972), 218–38.

[52] Susan Budd, *Varieties of Unbelief* (London: Heinemann, 1977), 97.

Methodism and nonconformity, and, second, the *patterns* of piety and biblical interpretation that were typically associated with these groups. Infidels and secularists were overwhelmingly skilled urban working class, the same class that made up the majority of Methodists and nonconformists.[53] By comparison, very few agricultural workers were members, at a time when they made up a significant percentage of the population.[54] There is a considerable literature on the subject of whether or not Methodism and nonconformity in general exercised an inhibiting or empowering influence upon working-class radicalism, a debate that has centred on the so-called Halévy thesis that Methodism stopped Britain from succumbing to revolution.[55] In one of the most stringent expressions of that thesis, Thompson famously branded Methodism as little more than the 'chialism of despair', a pathetic sop that smothered the nobler passions of working-class socialism.[56] The details of this debate do not concern us, yet it is important to note that later scholars have tempered the Halévy thesis, and have noted many contrary tendencies in working-class Methodism and nonconformity, so that, far from inhibiting political and religious radicalism, Methodism and nonconformity often actively promoted it. As Clark notes, to be a Methodist or nonconformist during this period suggested a degree of defiance towards the establishment, and Methodism in particular was, with good reason, associated with political radicalism.[57] A number of cases have been documented where individuals moved through Methodism and Primitive Methodism to secularism and atheism, before sometimes making the transition back again.[58] Such patterns become intelligible when we recall the close connection between political and religious radicalism in this period, and the shared interests of secularists, infidels, and nonconformists, who each campaigned for disestablishment and legal equality with their Anglican neighbours.[59] Atheism, then, can be partially explained by the degree of dislike a skilled working-class individual had towards the establishment, and the degree of connection

[53] Bebbington, *Evangelicalism*, 113–14.   [54] Royle, *Infidels*, 237, 239.
[55] For an overview of the arguments, see Gerald W. Olsen, ed., *Religion and Revolution in Early-Industrial England* (Lanham: University Press of America, 1990).
[56] E. P. Thompson, *The Making of the English Working Class* (Harmondsworth: Penguin, 1980), 427.
[57] Clark, *English Society*, 379; Edward Hobsbawn, 'Methodism and Revolution', in *Religion and Revolution in Early-Industrial England*, ed. Gerald W. Olsen (Lanham: University Press of America, 1990), 150.
[58] Cf. Iain McCalman, *Radical Underworld* (Oxford: Clarendon Press, 1993), 50–4; Perkin, *Modern Society*, 353–5, 205–6; Larsen, *Crisis of Doubt*, 72–108, 136–72.
[59] Royle, *Infidels*, 1.

they made between Christianity and their social and economic marginal-isation. Anglicans – especially those living within an agricultural setting with its traditional nexus of obligations – were, in an important way, *part* of the establishment, and therefore had little political reason to challenge Christianity.

These political factors are not enough, in and of themselves, however, to explain the strange convergence of Methodism, nonconformity, and atheism, and it is at this point that the biblical presuppositions we have been examining became operative. Out of one hundred and fifty available biographies of secularists, forty-eight out of fifty-eight list *two books* as being instrumental in their conversion to secularism. The first is, not unexpectedly, Paine's *Age of Reason*. The second, however, was not some equally scurrilous work, but the one work which might be supposed to protect one from atheism: *the Bible*. It was the Bible, and Paine's *Age of Reason*, that seem to have driven most Christians to atheism.[60] Yet this is only partly true, for it is not books that convert, but books read in conjunction with certain modes of interpretation. We noted earlier how nonconformity and Methodism increasingly came to reject confessional statements and theological systems in favour of unguided Bible reading. This pattern of biblical interpretation now bore bitter fruit, as noncon-formists and Methodists, searching their Bibles with an interpretive framework informed by the Lockean spirit of the age, and cut loose from Church tradition, sought coherent and consistent answers from the book they had been taught was the self-authenticating Word of God, and above error. When inconsistencies and factual errors were encountered, the logical option open to these conservative and often semi-educated Chris-tians was that the Bible had refuted its own authority, and was not the Word of God.[61] This was the experience of countless converts to atheism, including two of the most famous leaders of the movement, Charles Bradlaugh and Annie Besant.[62] Far from being innovative, Paine's *Age of Reason* merely acted as a spur to the serious Bible study that many already felt called to undertake for purely devotional reasons.

The presuppositions that converts to atheism continued to hold con-cerning Christianity in general and, in particular, the Bible, give add-itional weight to this interpretation. One might have thought that there

---

[60] Budd, 'The Loss of Faith', 109–10.
[61] Budd, 'The Loss of Faith', 110; Larsen, *Crisis of Doubt*, 239–40.
[62] See Timothy Larsen, *A People of One Book* (Oxford: Oxford University Press, 2011), 69–70, 75–6.

was a spectrum of belief, ranging from conservative-evangelical, through shades of liberalism, to atheism, which individuals progressed along as they gradually lost their faith. Yet it was not half-hearted or liberal Christians that typically made the transition to atheism, but those raised in evangelical households.[63] What is noticeable in the biographies and surviving works of the atheists of the nineteenth century is their *rejection* of liberal theology as an aberration of true Christianity. They generally accepted Erasmus Darwin's view of liberalism as a dishonest crutch for the weak, 'a feather-bed to catch a falling Christian'.[64] F. W. Foote, founder of *The Freethinker*, charged the authors of *Lex Mundi* with heresy, in the sure knowledge that Christianity could only be the biblicist, conservative movement he had known all his life, going so far as to elicit sympathy for conservatives like Moody and Gladstone. Of the latter he could say, 'When we want a sermon or an essay ... we know where to get it, and we like it unadulterated.'[65] This attitude arose as a consequence of the evangelical temper of the age. Evangelicalism established a high bar for Christian identity, far above mere churchgoing or participation in the Eucharist. The mark of a true Christian was her total emotional and intellectual assent to the truth of Scripture, and her experience of new life in Christ. Yet the consequence of this was that if one's experience or beliefs did not reach this high standard, then one was not truly a Christian, and the logic of evangelicalism then insisted that one be open about one's doubt, rather than remain as a hypocrite within the fold of the Church. Faith could become a zero-sum game, where one either had full faith in biblical Christianity or became an atheist.[66]

If secularists cared little for liberalism, they certainly knew a great deal about biblical theology, and the typical strategies they adopted against Christianity were bibliocentric in nature, relying upon literal interpretations and lower criticism.[67] Their literalism took three forms: mockery, the identification of internal contradictions and absurdities, and the noting of inconsistencies with contemporary science. Texts such as Exodus 33:23 ('I shall take away my hand, and thou shalt see my back parts') were taken out of their textual setting by atheists such as Foote to

---

[63] Cf. Budd, *Varieties*, 120.

[64] Cited in Jim Herrick, *Vision and Realism: A Hundred Years of the Freethinker* (London: G. W. Foote & Co, 1982), 24.

[65] Royle, *Radicals*, 298, 303–4.   [66] Larsen, *Crisis of Doubt*, 10–11.

[67] Budd, *Varieties*, 88.

stress their literal – blasphemous – sense.[68] Likewise, the literal sense was employed to show the 'contradiction' of texts such as Leviticus 23: 14, 21 ('it shall be a statute forever') and Romans 7:6 ('But now we are delivered from the law'), Proverbs 3:13 ('Happy is the man that findeth wisdom') and Ecclesiastes 1: 18 ('For in much wisdom is much grief').[69] Discussion of such contradictions was accompanied by attacks upon the consistency of Scripture with known fact, particularly the Book of Genesis. The creation narratives of Genesis 1–3, taken in their literal sense, were rejected on the basis of archaeology, geology, and palaeontology. Non-literal readings were explicitly denied. As Bradlaugh wrote of such spiritual, 'prayerful' readings, 'You must read prayerfully, that is, you must be prepared to cast away your senses every time they are opposed to your Bible.'[70]

These strategies were not adopted because they were considered the best suited to destroying faith, but because they arose naturally from the presuppositions that atheists continued to hold regarding the faith they rejected. Just as the freethinkers of an earlier time had pushed *sola scriptura* and the literal sense to their logical conclusion, so nineteenth-century secularists and atheists did what they had been taught to do as children: read the plain sense of a text presumed to be infallible, without the aid of any theological gloss. Yet to read the Bible without any conscious interpretive guide, save for a belief that its authority was guaranteed by its inerrancy, was to adopt the only hermeneutical framework left to hand: logical consistency, and correspondence with known fact. This is the framework which infidels used to interpret Scripture, taking passages literally, and independent of their theological and liturgical setting. It is worth considering the following passage from Foote, which describes his disgust for those Christians that continued to encounter Scripture within a primarily ecclesial and liturgical setting:

Almost every family has a copy of the Bible, but it is usually the best preserved book in the house ... Christians grow familiar with the judicious selections read aloud from the pulpit, but the rest of the holy volume remains to them a blank. Hence the surprise – which we ourselves have frequently witnessed – they exhibit when a sceptic cites an awkward text.[71]

---

[68] Joss L. Marsh, '"Bibliolatry" and "Bible-Smashing": G. W. Foote, George Meredith, and the Heretic Trope of the Book', *Victorian Studies* 34 (1991), 311–13.

[69] F. W. Foote and W. P. Ball, *The Bible Handbook* (London: Progressive Publishing, 1888), 10, 14.

[70] Charles Bradlaugh, *The Bible: What It Is!* (London: 1857), 8–14.

[71] Foote and Ball, *Handbook*, iii.

Foote's comment uncovers the paradoxical nature of popular Protestant piety in nineteenth-century England. On the one hand, the majority of the population were members of Protestant churches, and roughly half of churchgoers were attending nonconformist and Methodist churches that laid particular stress upon Bible reading, and the importance of conscience and personal conviction of the Gospel.[72] Yet, in practice, few made serious study of their Bibles, and even fewer did so while suspending the theological presuppositions and systems of doctrine they had been raised with. The majority did what the Christians of Britain had always done: they encountered Scripture within the context of worship and teaching, or, in times of joy and trial, brought to mind those passages that spoke most to their hearts. Atheists like Foote demanded more, and desired a fully coherent and inerrant Scripture that did more than simply soothe the soul. In this, atheists were sometimes more faithful to their Protestant heritage than many of their God-fearing contemporaries. They did not reject Christianity because they were unchristian, then, but because they were Protestant, and, driven by disgust for a Church that supported a corrupt establishment, followed the path trod by their freethinking predecessors, taking *sola scriptura,* and the literal sense, to one of their logical conclusions.

It is in this that we witness the unusual *mirroring,* or *sympathy* between atheist and evangelical thought that has been noted by a number of commentators.[73] Both groups shared the same biblical hermeneutic, the same understanding of science and religion, and the same conception of what it was to be a Christian. This mirroring was found even within families. Charles Bradlaugh's brother – William Robert – was converted by Moody and Sankey, and established the Anti-Infidel League to harass his brother, advancing a proto-fundamentalist platform that rejected Darwin and biblical criticism. This brother, and the League he founded, were the reverse of all that the other stood for, 'almost to the point of caricature'.[74] Perhaps surprisingly, the idea that the atheism of this time was dependent on the evangelicalism it rejected is shared by the official historian of *The Freethinker.* While noting that freethought is a wider phenomenon, Herrick argues that the attack upon the Bible by atheists and freethinkers 'could lead to a mirror-image evangelical anti-

---

[72] See Chadwick, *Victorian Church,* Part II, 218–38.
[73] Royle, *Infidels,* 109–19; Royle, *Radicals,* 167–70; Larsen, *One Book,* 70; Budd, *Varieties,* 45.
[74] Royle, *Radicals,* 307.

Christianity, which depended as deeply upon knowledge of the Bible as its obverse. The relationship between freethought and Christianity could become a form of hostile dependence'.[75] Atheists like Foote could even rejoice in their Protestant heritage, noting of the Roman Catholic Church that

It has always tried to keep the sacred volume in the hands of priests ... But the Protestant Church, by putting the Bible in the people's hands, opened a broad road to heresy, and flung Christianity into the melting-pot![76]

The reason for this sympathy lay in the predominantly skilled working class makeup of nineteenth-century atheism. It was this class that constituted the majority of Methodism and nonconformity, a class whose religiosity was exemplified by simple Gospel magazines like *The Friendly Visitor*, *Band of Hope Review*, and *King's Own*. This piety raised the Bible into an oracle of all truth: a means of comfort, education, correction, and hope. It was this conservative, biblicist Christianity that atheists rejected, not by adopting principles contrary to the tradition they had been raised in, but by taking the presuppositions of a predominantly nonconformist, working-class culture to their logical conclusion: letting a supposedly inerrant Bible speak for itself, shorn of all theological tradition. Militant freethought, like its mirror image in conservative Protestantism, lived by the Bible alone: *homines unius libri*.[77] Atheist and conservative evangelical thought came to be locked in a strange dialectic: a sympathetic antipathy, and an antipathetic sympathy.

The first archbishop of Westminster, Nicholas Wiseman, had a strong interest in the spirit of Protestantism, and gave a warning to churches seeking to distribute the Bible 'indiscriminately' to the working people of industrial Britain. He warned that Scripture teaches us not to cast pearls before swine, and that there are different kinds of food for different people: meat for the strong, and milk for the weak. Scripture is the work of the Church, and finds its proper setting in its life and worship. To put Bibles into the hands of men and women who can barely read, and then ask them to verify the truth of the Gospel for themselves, is to invite only heresy or mockery.[78] Wiseman understood well that mockery – and the unbelief that accompanies it – were not extrinsic to Protestantism, an

[75] Herrick, *Vision and Realism*, 19.
[76] G. W. Foote, *The Freethinker*, 13 March 1887. Quoted in Herrick, *Vision and Realism*, 21.
[77] Marsh, 'Bibliolatry', 316–17.   [78] Larsen, *One Book*, 51–2.

alien influence affecting it from outwith, but arose from tendencies intrinsic to it. The phenomenon of nineteenth-century atheism should not be understood as arising primarily from irreligious Enlightenment sources, then, but from within Protestantism itself. It arose from the teaching that the Bible was the self-authenticating Word of God, that a Christian was someone who gave full emotional and intellectual assent to the faith, and that Scripture should be interpreted in the literalistic and tradition-independent manner favoured by Locke. Yet this form of Christianity was highly vulnerable, for serious Bible study revealed textual contradictions and discrepancies with known fact that cast doubt on the Bible's infallibility. In a largely traditional, agricultural society, such doubts were lessened by inherited patterns of churchgoing, and deference to figures of authority. Yet in an urban industrial setting, stricken by poverty, oppressive laws, and the indifference of the establishment, such doubts took on a strongly political temper, as individuals grew in resentment against a corrupt, undemocratic government, supported by an Established Church they believed to be founded upon a lie.

ORIGINS AND ENDS

During the first half of the nineteenth century, atheist attacks were so obscure and aberrant that no respectable, educated person would read their publications, let alone countenance their views.[79] The hallmarks of infidelity – political radicalism and atheism – were doubly unattractive, for to support such a cause was to make oneself both a traitor and a fool. It entailed abandoning one's loyalty to the constitution and the Crown, and the adoption of a philosophical stance that could offer no credible scientific alternative to the divine origin of creation.[80] These two factors – loyalty to the constitution and a belief in direct divine creation – were preserved through the use of natural theology, which used the discoveries of science to demonstrate the existence, power, benevolence, and moral government of the Creator, who created a fixed social and political order that demanded obedience. These beliefs, generated and sustained by a literal, univocal and perspicuous conception of Scripture, and the disruptive and substitutionary nature of divine causality, were successful at wedding science and theology into a united worldview, in which science

---

[79] Owen Chadwick, 'The Established Church Under Attack', in *The Victorian Crisis of Faith*, ed. Anthony Symondson (London: SPCK, 1970), 92–3.
[80] Cf. Royle, *Infidels*, 125.

justified Scripture and Scripture justified the methods and conclusions of science. Yet they also left the Christian faith dangerously dependent on the continued acquiescence of science. We will now examine how the presupposition of the disruptive and substitutionary nature of divine activity came to structure arguments for an immediate special creation in late eighteenth- and nineteenth-century Britain, and the political uses it was put to. The subversion of this presupposition in the wake of unprecedented intellectual change would provide the intellectual conditions for the gradual adoption of anti-Christian and atheist forms of thought among the middle classes.

The development of natural theology for apologetic and political purposes, first undertaken at the Restoration, reached its apogee in the work of William Paley. Paley is of great importance for any understanding of the structure of nineteenth-century thought, as he transmitted many of the presuppositions of the eighteenth-century English Enlightenment to the nineteenth.[81] Although some have argued that Paley's views were outdated after the critique of Hume, this was not how it was seen at the time. While Hume's scepticism was viewed with anxiety, it was also met with incomprehension and disgust, and it was not until the mid-nineteenth century that his influence was felt significantly.[82] Paley intended his works to form an apologetic system of sorts, offering verification of the truth of natural religion, revealed religion, and a justification of the moral and political obligations that arise from both.[83] While the justification of moral and political obligations might appear misplaced in this list of interests, it reveals the social and political intention of Paley's work, an intention that finds its basis in the teleological framework of his most famous work, *Natural Theology*. Paley's purpose in this work is to demonstrate the existence, power, benevolence, and wisdom of a personal God, through reference to the natural world. This is accomplished through the use of analogy. The intricacy and adaptation of living creatures are famously compared to a watch that is found on a heath. Just as one would, upon inspection of the watch, note signs of design and contrivance, so do we, upon noting the order and careful design of living creatures, come to the conclusion that they too are works of design,

[81] D. L. Le Mahieu, *The Mind of William Paley* (Lincoln: University of Nebraska Press, 1976), x; Charles C. Gillispie, *Genesis and Geology* (Cambridge, MA: Harvard University Press, 1951), 35.

[82] Brooke, *Science and Religion*, 262, 284. Cf. Peter Addinall, *Philosophy and Biblical Interpretation* (Cambridge: Cambridge University Press, 1991), 209.

[83] Cf. William Paley, *Natural Theology* (Oxford: Oxford University Press, 2006), 3–4.

created by a wise and powerful Creator.[84] The creation in question, of course, is an immediate one, with God acting directly to create each species in its current form, without mediation of natural causes. The majority of Paley's work is thereafter taken up with detailed descriptions of anatomy, botany, animal psychology, and even astronomy, scouring the heavens and the earth for evidence of the wise design of God. When we examine creation in this way 'The world from thenceforth becomes a temple, and life itself one continual act of adoration.'[85] The moral and spiritual order of the universe is manifest in all things, and it is ours

To hope and to prepare; under a firm and settled persuasion, that, living and dying, we are his; that life is passed in his constant presence, that death resigns us to his merciful disposal.[86]

God is in his heaven, and all things on earth are created and ordered to fulfil their ordained purpose: to manifest his glory, and to play their allotted role in his providential plan. If the Reformation had stripped natural phenomena of their power to symbolise, the natural theological worldview of Paley and others helped to re-enchant it. While natural objects no longer referenced moral truths or other objects, their order and beauty nevertheless signified the power, wisdom, and benevolence of the Creator. Natural phenomena became signs of the existence and attributes of God, without – for now – doing any violence to scientific description.

There, remained, however, the problem of the relation between the natural and human worlds. For those tempted by the state of human society to doubt the goodness of God, Paley is clear that the Creator is not impugned by economic and political inequality, for the gifts of nature always outweigh gifts of fortune:

How much, for example, is activity better than attendance; beauty, than dress; appetite, digestion, and tranquil bowels, than the artifices of cookery, or than forced, costly, and farfetched dainties?[87]

Distinctions and honours encourage industry, and power and authority are as burdensome for the one who possesses them as the one who is subject to them.[88] This theme is continued in Paley's *Principles of Moral and Political Philosophy*. The inequality of wealth that exists in a society,

---

[84] Paley, *Natural Theology*, 6–15.   [85] Paley, *Natural Theology*, 278.
[86] Paley, *Natural Theology*, 283.   [87] Paley, *Natural Theology*, 262.
[88] Paley, *Natural Theology*, 263.

while an evil in and of itself, is justified because it is an indirect consequence of otherwise beneficial forces.[89] As a man who had known the pain of poverty in his youth, Paley is careful to stress the right of the poor to receive care from the rich. Yet this is an *imperfect* right, meaning that it is not enforceable. If the rich do not abide by their duties then they are blameworthy, but the poor cannot force their benefaction.[90] In the same way, while the duty of obedience to a corrupt or tyrannical government is not absolute, if a regime cannot be resisted or changed without public inconvenience – that is, a great upheaval or potential violence – it is the will of God that the established government be obeyed.[91] Moreover, in spite of his concern for the poor, Paley believes that the lower classes are dangerous. Their opinions are ill formed, and liable to be carried away by frenzied passion. It is thus desirable that the nobility should be incorporated into government within the House of Lords, for the nobility:

Averse to those prejudices which actuate the minds of the vulgar; accustomed to condemn the clamour of the populace; disdaining to receive laws and opinions from their inferiors in rank; they will oppose resolutions which are founded in the folly and violence of the lower part of the community.[92]

While Paley's views on government and class were not monochrome, their overall tendency was to support the prevailing constitution, and to do so by reference to the will of God, and the providential order of creation.[93] It is not by chance that he took time to write against the revolutionary politics of Thomas Paine. The timeliness of Paley's views won him great acclaim, and his works found institutional support when they were adopted by a number of Cambridge colleges.[94] His esteem was such that the King was said to have copies of his works in all his residences.

Paley's thought transmitted to the nineteenth century four assumptions that would prove fatal for Christian thought: the interdependence of

---

[89] William Paley, *Collected Works,* vol. IV (London: Thomas Davison, 1825), 75.
[90] Paley, *Collected Works,* vol. IV, 61–4.   [91] Paley, *Collected Works,* vol. IV, 339–40.
[92] Paley, *Collected Works,* vol. IV, 388–9.
[93] Cf. J. C. D. Clark, 'Religion and Origins of Radicalism in Nineteenth-Century Britain', in *English Radicalism 1550–1850,* ed. Glenn Burgess and Matthew Festenstein (Cambridge: Cambridge University Press, 2007), 262.
[94] While read at Cambridge, there is debate over when, if ever, Paley's works were compulsory reading. See Aileen Fyfe, 'William Paley's Natural Theology in the University of Cambridge', *British Journal for the History of Science* 30 (1997), 321–35. For a description of the relationship between natural theology, pedagogy and politics at Oxbridge in the early nineteenth century, see James A. Secord, *Victorian Sensation* (Chicago: Chicago University Press, 2000), 223–4.

science and religion, the literal truth of Genesis, the fixity of species, and the close connection between natural theology and the preservation of moral and political order. As in the Restoration period, scientific research offered examples of the direct agency of God in creation, which helped to wed science to theology in an age where there was a gradual trend towards purely naturalistic descriptions of reality. Yet the benefits to *science* from its alliance with religion were perhaps even more significant. In this period of British history, there was no way for science to offer *ultimate* explanations for its descriptions of the natural world without some reference to a divine origin, and the teleological purposes of the Creator.[95] This was a distinctively British phenomenon, as continental science, which derived much of its methodological impetus from Descartes, typically offered explanations of the natural world without reference to teleology or providence.[96] The result was that many, if not most, British scientists during the first half of the nineteenth century reserved a place for immediate divine activity within nature.[97] In addition to supplying ultimate explanations of the natural world, natural theology offered intellectual coherence to the humanities and sciences, unifying their differing descriptions of reality.[98] In the great tree of knowledge, the common root of all disciplines was the providential wisdom of Almighty God, who created the world, and ordered all things to manifest his glory and accomplish his will. The prominent place afforded the Creator and his agency in scientific literature was not only, however, the result of intellectual necessity, but business acumen. For the majority of the nineteenth century, the most popular publications were religious in nature. A doxological accent, emphasising the role of the Creator and the value of scientific research for a greater appreciation of his glory, was one way in which scientists could appeal to a mass readership.[99] These considerations led to the rise of edifying scientific works such as Charles Kingsley's *Glaucus, or the Wonders of the Shore*, which were at one with the respectable evangelical temper of the age.[100] The apologetic potential of such works was so great that the Society for the Promotion of Christian Knowledge began to issue its own range of cheap scientific works with a theistic emphasis. The particular union of scientific knowledge and

---

[95] Turner, *Without God*, 57.   [96] Le Mahieu, *Paley*, 39–41.
[97] Alvar Ellegård, *Darwin and the General Reader* (Göteborg: Göteborgs Universitet, 1958), 12.
[98] Budd, *Varieties*, 127–8.   [99] Ellegård, *General Reader*, 113.
[100] Bebbington, *Evangelicalism*, 57.

religious piety promoted by these publications, however, was one that committed science to the support of a six-day creation and the fixity of species, and the Christian faith to a particular constellation of scientific conclusions and methodologies. While this would later prove calamitous for the intellectual prestige of the Christian faith, the union of science and religion within a natural theological framework was considered essential to the very existence of the British constitution. Natural theology's demonstration of the power and purpose of God in creation found its correlate in the providential ordering of civil society, where the rich held property and station by the grace of God. Lest it be thought that this was a minority view, we need only consider the now omitted third verse of that quintessentially British hymn, *All Things Bright and Beautiful*:

> The rich man in his castle,
> The poor man at his gate,
> God made them high and lowly,
> And ordered their estate.

Cecil Alexander was no bigot. Rather, when she penned these lines, she gave expression to the basic natural theological assumptions of her age, assumptions that were shared by men like the distinguished scientist and theologian William Buckland, who claimed that science *proved* that social inequalities were ordained.[101] It was these assumptions that drove much of the support for the fusion of science and religion in natural theology, for if God did not create the world in six days through his direct activity, and did not ordain the ends of human and animal life, then his moral government and providential care could be called into question, as could the 'natural' class relations of nineteenth-century Britain.[102] The defence of the establishment resided not only upon force of law and the rebuke of the priest, but upon the teleological framework of natural theology. It was for these reasons that atheists such as Holyoake, realising the significance of Paley for the preservation of the religious and political order, sought to undermine his thought through dedicated attacks.[103] Natural theology, then, served a wide range of intellectual, theological, scientific, and political ends, and should not be parodied, as some paint it, as a craven attempt to halt the advance of science, but as an important unifying

---

[101] Gillispie, *Genesis and Geology*, 201.
[102] A. Hunter Dupree, 'Christianity and the Scientific Community in the Age of Darwin', in *God and Nature*, ed. David C. Lindberg and Ronald L. Numbers (Berkeley: University of California Press, 1986), 354; Gillispie, *Genesis and Geology*, 227–8.
[103] E.g. G. J. Holyoake, *Paley Refuted in His Own Words* (London: J. Watson, 1851).

principle that bridged disciplinary boundaries between Christian theology, natural science, political theory and apologetics.[104] It sustained the image of a harmonious natural, intellectual, and social world, created and ordered by a loving, personal God, whose rational purposes and moral will could be discovered and discerned in all things.

WALKING APART

As the nineteenth century wore on, this idyllic conception, representing a unity of biblical hermeneutics, science and moral and political order, would come under increasing strain. Over and against the image of a recent, special creation, whose truth was secured by Genesis and the findings of science, came scientific developments that cast doubt on the prevailing biblical and natural theological worldview. It is not necessary to elaborate fully upon the developments in geology, biology, and biblical criticism that exposed weaknesses in the presuppositions we have been examining, and converted them into the basis of atheist thought.[105] Yet in order to understand how the presupposition of a literal, univocal and perspicuous Scripture, and a disruptive and substitutionary understanding of divine activity would negate themselves, and come to structure future atheist thought, we must identify the salient changes that converted these Christian presuppositions into the foundations of atheism. It will become clear that, if not for the theological strategies adopted at the Restoration, these scientific developments would not have led to the development of atheism in the way they did.

Geology was unusual among the sciences of the nineteenth century due to its novelty, high public profile and methodology. While other sciences studied the existing order of nature, geology was the first to examine its *history*.[106] This approach was the product of an age that, as Glover notes, was increasingly developing an historical understanding of texts, knowledge and human society.[107] As the catastrophism of earlier geology gave

---

[104] William J. Astore, *Observing God* (Aldershot: Ashgate, 2001), 50–1. Cf. Addinall, *Biblical Interpretation*, 4, 13.

[105] For classic studies, see Andrew L. Drummond and James Bulloch, *The Church in Victorian Scotland* (Edinburgh: Saint Andrew Press, 1975); Andrew L. Drummond and James Bulloch, *The Church in Late Victorian Scotland* (Edinburgh: Saint Andrew Press, 1978). See previous citations for Gillispie, Chadwick, Brooke and Cantor and Secord.

[106] Gillispie, *Genesis and Geology*, 39–40.

[107] Glover, *Evangelical Nonconformists*, 13–14.

way to uniformitarianism through the work of the Scots James Hutton and Charles Lyell, it became clear that the time necessary for natural forces to form the geological formations we now observe must have been very much greater than those calculated by Bishop Ussher and others. As such, the prevalent six-day interpretation of Genesis would have to be adjusted. A variety of hermeneutical strategies were developed, with two approaches becoming prominent. A variant literal reading favoured by Thomas Chalmers and William Buckland – now known as gap creationism – suggested a period of many thousands or millions of years between the first and second verses of Genesis. Popular science writers such as Hugh Miller, on the other hand, promoted a non-literal reading now known as day-age creationism, which argued that the 'days' of Genesis 1 should be interpreted as ages spanning thousands, or millions, of years. Miller could even suggest that the findings of geology, far from harming the faith, actually strengthened it. While Paley could not disprove the eternity of the world, geology demonstrated that rock formations and animal life had arisen at specific points in history, supporting creation *ex nihilo*, and on-going, disruptive divine activity within creation.[108]

The future of science and Christianity did not lie in unity, however, but in divorce, and the exegetical strategies of writers like Miller only resulted in the growth of competing harmonisations, which strained to account for the geological data, and hopelessly contradicted each other. As Charles Goodwin, one of the *septem contra Christi*, put it in *Essays and Reviews*:

The conciliators are not agreed among themselves, and each holds the views of the others to be untenable and unsafe. The ground is perpetually being shifted, as the advance of geological science may require. The plain meaning of the Hebrew record is unscrupulously tampered with, and in general the pith of the whole process lies in divesting the text of all meaning whatever.[109]

The continuation of these efforts served to further undermine the faith, as one biblical and natural theological interpretation after another was refuted by the geological and palaeontological record. For broad churchmen like Goodwin, who had been raised on the traditional Paleyan worldview with its literal understanding of Genesis, the only reputable

---

[108] E.g. Hugh Miller, *The Testimony of the Rocks* (Boston: Gould and Lincoln, 1857), 211–36.
[109] Charles W. Goodwin, 'On the Mosaic Cosmogony', in *Essays and Reviews* (London: J. W. Parker & Son, 1860), 211.

option left was to accept that Genesis was myth rather than fact, and abandon harmonisation forever.

Uniformitarianism in geology, and a new appreciation for the history of the natural world, inevitably led to speculation concerning the origins of animal life. The first work to popularise these speculations widely was *Vestiges of the Natural History of Creation*.[110] Penned anonymously by Edinburgh publisher Robert Chambers, *Vestiges* advanced a simplified version of the transmutation theory of Lamarck, augmented by a bewildering array of scientific, anthropological, and mythical references. The work was a great popular success, read across society from autodidact working-class radicals to the Royal Family itself. There were, however, four serious problems with the work, which would hinder the open acceptance of evolutionary theories by respectable society. First, it was published anonymously, thereby tainting the sincerity of its views. Second, its argument, clearly the work of an amateur, did not offer sufficient evidence to garner the respect of professional scientists. Third, the work took on a subversive air thanks to its appropriation by working-class radicals and atheists, who saw in it a scientific rebuttal of the prevailing natural theological worldview that justified social and political inequality.[111] In contrast to the paternalistic worldview of Paley, evolution suggested that complexity and order were not imposed upon a pliant, disorderly world *from above*, but arose spontaneously *from below*. By denying the divine right of the prevailing social order, and removing God from the immanent processes of the world, radicals and atheists had a theory of origins that justified a fully democratic, secular society.[112] These conclusions, of course, were not Chambers'. Indeed, he had written the *Vestiges* as a work of natural theology, and believed that he had done the Creator a service by showing how his power and wisdom were so great as to fashion a self-creating creation. Yet, in his desire to refute the notion of a disruptive and substitutionary form of divine activity in creation, his work demonstrated how natural theology could become a Trojan Horse, and inadvertently support atheism.[113] The very science that Paley had used to substantiate the design argument now threatened to disprove design itself. The fourth and final death-knell for the acceptance of *Vestiges* was the time of its publication. Chambers' work was published

---

[110] Robert Chambers, *Vestiges of the Natural History of Creation* (London: John Churchill, 1844).

[111] Desmond, 'Artisan Resistance', 88.   [112] Marsh, 'Bibliolatry', 97.

[113] Brooke, *Science and Religion*, 222–23.

at a time of political instability, when high corn prices and Chartist protest caused anything which cast doubt upon Christianity to be viewed as dangerous.[114]

If evolutionary theories were to be accepted by respectable society, they had to be presented with convincing scientific evidence, and advanced by a reputable author whose theories could not be mistaken as an attempt to overthrow the prevailing social order. These needs were met in Charles Darwin's *On the Origin of Species*. This work, by a distinguished scientist, with no trace of radical intent, supplied the evidence necessary to substantiate a strong case for evolution. Darwin showed that the order and adaptation displayed by organisms was not the result of direct creative acts by God, but the result of immanent natural processes. As such, his theory appeared to divorce direct teleological ordering from biology, removing the agency of God – at best – to a remote past. Darwin's research overthrew the design argument in its Paleyan form, along with its accompanying social and political dimensions, and had unprecedented effects upon the relationship between science and faith in Britain. First, his discovery demonstrated that a literal reading of Scripture, so important for traditional Protestant hermeneutics, could not be applied to Genesis 1–3 without producing conflict with current science. Second, the theory of evolution did irreparable damage to the design argument, which had accounted for adaptation by reference to immediate special design, and the teleological purposes of the Creator. After Darwin, descriptions of natural phenomena no longer required reference to purpose, or the agency of a Creator in any significant sense. The genera and species of the animal world had not been established by a discrete act of divine intervention, but through millennia of mutation and adaptation to environment. Worst of all, humanity itself, the image of God, did not stand apart from the evolutionary process but was itself a product of it. As the design argument had wedded science to Christianity, Darwin's discovery led, third, to the possibility of real conflict between the two. Evolution disproved a recent, special creation, and destroyed much of the existing natural theological framework that united biblical hermeneutics and theology to the methods and discoveries of science. Science and theology increasingly came to be seen not as complementary and inseparable descriptions of the natural world, but as competing explanations of reality, where there could be only one victor.

[114] Jim Endersby, introduction to *On the Origin of Species*, by Charles Darwin (Cambridge: Cambridge University Press, 2009), xxv.

The close connection of faith and science brought about by the natural theological presupposition we have been examining did not only have consequences for faith, however, but also for science. The fixity of species, and the special creation of animal life by God, were not simply religious doctrines, but had become scientific theories.[115] By unifying science and religion, a disruptive and substitutionary conception of divine activity had conflated the methods and conclusions of each, so that the theological claims of an immediate creation and the fixity of species became scientific theories to be pitted against evolution. The struggle over evolution should not be seen as a contest between Christianity and science, then, but as a struggle *within* science itself, a painful *disentanglement* of Christianity from science, accomplished by the rejection of natural theology and teleology from scientific description.[116] This entanglement ensured that the debate over Darwin's theory would not be a simple contest between clergy and scientists, but be contested by scientists themselves for many years to come.[117]

This is not how it often appeared at the time, however, and it became common among some sections of the scientific community to posit a genuine conflict between science and religion. In addition to the debate over evolution, a belief in the conflict of science and religion must be understood against contemporary Papal policy, and the growth of Roman Catholicism in Britain. In 1850, the Roman Catholic diocesan system was re-established in Britain, prompting widespread protest and alarm. The threat from Roman Catholicism to science was highlighted in 1864, when Pius IX issued the encyclical *Quanta Cura*, with its infamous appendix the *Syllabus Errorum*. Among the errors condemned by this document were the propositions that 'Human reason, without any reference whatsoever to God, is the sole arbiter of truth and falsehood' and 'Philosophy is to be treated without taking any account of supernatural revelation.'[118] Propositions such as these lay at the heart of a robust and methodologically independent science, and their condemnation increased the perception that Christian theology and science were in conflict. Importantly, they also provided the occasion for attacks upon Anglican clergy. The issuing of *Quanta Cura* came in the same year as a number of pious British scientists signed a public letter attacking the way in which some of

---

[115] Dupree, 'Scientific Community', 360.   [116] Gillispie, *Genesis and Geology*, ix.
[117] Endersby, introduction, lxi.
[118] 'The Syllabus of Errors Condemned by Pius IX', last modified 2002, accessed 15 September 2015, www.papalencyclicals.net/Pius09/p9syll.htm.

their colleagues were using science to undermine the Christian faith. The scientific community was becoming increasingly divided between those who viewed science as confirming the teleological order of a divine Creator, and those who sought a purely naturalistic description of the world. The opposition of ordained scientists such as Adam Sedgwick, taken with the initial rebuke of church leaders like Bishop Wilberforce, gave rise to the fear among scientists that the integrity of British science, and scientists themselves, was being compromised by interference from Christian clergy of all stripes.[119] This opposition had an added sectarian and class dimension. A new generation of scientists, among them many nonconformists, were seeking a position in the science of their day without the institutional and financial support of an older generation of Anglican scientists. They resented the Oxbridge, Anglican-dominated intellectual landscape of the age, and cast themselves as earnest outsiders searching for truth, fighting against the ecclesiastical biases of the age.[120]

The man who would come to typify these changes, and play an important role in transmitting the biblical and natural theological presuppositions we have been examining to wider society, was Thomas Huxley. In Huxley, three traditions converged: middle class religious scepticism, plebeian nonconformity and scientific opposition to natural theology. These three traditions converged to produce the Victorian age's foremost advocate for the ejection of theology from science, and a critical approach towards religion. Unlike the majority of scientists in his day, Huxley's upbringing was economically and socially precarious. He held his first apprenticeship in the slums of London, and trained with nonconformist medics often bitter at their perceived exclusion from the Anglican medical establishment.[121] Early in his career he fell in with the culturally elite *Westminster Review* set, and carved out a reputation for himself as a gifted essayist and critic.[122] The science of his day was still dominated by men like Richard Owen, who believed that the purpose of anatomy and palaeontology was to reveal

---

[119] For a similar argument see Harrison, *Territories*, 142 and 173.
[120] For Huxley, see Adrian Desmond, *Huxley: Evolution's High Priest* (London: Michael Joseph, 1997), 3–4; Paul White, *Thomas Huxley: Making the 'Man of Science'* (Cambridge: Cambridge University Press, 2007), 32–66.
[121] Adrian Desmond, *Huxley: The Devil's Disciple* (London: Michael Joseph, 1994), 3–7.
[122] Desmond, *Devil's Disciple*, 185–7.

the unity which underlies the diversity of animal structures; to show in these structures the evidences of a predetermining will, producing them in reference to a final purpose.[123]

This platonic, teleological, and natural theological understanding of science as revealing the mind of the Creator was immensely popular, and helped to defend Christianity against the proto-evolutionary theories of Lamarck and Chambers. Owen's efforts at suppressing such politically dangerous theories earned him the esteem of the establishment, and he was rewarded with a state pension for his troubles. For Huxley, there were two problems with this natural theological approach towards science. First, it fettered the consciences of scientists, who had to adopt an informal confession of faith before entering the laboratory. Second, it hindered the advance of science, for it presumed in advance that there was a purpose for every anatomical feature, and that every species was ordered according to a perfect divine archetype. In later life, Huxley would record how difficult the earlier decades of the nineteenth century had been for scientists, where one risked social ostracism if one cast doubt on the scriptural record, and where 'Noah and his ark' barred science's path at every turn.[124] Huxley desired a pure form of science, unencumbered by theological presuppositions that could not be empirically verified. For Huxley, there were not two kinds of knowledge, not 'two weights and two measures' – however coordinated – but only one knowledge, and only one method.[125] This knowledge and method is science. Science cannot allow its explanations of natural phenomena to be compromised by theological assumptions and categories, but must attain to an objective, impartial description of reality. Its sense must be univocal and universal:

If scientific language is to possess a definite and constant signification whenever it is employed, it seems to me that we are logically bound to apply ... the same conceptions as those which are held to be legitimate elsewhere.[126]

If science is to make sense at all, it can only have one sense, one that is open to all. As Desmond has written of him, Huxley advanced 'a low-caste Dissenting image of science. The testimony of Nature was for all to

---

[123] Desmond, *Devil's Disciple*, 29.

[124] Thomas H. Huxley, *Collected Essays*, vol. II (Cambridge: Cambridge University Press, 2011), 215–16.

[125] Thomas H. Huxley, *Lay Sermons, Addresses and Reviews* (Cambridge: Cambridge University Press, 2009), 22; Huxley, *Collected Essays*, vol. II, 148.

[126] Huxley, *Lay Sermons*, 151.

hear. No priesthood had privileged 'access to her deepest secrets . . . Every man his own pastor'.[127] Huxley's rejection of teleology and theology from science did not, however, represent a rejection of religion, and it is here that we see Huxley's conscious dependence upon the religious categories of Protestantism.[128] Huxley claimed that his approach towards Christianity was simply an outworking of the individual's right to a personal interpretation of Scripture, and that agnosticism's indifference to the dogmas and creeds of the Church was an extension of the Reformers' indifference to Church authority.[129] Science continues the Reformers' work, for just as they shattered idols of wood and stone, so science now shatters the idols of 'books and traditions and fine-spun ecclesiastical cobwebs'.[130] Although such language and imagery might be interpreted as ironic, mocking or disingenuous, it was morally earnest, and attempted to associate the scientific spirit with all that was good in Britain's Protestant heritage.[131] Like the freethinkers of the eighteenth century, Huxley saw himself as extending the aims and ambitions of the Reformation against the pretensions of the clergy, who sought to aggrandise themselves through Church authority, and the manipulation of a specialised theological tradition. This is confirmed when one turns to examine Huxley's – often surprising – attitude towards Scripture. Huxley declares the Bible to be an 'undefiled spring', and urges his readers to drink from it.[132] He believed that returning to Scripture would reform British Christianity, and bring it in line with the advances of modern scholarship:

It is so certain, to my mind, that the Bible contains within itself the refutation of nine-tenths of the mixture of sophistical metaphysics and old-world superstition which has been piled upon it by the so-called Christians of later times.[133]

Like earlier freethinkers and nonconformists, Huxley believed that the way to restore the true sense of Scripture was to abandon the hermeneutical and confessional traditions of the Church, and simply read the text for what it is. This will yield a 'scientific theology', which will not suffer from the deficiencies of interpretation preserved by 'clericalism' and

---

[127] Desmond, *Devil's Disciple*, 252.
[128] Cf. Thomas H. Huxley, *Collected Essays*, vol. IV (Cambridge: Cambridge University Press, 2011), 162–3.
[129] Thomas H. Huxley, *Collected Essays*, vol. V (Cambridge: Cambridge University Press, 2011), 267, 245–6.
[130] Huxley, *Lay Sermons*, 20.   [131] White, *Man of Science*, 102–3.
[132] Huxley, *Collected Essays*, vol. V, 269.   [133] Huxley, *Collected Essays*, vol. V, 268–9.

'ecclesiasticism'.[134] There is no greater example of this than Huxley's attitude towards the interpretation of Genesis 1–3. For Huxley, all non-literal interpretations of the text are irrational and arbitrary, and the only legitimate reading is that 'which has been instilled into every one of us in our childhood'.[135] Huxley is scathing of those who believe that the days of Genesis 1 are made up of 'periods that we may make just as long or as short as convenience requires',[136] and believes that allegorical readings of Genesis risk imperilling the entire text of Scripture:

> But the faithful who fly to allegory in order to escape absurdity resemble nothing so much as the sheep in the fable who – to save their lives – jumped into the pit. The allegory pit is too commodious, is ready to swallow up so much more than one wants to put into it.[137]

Due to 'A certain passion for clearness,' Huxley simply desires to know what the author of the text means, and has more sympathy with the Jesuit who says that God would not be so cruel as to write 'day' but mean something else, than he has with the Anglican, who flies in the face of common sense and says that 'day' can mean anything he likes.[138]

What is key for our purposes is recognising not the *novelty* of these positions but their *dependence* upon the biblical and natural theological presuppositions we have been examining. Recapitulating and advancing the biblical and natural theological presuppositions he derived from nonconformity and plebeian unbelief, Huxley would strengthen and transmit four key assumptions to later atheist thought. The first was what might be termed methodological monism. There is only one method with which to discern truth, and that is science. This monism had the effect of ejecting teleology from science and the investigation of origins, for science, in its true form, can say nothing of purpose or design. The same approach was extended to Scripture. If knowledge of the Bible is possible at all, its words cannot depend for their meaning on the particular confessional viewpoint that one adopts, or the exigencies and needs of the reader. Its sense must be stable and accessible to all. For this reason, theological tradition and Church authority should be rejected, as they hinder our appreciation of Scripture's meaning. Developing trends originating in the seventeenth century, Huxley believed that Scripture, like

---

[134] Huxley, *Collected Essays*, vol. V, 312–14.
[135] Cf. Huxley, *Collected Essays*, vol. IV, 155–6, 63.
[136] Huxley, *Collected Essays*, vol. IV, 63–4.   [137] Huxley, *Collected Essays*, vol. V, 324.
[138] Huxley, *Collected Essays*, vol. IV, 232; Huxley, *Collected Essays*, vol. II, 137–8.

science, should be univocal.[139] This univocity led to a second key assumption that Huxley would transmit to later atheist thought, that Genesis 1–3 should be interpreted literally. To admit a plurality of meanings might save clerics from embarrassment over a few chapters, yet it throws the whole of Scripture into doubt. After all, if Genesis can be interpreted allegorically, then why not the Gospels and the Incarnation? Although Huxley's relationship with liberal and broad churchmen was complex, his methodological monism, and preference for literal and univocal readings of Scripture would lead, third, to the belief of future atheists that conservative evangelical and fundamentalist forms of faith are normative for Christians, something seen, for example, in the thought of Bertrand Russell.[140] Huxley's methodological monism and biblical hermeneutics would also give rise to Huxley's fourth – and perhaps most important – gift to future atheism: the supposed conflict between science and the Christian faith. While Huxley frequently differentiated between false 'theology' or 'clericalism' and true 'religion', he nevertheless felt that a great deal – if not most – of contemporary Christianity was fundamentally opposed to the methods and findings of science. Given the historic beliefs of the Church with regard to origins and immediate divine activity within nature, and the continuing insistence upon devotional readings of Scripture guided by confession, creed and Church authority, Huxley believed there really *was* a conflict between science and much of contemporary Christianity. Huxley's advancement of the 'conflict thesis' concerning the relation of science and religion would prove a fundamental plank of future atheist thought, and would be appropriated and amplified by a multitude of lesser luminaries.[141] Yet where Huxley exhibited a residual respect for Scripture and the heritage of British Protestantism, his successors would not be so deferential, and would push the biblical and natural theological assumptions he held into atheism.

The belief of men like Huxley that there was a genuine conflict between evolutionary theory and the Christian faith was reinforced by the opposition of many nonconformist churches to Darwin. While geology could, with some difficulty, be accommodated within Genesis 1 through gap or day-age readings, the detailed narratives of Genesis 2 and 3 did not readily admit of alternative literal readings: *either* God had created a

[139] Vf. Henry W. Parker, *The Agnostic Gospel* (New York: John B. Alden, 1896), viii.
[140] See, e.g., Bertrand Russell, *Why I am Not a Christian and Other Essays* (London: Unwin Books, 1967), 13, 25, 33.
[141] Desmond, *Devil's Disciple*, xiii.

human couple in one discrete act in the remote past, *or* humans were the product of evolution and natural selection. In an important study, Ellegård has shown that Methodist and nonconformist churches were the most likely to oppose evolution, as 'Evangelical fundamentalism, political conservatism and a fairly moderate educational standard all worked to produce a strongly anti-Darwinian attitude'.[142] Ellegård's study lends additional force to the thesis examined earlier, that the proportionately higher rate of Methodists and nonconformists in atheist and secularist societies came as a result of the failure of these churches to resolve discrepancies between Scripture and science due to their rejection of theological tradition, and their privileging of the literal sense. In comparison to Methodists and nonconformists, Ellegård makes the following observation concerning the more moderate stance of the Church of England and the English Roman Catholic Church, who

relying on a much more developed theology than the others, on the experience of centuries of ideological argument, and in the ability of the Church rather than the individual to solve Scriptural perplexities ... could afford to give greater scope to the new physical theories than their Evangelical brethren.[143]

While it is the confrontation of Bishop Wilberforce with Thomas Huxley at the British Association meeting in 1860 that has entered the popular imagination as the preeminent expression of nineteenth-century Christian prejudice towards science, the Church of England very quickly accepted evolution. This new theological attitude was exemplified in Frederick Temple, Archbishop of Canterbury. For Temple, the issue between science and religion did not hinge upon the truth or falsehood of the text of Genesis, but on its correct interpretation.[144] The opposition of some within the Church towards evolution had arisen from the assumption that the interpretation of Genesis they had been taught as children was infallible.[145] In order to defend this interpretation, they inveigh against geology and evolutionary biology, only to concede surrender after surrender. It is this that lies at the root of unbelief, for

When men have to give up in such circumstances they generally give up far more than they need, and in some cases an unreasonable resistance has been followed by an equally unreasonable surrender.[146]

---

[142] Ellegård, *General Reader*, 38, 109.   [143] Ellegård, *General Reader*, 38.
[144] Frederick Temple, 'The Relations between Science and Religion', in *Science and Religion in the Nineteenth Century*, Tess Cosslett (Cambridge: Cambridge University Press, 1984), 200–1.
[145] Temple, 'Science and Religion', 211.   [146] Temple, 'Science and Religion', 211–12.

For Temple, the safeguard against unbelief is to *surrender* the notion that Scripture teaches science, and grasp that religion is not based on science or empirical investigation, but on the inward sense of moral and spiritual truth witnessed to by the Bible.[147]

While the evacuation of natural theology from science and the rejection of literal readings of Genesis allowed the churches to retain a measure of intellectual respectability, Temple identified the problems confronting post-Darwinian Christians, problems which would continue to endanger the intellectual plausibility of Christianity in Britain. The simple truth was that a large proportion of British Christians, of whatever educational or church background, *had* believed in the literal truth of Genesis, along with the natural theological framework which wed it to scientific discovery.[148] When these interpretations of the biblical and scientific evidence were shown to be false, many were driven, as Temple noted, to surrender all, for if something so fundamental as the origin of the universe could be shown to be false, how could a rational person trust anything in Scripture? Yet the theological framework offered by Temple and others was of little consolation to many thoughtful Christians looking for reasons to retain the faith of their youth. To claim that the substance of religion was a spirtualised morality was to cast doubt on the distinctive utility of orthodox Christianity, for morality, as Darwin suggested in *The Descent of Man*, could equally be accounted for in terms of natural patterns of kinship.[149] Indeed, to a modern reader, there is little between the Christianity of Temple and the earnest agnosticism of men like Huxley, and it is not surprising that Huxley could, at times, dismiss liberal theologians as an 'army of reconcilers', who unlike 'real' Christians such as Cardinal Newman, were dishonestly trying to accommodate an irrational faith with the modern world.[150]

The final movement in the conversion of the biblical and natural theological presuppositions we have been examining into atheism in Britain was the gentrification and growing respectability of unbelief. While, in its plebeian aspect, unbelief was primarily driven by biblical literalism and political radicalism, for the middle classes, unbelief was

---

[147] Temple, 'Science and Religion', 200, 204–15.
[148] Ellegård, *General Reader*, 95–6, 101.
[149] Charles Darwin, *The Descent of Man* (London: John Murray, 1901), 935–6.
[150] Cf. Huxley, *Collected Essays*, vol. V, 309–65; Jon H. Roberts, *Darwinism and the Divine in America* (Madison: University of Wisconsin Press, 1988), 218; James R. Moore, *The Post-Darwinian Controversies* (Cambridge: Cambridge University Press, 1979), 63–4.

primarily a manifestation of the collapse of the Paleyan natural theological worldview, which guaranteed the moral purpose of life, united science and faith, and underwrote middle class – Anglican – respectability against dissenters and the working class.[151] In the absence of an ordained teleology for the world and for human life, there was only a distant God and an indifferent universe, the gloomy realisation which lay beyond much of the 'doubt' of figures such as F. W. Newman, Leslie Stephen, Thomas Hardy and Darwin himself. It is within the context of a purposeless and indifferent world that the more familiar *moral* critique against the Christian faith must be viewed, as, without it, such critiques would have little purchase.[152] It was the growing irreligion of the middle classes that created the possibility, for the first time in British history, of a socially respectable unbelief, one which did not seek to incite revolution, or overthrow the constitution. The respectable face of unbelief even had its own name – *agnosticism* – coined by Huxley to explain his position during heated debates at the Metaphysical Society. While the crux of agnosticism was the denial that the theological claims of the clergy had any basis, agnostics such as Huxley, unlike their plebeian atheist cousins, were often careful to cultivate their relationship with liberal Anglicans, and, as we have seen, were not averse to adopting quasi-religious language and imagery to cast themselves as pious purifiers of religion.[153]

The departure of many middle class people from the Christian faith led to a growing convergence with the older plebeian tradition of unbelief, helped also by a growing moderation among atheists such as Holyoake.[154] By the end of the nineteenth century, atheist societies such as the Rationalist Press Association were primarily publishing the works of respectable middle class doubters such as Thomas Huxley, Matthew Arnold and Herbert Spencer.[155] The twentieth century saw the gentrification of unbelief continue, with academics from the ancient universities such as John McTaggert, Bertrand Russell and A. J. Ayer offering their patronage to the cause of atheism. Although men like Russell wrote some decades after Huxley's death, their thought did little to alter the fundamental presuppositions adopted and transmitted by him, and Russell

---

[151] Cf. Desmond, *High Priest*, 7.   [152] Cf. Erdozain, *Soul of Doubt*, 173–220.

[153] Andrew Pyle, *Agnosticism* (Bristol: Thoemmes Press, 1995), x. Cf. White, *Man of Science*, 100–134; Larsen, *One Book*, 206–9.

[154] See Michael Rectenwald, 'Secularism and the Cultures of Nineteenth-century Scientific Naturalism', *The British Journal for the History of Science*, 46, no. 2 (2013): 231–54.

[155] See Bill Cooke, *The Gathering of Infidels* (Amherst: Prometheus Books, 2004).

continued to preach the omnicompetancy of science, the normative status of naïve forms of Christianity, and the conflict between science and religion.[156] As he argues in *Religion and Science*, 'Between religion and science there has been a prolonged conflict, in which, until the last few years, science has invariably proved victorious.'[157] Russell taught that Christians had always believed in a recent six-day creation, and that the Church had only been forced to adopt non-literal interpretations of Genesis due to the pressures of science.[158] Like Huxley, however, Russell believed that such strategies were futile, for while non-literal interpretations may save theologians in one instance, it damns them in the other, for to write off one passage of Scripture is to endanger all.[159]

Due to the unique scientific, religious, philosophical and political nexus of nineteenth-century British life, it would be unbelief, rather than fundamentalism, that would arise from the presuppostions of a literal, univocal and perspicuous Scripture, and a disruptive and substitutionary conception of divine activity. Before we turn to examine Protestant fundamentalism in Chapter 3, it is important to end this chapter with some observations as to why Britain was more likely to produce agnostics and atheists than fundamentalists. The first reason is that, while evolution was most acceptable to liberals and broad churchmen, it was very quickly adopted by a broad range of theological constituancies. Assent to evolutionary theory did not, then, imply a specific theological or political position, and did not provoke any organised social and ecclesiastical dissent. While the Methodist and nonconformist churches were initially hostile, and continued their dispute with evolution until the 1880s, they too came to drop their opposition.[160] The second reason concerns the development of biblical criticism in Britain. The origins of biblical criticism in Britain lie in the writings of the eighteenth-century freethinkers, and the continuation of their work by Paine. Yet the adoption of biblical criticism as a *respectable* undertaking stems from two mid-Victorian sources: William Robertson Smith in Scotland, and Benjamin Jowett in England. Neither Robertson Smith nor Jowett had any atheistic or politically radical intent in advancing their new methods, and rightly presented themselves as standing within a long line of Protestant scholars who, faithful to the principle of *sola scriptura*, allowed Scripture to speak for

[156] See, e.g., Russell, *Why I am Not a Christian*, 13, 25, 29, 33, 35–6, 69.
[157] Bertrand Russell, *Religion and Science* (London: Oxford University Press, 1960), 7.
[158] Russell, *Religion and Science*, 51–2, 16.　　[159] Russell, *Religion and Science*, 11.
[160] Robert Currie, *Methodism Divided* (London: Faber & Faber, 1968), 115–16.

itself, unencumbered by the bias of Church doctrine.[161] While Jowett and Robertson Smith initially encountered formidable opposition, by the end of the nineteenth century, their critical method had gained wide acceptance, and, like evolution, did not lead to any large-scale church division.[162] While the 1920s saw an analogous fundamentalist reaction to that of America, such protest was always poorly supported, and did not possess the strong creationist and inerrantist flavour that came to characterise the American context.[163] The third reason lies, paradoxically, in the same factor which precipitated organised unbelief: the established churches. Many conservative evangelicals remained part of the Church of Scotland and the Church of England, and therefore retained access to higher education, and influence within their denominations. They were also regularly socialised with Christians of different theological persuasions, inhibiting any tendencies towards isolation.[164] The fourth reason why fundamentalism failed to develop as a powerful movement in Britain stems from the same reason why evolution and biblical criticism were accepted so readily. We have already examined the importance of Locke's philosophy for the development of religious thought in Britain. In particular, we have noted two important elements of that thought: an epistemology based on experience and reflection, and an accompanying philosophy of language. While Locke's philosophy of language strengthened the literal interpretation of Scripture, and the empirical element of his epistemology strengthened the acceptance of the design theory, the idealist element in his thought moved in a different direction. Because of the importance of ideas in Locke's philosophy, Britain was amenable to the construction of models and hypotheses with which to investigate and explain phenomena, even when such theories were not immediately verifiable through direct sense experience.[165] This openness had repercussions for the Christian faith and its unity with science, however, for the acceptance of geology and evolutionary theory meant

---

[161] Cf. Benjamin Jowett, 'On the Interpretation of Scripture', in *Essays and Reviews*, 340, 343; A. C. Cheyne, *Studies in Scottish Church History* (Edinburgh: T&T Clark, 1999), 130–2; Richard A. Riesen, '"Higher Criticism" in the Free Church Fathers', *Records of the Scottish Church History Society*, 20 (1980): 119–42.

[162] Glover, *Evangelical Nonconformists*, 285–6.

[163] Bebbington, *Evangelicalism*, 220–1, 224.

[164] Mark A. Noll, *Between Faith and Criticism* (Vancouver: Regent College Publishing, 1998), 62–4.

[165] Cf. Bebbington's assessment of a leading British conservative, who was kept from inerrancy and creationism by 'the familiar Anglo-Saxon empiricism stemming from the Enlightenment'. Bebbington, *Evangelicalism*, 189–90.

that a literal interpretation of Genesis could no longer be accepted as true, thus disproving a recent, special creation of life on earth, and effectively disproving the design theory. The natural theological presupposition that science could detect the disruptive and substitutionary activity of God now worked in reverse, demonstrating the *mutual exclusivity* of divine activity and natural processes. As Chapter 3 will show, the philosophical presuppositions of fundamentalist thought in America stem from a related, yet distinct, philosophical tradition, one which, in reaction to Locke, held that any scientific theory not directly observable, nor supported by the plain sense of Scripture, was not simply heretical but *unscientific*, thereby giving rise to a unique form of Protestant Christianity.

This chapter has charted the consequences of two presuppositions established in the wake of the Reformation and Restoration: a literal, univocal and perspicuous understanding of Scripture, and a disruptive and substitionary conception of divine activity in creation. While not exhausting the causal factors leading to irreligion and atheism, these presuppositions played a primary role, and their popularisation and preservation into the twentieth century would lay key intellectual foundations for the new atheism of today.

The biblical hermeneutics of Locke were adopted by nonconformists and institutionalised in their academies, a hermeneutic that increasingly removed the Bible from its confessional and institutional superstructure. The evangelical revival popularised this hermeneutic among unprecedented numbers of the working class, promoting lay Bible reading, yet further eroding the place of theological tradition. This development, which isolated the Bible from the theological tradition that ensured its canonicity, came to rely upon internal coherence and consistency with known fact as guarantors of Scripture's canonicity and authority. When errors and inconsistencies were discovered, the logic of this hermenetuic could lead to the conclusion that the Bible was not the Word of God, and this, taken with hostility against the establishment, led some skilled working-class people to become atheists, and attack Church and state. Middle class unbelief typically arose for related, yet distinct reasons. The natural theological worldview, exemplified by Paley, sought to prove the existence and moral government of a benevolent, personal God from the order and adaptation of living things. This natural theological worldview united faith and science, bringing benefits to both. Yet the design argument was predicated upon a literal reading of Genesis and a recent special creation. As geology and later evolution challenged these views, purpose and order seemed to empty out of creation, and many of the middle class were left adrift in an indifferent world. This movement was facilitated by the disentanglement of science from theology, aided by nonconformist scientists such as Thomas Huxley, who challenged Anglican dominance of science, and sought to safeguard the independence and professionalisation of their field. Yet Huxley achieved this not by rejecting theological assumptions, but by *inverting* the biblical and natural theological presuppositions we have been examining, so that a literal reading of Genesis proved the incompatibility of Christianity with science, and science and divine activity were competing explanations for natural phenomena. Huxley communicated these assumptions to a host of lesser figures, who, in turn, pushed them further into outright atheism. In time, atheists would achieve institutional support in the universities, and would transmit their belief in a literal, univocal and perspicuous Scripture, and the disruptive and substitutionary nature of divine activity, to ever wider audiences.

3

An Inductive Theology

Chapter 1 charted the genesis of two biblical and natural theological presuppositions: a literal, univocal and perspicuous understanding of Scripture and a belief that divine activity in nature disrupts and substitutes for natural causation. Chapter 2 then surveyed the ways in which these presuppositions became inverted in the face of social, political and intellectual change, coming to form the basis of a range of anti-Christian and atheist forms of thought. We now move from England to Scotland, and from atheism to Protestant fundamentalism, and examine how the same presuppositions were instrumental not only to the growth of atheism but, paradoxically, to the opposing worldview of Protestant fundamentalism.

This claim may be surprising, yet the connection between England and Scotland and between atheism and fundamentalism is the philosophy of Locke, and the reaction to his thought by David Hume and Thomas Reid. The intellectual origins of Protestant fundamentalist thought lie in the same hermeneutical and natural theological beliefs charted in Chapter 1, yet with one crucial difference: the addition of Scottish Common Sense philosophy, beginning with Reid. This philosophy was a reaction to the religious and philosophical scepticism of Hume, which had developed from difficulties within the thought of Locke. Common Sense philosophy strengthened the importance of perspicuity and immediate experience in relation to Scripture and science. The Scottish philosophy would go on to gain particular strength in America, where it influenced the nation's education system for much of the nineteenth century. This influence gave rise to an inductive ideology in both science and theology, one that was suspicious of hypotheses and theories and any attempt to extend knowledge beyond sense experience. Yet the success of this form of thought insulated a significant constituency of American Protestants from the theological consequences of geology, evolution and biblical criticism, which sought to look beyond appearances to uncover scientific and textual origins that ran counter to immediate experience. When wedded to changes within American culture, this inductive ideology became radicalised, and led to the development of doctrines of inerrancy and biblical hermeneutics that increased literalism, and a renewed emphasis upon God's disruptive and substitutionary agency within creation. With these changes, the conditions for fundamentalist and creationist forms of evangelical Christianity were set.

As with the growth of anti-Christian and atheist forms of thought, we do wrong if we fall into a number of related errors. First, it is not argued here that the biblical and natural theological presuppositions we have been examining exhaust the causal factors that gave rise to Protestant fundamentalism. What is argued, however, is that these presuppositions played a vital role in its development. Second, it is not argued that each presupposition played an equal role at every stage of its development. While playing an important role in creating the conditions for the methodological monism of what became known as Baconianism, the presupposition that God's activity in creation is disruptive and substitutionary only rose to prominence from the 1920s onward. What is argued, however, is that this presupposition was always present, and decisively shaped the future fundamentalist texts that form the subject matter of Chapters 4 and 5. The third error is considering Protestant fundamentalism as a purely social phenomenon or a purely intellectual one. Protestant fundamentalism is neither purely intellectual nor purely social. Rather, its thought is the expression of its unique culture, and its culture is the instantiation of its thought. Protestant fundamentalist thought is the instrument and intellectual weaponry of a particular culture and form of life, just as the preservation and furtherance of that culture is the ultimate end of its thought. Another error is to see Protestant fundamentalism as a phenomenon that came into being fully formed at some period of the recent past. As with atheism, Protestant fundamentalism is the crystallisation of a wide range of social, political, theological and philosophical forces, which, under certain historical conditions, came together to radicalise conservative evangelical thought. Yet even under these conditions, we look in vain for any decisive factor – except, perhaps, six-day creationism – that would isolate Protestant fundamentalism from wider conservative evangelical thought. This admission is not a failure of analysis but an abiding feature of the religious culture in question.

THE SCOTTISH PHILOSOPHY

Like England, the Scottish Reformation had brought a new emphasis upon literal and univocal readings of Scripture, championing the unadorned text over the glosses of scholastic commentators. While this new hermeneutic influenced all of the Reformers, its effect was particularly pronounced on the theology of John Calvin, whose thought – examined briefly earlier – provided the foundation for future Scottish theology.[1] The Church of Scotland adopted this reading of Scripture at the Reformation, where it found confessional support in chapters XVIII and XX of the *Scots Confession*, and chapter II of the *Second Helvetic Confession*, which was approved by the Scottish Parliament. Scotland had also inherited from its southern neighbour a growing interest in natural theology and the physics of Newton. Newton received early support in Scotland, and his system received intuitional support in a number of Scottish universities, providing the basis for apologetic works by George Cheyne, Colin Maclaurin and Archibald Campbell.[2]

In spite of its adoption of similar hermeneutical and natural theological principles to that of England, because of its distinct social, political and religious context, the Church of Scotland was not beset like the Church of England with the same degree of conflict over the relation of Scripture to tradition, or to the authority of the Church. Instead, its difficulties related more specifically to Church polity and political authority. The Reformation of 1560 had attempted to introduce Reformed doctrine and Presbyterian polity to the country, yet had been only partially successful. The following century saw continued religious and political conflict, as the nation struggled to find a resolution to the competing claims of Presbyterians, Episcopalians and the King. While the Revolution of 1688 and the Claim of Right created an Established Presbyterian Church of Scotland, the political and religious climate of the nation remained tense, as Presbyterianism struggled to gain a foothold in the North and Northeast, where Roman Catholicism and Episcopalianism favoured the exiled Stuarts.

At the turn of the eighteenth century, there was little sign of the Enlightenment that had already begun in England, and that would soon propel Scotland into the forefront of European thought. The Church of Scotland, anxious to preserve its constitutional position, enforced

[1] Cf. McGrath, *Intellectual Origins*, 44–57, 153–8.
[2] See Jeffrey M. Suderman, 'Religion and Philosophy', in *Scottish Philosophy in the Eighteenth Century*, ed. Aaran Garrett and James A. Harris (Oxford: Oxford University Press, 2015), 204–6.

religious and moral conformity through its church courts, acting with magistrates to curb social and political dissent. In 1697, Paisley had witnessed the last major witch trials in Europe. In the same year, Thomas Aitkenhead, student of Divinity at the University of Edinburgh, was hung on the road to the Port of Leith, charged with blasphemy after repeating arguments he had found in the works of early freethinkers.

Scottish education at this time was largely conservative. In the first half of the eighteenth century, the philosophical curriculum was still dominated by a mixture of Cartesian and scholastic teaching, while the theological curriculum was still heavily indebted to European Protestant scholasticism and the Westminster divines. New ideas, however, were beginning to make themselves felt. Central to this intellectual renewal were the universities, which, somewhat unusually, made metaphysics and epistemology the foundation of their arts degrees.[3] Unlike our own day, Scottish universities at this time were charged not only with research and knowledge transfer but the humanitarian aim of producing better citizens, armed with the moral, philosophical and political knowledge to play a constructive role in society. This created an environment in which philosophical knowledge was cherished, and considered invaluable for placing society on a secure footing. The origins of this unique philosophical environment were not purely academic, however, but arose from the principle of *sola scriptura*. By this point, the nation's parish schools, established at the Reformation to enable Scots to read God's Word for themselves, began to bear fruit, as an educated lay population had the skills to read sophisticated scientific and philosophical works.[4] By the mid-eighteenth century, the anxiety and defensiveness of the Church had also begun to wane. The Church of Scotland General Assembly came to be dominated by the Moderate party, who sought the advancement of their nation through an enlightened Calvinism that eschewed the perceived dogmatism and obscurantism of earlier divines. The social and political ascendancy of the Moderate party ensured that Scotland's Enlightenment would be cleric-led, and would not assume an anti-Christian spirit. Unlike France, and more so even than England, Scotland managed to achieve a successful synthesis of Christianity and enlightenment.

---

[3] George Davie, *The Scotch Metaphysics* (London and New York: Routledge 2001), 1–2.
[4] Popular debating societies sprang up across the country at this time, with one student society, the Rankenians, corresponding with Berkeley, who complimented them for their understanding of his philosophy. Davie, *Metaphysics*, 10.

Yet the social and intellectual success that Scotland enjoyed in wedding philosophy, Christianity and the developing sciences would be challenged by one of its own. David Hume, like John Toland, developed tendencies latent in the thought of Locke and drove a wedge between ideas and sensation.[5] As we saw in Chapter 1, Locke believed that the direct objects of knowledge were not objects but their *representations*. This left open the possibility of doubt concerning the existence of external objects and the causal relations among them. In developing these possibilities into a sophisticated form of scepticism, Hume seemed to imperil the prevailing intellectual synthesis. In addition to throwing causation and empirical knowledge into doubt, in his *Enquiry Concerning Human Understanding* and the posthumous *Dialogues Concerning Natural Religion*, Hume's philosophy attacked two apologetic and theological foundations for the prevailing biblical and natural theological synthesis. First, it attacked the miraculous events that served as confirmation of Scripture's authority. Second, it undermined the arguments that demonstrated the existence and providence of a Creator by incorporating his disruptive and substitutionary activity into scientific and apologetic models. While, as noted earlier, Hume's success and popularity at this time has been overstated, his arguments provoked a response. This response would have dramatic effects upon Protestant theology, and, in the course of time, would inadvertently give rise to fundamentalism.

Much like Kant after him, Hume's writing roused Church of Scotland minister Thomas Reid from his philosophic slumber and motivated him to secure human knowledge upon a new footing. Reid responded to Hume for two reasons. First, Hume's critique of causality and induction appeared to throw the developing sciences into doubt. Reid was related to the accomplished Gregory family, who held a number of academic chairs in science and mathematics. Reid shared their interest, and he conducted rudimentary botanical experiments in the manse glebe of his parish at New Machar. It was during his early days of ministry that he became aware of the works of le Comte de Buffon, whose proto-evolutionary theories, and scepticism regarding the objectivity of scientific categories, engaged him greatly.[6] Hume's philosophy only seemed to confirm a

[5] Davie, *Metaphysics*, 16–17; Herbert Hovenkamp, *Science and Religion in America* (Philadelphia: University of Philadelphia Press, 1978), 6–7.
[6] Paul Wood, introduction to Thomas Reid, *Thomas Reid on the Animate Creation* (Edinburgh: Edinburgh University Press, 1995), 3–9; Suderman, 'Religion and Philosophy', 227–33. Cf. Hovenkamp, who argues wrongly that Scottish Realists had no real interest in science. Hovenkamp, *Science and Religion*, 17–18.

worrying growth in theories that challenged the certainty and status of the new sciences. Yet this scepticism also endangered the Christian faith itself. Reid himself lectured on the design argument, and Hume's attack on causality and induction threatened the basis of the inductive methods used in this and other apologetic arguments. The concerns of Reid and others were furthered by Hume's personal infidelity, which appeared to confirm the trajectory of his views. These views were particularly threatening given the perceived irreligion of the age.[7]

Reid's approach was to attack Hume's scepticism at its source, and critique the distinction between sense impressions and ideas. For Reid, Hume's thought was merely the end product of a long tradition in philosophy, which he called 'the way of ideas'. He traced the genealogy of this tradition from Plato through to Descartes, and from Descartes to Locke, Berkeley, and Hume.[8] This form of philosophy, according to Reid, despises the common experience of humanity, and separates philosophy into an illusionary realm of its own.[9] Central to this error is the belief, seen in Locke's influential philosophy, that the objects of knowledge are not external phenomena or mental states, but ideas.[10] For Reid, if the immediate objects of consciousness are not objects themselves, the door is held open to scepticism regarding the existence of the external world and our knowledge of it.[11] According to Reid, Hume's argument that ideas are the immediate objects of consciousness is dependent upon his perversion of everyday language, and his equation of the word 'perception' with sense *as well as* emotions, ideas, and interior states.[12] If Hume had paid attention to the ordinary uses of language, however, he would have learned that no distinction is made in everyday usage between perceiving an object and judging that it exists.[13] Rather, to perceive an object, and to be convinced of its existence, naturally accompany one another.[14] As Reid puts it,

No man seeks a reason for believing what he sees or feels; and, if he did, it would be difficult to find one. But though he can give no reason for believing his senses, his belief remains as firm as if it were grounded on demonstration.[15]

---

[7] See James McCosh, *The Scottish Philosophy* (London: Macmillan & Co, 1875), 12–14.
[8] Thomas Reid, *An Inquiry into the Human Mind on the Principles of Common Sense* (Edinburgh: Edinburgh University Press, 1997), 16–24.
[9] Cf. Reid, *Inquiry*, 15–16.   [10] E.g. Reid, *Inquiry*, 215.   [11] Reid, *Inquiry*, 23.
[12] Thomas Reid, *Essays on the Intellectual Powers of Man* (Indianapolis: Hackett Publishing, 1983), 135–7.
[13] Reid, *Intellectual Powers*, 148–9.   [14] Reid, *Intellectual Powers*, 215.
[15] Reid, *Intellectual Powers*, 201–2.

Rejecting the notion that ideas form the immediate objects of consciousness, Reid instead argued that the mind is cognisant of objects themselves.
Rejecting empirical theories tainted with idealism, he praises, and claims
to accept, the method of Francis Bacon, which presupposes that the
relations between objects are not illusionary but are discoverable through
patient observation, or the 'strict and severe method of induction'. True
science and philosophy are little more than disciplined common sense, so
that 'The learned and the unlearned, the philosopher and the day-
labourer, are upon a level.'[16] Because the objects of consciousness are
objects themselves, and because philosophy and science arise from the
same principles as common sense, Reid is happy to grant a limited
authority to personal testimony and the recollections of memory.[17]
Memory is as much a gift of nature as the senses, and there is no reason
to accept the testimony of one and not the other.[18] Although not Reid's
intention, this defence of testimony and memory would, at a later time,
contribute to the defence of the accuracy of the Gospels by conservative
evangelicals.[19]

While Reid's thought can be understood as a reaction against Locke
and his influence upon Hume, in important respects, Reid actually
strengthened the empirical element of this tradition, against the idealistic
element that was present in Locke and his successors.[20] Instead of sense
experience being mediated by ideas – ideas that left room for doubt over
external reality and causation – Reid defended the general trustworthiness
of sense, memory and testimony. Reid sought to further legitimise his
position by directly relating it to the inductive method of Bacon, one that
stressed immediate sense experience and unadorned fact over speculation
and hypotheses.

The development of what would come to be known as Scottish
Common Sense philosophy would have dramatic, and unexpected, consequences for Protestant Christianity. While, as Harris argues, there is no
indication in Reid's writings that he favoured the application of Common
Sense principles to biblical hermeneutics, it is not by chance that Reid's
ideas, while claiming to describe the common sense of all humanity, arose

---

[16] Reid, *Intellectual Powers*, 258.   [17] Reid, *Intellectual Powers*, 202–5.
[18] Reid, *Intellectual Powers*, 261.
[19] David B. Calhoun, *Princeton Seminary*, vol. I (United States: Banner of Truth Trust,
1994), 87.
[20] Cf. George M. Marsden, *Understanding Fundamentalism* (Grand Rapids: Eerdmans,
1991), 14–15; cf. Bruce Kuklick, *A History of Philosophy in America 1720–2000*
(Oxford: Clarendon Press, 2001), 49.

as the philosophy of a Reformed and Presbyterian society.[21] The democratic and anti-specialist principles of Common Sense philosophy were
the correlate of the principle of *sola scriptura*, with its emphasis upon the
perspicuity of Scripture, and the inadmissibility of theological tradition.[22]
Common Sense put all classes of society on the same intellectual footing,
so that no one – whether philosopher, priest or minister – could reasonably cast doubt upon the fundamental beliefs of ordinary men and
women, whether these related to the facts of sense experience or the basic
truths of religion. The defence of common sense provided a philosophical
framework for this Reformed and Presbyterian ideology. Despite his
intentions, then, Reid's thought would lead to the development of four
operative principles within future Protestant fundamentalism:

    (i)   Realism: that the objects of knowledge are objects themselves,
         not ideas
   (ii)   Common Sense: that knowledge arises from self-evident, universal
         principles inherent in the human mind
  (iii)   Baconianism: that science must be based on direct sense data, not
         hypotheses
  (iv)   Evidentialism: that faith requires justification by *a priori* and *a
         posteriori* evidences[23]

The legacy of Reid was not immediately established; it relied on a range of
lesser figures to transmit – and distort – his thought. Among the most
successful in his day was James Beattie, professor of Moral Philosophy
and Logic at Marischal College, Aberdeen. In *An Essay on the Nature
and Immutability of Truth*, Beattie followed Reid in his defence of realism, and his critique of Humean scepticism as arising from a perversion of
everyday language.[24] Yet Beattie's chief concern in his *Essay* is not the
effect of scepticism upon philosophical and scientific certainty, but upon
religion and morals. As he writes of sceptical writers:

Their writings tend to subvert the foundation of human knowledge, to poison the
sources of human happiness, and to overrun that religion which the best and
wisest of men have believed to be of divine original. . .[25]

[21] Harris, *Fundamentalism and Evangelicals*, 118.
[22] George M. Marsden, *Fundamentalism and American Culture* (Oxford: Oxford
University Press, 1980), 110–1.
[23] See Harris, *Fundamentalism and Evangelicals*, 98–101.
[24] James Beattie, *An Essay in the Nature and Immutability of Truth* (Bristol: Thoemmes
Press, 2000), 7.
[25] Beattie, *Immutability of Truth*, 251.

Due to his fear that religion and morals will wither from sustained sceptical assault, Beattie deploys a further line of common sense defence not used by Reid. It is not only the existence of external objects that is certain and self-evident, argues Beattie, but a host of other innate ideas. Included in these are 'Injustice ought to be blamed and punished' and, crucially, 'There is a God.'[26] Of these, Beattie tells us:

these feelings and suggestions are such, and affect me in such a manner, that I cannot help receiving them, and trusting in them.[27]

Beattie is clear, however, that these innate ideas are not opposed to reason. On the contrary, each works with the other to disclose truth to us. Like innate ideas, reason is a gift from God. Yet when reason is used to attack our fundamental instincts concerning reality it falls into error, for the certainty of these instincts is a gift from God also.[28]

In Beattie, we see the way in which Reid's philosophy could be used to defend a range of attitudes, ideas and beliefs that Reid himself would not necessarily have recognised. Further, we see the way in which religious belief could become entangled with a particular conception of reason. While Beattie's philosophy had its brief moment in the sun, it would take the work of another Scot, and the unique cultural context of the New World, to wed Common Sense philosophy to the biblical and natural theological presuppositions we have been examining, and become the intellectual basis of contemporary fundamentalism.

AN EVANGELICAL EMPIRE

We now turn to trace the intellectual, social and political factors that came to strengthen a literal, univocal and perspicuous understanding of Scripture and a disruptive and substitutionary conception of divine agency in nature. While Common Sense philosophy had its origins in Scotland, it would enjoy its greatest success in America. It would become the unofficial philosophy of nineteenth-century America, giving rise to the phenomenon of 'Baconianism', an inductive ideology that sought to apply a common method to Scripture and nature alike. In doing so, it strengthened the biblical and natural theological framework inherited from Britain, creating a powerful synthesis that came to structure much of evangelical theology.

[26] Beattie, *Immutability of Truth*, 19.   [27] Beattie, *Immutability of Truth*, 19.
[28] Beattie, *Immutability of Truth*, 28.

Britain's North American colonies had more in common with Scotland than they did with England. Like Scotland, the absence of court and parliament, and the relative absence of nobility, meant that culture was in the hands of the upper middle class. Americans shared with Scots an aversion to Episcopalianism, which was associated in the minds of both nations with the encroachment of political and religious tyranny.[29] The limited influence of the Anglican Church in North America, and the hesitance of the British government to order the installation of American bishops, meant that religious provision was often piecemeal, and irreligion was common.[30] The outbreak of the American Revolution only increased popular and educated unbelief, as radical political and religious tracts were imported from Europe, and used to support republican ideals against the Crown. Farmhands read Thomas Paine, and heterodox thinkers such as Elihu Palmer attempted to propagate anti-Christian ideas through outdoor preaching and polemical writings.[31] Two events ensured, however, that it would not be an anti-Christian enlightenment that would lay the foundation for American intellectual life, but a clerical, Protestant enlightenment, and one of a uniquely Scottish and Common Sense kind.

The first pivotal event was the introduction of Scottish Common Sense philosophy into America. Prior to his arrival in America, James Witherspoon had made a name for himself in Scotland for the biting criticisms of the Moderate party made in his *Ecclesiastical Characteristics*.[32] After involvement in a damaging court case, it was with relief that Witherspoon received a second invitation to become president of the College of New Jersey. The college at that time was in the grip of a dispute between Old and New Schools and was dominated by Berkeleian philosophy.[33] Witherspoon's first task was to strengthen orthodoxy in the college and dismiss those staff that were espousing Berkeleian and radical Lockean views, which Witherspoon – following Reid's critique of 'the way of ideas' – directly connected with

[29] Henry F. May, *The Enlightenment in America* (New York: Oxford University Press, 1976), 342–3.

[30] Amanda Porterfield, *Conceived in Doubt* (Chicago: Chicago University Press, 2012), 6–7.

[31] Susan Jacoby, *Freethinkers: A History of American Secularism* (New York: Henry Holt and Company, 2004), 52–5.

[32] James Witherspoon, *Ecclesiastical Characteristics* (Glasgow, 1753).

[33] James H. Moorhead, *Princeton Seminary in American Religion and Culture* (Grand Rapids: Eerdmans Publishing Co., 2012), 16–17.

scepticism and irreligion.[34] In its place, Witherspoon introduced the philosophy of Hutcheson that he had earlier lampooned in the *Characteristics*, and later introduced teaching on Reid's Common Sense Realism.[35]

The second pivotal event that inhibited the advance of anti-Christian ideas was, paradoxically, the French Revolution. While American philosophy at this time, following Britain, was dominated by Locke and the other British empiricists, the advent of the French Revolution, and the excesses of the Terror, produced great mistrust and suspicion regarding the effect of enlightenment ideas upon irreligion and political radicalism. For a young nation, struggling to maintain unity after a revolution, and seeking to prove to their British critics that they were fit to govern, the nation grew increasingly suspicious of the destabilising effect of anti-Christian ideas. Given the predominance of Lockean and Berkeleian philosophy at this time, the narrative of Reid and Witherspoon – that the idealistic elements in Locke's thought gave rise to scepticism and irreligion – gained increasing plausibility, and Locke's dominance began to be challenged by Scottish Common Sense Realism.[36]

It was not only a fear of scepticism and irreligion, however, that prompted this change. The Scottish philosophy was useful to the young republic because it successfully synthesised three principles central to its intellectual life: empiricism, the self-evident nature of certain political and moral truths and the reasonableness of evangelical Christianity.[37] It was also democratic and anti-elitist, as all right-thinking people, regardless of class or educational attainment, possessed the capacity to understand fundamental truth. Such a philosophy afforded a straightforward and robust epistemological foundation for the stability and territorial expansion of the republic.[38] It also justified the existence of an intuitive moral sense independent of tradition, necessary to hold together peoples from a variety of national and religious backgrounds.[39]

Witherspoon's promotion of Common Sense philosophy was continued by his successors, and, from Princeton, the Scottish philosophy

[34] Kuklick, *Philosophy in America*, 47–9.
[35] Mark A. Noll. 'The Irony of the Enlightenment for Presbyterians in the Early Republic', *Journal of the Early Republic* 5, no. 2 (1985), 153–5.
[36] Theodore Dwight Bozeman, *Protestants in an Age of Science* (Chapel Hill: University of North Carolina Press, 1977), 23–4; Jacoby, *Freethinkers*, 46–7; May, *Enlightenment in America*, 207, 232–3.
[37] Marsden, *Understanding Fundamentalism*, 128–9.
[38] Cf. May, *Enlightenment in America*, 346.   [39] Noll, 'Common Sense Tradition', 218.

spread to Harvard, Yale, Pennsylvania, Columbia and Brown, becoming 'the official philosophy of nineteenth century America', taught in colleges and schools across the country.[40] It should not, of course, be thought that this influence was principally extended through first-hand familiarity with the works of Reid. Rather, it was through his popularisers – chiefly Beattie, James Oswald and Dugald Stewart – that Common Sense philosophy extended its influence. In many instances, professors and schoolteachers would read works of Common Sense philosophy before producing edited or simplified volumes for their students, thereby domesticating the Scottish tradition, and adapting it for American needs. As the majority of teachers and educational institutions had ecclesiastical ties, this meant that the form of Common Sense philosophy imbibed by students was interwoven with evangelical Christianity, so that all disciplines – including, crucially, natural science – were seen to be part of a single body of truth, confirmed and advanced by a single, self-evident method.[41]

Nowhere was the influence of this philosophy felt more strongly than theology, where it would definitively shape evangelical hermeneutics, and approaches towards the relation of science and religion. Common Sense principles became associated with the method of induction developed by the scientist lauded by Reid as the originator of his own philosophical method: Francis Bacon. As we saw earlier, Bacon's thought was developed in response to the collapse of meaning in nature brought about by the Reformation. This, taken with the recovery of Augustinian anthropology and its development by Calvinist theology, prompted Bacon to be extremely sceptical about the capacity of human beings to know anything about the natural world.[42] In the *Novum Organon*, Bacon sought to develop a new inductive method that would replace the inherited authority of Aristotelian scholasticism and ancient scientific authorities, establishing natural philosophy on a humble – yet secure – empirical basis:

The syllogism consists of propositions, propositions consist of words, and words are counters for notions. Hence if the notions themselves (this is the basis of the

---

[40] May, *Enlightenment in America*, 121; Hovenkamp, *Science and Religion in America*, 19–20; Harris, *Fundamentalism and Evangelicals*, 126–7; McCosh, *Scottish Philosophy*, 188.

[41] Cf. Marsden, *Understanding Fundamentalism*, 14, 17; Kuklick, *Philosophy in America*, 59–62. Moorhead, *Princeton Seminary*, 200–1.

[42] See Peter Harrison, *The Fall of Man and the Foundations of Science* (Cambridge: Cambridge University Press, 2007), 7.

matter) are confused and abstracted from things without care, there is nothing sound in what is built on them. The only hope is true induction.[43]

Central to this method were significant restraints upon the use of theories and hypotheses in the practice of science and the construction of knowledge. Bacon claimed to:

reject in general the work of the mind that *follows* sensation; and rather to open and construct a new and certain road for the mind from the actual perceptions of the senses.[44] [my emphasis]

The rhetoric of induction, and its accompanying suspicion of theories and hypotheses, was famously adopted by Newton in the *General Scholium* of the second edition of the *Principia*, 'I do not feign hypotheses' (*hypotheses non figno*).[45] It was this inductive rhetoric, as we have seen, that Reid invoked against Hume, as he sought to defend Common Sense Realism against scepticism. Scottish Common Sense philosophy would bring this influence to America, where it would enjoy unparalleled success.

The principles of 'Baconianism', as it came to be called, were rarely outlined in full, and it was less a coherent philosophy and more an ideology and habit of mind.[46] Daniels' three characteristics of Baconianism provide a helpful summary. First, Baconianism was empirical, arguing that all scientific statements should rest solidly on observed fact. Second, it was anti-theoretical, believing that hypotheses should be avoided, and that scientific method should not be extended beyond immediate observation. Third, it was taxonomic, holding that science chiefly consisted of the collection and orderly presentation of facts.[47] This conception of science was not only applied to natural phenomena, however, but also to the Bible. Baconianism viewed the contents of Scripture as facts among other facts, and as trustworthy as the facts of sense experience that formed the basis of science. As such, they did not require any special method of interpretation, but simply the application of common sense. When this was done, the facts of Scripture were perspicuous, and divergent interpretations could only be the result of

[43] Francis Bacon, *The New Organon*, trans. Lisa Jardine and Michael Silverthorne (Cambridge: Cambridge University Press, 2000), 35.
[44] Bacon, *Organon*, 28.
[45] Isaac Newton, *Philosophiae Naturalis Principia Mathematica*, trans I. Bernard Cohen and Anne Whitman (Berkeley: University of California Press, 1999), 943.
[46] George H. Daniels, *American Science in the Age of Jackson* (New York: Columbia University Press, 1968), 27.
[47] Cf. Daniels, *American Science*, 65.

deviance from this method.[48] The equivalence of the facts of Scripture and the facts of nature, and the single method used to uncover and order them, led to the apotheosis of Baconian method as a divinely-inspired, and singularly Protestant, method. Bacon became something like a Protestant saint, whose scientific prowess arose naturally from his obedience to the principle of *sola scriptura*, and his devotion to the plain meaning of Scripture.[49]

For much of the nineteenth century, this inductive ideology successfully synthesised Christianity with the sciences in a manner analogous to the British context. As there was one truth, and one method for apprehending this truth, science was not in conflict with faith, but its handmaid. Science testified to the glory, power, and wisdom of God, and each new discovery only amplified the mind's worship of the Creator. In a nation without an established church to enforce Christianity with legal sanction, science therefore served an apologetic function, ensuring social and intellectual conformity with the faith.[50] Danger only arose when the natural world was approached without the strict inductive method of Bacon, and the mind allowed to wander into vain hypotheses not substantiated by direct sense experience.[51] Common Sense principles ensured that this did not occur, and that scientific knowledge would not be enlisted for anti-Christian purposes.[52] Due to its apologetic and theological functions, science in mid-nineteenth century America was a 'doxological science', fulfilling an analogous function to contemporary scientific writing in Britain.[53]

Yet how did Baconianism and the rhetoric of induction affect theology? And how was it mediated to the later fundamentalist tradition? The key figure in this mediation was one of Witherspoon's successors at Princeton: Charles Hodge. For Hodge, the foundation of all theology was the plenary inspiration of Scripture. Inspiration means that the Bible's ultimate author is the Holy Spirit. It is infallible, and its revelation exhausts all that God would have us know.[54] Inspiration for Hodge 'is not confined to moral and religious truths, but extends to the statement of

[48] Marsden, *Understanding Fundamentalism*, 56; Bozeman, *Age of Science*, 132–59.
[49] Bozeman, *Age of Science*, 130.
[50] Bozeman, *Age of Science*, 133; Turner, *Without God*, 50.
[51] Hovenkamp, *Science and Religion in America*, 44.
[52] Bozeman, *Age of Science*, 101–3.
[53] Bozeman, *Age of Science*, 75; Roberts, *Darwinism and the Divine*, 9.
[54] Charles Hodge, *Systematic Theology*, vol. I (London and Edinburgh: Thomas Nelson & Sons, 1880), 152.

facts, whether scientific, historical or geographical'.[55] Inspiration, moreover, extends to the very words used to represent these truths, so that
inspiration is not only plenary but verbal.[56] Following the biblical and
natural theological assumptions of the age, Hodge argues that the correct
method for interpreting Scripture is a Baconian one, which uses the same
methods as the natural sciences:

> As the facts of nature are all related and determined by physical laws, so the facts
> of the Bible are all related and determined by the nature of God and of his actions.
> And as He wills that men should study his works and discover their wonderful
> organic relation and harmonious combination, so it is his will that we should
> study his Word, and learn that, like the stars, its truths are not isolated points, but
> systems, cycles and epicycles, in unending harmony and grandeur.[57]

The theologian discovers these laws by utilising the inductive method,
whose purpose is not to manufacture, presume, or modify, but to take the
statements of Scripture for the facts they are.[58] This is because Hodge –
quoting Chillingworth – believed that it was the Bible, and the Bible
alone, that was the religion of Protestants.[59] The Bible is to the theologian
what nature is to the man of science: 'it is his store-house of facts, and his
method of ascertaining what the Bible teaches, is the same as the which
the natural philosopher adopts to ascertain what nature teaches.'[60] From
this perspective, the purpose of doctrine is merely, like the Baconian
scientist, to collate, summarise and present the teaching of Scripture. To
try and 'look behind' the plain meaning of the text for alternative meanings is therefore not simply wrong, but *unscientific*.

As theology's method is one of strict scientific induction, a method in
which the historical and social context of the researcher are presumed to
have no relevance for their findings, Hodge's *Systematic Theology*, in its
many thousands of pages, considers the issue of interpretation in under
two. For Hodge – following the Common Sense teaching he received at
Princeton – Scripture should be read in its 'plain historical sense', and as a
unity. When this is done, all right-thinking people will agree on the
necessary truths of doctrine and practice. This argument provides a
'decisive proof' for the perspicuity of the Bible, and the legitimacy –
indeed the necessity – of 'allowing the people the enjoyment of the divine
right of personal judgement'.[61]

[55] Hodge, *Systematic Theology*, vol. I, 163.   [56] Hodge, *Systematic Theology*, vol. I, 164.
[57] Hodge, *Systematic Theology*, vol. I, 3.   [58] Hodge, *Systematic Theology*, vol. I, 9–10.
[59] Hodge, *Systematic Theology*, vol. I, 11.   [60] Hodge, *Systematic Theology*, vol. I, 10.
[61] Hodge, *Systematic Theology*, vol. I, 187–8.

Hodge's emphasis on the plain sense of Scripture, and his faith in the capacity of all right-thinking people to reach agreement on the fundamental doctrines of the faith, rested upon a conception of language derived from the hermeneutical practices examined in Chapter 1. Like the Restoration divines influenced by Locke, Hodge believed that Scripture's true sense is literal and univocal. Yet this was now supplemented by a Common Sense belief, shared by many evangelicals, in the inert and static meaning of words.[62] This theory of language meant that, for Hodge, the univocal meaning of Scripture extends even to its figurative language, for 'figurative language is just as definite in its meaning and just as intelligible as the most literal'.[63] This is because the Bible 'is a plain book. It is intelligible by the people'.[64] The perspicuity of Scripture was so total for Hodge that it could not be said that the Church or its tradition mediated theology in any way whatsoever. Rather, the Bible gave all people immediate access to the teaching of the Holy Spirit.[65]

The belief that the contents of Scripture are facts among other facts, and that the correct way to interpret these facts is through a plain, and univocal reading of its perspicuous text, had momentous consequences for Hodge's conception of the relation between science and religion. As Scripture and nature are both God's works, the facts of nature cannot contradict Scripture. If an interpretation of Scripture contradicts established fact that interpretation must be rejected. Hodge argued that the Church must be careful not to repeat the mistakes of the past, when the Copernican theory was rejected by both Protestant and Roman Catholic theologians.[66] Indeed, true science can help the Church in its task of interpreting Scripture, as it can rule out certain interpretations of its text.[67] Yet, at this point, Hodge – drawing upon a Common Sense distaste for hypotheses – introduces a crucial distinction, which would be repeated in later fundamentalist thought: the *facts* of science are distinct from the *theories* of science. As Hodge puts it:

There is a great distinction between theories and facts. Theories are of men. Facts are of God. The Bible often contradicts the former, never the latter.[68]

---

[62] See John Lardas, *Secularism in Antebellum America* (Chicago: University of Chicago Press, 2011), 104–5.
[63] Cited in Moorhead, *Princeton Seminary*, 214–7.
[64] Hodge, *Systematic Theology*, vol. I, 183.   [65] Moorhead, *Princeton Seminary*, 211.
[66] Hodge, *Systematic Theology*, vol. I, 56–7.
[67] Hodge, *Systematic Theology*, vol. I, 170–1.
[68] Hodge, *Systematic Theology*, vol. I, 170–1.

Following Scottish Common Sense philosophy, and a Baconian mistrust of hypotheses, no *theory* can negate a traditional interpretation of Scripture, for 'the great body of what passes for philosophy or science is merely human speculation'.[69] In spite of this distinction, however, Hodge nevertheless believes that it is necessary to prove the existence of God through reason alone, and is happy to receive the support of proofs – especially the teleological or design argument – that, Hodge believes, confirm the teaching of Genesis.[70]

Hodge's defence of the design argument, and the ability of science to support a recent special creation with its accompanying conception of immediate divine activity, would be of crucial importance for the future, and in his thinking we see the basic structure of future fundamentalist and creationist thought. The two pillars of this structure are the verbal inspiration of Scripture – with its infallible authority in religious, scientific and historical matters – and a Baconian, Common Sense understanding of biblical hermeneutics and the scientific method. Hodge believed in the existence of a single faculty of reason, possessed by all people, which could be used to answer both scientific and theological questions. There is no sense in his thought that reason could take different forms within different disciplines, or that different objects required different kinds of enquiry.[71] This unitary understanding was a direct development of the biblical and natural theological presuppositions examined in Chapter 1, now amplified by Scottish Common Sense philosophy. This unitary understanding had three effects. First, it reinforced the belief that divine activity in nature disrupts and substitutes for natural causation. God's causal activity was functionally equivalent to physical force, and could be verified through gaps in scientific understanding, and thereby incorporated into scientific models. Second, it produced a conception of the relation between science and faith in which the former served the latter. This led, third, to a situation in which the theories of science could not easily be permitted to overturn traditional interpretations of Scripture.

Through his teaching, preaching and publications, Hodge transmitted Scottish Common Sense and Baconian ideas to ministers and pastors across the nation. The synthesis of science and theology he championed, while reasonable and advantageous in the short-term, would ultimately prove disastrous for American evangelicalism. The biblical and natural

---

[69] Hodge, *Systematic Theology*, vol. I, 57–8.
[70] Hodge, *Systematic Theology*, vol. I, 202, 215–33.
[71] Cf. James Barr, *Fundamentalism* (London: SCM Press, 1977), 274.

theological presuppositions that underlay it would, in time, have to bear the strain of unprecedented intellectual and social change, developments that would break apart the evangelical empire of the United States, and give rise to two different attitudes towards culture, and two very different conceptions of science.

THE SHOCK OF THE NEW

Thus far, we have traced the ways in which the biblical and natural theological presuppositions we have been examining were strengthened by Scottish Common Sense philosophy in an American context and led to the development of a unitary method in both theology and science. We will now see how the intellectual challenges of Darwinism and biblical criticism, and the social challenges of industrialisation, immigration and secularisation, undermined traditional evangelical culture and radicalised its theological presuppositions. This led to the formulation of defensive accounts of inerrancy, and the adoption of a strong anti-modern polemic in some conservative evangelical constituencies. Under these social and intellectual conditions, the presupposition of a literal, univocal and perspicuous Scripture, and an understanding of divine activity as that which disrupts and substitutes for natural causation, became instrumental to the genesis of fundamentalism. While the latter of these assumptions was secondary to the first during the first decades of fundamentalism's existence, it would become increasingly important as the twentieth century progressed. When conservative evangelicalism was dominant in American life, emphasis upon direct divine activity was not of great importance. Yet as evangelicals lost social and political power, a reading of Scripture that emphasised the unmediated punitive and providential power of God became socially and psychologically attractive. The story of how this occurred is a further example of how the function and significance of beliefs change under different social conditions.

The shocks encountered by American culture in the second half of the nineteenth century were dramatic and sudden, ushered in by war, evolutionary theory, biblical criticism and rapid industrialisation.[72] The American Civil War took the lives of over 600,000 men, and did irreparable damage to the position of the Bible in American life. Each side

---

[72] Bradley J. Longfield, *The Presbyterian Controversy* (New York and Oxford: Oxford University Press, 1991), 12–17; Cole, *History of Fundamentalism*, 16–30; Marsden, *American Culture*, 21–2.

marshalled God to their side, and each put forward opposing biblical arguments as to the justice of their cause. This spoke against the perspicuity of Scripture, for if, as Hodge argued, all necessary matters were clear to right-thinking people, how could Christians have become so divided?[73] The wake of the Civil War also brought social, political and economic division between North and South. The latter lost its infrastructure, economic base and political influence in the war, and the policies of the North during the Reconstruction angered many Southerners, who witnessed the dissolution of their traditional way of life. This instigated a reactionary religious and social conservatism among a significant part of the South's population, a conservatism that would prove important during the later fundamentalist controversy.[74]

Although not foreseen at the time, one of the most significant intellectual factors in the generation of future fundamentalism was the publication of *On the Origin of Species*. Like Britain, the majority of objections to Darwin's theory were purely scientific, or, more commonly, arose from concerns regarding the effects of Darwin's ideas upon the apologetic schema used to justify Christianity and aid its integration with science.[75] Central to the debate was the extent to which Darwin's theory accommodated teleology and divine agency. While Asa Grey, one of Darwin's leading American proponents, believed that Darwin had not precluded design from his theory, Charles Hodge saw the rejection of teleology as being at the centre of Darwin's theory:

It is however neither evolution nor natural selection which gives Darwinism its peculiar character and importance. It is that Darwin rejects all teleology or the doctrine of final causes... [And] it is this feature of his system which brings it into conflict not only with Christianity, but with the fundamental principles of natural religion.[76]

Prefiguring certain sections of future fundamentalist thought, Hodge was in no doubt what Darwinism was: 'What is Darwinism? It is atheism.'[77] Darwin was problematic to men like Hodge for two reasons. First, by proposing a natural mechanism for the development of life, including human beings, Darwin had closed off the largest domain of direct divine activity within nature, leaving few places – if any – where God's direct

[73] Moore, *Post-Darwinian*, 54–5; Cole, *History of Fundamentalism*, 18.
[74] Marsden, *American Culture*, 103.   [75] Roberts, *Darwinism and the Divine*, 20.
[76] Charles Hodge, *'What Is Darwinism?' and Other Writings on Science and Religion*, ed. Mark A. Noll and David N. Livingstone (Grand Rapids: Baker Books, 1994), 92.
[77] Hodge, *What Is Darwinism?*, 156.

agency could be seen. Second, Darwin sought to overturn the plain sense of Scripture by a mere *theory*, flying in the face of common sense. As such, although Hodge adopted a natural theological line of attack in *What Is Darwinism?*, it is likely that he rejected Darwin for primarily biblical and philosophical reasons, his Common Sense presumptions viewing evolution as anti-Scriptural and irrational, given the 'self-evident' signs of design in nature.[78] What is remarkable in light of later developments, however, is that there was little opposition to Darwin's theories based on a literal six-day reading of Genesis. The majority of Christians – whether scientists or otherwise – accommodated evolution within Genesis by adopting day-age or gap interpretations.

While scientists and theologians accommodated evolutionary theory in a variety of ways, the realisation that science could overturn traditional interpretations of Genesis, which had been defended by Baconian principles, did great damage to the position of Common Sense philosophy in America. Common Sense philosophy struggled to accommodate evolution for two reasons. First, as the concept of evolution developed by taking multiple inferences from a variety of scientific fields, and synthesising them into a theory that was not immediately verifiable through direct sense experience, it demonstrated that theories and ideas played an important role in the construction of knowledge. As evolution broke the exclusive connection between direct sense experience and knowledge, so it, second, broke the connection between common sense and knowledge. Reid's philosophy had been constructed around the principle that the beliefs and reasoning of ordinary people were not fundamentally different from those of philosophers and scientists. Yet the fact of evolution drove a wedge between what was verifiable and intuitive to ordinary people, and what was verifiable by specialists. This gulf, when allied to the rhetoric of biblical and scientific perspicuity championed by conservative evangelicals influenced by Baconianism, would, in time, result in an anti-specialist and anti-elitist mind-set developing within certain sections of the conservative evangelical community.[79]

While Common Sense philosophy struggled to accommodate evolution, the Scottish philosophy's old enemy, idealism, found this accommodation far easier to achieve, and over the next decades Common Sense philosophy would lose its pedagogical dominance, except, crucially, within conservative evangelical circles.[80] Idealism, however, did not

---

[78] Cf. Roberts, *Darwinism and the Divine*, 210.
[79] Cf. Marsden, *American Culture*, 20–1.   [80] Noll, 'Common Sense Tradition', 232–3.

arrive in America unaccompanied. The divorce between everyday common sense and knowledge was exacerbated by the arrival of biblical criticism from Germany. Just as evolutionary theory had challenged traditional Protestant readings of Genesis, and offered an alternative, compelling vision for the development of human life, so German biblical criticism began to cast doubt upon traditional interpretations of Scripture, and its authority as the sole source of doctrine. Modernist, or liberal theology spread quickly from the 1880s onward, often in the wake of the movement from Common Sense philosophy to idealism.[81] While this movement had antecedents within New England theology, it took on a far more menacing figure due to the unprecedented social and intellectual changes that were contemporaneous with it.[82] While far from uniform, a number of common resemblances differentiated modernist theology from conventional evangelicalism: first, a tendency to view experience, rather than Scripture, as the ground of religious certainty; second, the identification of the Kingdom of God with the progress of civilisation, and, especially, science; third, a conception of morality as the essence of Christianity; and, fourth, a tendency to reduce God's activity in creation to natural processes.[83] For such a worldview, evolution provided the perfect metanarrative: the steady perfection of creation through the work of natural law rather than miraculous interventions, with God progressively revealing new truths to the Church and wider society. Evangelicals were now confronted with increasing numbers within their own denominations who no longer viewed Scripture as the inerrant, self-authenticating ground of faith, who rejected many of the miraculous events recorded in its pages, and were happy to accept many of the social changes challenging evangelical culture as manifestations of God's progressive plan for humanity. Modernism found particular support in New England and the wealthy Divinity Schools of the North, lending an additional North-South and social-political dimension to the substantive theological issues.

Archibald Hodge and Benjamin Warfield responded to these challenges in what would become a classic defence of the conservative evangelical understanding of Scripture. For an article that would become associated with Protestant fundamentalism, it is perhaps surprising that Hodge and Warfield begin their argument by stressing the *humanity* of

---

[81] Kuklick, *American Philosophy*, 99; Marsden, *American Culture*, 25.

[82] See Gary Dorrien, *The Making of American Liberal Theology: Imagining Progressive Religion 1805–1900* (Louisville: Westminster John Knox Press, 2001), 2.

[83] Cf. Marsden, *American Culture*, 24.

Scripture, conceding the various personal, social and historical factors that came together to produce it. Yet, in making this concession, the authors balance it with a strong account of providence and concurrence, the Holy Spirit accompanying and ordering these human elements to produce the words that he willed.[84] This providential ordering is the substance of Scripture's inspiration. Because thought cannot be expressed save in language, the inspiration of the Holy Spirit is verbal and plenary, and is not reducible to the ideas represented by the words of Scripture.[85] While belief in inspiration and inerrancy might be thought to be a matter for faith alone – a deduction from the fact of Scripture's divine authorship – Hodge and Warfield nevertheless believe that inspiration and biblical authority can be proved *inductively*, and that 'if the Scriptures do fail in truth in their statements of whatever kind, the doctrine of Inspiration which has been defended in this paper cannot stand'.[86] This inductive element of Hodge and Warfield's thought reflects the need for a self-authenticating Scripture introduced at the Reformation, now strengthened by the Common Sense beliefs of Princeton theology. While providing a precedent for the harmonisation that would come to typify fundamentalist apologetics, an inductive approach towards Scripture, on the face of it, nevertheless allows the authors to take a remarkably open-minded attitude towards the dating, authorship and documentary history of biblical texts:

the defenders of the strictest doctrine of Inspiration should cheerfully acknowledge that theories as to the authors, dates, sources and modes of composition of the several books, which are not plainly inconsistent with the testimony of Christ or His Apostles as to the Old Testament, or with the apostolic origin of the books of the New Testament, or with the absolute truthfulness of any of the affirmations of these books so authenticated, cannot in the least invalidate the evidence or pervert the meaning of the historical doctrine of Inspiration.[87]

Yet this openness to at least some level of biblical criticism is tempered by a number of additional principles that, like the elder Hodge's distinction between facts and theories, made any significant revision to the doctrine of verbal and plenary inspiration almost impossible to accomplish. To the determined biblical critic, Hodge and Warfield laid down the following challenge:

---

[84] A. A. Hodge and B. B. Warfield, 'Inspiration', *The Presbyterian Review* 6 (1881): 228–32.
[85] Hodge and Warfield, 'Inspiration', 232–5.
[86] Hodge and Warfield, 'Inspiration', 244.   [87] Hodge and Warfield, 'Inspiration', 236.

With these presumptions, and in this spirit, (1) Let it be proved that each alleged discrepant statement certainly occurred in the original autograph of the sacred book in which it is said to be found. (2) Let it be proved that the interpretation which occasions the apparent discrepancy is the one which the passage was evidently intended to bear. It is not sufficient to show a difficulty which may spring out of our defective knowledge of the circumstances. The true meaning must be definitely and certainly ascertained, and then shown to be irreconcilable with other known truth. (3) Let it be proved that the true sense of some part of the original autograph is directly and necessarily inconsistent with some certainly known fact of history, or truth of science, or some other statement of Scripture certainly ascertained and interpreted. We believe that it can be shown that this has never yet been successfully done in the case of one single alleged instance of error in the WORD OF GOD.[88]

There are three defences advanced here, with the second and third closely related. The first is the most difficult to overcome, that of demonstrating that the original autographs inspired by the Holy Spirit contain a passage which contradicts another statement of Scripture, or contradicts accepted fact. Here, paradoxically, the tangled history of the formation of the canon and the biblical text works *in favour* of conservative evangelicalism, placing an indefinite number of revisions and alterations between the original autographs and the Bible as we now possess it, thereby protecting the doctrine of inspiration behind the mists of history. Yet even if the original autographs *were* to be found, the biblical critic is then presented with a second hurdle, that of showing that the apparent discrepancy resides in the 'true meaning' of the text, and not in a faulty interpretation. This second defence is closely related to the third, that of demonstrating that the original autograph, properly interpreted, 'is directly and necessarily inconsistent with some certainly known fact'. The requirement for 'direct' and 'necessary' contradiction echoes the Common Sense distinction between facts and theories drawn by the earlier Hodge, and has two consequences. First, it makes textual inconsistency almost impossible to prove, as context, and the presumed intention of the human author, provide endless possibilities for alternative, harmonious readings, something which Hodge and Warfield make full use of in their defence of a Roman census at the time of Christ's birth, and his nativity during the reign of Tiberius.[89] In these defences, we witness two authors, indebted to Common Sense Realism, making an inconsistent and largely hypocritical use of theories, hypotheses, and speculations to argue away *prima facie*

---

[88] Hodge and Warfield, 'Inspiration', 242.
[89] Hodge and Warfield, 'Inspiration', 247–50.

biblical contradictions that would be observable by any person of reasonable intelligence. As long as a saving hypothesis, theory or speculation can be thought of, however implausible, a 'direct' and 'necessary' contradiction is averted. Second, this tendency to rationalise inconsistency has implications for the relation of science and religion. Because inconsistency requires 'direct' and 'necessary' contradiction, Hodge and Warfield have no difficulty in asserting that contemporary science demonstrates the accuracy of the first two chapters of Genesis. Although Hodge and Warfield, perhaps owing to their high sense of providence, could accommodate a conservative version of Darwinism within their thought, as we shall see, their arguments and methods would be used at a later date to prove the scientific authority of a literal reading of Genesis, and the unscientific nature of the theory of evolution.

In and of themselves, however, inerrancy, a preference for literal readings of Scripture, and Common Sense assumptions did not *necessarily* entail the rejection of evolutionary theory, and the great majority of contemporary evangelicals accommodated themselves to evolutionary theory. Why, then, did later fundamentalists turn to six-day creationism? The answer is complex and lies in the unprecedented social and economic changes that occurred during the late nineteenth and early twentieth centuries, and their effect on the biblical and natural theological presuppositions we have been examining. These would result in the isolation of evangelical culture and Common Sense principles from wider society, and the radicalisation of its understanding of science and religion. Unlike Britain, America's industrialisation occurred at a much later date, and progressed far more rapidly.[90] In 1880, forty-four percent of the American population were still employed in agricultural labour, and only twelve percent lived in cities.[91] Yet by the turn of the twentieth century, the urban population, aided by massive immigration from Europe, had surpassed that of the rural population, shifting power away from traditional centres to the new. This combination of urbanisation and immigration increased social pluralism and changed American self-identity, thereby weakening the dominance of evangelical Protestants. It also brought about greater secularisation, as the public sphere accommodated itself to the presence of large numbers of non-Protestant Americans.

The increasing pluralisation of American society, taken with the same professionalisation of science witnessed in Britain, led to changes in the

---

[90] Julie S. Jones, *Being the Chosen* (Farnton: Ashgate, 2010), 35.
[91] Cole, *History of Fundamentalism*, 12n8.

provision of education. Prior to the Civil War, the vast majority of America's colleges and schools had denominational ties, and the majority of college presidents were clergymen. The movement towards modern, German-influenced research universities favoured academic specialists rather than generalist clergymen, and the trustees of many leading universities chose to sever ties with their founding churches.[92] It was this secularisation of education that gave rise to the American progenitors of the 'conflict thesis' concerning science and religion: Andrew Dickson White and John William Draper. White was instrumental in the founding of Cornell University, and wrote his most well known work *A History of the Warfare of Science with Theology in Christendom* after his conflict with churchmen over Cornell's status as a non-denominational college.[93] While not anti-Christian, White's book presented history as the process whereby dogmatic theology is displaced by the forces of reason, bringing with it intellectual progress and social emancipation.[94] The work was joined by that of Draper, who summed up the relationship between science and religion in this way:

The history of science is not a mere record of isolated discoveries; it is a narrative of the conflict of two contending powers, the expansive force of the human intellect on one side, and the compression arising from traditionary faith and human interests on the other.[95]

On one side stood truth, knowledge and the greatness of the human mind, and on the other stood obscurantist religion and personal selfishness. While hopelessly biased, 'a tract, not a history',[96] the works of Draper and White provided Americans with a conflict narrative analogous – although more simplistic – to that offered in Britain by Huxley. This narrative played a role in alienating certain sections of the intellectual elite from Christianity, who as writers, professors and educational leaders, attempted to further secularise the education sector. These developments furthered the impression among evangelicals that Christianity was being displaced as a vital constituent of education, and provided a focus for growing conservative reaction.[97]

---

[92] See Noll, *Faith and Criticism*, 12–14.   [93] Moore, *Post-Darwinian*, 33–5.

[94] Andrew D. White, *A History of the Warfare of Science and Theology* (New York: Dover Publications, 1960), v–xii.

[95] John W. Draper, *History of the Conflict between Religion and Science* (London: Kegan Paul, Trench & Co, 1887), vi.

[96] Chadwick, *Victorian Church*, vol. II, 14.   [97] Marsden, *American Culture*, 160.

This time of rapid change has been described as the 'Golden Age' of American unbelief, headed by the orator and wit Robert Ingersoll. American unbelief was, paradoxically, the *correlate* of the dominance of evangelical religion. While the First Amendment of the Constitution maintained a separation between Church and state, the dominance of evangelicalism at both local and national level meant that evangelicalism 'was virtually a religious establishment'.[98] There were a number of cases in which this informal establishment had analogous results to those in Britain, where certain individuals felt sufficiently marginalised and disenfranchised as to blame Christianity for their plight.[99] Yet in spite of growing hostility towards Christianity among a section of the intellectual elite, unbelief in America would never achieve the popularity or cultural strength that it achieved in Britain. This anomaly requires comment. The first reason for the relative failure of unbelief was the most significant difference in the religious complexion between Britain and America: the absence of an established church. While the tone of government administrations during the nineteenth century was often of a broad evangelicalism, the absence of a formal religious establishment, enforced by law, meant that religious power was not associated with political power as it was in Britain.[100] This ensured that any working class or racial disquiet against the prevailing political and economic order could not be so readily associated with Christianity as it was in Britain. This had the effect, second, of ensuring that popular unbelief could never achieve a political consensus that would aid in recruitment and mobilisation.[101] The absence of a state church and a unified anti-Christian political agenda had the effect, third, of channelling working class energy away from radical politics into alternative forms of religious expression, ranging from Mormonism to premillenialism and, later on, Pentecostalism. The fourth reason for the failure of unbelief to develop in America was the First World War and the Russian Revolution. The war led to an outpouring of religiously-heightened nationalism, while the Russian Revolution had a similar effect upon public opinion as the French Revolution had before, cementing the connection between atheism and political disorder, and

---

[98] Marsden, *American Culture*, xxx, 6–7.   [99] E.g. Jacoby, *Freethinkers*, 18–20, 66–103.

[100] Sidney Warren, *American Freethought 1860–1914* (New York: Columbia University Press, 1943), 184. Also see Marty's comment that infidelity in American never grew in strength because 'There was progressively less to be infidel about'. Martin E. Marty, *The Infidel* (Cleveland: Meridian Books, 1961), xxx.

[101] Jacoby, *Freethinkers*, 151–3.

confirming America's role as the God-appointed guardian of political and economic freedom.[102]

While unbelief never attained the success it enjoyed in Britain, the sociological, educational, and theological pluralism of the closing decades of the nineteenth century produced a serious reaction among conservative evangelicals. Evangelical Protestant culture primarily consisted of white Americans of British or North European descent. These were the first to settle America, and their culture had dominated social and political life in the country since the late eighteenth century. They now saw that dominance disappearing, sapped by social and intellectual changes that threatened their cultural and political superiority. Worse, the new culture appeared to them to be anti-Christian, governed by materialist and capitalist principles that produced ruthless competition and class tensions. This was alien to their image of their nation as being united under God, exemplified by a 'small-town' mentality where anonymity was frowned upon, and where personal actions were interpreted in a traditional nexus of rights and obligations.[103]

Earlier hopes that evangelicalism would fully convert American culture began to dissipate, and were replaced by growing malaise, and fear for the future. This cynicism towards society found expression in the growth of premillennialism among evangelicals. Ever since the work of Sandeen, there has been a conversation in the literature concerning the influence of premillennialism on Protestant fundamentalism in America. The consensus view is that while premillennialism played a role in the genesis of fundamentalism, it came to be of less importance as time wore on, and did not play any significant role in the controversy of the 1920s that would propel fundamentalism into the public consciousness.[104] Although premillennialism has a long history within Christian theology, the form that came to influence fundamentalism most strongly was premillennial dispensationalism. This form of premillennialism originated with the founder of the Plymouth Brethren, John Nelson Darby, before spreading to America, where it became influential within popular revivalism. The relevance of revivalist premillennialism for fundamentalism was twofold. First was its dualistic worldview and cultural pessimism, which rejected

---

[102] Jacoby, *Freethinkers*, 227–8, 240.
[103] Marsden, *Understanding Fundamentalism*, 10–1, 27–8; Joel A. Carpenter, *Revive Us Again* (New York and Oxford: Oxford University Press, 1997), 10.
[104] Cf. Sandeen, *Roots*, 268–9; Marsden, *American Culture*, 136; Longfield, *Presbyterian Controversy*, 220.

the widespread belief in progress for a belief in an immanent apocalyptic battle between God and Satan. Second was its biblical hermeneutic, which, strengthening the biblical and hermeneutical tendencies we have been examining, adopted a hyper-literalist reading of Scripture and, in particular, the Book of Revelation. For premillennial dispensationalists, allegorical readings were beneath the dignity of Scripture, for to speak authoritatively was to give perspicuous and historically accurate teaching.[105] Premillennialist revivalism had little time for ambiguity or contextually-sensitive interpretations of biblical texts, and was more likely to view Scripture and society through the dualisms of saved and lost, elect and worldly, God and Satan.[106] Premillennial dispensationalist thought reached its zenith in the wildly successful *Scofield Reference Bible*, which popularised its hyper-literal reading of Scripture. Initially, scholars of the Princeton School had been contemptuous and dismissive of premillennialism. Yet, from the end of the nineteenth century, there would be an increasing coalescence between it and the Reformed theology of the Princeton school, due to their mutual antipathy towards modernism, and their growing isolation from wider culture.[107] For this reason, fundamentalism in America would come to be characterised by both the unambiguous Gospel of revivalist premillennialism, as well as the high-culture intellectualism of Princeton theology.[108]

An increasing pessimism towards contemporary culture, and a fear that Christianity was being eroded from within and attacked from without, fostered a new spirit of cooperation between conservative evangelicals of all denominations, and would give rise to the publishing event that would become synonymous with future fundamentalism. After hearing the attack of A. C. Dixon upon the Chicago School of Divinity for its advancement of liberal theology, Lyman Stewart, successful oil capitalist and devout evangelical, hatched upon the idea of financing a sustained defence of evangelical orthodoxy against its liberal, Roman Catholic and infidel opponents. The result was *The Fundamentals*, a fourteen-volume series with articles from a range of American and British evangelicals of all denominations. These were distributed – free of charge – to all ministers, divinity students and Sunday school teachers in America and

---

[105] Sandeen, *Roots*, 13; Marsden, *American Culture*, 162–3.
[106] Marsden, *American Culture*, 224.
[107] Dorrien, *Liberal Theology*, 344–5; Noll, *Faith and Criticism*, 37–8.
[108] Marsden, *American Culture*, 47–8.

Britain.[109] Despite what is sometimes thought, *The Fundamentals* do not represent a coherent or systematic presentation of fundamentalist thought, which, at this stage, was still in its infancy.[110] Rather, the series fulfilled two ideological and social functions. First, it popularised the idea that orthodox Protestant theology was under attack by modernist theology and an irreligious society, and that its erosion heralded the collapse of civilisation. Second, they galvanised lay support, and provided the inspiration and theoretical tools for church members to challenge and reject liberal theology. This lay mobilisation went hand in hand with a recurring theme in the series, that of the honest, common sense Christian versus the effete, arrogant intellectual, out of touch with reality. Of the many thousands of letters received by the editors, it is telling that the only letter published in the fourteen volumes themselves was from a church member thankful for the means to attack educated elites who were destroying the faith.[111]

The publication of *The Fundamentals* coincided with a growing tension within northern denominations, yet it was not until America's entry into the First World War that the tensions precipitated by social and intellectual change would become acrimonious and schismatic.[112] In a context already marked by mistrust and fear over biblical criticism, and the erosion of evangelical culture, the experience of war heightened social anxiety, and increased mutual suspicion.[113] The suspicion and fear of evangelicals that the modern world was increasingly godless were confirmed by the Russian Revolution, which demonstrated that atheism could overtake entire nations, abolishing private property, and persecuting the faith.[114] This provoked a conservative reaction, leading to a resolve among conservative evangelicals to halt the advance of heterodoxy. When Harry Emerson Fosdick preached his sermon 'Shall the Fundamentalists Win?' at First Presbyterian Church in New York in 1922, the scene was set for the fundamentalist controversy of the 1920s.

While the details of this controversy are largely irrelevant to this study, it is important to briefly examine two examples of how conservative

---

[109] Reuben A. Torrey and Andrew C. Dixon, eds., *The Fundamentals: A Testimony to the Truth* (Grand Rapids: Baker Books, 1917).

[110] Marsden, *American Culture*, 122.

[111] Michael Lienesch, *In the Beginning* (Chapel Hill: University of North Carolina Press, 2007), 24.

[112] Marsden, *American Culture*, 141, 149.

[113] Marsden, *Understanding Fundamentalism*, 53–5.

[114] Jacoby, *Freethinkers*, 227–8, 240.

evangelicalism, and the hermeneutical and theological presuppositions that supported it, became radicalised by the fundamentalist controversy. We can best examine this radicalisation by considering two leading conservative evangelicals of the day: Reuben Torrey and J. Gresham Machen. Torrey was an influential preacher, writer and editor of *The Fundamentals*, who became one of the first deans of the Bible Institute of Los Angeles. Torrey's writings exemplify the Common Sense hermeneutic adopted by Hodge, a hermeneutic which meant that, as he put it, 'In ninety-nine out of a hundred cases, the meaning that the plain man gets out of the Bible is the correct one.'[115] Torrey's Common Sense hermeneutic is illustrated by *What the Bible Teaches*, in which 'the methods of modern science are applied to Bible study', through a 'careful, unbiased, thoroughgoing, inductive study and statement of Bible truth'.[116] The result of this method is that Scripture's teaching is refined into a series of succinct, unambiguous, logical propositions supported with proof texts, a method which was intended to convince doubters of the single, coherent philosophy present throughout Scripture.[117] It is of some relevance that Torrey's commitment to Baconian induction led him to reject Darwinian evolution.[118]

This commitment to Baconian inductivism was also shared by Torrey's contemporary, J. Gresham Machen, yet was there allied with a concern to preserve direct divine agency within history.[119] Machen's biography illustrates well the motivations that led intelligent evangelicals to become alienated from the culture of their day, and begin the pattern of separatism that would come to characterise later fundamentalism. Machen grew up in Baltimore, which – while nominally part of the Union during the Civil War – had strong Confederate sympathies. Machen's mother was an active member of the United Daughters of the Confederacy, and he was raised as a respectable Southerner. Yet in a town situated between North and South, Machen would have been sensitive to the challenges that modern culture – urban, anonymous, secular – posed to a traditional pattern of evangelical life. In his most famous work, *Christianity and Liberalism*, Machen took the Princeton theology of inerrancy and literalism and radicalised it, ranging it against the godless theology of

---

[115] Cited in Marsden, *American Culture*, 61.
[116] Reuben A. Torrey, *What the Bible Teaches* (London: James Nisbet, 1902), 1.
[117] Torrey, *What the Bible Teaches*, 1–2.
[118] Reuben A. Torrey, *Difficulties in the Bible* (London: James Nisbet, 1900), 29–39.
[119] Longfield, *Presbyterian Controversy*, 48.

modernism. Although a polemical work, Machen's book was perceptive and prescient, correctly identifying theological liberalism as a response to the pressures of biblical criticism, and the social and technological changes taking place in American society.[120] Machen argues that these intellectual and social changes have overturned the direct, disruptive activity of divine power in creation, and introduced the principle of naturalism into theology:

> The many varieties of modern liberal religion are rooted in naturalism – that is, in the denial of any entrance of the creative power of God (as distinguished from the ordinary course of nature) in connection with the origin of Christianity.[121]

Liberalism is not simply another form of Christianity, however, but is a different religion altogether, one whose true nature is hidden by the duplicitous use of traditional terms and categories by liberal clergy.[122] Due to the dialectical relationship between belief and social practice, theological liberalism, according to Machen, will precipitate the continued erosion of evangelical culture. In place of the spiritual adventure and the noble individualism of evangelical life, America will become one great 'Main Street', where 'materialistic utilitarianism' will sap society of its vitality and creativity, aided by a secular education system that will become 'an instrument in destroying human souls'.[123] The only solution left, according to Machen, is to take a stand for historic Christianity, and its commitment to a robust account of divine intervention in nature and history. This is the only force capable of saving American life. In Machen, we see the close connection between an interventionist conception of divine activity, biblical inerrancy, and a polemical political agenda. As hyperbolic as his arguments might appear, they represent an astute understanding of the dialectical relationship between changes in social practice and changes in theology, and a realisation that evangelical theology could not survive when separated from a specific form of social life.[124]

The hermeneutical approach of Torrey, and the concern for disruptive divine activity seen in Machen, characterise the way in which the presuppositions of nineteenth-century American evangelicalism were

---

[120] Longfield, *Presbyterian Controversy*, 36–8, 47.
[121] J. Gresham Machen, *Christianity and Liberalism* (Grand Rapids: William B. Eerdmans, 2009), 2.
[122] Machen, *Christianity and Liberalism*, 1–2.
[123] Machen, *Christianity and Liberalism*, 12.
[124] See Machen, *Christianity and Liberalism*, 8–13.

strengthened and radicalised in the wake of intellectual and social change. Yet the intellectual and social nexus established by Protestant fundamentalism did not necessarily give rise to anti-evolutionary views, and, when it did, it was always secondary to the principal target of modernism. In order for the issue of evolution, and a disruptive and substitutionary understanding of divine activity to assume greater importance for fundamentalists, the talents of a brilliant orator, and the sting of public humiliation, would be necessary.

DEATH IN TENNESSEE

William Jennings Bryan, three-time presidential candidate, would speak from 60 to 120 days each summer, often addressing crowds of over 5000 at a time.[125] In the early 1920s, his newspaper column was syndicated across the country, and it reached between twenty and twenty-five million readers. Prior to 1918, he had issued only sporadic comments regarding evolution. Yet having read Vernon Kellog's *Headquarters Nights*, and Benjamin Kidd's *The Science of Power*, Bryan came to make a direct connection between Darwin's theory of evolution and German military aggression, as well as a host of domestic evils. For Bryan, evolution presented three serious problems. First, it instilled in the modern mind the dicta of 'might makes right' and 'survival of the fittest', leading to unrestrained competition between nations, and social and economic conflict between classes. Second, by teaching that humanity was not specially created, evolution led men and women to view themselves as animals, causing them to descend into sexual immorality. Third, by contradicting Scripture, evolution endangered the faith of millions. What was most remarkable of all for Bryan, however, was that evolution was nothing more than a *theory*, a fantasy, which, rejecting common sense observation, entered a world of speculative delusion.[126] In short, then, Bryan came to believe that evolution was wrong because it was unscientific, and *wicked* because it destroyed faith and morals.[127] Like Machen and others, Bryan realised that the soul of America was in the balance.

Prior to Bryan's intervention, evolution had been a secondary issue to the fundamentalist cause. The majority of conservative evangelicals continued to hold to the same day-age and gap readings adopted by the

---

[125] Lienesch, *In the Beginning*, 62.
[126] Marsden, *American Culture*, 169; Longfield, *Presbyterian Controversy*, 54–6.
[127] Longfield, *Presbyterian Controversy*, 56.

generation that grappled with geology and Darwin. Yet starting with his widely reported speech 'The Menace of Darwin', Bryan raised awareness of evolution in the minds of the public, and began to forge it into a symbol around which fundamentalists could rally. While evolution was not an instinctive enemy, nevertheless, it presented a recognisable social image: that of an effete, educated professional, telling ordinary men and women that a tiny minority knew better than millions of God-fearing Americans who loved their Bible.[128] Bryan tapped into a populist 'folk epistemology' – part democratic sentiment, part Common Sense religiosity – to challenge the class of academics and educators who had spurned denominational affiliation and rejected the Bible from class and seminar room.[129]

If Bryan had made his attack even two decades earlier it would have fallen largely on deaf ears, as the delay between the publication of *The Origin of Species*, and its transmission to the public, had not yet been overcome. Yet, by the 1920s, evolutionary theory had become increasingly common in schools and colleges. During his lecture tours, and through his copious correspondence, Bryan became aware of increasing numbers of college students losing their faith, or engaging in promiscuity after encountering the theory of evolution from a sceptical teacher or biology textbook. Bryan's concern was typical of a growing evangelical alarm at the direction of public education, an alarm that prompted hyperbolic works such as T. T. Martin's *Hell and the High Schools*, which argued that the teaching of evolution was more heinous than German war crimes, and that public schools had become little more than entranceways into Hell itself.[130]

By the 1920s, increasing concern at the erosion of evangelical culture and the pernicious effects of evolution had resulted in a flurry of anti-evolution laws by – largely southern – legislatures. Among them was Tennessee, which banned the teaching of evolution in all public schools. The American Civil Liberties Union announced that it would fund a case testing the constitutionality of this act. After a group of local businessmen in Dayton, Tennessee realised the economic benefits of a high-publicity court case, a young teacher called John Scopes was approached to stand

[128] Lienesch, *In the Beginning*, 70–1.
[129] Marsden, *Understanding Fundamentalism*, 165–8; Lienesch, *In the Beginning*, 72–3.
[130] T. T. Martin, *Hell and the High Schools* (Kansas City: Western Baptist Publishing, 1923).

as a defendant.[131] The resulting Scopes 'Monkey Trial' was more than simply a court case, however. With extensive coverage in national news, it became a microcosm of the social, intellectual and theological changes taking place in American life. For the anti-evolutionists, it was an opportunity for evolution to be publicly discredited, and its supporters punished. For their enemies, it was a battle to move American culture into the modern, scientific world. For the defence stood Clarence Darrow, eminent city lawyer, humanist and wit, while the star witness for the defence was 'the great commoner' himself, William Jennings Bryan, who represented the morally concerned citizen and ordinary Christian. While the prosecution won the case, Bryan's lacklustre performance drew widespread scorn and mockery. Worse still – and vitally important for the future of fundamentalist thought – Bryan revealed under cross-examination that he did not hold to a literal six-day reading of Genesis 1, but held instead to a conventional gap reading.[132] In a final, bitter twist, Bryan, exhausted from the case and from other speaking engagements, died five days after the close of the trial.

It was not only Bryan who died in the wake of the Scopes trial, however, but the image of America as a Bible-believing, evangelical nation. The trial had four consequences for fundamentalism and the incipient anti-evolution movement. First, scientific beliefs based on Baconian induction, which had been respectable only a few decades before, were now openly scorned, and fundamentalists and anti-evolutionists were portrayed as fools.[133] Second, this reaction demonstrated to fundamentalists that the evangelical culture they had been raised in no longer commanded respect among the country's elite, and that they had lost their dominant social position. Third, the mocking of their beliefs, and the loss of their cultural position, led to a severe social dislocation among fundamentalists, who now began to isolate themselves from wider society in order to protect their culture and beliefs. Although fundamentalism is sometimes thought to have gone into decline after the trial, this was merely a strategic retreat. Fundamentalist leaders now focussed upon building and maintaining a separate world of schools, colleges, journals and radio stations, supported by an organised and

---

[131] Ironically, it is doubtful whether Scopes broke the law by reading the chapter on evolution from G. W. Hunter's *Civic Biology* (New York: American Book Company, 1914).

[132] See Ronald L. Numbers, *The Creationists* (Cambridge, Mass.: Harvard University Press, 2006), 58.

[133] Marsden, *American Culture*, 218.

highly motivated lay membership.[134] As a once dominant culture now pushed into an embattled minority, fundamentalists would come to hold a unique mind-set: persecuted outsiders and a silent majority.[135] Fourth, this context of social, political, and intellectual marginalisation created the conditions necessary for the growth of the scientifically aberrant phenomenon of six-day creationism. Like the generation of theologians that first considered Darwin, the vast majority of anti-evolutionists – including Bryan – subscribed to day-age or gap readings of Genesis. As such, they generally believed in a pre-Adamic creation, and an old earth. In the 1920s, six-day creationism was limited to a very small number of – typically self-taught – individuals, the most influential of which was George McCready Price. Price had initially been drawn to evolution, but was dissuaded from following Darwin when he realised that when facts were stripped of the interpretations typically placed upon them, the evidence for evolution evaporated.[136] As such, Price, like many of the men examined in this chapter, made the fundamental Common Sense distinction between direct sense observation and ideas, rejecting the latter as speculation when they exceeded direct reference to experience. Price's brand of 'inductive geology' found expression in his most influential work, *The Fundamentals of Geology*, which was dedicated – perhaps unsurprisingly – to Bacon and Newton.[137] While Price failed to be taken seriously among scientists, there were signs that his six-day creationism and flood geology were making progress among fundamentalists. While it would have been hard to foresee at the time, Price's ideas would only grow in popularity, wedding the anti-evolution sentiment of the 1920s to a young earth, and a literal six-day creation.

The creationist tendency in American fundamentalism will be examined shortly, yet it is important to conclude this chapter with some observations as to why the biblical and theological presuppositions we have been examining would give rise to fundamentalism and six-day creationism rather than atheism within an American context. The first factor was that which frustrated the growth of organised unbelief in America: an established church. British evangelicals were never denied access to top universities, and could expect representation in the governance of both the Church of England and the Church of Scotland.

[134] See Douglas Carl Abrams, *Selling the Old-Time Religion* (Atlanta and London: University of Georgia Press, 1998).
[135] Marsden, *American Culture*, 6–7.   [136] Numbers, *Creationists*, 91–3.
[137] Numbers, *Creationists*, 107–8.

In addition, the participation of many evangelicals within the established churches ensured that they had social contact with parties possessing very different views, so that isolation and permanent division were considerably harder to achieve. The absence of such ameliorating factors in America meant that social, political and intellectual marginalisation was easier, allowing culturally aberrant beliefs and practices to gain plausibility within separatist evangelical communities.[138] Second, on an intellectual level, six-day creationism possessed a deep congruence with that feature of Protestant theology that separated it most strongly from its Roman Catholic ancestry: its literal and univocal understanding of Scripture. Conceiving of the days of Genesis as twenty-four hour time periods accorded better with the mistrust of non-literal readings of Scripture that we have examined previously. Third, this aspect of fundamentalism went hand in hand with another prevailing feature of Protestant hermeneutics, an insistence upon the perspicuity of Scripture, and a corresponding mistrust of non-intuitive, specialist interpretation. The possibility of non-literal readings of Genesis 1–3 could only arise once one had some familiarity with evolutionary theory, or an awareness of the rich hermeneutical alternatives afforded by Christian tradition. Both were often beyond the reach of American Christians, and their difficult and sometimes non-intuitive nature flew in the face of the supposed clarity of Scripture, and the capacity of all people to read and understand its text. Fourth, six-day creationism accorded better with the conception of science and religion that developed in nineteenth-century America, and which traced its heritage back through Scottish Common Sense philosophy to Restoration England. As we have seen, this conception was founded on an equivalence between the facts of Scripture and the facts of nature, an approach facilitated by the physical effects of God's disruptive and substitutionary activity within nature. This equivalence of fact gave rise to an equivalence in methodology, with the same inductive, tradition-independent method being applied to the study of both. Fifth, six-day creationism drew upon a strong apologetic need within American evangelicalism. The missional impulse, already present, took on new significance as evangelical culture began to be secularised towards the end of the nineteenth century. Appeals to natural phenomena and the discoveries of science to support the literal truth of Genesis allowed six-day creationists to claim that they possessed proof of the infallibility and

---

[138] Noll, *Between Faith and Criticism*, 62–4, 85–90.

perspicuity of Scripture, independent of theological tradition or Church authority. Sixth, the marginalisation of conservative evangelicals, and their sense of powerlessness, increased the importance of appeals to direct and forceful exertions of divine power upon creation. A literal reading of Genesis 1–3 revealed a God who was active within the world, and that individuals and entire cultures could be judged, condemned, and over-thrown should his patience be mocked. These features of evangelical Protestantism were strengthened by Common Sense Baconian principles, and radicalised through the marginalisation of evangelical Protestantism within American society. It was this unique convergence of intellectual and social factors that pushed the biblical and natural theological presup-positions we have been examining into fundamentalism and six-day creationism, forms of thought that, despite their recent history, have become for many the normative expression of authentic Christianity, thereby confirming the problematic position of Christianity within British and American culture.

In this chapter, we have charted the way in which the presupposition of a literal, univocal and perspicuous, Scripture, and the disruptive and substitutionary nature of divine activity in creation were converted – under the influence of Scottish Common Sense philosophy and the unique social and political conditions of America – into fundamentalism and creationism. Seeking to re-establish the legitimacy of everyday beliefs and the use of induction in science and apologetics in the wake of Hume's development of Locke, Thomas Reid formulated an epistemology that limited the influence of ideas and theories in the formation of know-ledge. Common Sense thought gave a philosophical superstructure to many of the key hermeneutical and epistemological beliefs of the Scottish Reformation, and, in particular, strengthened the principle of perspicuity. In the aftermath of the American Revolution, this Common Sense phil-osophy was useful to a society that lacked a shared ecclesial or ethnic identity, supplying it with an authoritative foundation for religion and morality independent of tradition and Church authority. At the height of its influence, Common Sense philosophy supported the adoption of a unitary method within both science and theology, a method that presup-posed that the facts of Scripture and the facts of nature were self-evident to all right-thinking people, and did not require interpretation. Yet biblical criticism and the theory of evolution threw this understanding of nature and Scripture into doubt, as theologians were forced to adopt readings of Scripture that were not fully literal, and required complex interpretation. Over the following decades, societal changes increased the intellectual and social marginalisation of a once dominant evangelical culture, leading to defensive accounts of inerrancy, and the fundamentalist controversy of the 1920s. This period of tension and conflict culminated in the Scopes trial, where fundamentalism and anti-evolutionism were publically ridiculed. This cemented the connection in the minds of many conservative evangelicals between evolution and religious and social marginalisation, leading to a more literal, anti-evolutionary reading of Scripture, and a new prominence for disruptive and substitutionary understandings of divine activity in nature. With this constellation of theological, scientific and political factors now in place, the intellectual and social structure of Protestant fundamentalism was complete.

4

The Secret Sympathy

Chapters 1–3 have charted the genesis and effect of two presuppositions: a literal, univocal and perspicuous understanding of Scripture and a disruptive and substitutionary conception of divine activity in nature. We will now analyse the way in which these two presuppositions structure new atheist and Protestant fundamentalist thought. These presuppositions – the products of a common Protestant heritage – have given rise to a range of shared beliefs and practices among new atheists and fundamentalists, such as a common biblical hermeneutic, the normative status of fundamentalist Christianity, the futility of academic theology, the incompatibility of evolution and design and the destructive effects of evolutionary thought upon the Christian faith.

The range of atheist and Protestant fundamentalist texts surveyed in this section was described in the Introduction, but will be rehearsed here for the ease of the reader. Protestant fundamentalism represents the least problematic use of the word 'fundamentalist', as the term is native to conservative evangelicals, and, crucially, was used for many years as a means of self-designation. Nevertheless, Protestant fundamentalism does not represent a unified body of ideas, attitudes or social practices. For the purposes of analysis, the following criteria have been used in the selection of texts: a belief in biblical inerrancy, a belief that Scripture's sense is literal, univocal and perspicuous, the rejection of evolution on biblical grounds and a strong antipathy towards contemporary Western culture. These criteria guard mainstream evangelicals from being tarred as 'fundamentalist', and, by considering such extreme texts, set appropriate hurdles for the verification of this work's claims. Other criteria could be utilised, of course. Yet for the purposes of the following analysis, which seeks to ascertain the cogency of comparisons between new atheism and Protestant fundamentalism, these criteria suffice. In relation to atheism, it must be stressed that the range of atheist texts examined in this chapter only relate to *new atheism*, and not atheism in general. While, as we have seen, there is debate over the use of the phrase 'new atheism', the criteria used for selection of material in this chapter is relatively straightforward: popular anti-Christian texts written in English since 2001, along with earlier works – such as those by Richard Dawkins – which shed light on the texts in question. The following argument does not claim that all Protestant fundamentalist and all new atheist writers share the same beliefs, only that they share the two presuppositions we have been examining, along with a range of accompanying beliefs.

The examination conducted in this chapter is not an end in itself, however, but lays the foundation for the critical analysis of Chapter 5. This concluding analysis will reveal that the shared intellectual structure of both groups derives from a common Protestant culture in disintegration, producing tensions in each form of thought that renders them unstable, and forcing them to adopt regulating principles that contradict their fundamental presuppositions.

CONTEMPORARY CONTEXT

Before an analysis of the shared structure of new atheist and Protestant fundamentalist thought can be made, it is important to place them in context by briefly recounting their recent history. Both groups entered the 1930s in a state of relative hibernation. American fundamentalists, wounded from the humiliation of the Scopes trial, largely retreated into a private world. Yet during this time they were not passive but active: consolidating their membership, acquiring and developing a network of private schools and colleges and establishing a range of mass communication enterprises. Fearing the ire of millions of conservative Christians, publishers largely dropped evolution from school textbooks, or downplayed its significance.[1] While there was a slight rise in Protestant fundamentalism in Britain during the 1930s, numbers were chronically small, and the movement exerted no real influence on public life.[2] In a similar way, while atheism maintained a working-class contingent, and had representation in the universities and wealthier ranks of society, it too

---

[1] Numbers, *Creationists*, 264–5.   [2] Bebbington, *Evangelicalism*, 217–23.

was largely marginalised within the public sphere. In America, atheism was strongly connected with Soviet Russia, which only added to atheism's perception as being the antithesis of American values.[3] America's religious identity was confirmed in 1956, when Congress adopted 'In God We Trust' as the official motto of the United States. In Britain, while the prestige of the traditional denominations had declined, and continuing concerns were raised about church attendance, the cultural pre-eminence of Christianity remained largely secure.

This situation was to change from the late 1950s onward in the face of unprecedented political and social change. In 1957, Soviet Russia successfully launched Sputnik 1, the first artificial satellite to orbit the Earth. This technological achievement raised grave concerns regarding the state of American science and forced the government and scientific profession to alter their policy regarding the appeasement of fundamentalists. Evolutionary teaching in schools increased, culminating in *Man: A Course of Study*, which became influential in both Britain and America.[4] These developments reawakened concern for the decline of evangelical teaching in schools and created a new audience for anti-evolutionary theories. Fundamentalist interest in anti-evolutionary theories was further increased by the cultural revolution of the 1960s, which saw the rejection of those elements of fundamentalist morality that continued to subsist in wider culture.[5] These concerns – to undermine evolution and to win American society back for God – coalesced in the unprecedented success of Whitcomb and Morris's *The Genesis Flood*.[6] This text – whose themes shall be examined later – resurrected the flood geology of George McCready Price, and argued for a recent six-day creation. It presented a thorough rejection of uniformitarianism in geology, and, by extension, the time-scale necessary for the evolution of species by variation and natural selection. The success of the work – which would sell 200,000 copies over the next quarter-century – largely rested on its supposedly literal reading of Genesis, which was closer to fundamentalist hermeneutics than the day-age and gap readings which had been developed in the nineteenth

---

[3] Jacoby, *Freethinkers*, 227–8.

[4] Susan Friend Harding, *The Book of Jerry Falwell* (Princeton: Princeton University Press, 2000), 211–2.

[5] Robert Inchausti, 'Thomas Merton's Apologies to an Unbeliever', in *'God Is Dead' and I Don't Feel So Good Myself*, ed. Andrew David (Eugene: Cascade Books, 2010), 3–4.

[6] John C. Whitcomb and Henry M. Morris, *The Genesis Flood* (Phillipsburg: P&R Publishing, 1961).

century.[7] The success of *The Genesis Flood* as compared with the work of McCready Price, which employed a similar hermeneutic, is testament to the growing defensiveness of conservative evangelicals, and the increasing polarisation of religious identities after the social change of the 1960s. During this period, creationism began to grow, so that, by 1991, a Gallup poll recorded that 47 per cent of Americans believed in a recent, special creation of the earth and animal life.[8] The growth of support for creationism, taken with a resulting rise in creationist teaching in public schools, initiated a series of high-profile re-runs of the Scopes trial, where state law after state law supporting creationist teaching was struck down by the higher courts.[9] These cases secured the public profile of six-day creationism in America, which – owing to the dominance of American culture – also became part of the public imagination in Britain.

The fifties and sixties also saw changes in the public prominence of atheism and non-religion. Madalyn Murray O'Hair enjoyed success in removing prayer and Bible reading from public schools in America in 1963, and humanism gained greater public acceptance in Britain after the historic broadcasts of Margaret Knight on BBC Radio.[10] Yet it was not until the Terrorist attacks of September 11, 2001 that atheism came of age in Britain and America.[11] This event had three effects. First, it gave traditional arguments against religion a political and social relevance they had lacked for over a hundred years. Second, it energised atheists, and gave them the warrant and impetus to increase their lobbying and public critique of religion. Third, it handed atheists unprecedented media coverage, as the question of religious fundamentalism took centre stage in the public life of Britain and America. This resulted in a gamut of publishing opportunities for atheists, whose books became bestsellers on both sides of the Atlantic. These works quickly generated controversy due to their uncompromising hostility towards religion and their call for an end to religious influence in public life. This increase in the frequency and hostility of atheist activity led Gary Wolf of *Wired* magazine to refer to the 'New Atheists', a name that has endured ever since.[12] Yet while the

---

[7] Harding, *Falwell*, 214.   [8] Harding, *Falwell*, 213.
[9] The legal history of these cases is not directly relevant to what follows and will not be discussed further. The standard work charting the legal history of creationism in twentieth-century America is Larson, *Trial and Error*.
[10] See Callum G. Brown, '"The Unholy Mrs Knight" and the BBC', *English Historical Review* 128 (2012): 345–76.
[11] Alister McGrath, *Why Faith Won't Go Away* (London: SPCK, 2011), vii–viii.
[12] McGrath, *Why Faith Won't*, 3.

primary cause for the growth of atheist activity was an attack by Islamic militants, it is not Islamic theology that would become the primary target of new atheist writers, but Christianity. Islam provided the *occasion* for the genesis of new atheism, but its historical lineage and intellectual structure came from Protestantism, and the problems concerning Scripture, natural theology, evolution and the political and moral authority of Christianity whose genealogy was examined in Chapters 1–3.

The attack of new atheists upon Christianity elicited a great number of responses. One of the more unusual was the allegation that new atheists, in their attacks upon religion, replicated in some way the behaviour or worldview of fundamentalist Christianity. These allegations typically take the form of brief comparisons between the supposed extremism of fundamentalism and atheism, often coupled with some reference to 'atheist fundamentalism'.[13] Here, the comparison is in terms of a shared intolerance, intransigence and uncompromising attitude towards difference. As such, it is primarily a psychological similarity – and not an intellectual one – that is being suggested. Sometimes, however, this general psychological comparison is accompanied by more specific accusations. Armstrong, for example, notes six areas of similarity. Each group:

- Adheres to 'scientific rationalism'
- Is intolerant and reductive, believing that they alone possess truth
- Reads Scripture literally and rejects allegory
- Has a crude understanding of Biblical inspiration
- Conceives of Christian ethics as a set of rules
- Believes the Bible must teach accurate science[14]

The only material difference between the two groups, argues Armstrong, is that one affirms what the other denies. Similar comparisons have also been made by Stahl.[15] Other commentators focus on more specific comparisons. Cunningham accuses both groups of possessing the same defective conception of evolution as being mutually exclusive of design.[16]

---

[13] E.g. De Botton, *Religion for Atheists*, 12; Vernon, *After Atheism*, 4, 7, 55–6; Hart, *Atheist Delusions*, 4, 231–2; Roy A. Varghese, preface to Anthony Flew, *There Is a God* (New York: HarperOne, 2008), xvi. Robertson includes somewhat more detail, yet his comparison is based largely on the use of intemperate and aggressive language by both groups. See Robertson, *Dawkins Letters*, 78–83.

[14] Armstrong, *Case for God*, 290.

[15] William A. Stahl, 'One-Dimensional Rage', in *Religion and the New Atheism: A Critical Appraisal*, ed. Amarnath Amarasingam (Leiden: Brill, 2010), 97.

[16] See, e.g., Cunningham, *Pious Idea*, 265–376.

Spencer notes a similar emphasis upon evolution, while also detecting a shared conception of the nature of Christianity, and a common antipathy towards non-fundamentalist Christians.[17]

While such comparisons are intriguing, they present a number of difficulties. First, they are generally made in passing, and it is not always clear whether they should be taken seriously, or considered as little more than insults. Second, when commentators enter into more sustained discussion, very little detail is provided. Due to these deficiencies, comparisons between fundamentalists and atheists are in danger of being dismissed for three reasons. First, given that the majority of comparisons relate to the uncompromising and intemperate tone of both atheists and fundamentalists, it could be argued that *any* strongly held belief could be denounced as 'fundamentalist'. Dawkins argues that it is easy to confuse fundamentalism with passion and strength of feeling, and that the term is at risk of losing any real meaning if it is applied in this way. This would then make it unavailable in situations where it is warranted. The difference between atheists and fundamentalists, argues Dawkins, is that the former are willing to change their views in the light of new evidence.[18] This argument is echoed by Grayling, who argues that it is not possible for an atheist *not* to be 'fundamentalist' about her atheism, in the sense that she cannot at once believe and not believe it.[19] Second, apparent similarities between Protestant fundamentalists and new atheists could be accounted for in the way in which *any* debate presupposes common areas of agreement. For example, if one person affirms the existence of unicorns and another denies it, both could be said to hold the same conception of unicorns. Otherwise, they would be at cross-purposes, and discussing different subjects. If the similarity ends there, however, then the comparison could be dismissed as trivial at best. A third argument against the cogency of comparisons between new atheists and Protestant fundamentalists comes from atheists who seek to refute the 'dependence theory', that atheism is somehow parasitic upon the religion it rejects. Concerned that the etymology of 'atheism' suggests some such form of dependence, Baggini argues that, while atheism would be called by another name in the absence of theism, its content would be the same, as it is simply the absence of belief in gods. Atheism may deny the existence of particular gods at particular times, yet this does not imply any dependence upon

---

[17] Spencer, *Origin of the Species*, 251.
[18] Richard Dawkins, *The God Delusion* (London: Black Swan, 2006), 18–19, 319–23.
[19] A. C. Grayling, *Against all Gods* (London: Oberon Books, 2007), 23–30.

what is denied.[20] For these reasons, it could it be argued that the apparent dependence of atheism – of whatever kind – upon the religion it rejects is only illusory, and based on a confusion between belief and the absence of belief.

The implausibility of a connection between atheism and fundamentalism is strengthened when we consider the accounts new atheists and Protestant fundamentalists give of their own beliefs. On the surface, these would seem to confirm the stereotype of rational, scientific atheists versus bibliocentric, irrational fundamentalists. For Dawkins, scientists are those who are tasked with discovering what is true, and they do so through observation, the collection of evidence and the making of predictions.[21] Scientists determine the truth of things directly through the senses, or indirectly through special instruments. These observations then lead to the construction of models, a method of science that has come to be known as the hypothetico-deductive method.[22] This hypothetico-deductive method first forms a hypothesis on the basis of existing data, deduces a prediction from this hypothesis and then tests the prediction against further data. The better a theory explains the evidence, the more claim to truth it possesses. Truth is the degree to which a given statement corresponds with reality, and reality is what is observable though the senses and special instruments, or deducible by reason.[23] Following this method, scientists like new atheist Victor Stenger have come to the conclusion that only matter exists, and that all forms of spiritual reality are fictional.[24]

New atheists view the theory of evolution by natural selection as holding a position of pre-eminence among all the discoveries made using the scientific method. Whereas our existence once represented the greatest of all mysteries, this mystery has been solved once and for all by science, which Dawkins believes has shattered the mythical speculations of religion and substituted them for fact.[25] Darwin's discovery is not only of paramount importance for the question of origins, however, but is of universal significance, for it unifies science and meaning. In unifying all

[20] Julian Baggini, *Atheism: A Very Short Introduction* (Oxford: Oxford University Press, 2003), 7.

[21] Richard Dawkins, *A Devil's Chaplain* (London: Phoenix, 2003), 284–5.

[22] Richard Dawkins, *The Magic of Reality* (London: Bantam Press, 2011), 12, 19; Victor J. Stenger, *God: The Failed Hypothesis* (Amherst: Prometheus Books, 2007), 12.

[23] Dan Barker, *Godless* (Berkeley: Ulysses Press, 2008), 119.

[24] Victor J. Stenger, *The New Atheism* (Amherst: Prometheus Books, 2009), 21.

[25] Richard Dawkins, *The Blind Watchmaker* (London: Penguin Books, 2006), xvii.

156 Atheism, Fundamentalism and the Protestant Reformation

aspects of human knowledge, and providing each with an incontestable foundation, it provides humanity with an objective basis for knowledge and discourse. In the words of Dennett, evolution offers a 'stable system of explanation that does not go round and round in circles or spiral off in an infinite regress of mysteries'.[26]

While science is objective, transparent and universal, religion is the enemy of free debate and enquiry.[27] Dawkins argues that religious believers wallow in obscurity and mystery, rather than using mystery as a spur to understanding.[28] The sciences are the only way to keep us from deluding ourselves about reality, and, if we do not follow them to the letter, Loftus worries that objectivity will disappear, and humanity will never be able to reach agreement on anything.[29] Unlike science, which is founded on evidence, new atheist writers are agreed that faith is belief in the *absence* of evidence.[30] In the words of Harris, 'Faith is what credulity becomes when it finally achieves escape velocity from the constraints of terrestrial discourse – constraints like reasonableness, internal coherence, civility and candor [sic].'[31] For this reason, science is the opposite of religious faith, and there exists a genuine conflict between them.[32]

When we turn to consider Protestant fundamentalists, the differences from new atheism could not, on the surface, be any clearer. The foundation of Protestant fundamentalist thought is the inerrancy of Scripture. Scripture takes precedence over all other sources of knowledge. As Taylor puts it, 'God's Word is the standard by which we judge all other academic pursuits. We can confidently use the Bible in this way, knowing it will not let us down.'[33] Indeed, it is Scripture itself that is responsible for science, for it was the rediscovery of Scripture at the Reformation that made science possible. As Morris puts it:

---

[26] Daniel C. Dennett, *Darwin's Dangerous Idea* (London: Allen Lane, 1995), 25.

[27] Sam Harris, *The End of Faith* (London: The Free Press, 2006), 45.

[28] Richard Dawkins, *Unweaving the Rainbow* (London: Penguin Books, 2006), 17.

[29] John W. Loftus, introduction to *The End of Christianity*, ed. John W. Loftus (Amherst: Prometheus Books, 2011), 15.

[30] E.g., Peter Boghossian, *A Manual for Creating Atheists* (Durham, N.C.: Pitchstone Publishing, 2013), 21–3; Barker, *Godless*, 117; Grayling, *Against all Gods*, 15; Victor J. Stenger, *God and the Folly of Faith* (Amherst: Prometheus Books, 2012), 18; Stenger, *New Atheism*, 15.

[31] Harris, *End of Faith*, 65.

[32] Boghossian, *Manual*, 157; Christopher Hitchens, *God Is Not Great* (London: Atlantic Books, 2008), 253–72; Stenger, *New Atheism*, 73.

[33] Paul F. Taylor, *The Six Days of Genesis* (Green Forest: Master Books, 2007), 23.

The biblical world outlook *is* the scientific world outlook – namely that the universe had a beginning and that its processes and system are reliable and intelligible, operating in accordance with fixed laws that can be discovered and used.[34]

Because the biblical understanding of reality is identical to the scientific, all the great scientists of the past drew their methods and inspiration from Scripture.[35] Because Scripture is inerrant, Christians should hold a biblically-founded scepticism towards all claims made by the nonreligious, safe in the knowledge that all true science will agree with Scripture, because God made both.[36]

The Protestant fundamentalist understanding of science is different from that held by new atheists, and flows directly from the presuppositions bequeathed by Scottish Common Sense Realism.[37] Central to the fundamentalist understanding of science is the distinction between facts and their interpretation. This takes the form of a distinction between observational and historical science, or, as it is sometimes rendered, empirical and origins science. Observational or empirical science is based upon direct sense experience and repeatable experiments.[38] Historical or origins science, however, is not based on direct sense experience or experiments, but is an interpretation of present evidence based on subjective factors that direct and inform this interpretation. Because of this, it cannot yield objective knowledge.[39] As the official guide to the Creation

---

[34] Henry M. Morris, *The Long War against God* (Green Forest: Master Books, 2000), 304–5.

[35] See generally Henry M. Morris, *Men of Science – Men of God* (San Diego: Master Books, 1988).

[36] Roger Patterson, 'Self-Refuting Skepticism', in *A Pocket Guide to Atheism*, ed. Ken Ham (Petersburg: Answers in Genesis, 2014), 67; Henry M. Morris, *Biblical Creationism* (Green Forest: Master Books, 2013), 14.

[37] Understanding of Protestant fundamentalism has been hindered by the dislike that many commentators have of its worldview, a dislike that has resulted in dismissive descriptions of their philosophy of science. Such attitudes hinder academic inquiry. See George M. Marsden, 'Understanding Fundamentalist Views of Science' in *Science and Creationism*, ed. Ashley Montagu (Oxford: Oxford University Press, 1984), 96, 108; Francis Harold, Raymond Eve, and John Taylor 'Creationism: American-Style', in *The Cultures of Creationism*, ed. Simon Coleman and Leslie Carlin (Aldershot: Ashgate, 2004): 67–84.

[38] Ken Ham, *The Lie* (Green Forest: Master Books, 2012), 48; David A. DeWitt, *Unravelling the Origins Controversy* (Lynchburg: Creation Curriculum, 2007), 38.

[39] E.g. Ham, *The Lie*, 25; Roger Patterson, *Evolution Exposed* (Hebron: Answers in Genesis, 2007), 20, 24–9; Whitcomb and Morris, *Genesis Flood*, xxvii; Henry M. Morris, *The Beginning of the World* (Green Forest: Master Books, 1999), 12; Jonathan Sarfati, *Refuting Evolution* (Brisbane: Answers in Genesis, 2002), 29.

Museum puts it 'The evidence is in the *Present* . . . but what happened in the *Past?*'[40] Protestant fundamentalists claim to accept the factual data of the sciences, but because the theory of evolution and uniformitarian geology cannot be confirmed by direct sense experience, and relate to unrepeatable events that happened over great lengths of time, fundamentalists reject them as pseudo-science, and view them as little more than speculations.[41] Any claim that cannot be confirmed by sense experience is like a subjective gloss placed over reality, a belief illustrated by the following critique of secular museum exhibits supporting evolution: 'The evidence is *in the glass case. The hypothetical story of evolution can only be seen pasted on the glass case.*'[42] Because science cannot give us objective knowledge regarding events in the distant past, there is an important sense in which evolution and creation are *both* based on faith and involve biases and presuppositions.[43] As Patterson argues, 'Neither creation nor evolution is directly observable, testable, repeatable, or falsifiable . . . Starting from two opposite presuppositions and looking at the same evidence, the explanations of the history of the universe are very different.'[44] Nevertheless, as Sarfati puts it, 'It is not really a question of who is biased, but what bias is the correct bias with which to be biased!'[45] Creationist bias is to be preferred to evolutionary bias for two reasons. First, while no human science can give us knowledge of origins, Christians possess an *eyewitness testimony* of creation: God's inerrant Word.[46] The Bible contains the words of the one person who was there, and God's Word should be trusted over the speculations of human beings.[47] Second, creationism offers a better model with which to understand the scientific data, and is more amenable to everyday

[40] Answers in Genesis, *Journey through the Creation Museum* (Green Forest: Master Books, 2008), 24.

[41] E.g. Morris, *Long War*, 32; Duane T. Gish, *Evolution? The Fossils Say No!* (San Diego: Creation-Life Publishers, 1973), 42; Ham, *The Lie*, 35; Ian McNaughton and Paul Taylor, *Darwin and Darwinism 150 Years Later* (Leominster: Day One, 2009), 5; Elizabeth Mitchell, 'What Are the Tactics of the New Atheists?', in *A Pocket Guide to Atheism*, ed. Ken Ham (Petersburg: Answers in Genesis, 2014), 40; Whitcomb and Morris, *Genesis Flood*, 130–1; Henry M. Morris, *Defending the Faith* (Green Forest: Master Books, 2000), 93; Morris, *Beginning*, 12; Duane T. Gish, *Evolution: The Fossils Still Say No!* (El Cajon: Institute for Creation Research, 1995), 3; Sarfati, *Refuting Evolution*, 29.

[42] Ham, *The Lie*, 73.

[43] DeWitt, *Unravelling*, 42–5; Ham, *The Lie*, 36; Sarfati, *By Design*, 223.

[44] Patterson, *Evolution Exposed*, 24.   [45] Sarfati, *Refuting*, 17.

[46] Patterson, *Evolution Exposed*, 27; Whitcomb and Morris, *Genesis Flood*, 213.

[47] Ham, *The Lie*, 35.

intuitions regarding ourselves and our world.[48] It also has the advantage that, unlike evolution, it does not reject the possibility of divine agency in advance.[49]

THE BIBLE: LITERAL, UNIVOCAL AND PERSPICUOUS

Given the differences between these two worldviews, the cogency of comparisons between new atheists and Protestant fundamentalists would seem to be at best doubtful, and, at worse, dishonest and unhelpful. Yet when we move past what each group claims about itself, and turn to consider the specific areas of disagreement that divide them, a very different picture begins to emerge. It is then revealed that while one affirms what the other denies, new atheists and Protestant fundamentalists share *the same* conception of Scripture, *the same* biblical hermeneutic, *the same* understanding of religion, *the same* dismissive attitude towards non-fundamentalist Christians, *the same* conception of divine agency, *the same* belief that evolution disproves Christianity, *the same* rejection of postmodernity and the same interest in preserving fundamentalist conceptions of the Christian faith. These shared attitudes and beliefs arise from two presuppositions that are common to both groups, and have been inherited from their shared Protestant heritage: a literal, univocal and perspicuous reading of Scripture and a disruptive and substitutionary conception of divine activity in nature. Both groups are the heirs of Protestant Christianity, a Protestantism which, in the face of pluralisation and secularisation, has now broken apart into two opposing forms, forms that, paradoxically, continue to share the same intellectual structure.

The first area of agreement between new atheists and Protestant fundamentalists is that most Protestant of subjects: the Bible and its correct interpretation. Both groups hold to the presupposition of a literal, univocal and perspicuous Bible, and this presupposition supports, in turn, a common understanding of the Christian faith and the dismissal of academic and moderate forms of Christianity. In addition, it contributes towards the new atheist understanding of God as a quasi-mortal, spatio-temporal being.

---

[48] DeWitt, *Unravelling*, 42–5; Paul Garner, *The New Creationism* (Darlington: Evangelical Press, 2009), 240; Whitcomb and Morris, *Genesis Flood*, 136–211; Philip E. Johnson, *The Wedge of Truth* (Downer's Grove: Inter-Varsity Press Books, 2000), 156.

[49] Dominic Statham, *Evolution: Good Science?* (Leominster: Day One, 2009), 135; Philip E. Johnson, *Darwin on Trial* (Downer's Grove: Inter-Varsity Press, 1993), 28; Ham, *The Lie*, 50–2.

As noted earlier, the inerrancy of Scripture is the foundation of the Protestant fundamentalist worldview. For Morris and Clark, inerrancy is not a doctrine of the Church, but Scripture's own doctrine concerning itself, a self-attestation ratified by the approval of Jesus Christ himself.[50] Given the danger of misrepresenting God's Word, the self-interpretation and perspicuity of Scripture is particularly important for fundamentalists. The basis of our knowledge of Scripture is what Scripture says about itself, and we do not need to look to any other source to understand it.[51] For Ham and Hodge, it is this understanding that separated the Reformers from the tradition and magisterium of the Roman Catholic Church.[52] While not everything in the Bible is immediately clear, fundamentalists consciously stand in the tradition of Tyndale, and are watchful not to place the Bible in the hands of a scholarly elite.[53] Despite difficulties, the perspicuity of Scripture can be relied upon, because this perspicuity is founded upon God, and God's intention is to be understood by his people. Because of this divine intention, the doctrine of perspicuity is occasionally moved into the doctrine of God itself, the reasoning being that, if God is clear and straightforward, Scripture must be also.[54]

Fundamentalist hermeneutics follow naturally from the inerrancy, perspicuity and self-interpretation of Scripture. The most common appeal is to what fundamentalists call the 'historical-grammatical approach', which seeks to identify the meaning words had in the language of their day, before taking them in their literal, or plain, sense.[55] More formally, for any given text, the reader should first take account of context, genre, the interpretation placed on the text by other sections of Scripture and the Church's historical view in order to determine its meaning.[56] In this way, many fundamentalists formally recognise the principles and practices employed by contemporary biblical scholarship. In practice, however, their reading of Scripture is founded upon what they call the plain or literal sense. As Boone says, at its most basic, the plain or literal sense

---

[50] Henry M. Morris and Martin E. Clark, *The Bible Has the Answer* (Green Forest: Master Books, 1999), 1–6; Morris, *Biblical Creationism*, 15; Morris, *Defending the Faith*, 17–19.

[51] Patterson, *Evolution Exposed*, 126–7; John D. Currid, *A Study Commentary on Genesis*, vol. I (Darlington: Evangelical Press, 2003), 40–1.

[52] Tim Chaffey, 'How Should We Interpret the Bible?', in *How Do We Know the Bible Is True?*, ed. Ken Ham and Bodie Hodge (Green Forest: Master Books, 2011), 128–9.

[53] Chaffey, 'How Should We Interpret', 123–4.

[54] Kurt Wise, *Faith, Form and Time* (Nashville: Broadman & Holman, 2002), 19.

[55] Chaffey, 'How Should We Interpret', 124–5; Patterson, *Evolution Exposed*, 127.

[56] Ken Ham, *Six Days* (Green Forest: Master Books, 2013), 71–4.

amounts to little more than the view that Scripture means what it says, and what it says is however a 'reasonable' or 'common sense' person would read it.[57] Positively, it is a belief in the univocity of Biblical texts, and that the meaning of Scripture is empirically referential; negatively, it is the rejection of polyvocity and allegory.[58] This is particularly important for passages that purport to be historical. The 'literal sense' means taking texts at their word, and affirming their reference to a past, present or future reality.[59] Any movement away from the literal sense would suggest that the events in question are false, an outcome that would render the text worthless.

Although fundamentalists can sometimes recognise a wider set of hermeneutical criteria that incorporate elements used within contemporary biblical scholarship, their stress upon the reading of Scripture that would be most acceptable to the ordinary person without theological training, taken with the perspicuity and self-interpreting nature of Scripture, gives rise to one of the most characteristic features of fundamentalist hermeneutics: the denial of hermeneutics. This is illustrated by the following question and answer from Morris and Clark:

Question: 'How can a person know how to interpret the Bible?'

Answer: *The proper way to interpret the Bible is not to interpret it at all! It was written to be understood and obeyed and should therefore be read like any other book of information and instruction. If God is truly the Author of the Bible, as Christians have always believed, then it is certainly reasonable to assume that He could say what He means!*[60]

In this hermeneutic, the meaning of texts is considered objective and fixed, and interpretation is the simple action of coming to hold this fixed and objective meaning within one's mind.

The high value placed by fundamentalists upon the inerrant and self-authenticating nature of Scripture is rendered problematic by the existence of apparent contradictions, errors, and *non sequiturs* within its text, and provokes robust response. In relation to the conclusions of modern biblical scholarship, any criticism that questions inerrancy is ruled out in advance as subjective and arbitrary.[61] If engaged with at all, biblical criticism is used only for apologetic purposes, using critical methods to

---

[57] Boone, *Bible Tells Them*, 13, 39–40.   [58] Boone, *Bible Tells Them*, 45.
[59] Barr, *Fundamentalism*, 49; Marsden, 'Views of Science', 106; Harris, *Evangelicals and Fundamentalism*, 151–5; Boone, *Bible Tells Them*, 57–8.
[60] Morris and Clark, *Bible Has the Answer*, 8.   [61] Currid, *Study Commentary*, 23–30.

defend inerrancy against the questioning of scholars.[62] For fundamentalists such as Ham, if the discoveries of biblical criticism were proved correct, Christianity, and all reality, would crumble:

> If the Bible is to be questioned and cannot be trusted, and if it is continually subject to reinterpretation based on what fallible humans believe, then we do not have an absolute authority. We do not have the Word of the One who knows everything, which means we have no basis for anything.[63]

Because they reject the methods of contemporary biblical criticism, fundamentalists typically affirm the traditional Mosaic authorship of the Pentateuch.[64] Indeed, the fundamentalist emphasis upon the written text of Scripture sometimes goes further, and leads to the belief that Adam and his descendants compiled the separate narratives of the Book of Genesis, until they were handed over to Moses for collation and editing.[65] The rejection of biblical criticism, taken with the inerrancy and self-interpretation of Scripture, leads fundamentalists to conceive of its pronouncements as forming a coherent unity. This has two consequences. First, it gives rise to the practice of proof-texting, where biblical verses are conceived of as propositions carrying context-independent meaning.[66] Second, it requires fundamentalists to engage in elaborate apologetic work to harmonise apparent contradictions. This is achieved by duplicating biblical events, rearranging narratives into alternative chronological forms, or interjecting non-textual hypotheses to account for inconsistencies. These strategies will be examined more closely in Chapter 5.

While new atheists – unsurprisingly – reject the inerrancy of Scripture, this rejection is not simplistic but complex, and heavy with assumptions drawn from the Protestant thought it rejects. As an example, we may consider the following quotation from Barker:

> I lost faith in faith. I was forced to admit that the Bible is not a reliable source of truth: it is unscientific, irrational, contradictory, absurd, unhistorical, uninspiring and morally unsatisfying.

This is an uncompromising rejection, yet one which, nevertheless, assumes that the Bible *should be* a source of scientific truth, a coherent

[62] See, e.g., Ron Rhodes, 'Has the Bible's Text Been Changed over the Years?', in *How Do We Know the Bible Is True?*, ed. Ken Ham and Bodie Hodge (Green Forest: Master Books, 2011), 272–3.
[63] Ham, *The Lie*, 68.   [64] e.g. Currid, *Study Commentary*, 31.
[65] Morris, *Biblical Creationism*, 19, 23; Currid, *Study Commentary*, 31.
[66] Harris, *Evangelicals and Fundamentalism*, 168–72.

whole without contradiction, giving historically precise information regarding past events, and consonant with contemporary conceptions of morality. New atheists such as Barker typically share the same presuppositions as fundamentalists regarding what Scripture should be, and, finding that it does not meet their expectations, reject it as worthless. These same assumptions are latent within the exegesis that accompanies almost all of their works. The favoured hermeneutical procedure of new atheists is to engage in proof-texting, lifting verses from different contexts, and bringing them into relation with each other to show their mutual incompatibility.[67] In the following example from Dennett, two texts are compared in order to demonstrate Scripture's supposed self-contradiction:

Every prudent man dealeth with knowledge: but a fool layeth open his folly.
    For it is written, I will destroy the wisdom of the wise, and will bring to nothing the understanding of the prudent.[68]

These are held to be contradictory because the 'wisdom', 'prudence' and 'knowledge' discussed in these texts are held to be synonyms of a single abstract noun, possessed of a univocal, objective meaning that is independent of the context in which it is used. For new atheists, such a reading of Scripture is natural, and any other hermeneutic – for example, one mediated by theological tradition – is denounced as arbitrary and dishonest. As Barker writes, 'People who are free of theological bias notice that the Bible contains hundreds of discrepancies.'[69] Like many Protestants before and since, Church tradition is seen by new atheists as a barrier to comprehending the meaning of Scriptural texts, rather than a necessary aid to exegesis. Tradition is conceived as arbitrary, relative, and biased, while those unburdened by tradition are considered objective, rational, and honest. As Long puts it:

If you undertake an honest, dispassionate, and emotionless analysis of the Bible, you can easily conclude that it's not the work of a supreme being.[70]

This hermeneutic is not, however, borne of honest ignorance, but is a conscious choice on the part of new atheists. Despite his antipathy towards religion, Hitchens expresses *respect* for the manner in which

---

[67] E.g. Harris, *End of Faith*, 85; Hitchens, *God Is Not Great*, 97–107, 109–22; Dawkins, *God Delusion*, 119–20; Barker, *Godless*, 222–42; John W. Loftus, *Why I Became an Atheist* (Amherst: Prometheus Books, 2008), 167–75.
[68] Daniel C. Dennett, *Breaking the Spell* (London: Penguin Books, 2007), 50–1. For another example, see Jason Long, *Biblical Nonsense* (New York: iUniverse, 2005), 146.
[69] Barker, *Godless*, 222.   [70] Long, *Biblical Nonsense*, 3.

fundamentalists read Scripture, as they, unlike non-fundamentalist Christians, read Scripture 'correctly', just as Hitchens was taught to do in Sunday School as a boy.[71] This reading, of course, is literal, univocal and perspicuous, and atheists are swift to defend it against theologians who would suggest alternative, non-intuitive readings.[72] As Grayling asks, making use of the common new atheist opposition between truth and metaphor, 'What are the principled grounds for saying what is true and what is metaphor in the texts and traditions?' At least fundamentalists have a consistent commitment to the literal sense.[73] Due to their consistency and clarity, Harris argues that fundamentalists cannot be criticised on theological grounds at all, as their understanding of Scripture's meaning cannot be rivalled by anyone.[74] To those who would accuse new atheists of having no real grasp of how to read Scripture, an appeal to perspicuity is made: 'What the Bible means *in plain English* is what most people read. If it embarrasses itself in plain English, then it fails to make its point.'[75] These hermeneutical beliefs have led a number of commentators to compare atheist readings of Scripture with those undertaken by fundamentalists.[76] As Beattie argues:

> The problem is that militant atheists are fundamentalists when it comes to interpreting Scripture. Sweeping aside the careful scholarship which should go into any research of ancient texts, they throw out quotations from the Bible with a literalistic zeal worthy of any Christian fundamentalist.[77]

This lack of interest in biblical studies has been documented by Moffat, and is detectable in all new atheist engagements with Scripture.[78] The lack of interest in biblical studies is not, however, a ploy by which to avoid serious engagement with Scripture, but stems from two related beliefs. First, new atheists share the belief of Protestant fundamentalists that critical study of the Bible is incompatible with faith.[79] This means that, if they engage with it at all, it is only as an ancillary to their own polemical attacks, mirroring the Protestant fundamentalist practice of only using

---

[71] Hitchens, *God Is Not Great*, 2.
[72] E.g. Dawkins, *God Delusion*, 275, 269, 280; Stenger, *Folly of Faith*, 121–2.
[73] A. C. Grayling, *The God Argument* (London: Bloomsbury, 2013), 29–30.
[74] Harris, *End of Faith*, 20.   [75] Barker, *Godless*, 185.
[76] John F. Haught, *God and the New Atheism* (Louisville: Westminster John Knox Press, 2008), 30–1; Robertson, *Dawkins Letters*, 102; Cunningham, *Pious Idea*, 378.
[77] Tina Beattie, *The New Atheists* (London: Darton, Longman and Todd, 2007), 81.
[78] See Russel Moffat, *Atheists Can Be W***ers Too* (Milton Keynes: AuthorHouse, 2009), 93–123 for examples.
[79] Barker, *Godless*, 38.

criticism to defend inerrancy. Second, because it has performed its task of illuminating the process of editing and redaction that produced Scripture's text, biblical studies is no longer needed, and can be wound up as an academic discipline.[80] Unlike modern scholarship, which does not function with the category of 'error', fundamentalists and atheists have no sustained interest in the academic study of the Bible for its own sake. On the contrary, they reject such study for the elementary question of whether the Bible is inerrant or not.[81]

New atheists and Protestant fundamentalists, then, share a number of biblical and hermeneutical beliefs: that Scripture should be inerrant, that its meaning should be literal, univocal and perspicuous, that fundamentalists are the best interpreters of its text, and that biblical studies is largely irrelevant to the task of exegesis. This conception of Scripture and hermeneutics gives rise, in turn, to a shared understanding of what true Christianity is. As Lash and Armstrong have argued, new atheists are clear that true religion is represented by fundamentalism.[82] According to Harris, the majority of religious people worldwide are fundamentalists, and if moderates in Europe view their form of religion as normative, they are, argues Dawkins, quite wrong: they are the exception.[83] This is because religions, according to Grayling, are 'by their nature fundamentalist', and the moderate forms of Christianity existing in the West are only the result of a loss of influence, and are not *truly* religion.[84] Prior to the modern period, Christianity was singular and monolithic, and has only changed its doctrine and practice due to atheist critique.[85]

What is even more surprising for our purposes, however, is how heavily new atheist understandings of religion are indebted to conservative evangelicalism. As Stahl, Beattie and Schaeffer have noted, new atheist understandings of Christianity bear all the hallmarks of a Western Protestant mindset, with an emphasis on the cognitive and individualistic nature of faith, biblical theology, and personal sin.[86] One common trope

[80] Hector Avalos, 'Why Biblical Studies Must End', in *The End of Christianity*, ed. John W. Loftus (Amherst: Prometheus Books, 2011), 107–10, 129.
[81] Cf. Barr, *Fundamentalism*, 55.
[82] Nicholas Lash, *Theology for Pilgrims* (Notre Dame: University of Notre Dame Press, 2008), 3–4; Armstrong, *Case for God*, 7.
[83] Dawkins, *God Delusion*, 358–60.   [84] Grayling, *God Argument*, 3, 14.
[85] David Eller, 'Christianity Evolving', in *The End of Christianity*, ed. John W. Loftus (Amherst: Prometheus Books, 2011), 23–51; cf. Moffat, *Atheists Can Be*, 56–7.
[86] Stahl, 'One-Dimensional Rage', 102; Beattie, *New Atheists*, 40–3; Donovan O. Schaefer, 'Blessed, Precious Mistakes: Deconstruction, Evolution, and New Atheism in America', *International Journal for Philosophy of Religion* 76 (2014), 76–7.

in new atheist texts is the distinction between nominal or cultural religion in opposition to personal faith, the latter of which is held to be normative. True religion for new atheists is the result of a personal, conscious assent, rather than an inherited, communal practice as in Roman Catholicism, and Dawkins and Boghossian condemn all traditions as particularly obnoxious sources of truth.[87] This Western Protestant attitude towards Christianity extends to doctrine also. Dawkins argues for the primacy of original sin and penal atonement in Christian theology, and the importance of an historical Adam, while Grayling and Dennett advance criticisms of transubstantiation in the Eucharist that would not have been out of place in the sixteenth or seventeenth centuries.[88] In relation to ethics and the Christian life, atheist hermeneutics sometimes lead to the conclusion that Old Testament law is still normative for Christians, and that the New Testament did not fundamentally change the conditional and works-based nature of salvation.[89] According to Barker, Jesus made it clear in Matthew 5:18 that not a jot or tittle of the Law would be annulled, and Christians are dishonest for suggesting that Old Testament purity regulations are not in force.[90] In this way, as Eagleton and Vernon argue, the god of new atheism remains a fearful and uncompromising law-enforcer, a divine bully ever ready to punish sinners.[91] Yet, given their hermeneutical assumptions, even this gloomy and fearful image elicits the grudging respect of new atheists. As compared to the nebulous God of love preached by liberals, a God who punishes sin with misfortune and natural disasters is at least comprehensible: 'The theology of wrath,' argues Harris 'has far more intellectual merit'.[92] If Christianity is true at all, thinks Loftus, it is conservative evangelicalism, rather than liberalism or Roman Catholicism, which is its purest expression.[93] The dependence of new atheism upon traditional Protestant forms of thought and practice is even occasionally celebrated. As Hitchens says:

---

[87] Dawkins, *God Delusion*, 25, 379–83; Dawkins, *Devil's Chaplain* 284–5; Boghossian, *Manual*, 47; Barker, *Godless*, 3; Loftus, *Why I Became*, 19.

[88] Dawkins, *God Delusion*, 283–7; Grayling, *God Argument*, 31–2; Dennett, *Breaking the Spell*, 227–8.

[89] Grayling, *Against All Gods*, 24; Long, *Biblical Nonsense*, 96–9, 146–9. Also see Barker's treatment of the Beatitudes as a table of prescriptive laws. Barker, *Godless*, 197–200.

[90] Barker, *Godless*, 164–5.

[91] Hitchens, *God Is Not Great*, 16; cf. Eagleton, *God, Faith, and Revolution*, 51; Vernon, *After Atheism*, 87–89.

[92] Sam Harris, *Letter to a Christian Nation* (London: Bantam Press, 2007), 47–8.

[93] Loftus, *Why I Became*, 12; cf. Harris, *Letter*, 4–5.

my particular atheism is a Protestant atheism. It is with the splendid liturgy of the King James Bible and the Cranmer prayer book – liturgy that the fatuous Church of England has cheaply discarded – that I first disagreed.[94]

Like his Protestant forbears, Hitchens delights in the success of the Reformers, who ended the tyranny of the priesthood by translating the Bible into the vernacular.[95] New atheist understandings of religion, then, have, as Beattie argues, a strongly 'Post-Protestant' flavour to them, a dependence that becomes explicable with the Protestant background of the majority of new atheist writers, and the genealogy charted in Chapters 1–3.[96]

The use of categories and beliefs drawn from conservative Protestantism is perhaps part of what Cunningham refers to as atheism's 'vulgar' character, that is, its failure to engage in the theological inquiry recognised by academic theologians and the mainstream Church.[97] This judgment is echoed by fundamentalists and atheists themselves, however, who, sharing a common understanding of Scripture, hermeneutics and the nature of religion, generally reject non-fundamentalist Christianity as confused, dishonest and worthless. At best, non-fundamentalist expressions of Christianity are dismissed by new atheists as the products of ignorance. Thus, Hitchens can praise the 'admirable but nebulous humanism' of Dietrich Bonhoeffer, and Harris believes that liberals only defend their faith against atheists because they – unlike fundamentalists – have no idea what Scripture actually teaches, a view echoed by Stenger.[98] More common, however, is the charge that non-fundamentalist Christians, led by theologians and educated clergy, purposefully deceive themselves and others so as to preserve their own power. This accusation of dishonesty is targeted at three areas: biblical hermeneutics, academic theology and the nature of God.

Following the understanding of Scripture and the Christian faith they share with Protestant fundamentalists, new atheists believe that no real progress is possible within Christian theology, because the meaning of Scripture is fixed forever. For this reason, Harris argues that an individual living in the fourteenth century was capable of knowing as much as anyone today regarding the Bible.[99] Because Christianity is monolithic

---

[94] Hitchens, *God Is Not Great*, 11.
[95] Hitchens, *God Is Not Great*, 125; cf. Dawkins, *God Delusion*, x.
[96] Beattie, *New Atheists*, 5.   [97] Cunningham, *Pious Idea*, xvii.
[98] Hitchens, *God Is Not Great*, 7; Harris, *End of Faith*, 17; Stenger, *New Atheism*, 129.
[99] Harris, *End of Faith*, 22.

and immutable, any deviation from traditional readings of Scripture is denounced as arbitrary and unwarranted, an unprincipled 'cherry-picking' that is undertaken without any reference to consistent criteria. This dishonest and arbitrary practice, however, nevertheless reveals the ultimate primacy of reason and personal autonomy over religion.[100] As Dawkins argues:

We pick and choose which bits of scripture to believe, which bits to write off as symbols or allegories. Such picking and choosing is a matter of personal decision, just as much, or as little, as the atheist's decision to follow this moral precept or that was a personal decision, without an absolute foundation.[101]

This non-biblical cherry-picking has arisen due to the scruples of liberals, who have been corrupted by secular trends. While no longer believing in Scripture, these individuals still desire to salvage some semblance of truth from its pages.[102] This dilution of religious truth has given rise to 'emasculated and feeble latitudinarian religious bodies like the Church of England' where 'strummed guitars and saccharine smiles' have replaced the honesty of hellfire preaching and the Crusades.[103] Because they no longer believe in the historicity of biblical narratives, liberal interpretations of Scripture are akin to discovering that the double helix structure of DNA is false, yet still asking what its meaning is for us today.[104] In short, as Harris puts it, 'Religious moderation is the product of *secular* knowledge and *scriptural* ignorance – and it has no bona fides, in religious terms, to put it on a par with fundamentalism.'[105]

Fundamentalists agree. According to Anderson, the liberal hermeneutic is without justification, and is an attempt to subvert evangelical truth and betray the Lord.[106] The liberal churches are more interested in counselling than studying the Bible, and their 'general apostasy' from Scripture will result in the dissolution of Christianity.[107] These criticisms are often accompanied by an alternative fundamentalist genealogy, which traces the development of anti-Christian hermeneutics through the ages. According to Morris, true Christianity has always preserved the literal sense of Scripture as normative. Yet, starting with Augustine,

---

[100] Dawkins, *God Delusion*, 280; Stenger, *Folly of Faith*, 121–2.
[101] Dawkins, *God Delusion*, 275.   [102] Harris, *End of Faith*, 17.
[103] Grayling, *Against all Gods*, 24, 32.   [104] Dawkins, *Unweaving the Rainbow*, 183–4.
[105] Harris, *End of Faith*, 21.
[106] David Anderson, *Creation or Evolution: Why We Must Choose* (Littlethorpe: J6D Publishers, 2009), 8.
[107] Morris, *Long War*, 44.

non-Christian philosophy was allowed to alter the plain sense of the Bible, introducing allegorical readings that allowed rapprochement between Church and world, but at the cost of rejecting God's Word. This process reached its infernal apogee during the Middle Ages with the Roman Catholic theology of Thomas Aquinas, where the Bible could mean anything one pleased.[108] Due to the rediscovery of Scripture at the Reformation, however, the Church recovered the true sense of the Bible, including, crucially, a six-day literal creation.[109] There has always been a war between the true reading of Scripture and the false, a war that is uncompromising. As Anderson frames it:

Literalism has slain its thousands, but liberalism its tens of thousands. It is not excessive literalism which has ruined the mainline denominations of the professing Christian church; it is liberalism.[110]

As Lash has noted, in the hermeneutical binary shared by both new atheists and Protestant fundamentalists, one either believes a text 'literally', or 'writes it off' as nonsense.[111] All alternatives are excluded. This is not, as we have seen, the product of simple ignorance, however, but arises from a range of philosophical and theological arguments, arguments that are shared by Protestant fundamentalist and new atheists, and which arise from the genealogy traced in Chapters 1–3.

We have noted already how the fundamentalist doctrine of perspicuity gives rise to the belief that any reasonable person can understand Scripture's contents, and the accompanying suspicion that specialists might usurp the individual's right of interpretation. This same suspicion is levelled by new atheists against academic theologians. New atheists typically view theology as, at best, a non-subject, and, at worst, an obfuscating mist to shield the errors and absurdities of the Christian faith. In contrast to theologians, who seek a way out of logical arguments against God's existence by changing definitions, and making hair-thin distinctions, the science of new atheists offers an empirical and objective way of moving beyond mere words.[112]

[108] Morris, *Long War*, 197–218.
[109] Joel R. Beeke, *What Did the Reformers Believe about the Age of the Earth?* (Petersburg: Answers in Genesis, 2014), 2–3.
[110] Anderson, *Why We Must*, 18.
[111] Lash, *Pilgrims*, 9. Lash's observation is matched almost word-perfect by Sam Harris. See Harris, *End of Faith*, 17–18.
[112] Stenger, *Failed Hypothesis*, 34.

All of us have been criticised for not paying enough attention to modern theology. We are more interested in observing the world and taking our lessons from those observations than debating the finer points of scriptures that are probably no more than fables to begin with.[113]

Grayling castigates theologians as 'master-wrigglers when skewered by logic', utilising concepts 'so elastic, multiple and ill-defined as to make it hard to attach a literal meaning to them', with the result that challenging their beliefs is like 'engaging in a boxing match with jelly'.[114] Lacking an empirical basis, theology cannot be considered a subject at all, and theologians have no authority that would qualify them as specialists. As Dawkins reminds his readers, theology, unlike science, has not made any true advance in eighteen centuries.[115] Echoing the thought of earlier freethinkers, Harris, Boghossian and Grayling argue that theology only manages to maintain a semblance of prestige through the use of mystery, where ineffability provides an excuse for poor reasoning, enabling theologians to avoid the attacks of reason, and defend their own corrupt privilege.[116]

It is not only the supposed lack of an empirical basis that marks theology out as a non-subject, however, but its supposed failure to represent what 'ordinary' Christians believe. For Dawkins, the theologies of Bonhoeffer, Tillich, or Holloway may be palatable, yet they bear no relation to what Christians actually believe.[117] It is at this stage that new atheists make a surprising move: they utilise Scripture to argue for a particular doctrine of God. This move consists of two stages. First, the new atheist critique of liberalism and academic theology is extended to undermine sophisticated conceptions of God. According to Grayling, cultured apologists for faith

seek to avoid or deflect criticism by slipping behind the abstractions of higher theology, a mist-shrouded domain of long words, superfine distinction and vague subtleties, in some of which God is nothing ('no-thing, not a thing') and does not even exist ('but is still the condition for the possibility of existence' – one could go on and on) – in short, sophistry ...[118]

This 'sophistry' is associated in the minds of the majority of new atheist writers with what they term the 'abstraction' of the Christian doctrine of God. As Stenger argues:

[113] Stenger, *New Atheism*, 12.
[114] Grayling, *Against all Gods*, 38; Grayling, *God Argument*, 4.
[115] Dawkins, *God Delusion*, 55, 79–80.
[116] Harris, *End of Faith*, 64–5; Grayling, *God Argument*, 20; Boghossian, *Manual*, 34–5n2.
[117] Dawkins, *God Delusion*, 15, 269.   [118] Grayling, *Against All Gods*, 9–10.

I am well aware that sophisticated theologians have developed highly abstracted concepts of a god that they claim is consistent with the teachings of their faiths. One can always abstract any concept so it is out of the realm of scientific investigation. But these gods would not be recognised by the typical believer.[119]

Here, divine transcendence – the non-identification of God with any object or immanent process – is denounced by new atheists as a response to the attacks of science, and not truly representative of the Christian faith. This denunciation of the Christian doctrine of God – thought by many new atheists to be a novelty – gives rise to a second move, the elaboration of an alternative materialist and anthropomorphic doctrine of God. This alternative doctrine of God, paradoxically, is believed by many new atheists to be more faithful to Scripture than the God of Christian orthodoxy. As strange as this argument may seem, it is made earnestly. New atheist writings often feature accounts of the formative years of their authors. One recurring image in these accounts is of God as a powerful father-figure, a spatial and temporal being who exists far from the Earth in a remote part of the universe.[120] For Dennett, there are only two kinds of god: a conscious, supernatural being, or a higher power or essence that does not exercise agency. The only respectable God is the former, and it is likely that, if such a being exists, it is possessed of a large body. This is because Dennett can think of no greater 'deformation' than the movement from the spatial and temporal God of anthropomorphism to the rarefied God of the theologians.[121] Dennett argues that if a personal creator God exists, and exercises providential care towards believers, then God must be material, as there is no other way for God to interact with creation.[122] This view is echoed by Barker, who argues that to exist at all means to be material, and that, if God were Spirit, he could not exert any force over creation, for force is material.[123] It is telling that, while Dawkins attempts to distance himself from attacks upon a 'Big Man in the Sky', he nevertheless cites with approval a quotation from Gore Vidal, which explicitly singles out such a material Sky-God for attack.[124]

These philosophical considerations are augmented by arguments based on the anthropomorphic language of Scripture, a line of reasoning

[119] Stenger, *Failed Hypothesis*, 11.
[120] E.g. Richard Dawkins, *An Appetite for Wonder* (London: Black Swan, 2014), 77; Dennett, *Dangerous Idea*, 18; Ludovic Kennedy, *All in the Mind* (London: Hodder and Stoughton, 1999), 3, 261–3; cf. Eagleton, *God, Faith, and Revolution*, 13, 28, 49.
[121] Dennett, *Breaking the Spell*, 204–7, 232–4.
[122] Dennett, *Breaking the Spell*, 190–3, 197–8.   [123] Barker, *Godless*, 125, 138–9.
[124] Dawkins, *God Delusion*, 57–8.

strongest among those atheists from conservative evangelical and fundamentalist backgrounds such as Loftus, Barker and Dennett. If we take the Bible seriously and at face value, argues Gericke, then God has a body that sees, smells and moves through space.[125] While theologians try and downplay these references by claiming that they merely make use of anthropomorphic imagery, Loftus reminds his readers that the word 'anthropomorphic' does not even appear in Scripture, and the text gives no reason to interpret it as such.[126] For this reason, the strategies of theologians are illegitimate, and when they try to explain such imagery away, they only demonstrate their belief in the absurdity of Scripture, and the desperate need to re-write it.[127] As the Church no longer believes in a God who is material, mutable, and possessed of a large body, the majority of Christians demonstrate that they do believe in the God of the Bible.[128] For this reason, new atheists like Dennett reject the apophatic tradition in its entirety, viewing it as a theological luxury of the sceptical middle classes, and one possessed of no practical import whatsoever. If Christians continue to use anthropomorphic imagery to describe a non-material God, they are in a state of contradiction, and further demonstrate the irrelevancy of their faith.[129]

The conception of God held by new atheists gives rise to the further belief that, if God does exist, God is infinitely complex, and his existence requires an explanation like any other phenomenon. This argument – the argument from complexity – is a common feature of new atheist thought. It draws upon a literal interpretation of anthropomorphic biblical imagery and the belief in divine materiality recounted earlier, and weds these to the universal scope of evolution by natural selection.[130] If God exists at all, God is massively complex, and given that the only process known to science capable of generating complex life is evolution, God must be the product of evolution. This being so, God cannot forestall an infinite regress of causes, and God therefore also requires a cause.[131] This idea is most famously expressed in the 'God Hypothesis' of Dawkins, that

[125] Jaco Gericke, 'Can God Exist if Yahweh Doesn't?', in *The End of Christianity*, ed. John W. Loftus (Amherst: Prometheus Books, 2011), 137–8, 140.

[126] Loftus, *Why I Became*, 128–30.   [127] Gericke, 'Can God Exist', 137–8, 140.

[128] Loftus, *Why I Became*, 98–9.   [129] Dennett, *Breaking the Spell*, 9, 232–4.

[130] See Loftus, *Why I Became*, 93–6. Dawkins has written of his belief that the theory of evolution by natural selection explains the origin of all life, no matter its point of origin within the universe. See Dawkins, *Devil's Chaplain*, 91–106.

[131] Dawkins, *God Delusion*, 177–86; Grayling, *God Argument*, 111; Stenger, *New Atheism*, 103; Loftus, *Why I Became*, 94.

there exists a supernatural intelligence that designed and created the universe, and that any intelligence capable of design comes into existence only as the product of evolution.[132]

These considerations largely confirm the view of Lash and Ward that the God displayed in many new atheist texts is a 'particular, specifiable, fictitious entity', a semi-mortal being existing within time and space.[133] This conception of God is not, however, the product of ignorance, but is held for a number of philosophical, biblical and theological reasons. At every stage, these beliefs are advanced with arguments that utilise theological categories. As with the other areas we have examined, then, new atheists are, paradoxically, heavily engaged in the task of theology. Yet this is not an effort of *positive* theology but *negative* theology. It is *a*theology, the use of theology to justify the rejection of theology. The first key assumption of new atheist atheology is one it shares with Protestant fundamentalism: a literal, univocal and perspicuous understanding of Scripture. This shared intellectual foundation, and the beliefs that arise from it, are the result of both group's dependence upon a decaying Protestant culture, and the biblical and theological genealogy charted in Chapters 1–3.

Both new atheists and Protestant fundamentalists, then, presuppose that the Bible's sense is literal, univocal and perspicuous, and this belief supports a number of others. This is not, however, the only presupposition bequeathed to each group by the Protestant heritage of Britain and America, and we must turn now to uncover the presupposition that lies behind the crucial flash point of evolution: that God's activity disrupts and substitutes for natural causation.

DIVINE ACTIVITY: DISRUPTIVE AND SUBSTITUTIONARY

This section elucidates the second shared presupposition found in new atheist and Protestant fundamentalist texts, that God's activity disrupts and substitutes for natural causation. This shall be done through an examination of one of the key areas of conflict between the two groups: evolution by natural selection. While any commonality on this issue may seem surprising – and even disingenuous – analysis will reveal that the position of each group arises from this shared presupposition regarding divine activity, and that this presupposition, along with the biblical

---

[132] Dawkins, *God Delusion*, 52. [133] Lash, *Pilgrims*, 7; Ward, *Almost Certainly*, 19–20.

presupposition previously examined, supports a range of other beliefs, such as the incompatibility of creation and evolution, the ability of science to detect or fail to detect divine activity, the exhaustive capacity of new atheist and Protestant fundamentalist worldviews, and a corresponding proclivity to reduce competing narratives to their own.

While the question of origins is central to the worldviews of both new atheism and Protestant fundamentalism, given how different these views of origins are, there would appear to be little else that the two groups had in common. For new atheists, evolution provides a complete system of meaning and description, one that explains 'the whole of life'. Evolution supersedes all previous accounts of origins, particularly religious ones.[134] According to Dawkins, Darwin's discovery undermined centuries of theistic explanations for the origin of life, explanations culminating in the design argument of Paley.[135] For Grayling, evolution disproves the activity of God in the formation of life, natural selection having no purpose or design that would warrant the conclusion of divine superintendence.[136] In contrast to the intelligence and agency of Paley's God, natural selection is a 'blind watchmaker'.[137] This being so, natural selection and design are mutually exclusive and are 'close to being irreconcilably different'[138] The improbability of design is strengthened by the waste of life that accrues as a result of evolution, along with instances of supposedly poor design. Hitchens reminds his readers that the history of life on earth has been one of boom followed by bust, and Harris wonders why an intelligent, loving designer would have utilised an evolutionary mechanism that would result in 99 per cent of all animal species dying out.[139] Hitchens cites 'junk' DNA, the appendix and the genito-urinary system of the human male as proofs against the existence of a designer.[140] Dawkins cites many other instances, and argues that while human beings may appear externally – from a non-scientific view – to be a paragon of design, internally, human beings are a mess of evolutionary dead-ends, failed experiments, and patch-up jobs. While this is explained well by variation and natural selection, it is a major problem for theology, and its belief in an intelligent designer.[141]

---

[134] Dennett, *Dangerous Idea*, 25; Dawkins, *God Delusion*, 141; Richard Dawkins, *The Selfish Gene* (Oxford: Oxford University Press, 2006), 1.

[135] Dawkins, *Blind Watchmaker*, 37.   [136] Grayling, *God Argument*, 113.

[137] Dawkins, *Blind Watchmaker*, 3.   [138] Dawkins, *God Delusion*, 85.

[139] Hitchens, *God Is Not Great*, 91; Harris, *Letter*, 75.

[140] Hitchens, *God Is Not Great*, 73–96.

[141] Richard Dawkins, *The Greatest Show on Earth* (London: Black Swan, 2010), 356–71, 375–96.

Evolution not only has consequences for the doctrine of creation, however, but for Scripture, salvation and the existence of God. According to Hitchens, because the account in Genesis 1–3 is at odds with science, it is demonstrated beyond any reasonable doubt that the Bible was written by 'ignorant men' and not by God, thereby endangering all of Scripture's contents, including the promise of salvation.[142] As Dawkins argues, if Adam and the Fall are only symbolic, then Jesus had himself tortured and killed in vicarious punishment for a symbolic sin committed by a non-existent person.[143] Non-literal readings are of no avail. While evolution is damaging to Christian accounts of creation and redemption, the absence of any place for divine agency in scientific accounts of the development of life casts serious doubt over the existence of God himself. By excluding design and divine agency from nature, and proving Scripture to be erroneous, Dennett contends that Darwin's dangerous idea has left religion without any justification.[144]

In contrast to the new atheist belief in the foundational significance of evolution, a literal reading of Genesis for Protestant fundamentalists is 'the foundation of all true history, as well as true science and true philosophy'.[145] It is foundational to Christology, and second only to the doctrine of God in terms of importance.[146] Given these beliefs, any comparison with new atheism would seem to be specious. Yet while Protestant fundamentalists reject evolution and a natural origin for the universe, this rejection is not a simple negation of the new atheist position, but one that, surprisingly, displays many of its assumptions and beliefs. Like new atheists, fundamentalists believe that the universe either came about by naturalistic processes or it did not, and that there is no third option.[147] According to Morris, 'evolution is naturalistic and materialistic by its very nature. It is merely an attempt to explain the origin of things without God.'[148] For Johnson, as a naturalistic form of explanation, evolution is mutually exclusive of creation, design and purpose.[149] Protestant fundamentalists also agree with new atheists that evolution is

---

[142] Hitchens, *God Is Not Great*, 90, 99. [143] Dawkins, *God Delusion*, 287.
[144] Dennett, *Dangerous Idea*, 18.
[145] Henry M. Morris, *The Genesis Record* (Grand Rapids: Baker Book House, 1998), 18–21.
[146] Morris, *Biblical Creationism*, 269.
[147] Henry M. Morris and John D. Morris, *The Modern Creation Trilogy*, vol. 1 (Green Forest: Master Books, 1996), 9.
[148] Henry M. Morris, *Science and the Bible* (Chicago: Moody Press, 1995), 39.
[149] Johnson, *Darwin on Trial*, 114–19.

intellectually problematic and dishonours God. For Morris, 'Evolution is the cruellest, most wasteful and most irrational method of 'creation' that could ever be imagined'[150] Ham argues that the waste and cruelty of evolution is beneath the dignity of a benevolent God, and even congratulates atheists for understanding this.[151] Moreover, if evolution is true, then Scripture – following the biblical hermeneutic recounted previously – is proved to be errant, thereby throwing the Christian faith into serious doubt. Summarising his own experience of such doubt, Upchruch writes 'If the Bible wasn't true for history or science, then there was no reason to trust it for spiritual purposes: if the Bible can't be trusted on what people can see, it is very unlikely that they will trust it on what they can't see.'[152]

The mutual agreement of atheists and fundamentalists over the issue of evolution has been noted by a number of commentators. Cunningham writes of the 'unholy alliance' that colludes to raise evolution into the enemy of faith, while McGrath argues that 'The Dawkinsian view of reality is a mirror image of that found in some of the more exotic sections of American fundamentalism.'[153] Alexander notes that 'Ironically, young earth creationists agree with Dawkins! The opposite extremes in a debate are often more similar than either pole is ready to admit.'[154] While moderate Christians may find the agreement of new atheists and Protestant fundamentalists on this matter surprising, and assume that it is hidden to the two parties, atheists and fundamentalists are well aware of their agreement, and view it as the simple apprehension of the exclusive nature of creation and evolution. As Anderson says, 'Dr Alexander writes that it is ironic that young earth creationists agree with Dawkins that evolution is inherently atheists. This is not ironic, it is simply true.'[155] Atheists and fundamentalists go further, however, and praise each other for the

---

[150] Morris, *Long War*, 58.   [151] Ham, *The Lie*, 118–20.

[152] John Upchurch, 'Confessions of a Former Atheist', in *A Pocket Guide to Atheism*, ed. Ken Ham (Petersburg: Answers in Genesis, 2014), 85. This idea is connected to the words of Christ in John 3:12, 'If I have told you of earthly things, and ye believe not, how shall ye believe, if I tell you of heavenly things?' See Morris and Clark, *Bible Has the Answer*, 7.

[153] Cunningham, *Pious Idea*, xv–xvi, 275; Ryan C. Falcioni, 'Is God a Hypothesis? The New Atheism and the Philosophy of Religion', in *Religion and the New Atheism: A Critical Appraisal*, ed. Amarnath Amarasingam (Leiden: Brill, 2010), 223; McGrath and McGrath, *Dawkins Delusion?*, 23–4. Also see Gunther S. Stent 'Scientific Creationism: Nemesis of Sociobiology', in *Science and Creationism*, ed. Ashley Montagu (Oxford: Oxford University Press, 1984), 136–41.

[154] Denis Alexander, *Creation and Evolution: Do We Have to Choose?* (Oxford: Monarch Books, 2008), 180–1.

[155] Anderson, *Why We Must*, 89.

intellectual honesty and coherence of their beliefs.[156] Long applauds creation scientists for their commitment to research programmes that seek to prove the truth of a literal reading of Genesis 1–3.[157] Inveighing against 'appeasers' like Stephen Jay Gould, who stress the complementarity of science and religion, Dawkins claims 'I do have one thing in common with the creationists. Like me, but unlike the "Chamberlain School", they will have no truck with NOMA and its separate magisteria. Far from respecting the separateness of science's turf, creationists like nothing better than to trample their dirty hobnails all over it.'[158] Johnson returns the compliment, and salutes Dawkins for his clarity over the issues, even adopting the phrase 'bling watchmaker thesis' instead of 'evolution'.[159] This recognition is possible because of an agreement over the terms of the debate. As Johnson writes of another atheist evolutionist, William Provine, 'Provine and I have become very friendly adversaries, because our agreement about how to define the question is more important than our disagreement about how to answer it.'[160] For Morris, Charles Darwin, Bertrand Russell and all those who reject Christianity due to evolution understand more about exegesis and biblical theology than most Christians.[161] As Young argues, 'The man who says "I believe that Genesis purports to be a historical account, but I do not believe that account", is a far better interpreter of the Bible than the man who says, "I believe that Genesis is profoundly true, but it is poetry".'[162]

The agreement between both groups on the issue of evolution is not incidental, but arises from the two presuppositions they share. The first of these is the belief in a literal, univocal and perspicuous Scripture that was examined in the last section. This gives rise to the belief that Scripture teaches a six-day literal creation, and cannot be reconciled with evolution by natural section. New atheists read Genesis 1 as presenting an account of the creation of the world and all life in six literal days. For Harris, 'Any honest reading of the biblical account of creation suggests that God created all animals and plants as we now see them', without the mediation of evolution. Indeed, if we read Scripture truthfully, we should all agree

---

[156] See, e.g. Dennett, *Dangerous Idea*, 18; Hank Hanegraaff, *The Farce of Evolution* (Nashville: Word Publishing, 1998), 19; Anderson, *Why We Must*, 11–2, 44–5; Ham, *The Lie*, 118–120; Morris, *Long War*, 58–9, 119.

[157] Long, *Biblical Nonsense*, 77.   [158] Dawkins, *God Delusion*, 92.

[159] Johnson, *Darwin on Trial*, 167–8.   [160] Johnson, *Darwin on Trial*, 165.

[161] Henry M. Morris and John D. Morris, *The Modern Creation Trilogy*, vol III (Green Forest: Master Books, 1996), 182–5.

[162] Edward J. Young, *In the Beginning* (Edinburgh: Banner of Truth Trust, 1976), 19.

with a six-day creationist interpretation.[163] This forms the basis for the rejection of Genesis on the grounds of science. According to Long:

> Anyone with a decent background in natural science who undertakes an impartial but critical look at the first chapter of Genesis should have no trouble denouncing its claims as rubbish.[164]

Dawkins, Loftus, Hitchens and Stenger all assent to this view.[165] For Protestant fundamentalists, no interpretation of Genesis 1 is possible apart from a literal six-day creation. For Kelly, there is no indication that the text is poetic, as its verb forms are fully consonant with an historical narrative.[166] Moreover, the Hebrew for day – *yom* – in this context does not lend itself to a non-literal interpretation.[167] Similarly, gap readings – which interpret a vast period of time, including a time of cataclysm, between Genesis 1:1 and 1:2 – are dismissed as an 'exegesis of desperation'.[168] The rejection of non-literal interpretations of Genesis 1–3 is strengthened by Scripture's own interpretation, for no biblical allusions to the Book of Genesis treat it as allegorical or poetic, despite proto-evolutionary ideas being present in the ancient world.[169] According to Whitcomb, non-literal interpretations of Genesis only entered into the Church through pagan philosophy, which sought to subvert God's Word with the word of man.[170] The Reformation restored the true, literal interpretation of Scripture to the Church, and Luther and Calvin accordingly believed in a literal six-day creation. The hermeneutic restored at the Reformation was, of course, the natural, common sense hermeneutic of any reasonable person, and anyone that opened the Book of Genesis would come to the conclusion that it taught a literal six-day creation.[171] Like the introduction to any other book, it lays the foundation for all that follows.[172]

---

[163] Harris, *End of Faith*, 19.   [164] Long, *Biblical Nonsense*, 37.

[165] Dawkins, *Magic of Reality*, 34–5; Loftus, *Why I Became*, 277–9; Hitchens, *God Is Not Great*, 90, 99; Stenger, *Failed Hypothesis*, 52.

[166] Kelly, *Creation*, 37–40; Don de Young, *Thousands … Not Billions* (Green Forest: Master Books, 2006), 158–170; Morris, *Biblical Creationism*, 19–20.

[167] Douglas F. Kelly, *Creation and Change* (Ross-shire: Mentor Books, 2010), 96–106.

[168] Kelly, *Creation*, 84–5.

[169] Kelly, *Creation*, 114–8; Currid, *Study Commentary*, 40–1; Morris, *Biblical Creationism*, 213–14; Morris, *Long War*, 151.

[170] John C. Whitcomb, *The Early Earth* (Grand Rapids: Baker Book House, 1997), 36.

[171] John MacArthur, *Battle for the Beginning* (United States: W Publishing Group, 2001), 22; Anderson, *Why We Must*, 25.

[172] Taylor, *Six Days*, 15.

While the biblical-hermeneutical presupposition of a literal, univocal and perspicuous Scripture forms an important part of new atheist and Protestant fundamentalist thought, another element is needed to complete the logical structure underlying their agreement on the issue of evolution. This is supplied by a second presupposition, that God's activity disrupts and substitutes for natural causation. It is this presupposition that gives rise to a belief in the mutual exclusivity of divine activity and natural processes, while also supporting a range of other beliefs. Among these are the incompatibility of creation and evolution, the ability of science to detect divine activity, the rejection of theistic evolution, the belief of each respective group that its worldview exhausts reality and that competing narratives must be reduced to its own.

As examined earlier, new atheist readings of Scripture, taken with a belief in the universal application of evolution by natural selection, give rise to the view that, if God exists, he is most likely corporeal, and the result of a long evolutionary process. This conception of God also functions as the basis for empirical arguments against his existence that operate on the presupposition that the activity of such a being must supplant or disrupt natural processes, and that, as such, science can detect his activity, a line of argument that may be characterised as natural atheology. Take the following passage from Stenger:

My analysis will be based on the contention that God should be detectable by scientific means simply by virtue of the fact that he is supposed to play such a central role in the operation of the universe and the lives of humans. Existing scientific models contain no place where God is included as an ingredient in order to describe observations. Thus, if God exists, he must appear somewhere within the gaps or errors of scientific models.[173]

For new atheists like Stenger, if God exists, then God's activity must be empirically detectable as a constitutive element of the universe and its operations. Much like the design argument of old, God can be known through his effects, and is therefore 'discoverable in principle if not in practice' by science.[174] The form of activity envisioned here, however, is very limited. It cannot take the form of general concurrence, or the creation and preservation of regularities in nature, nor the non-invasive providential ordering of objects and chains of events. All of these forms of activity are undetectable by science, and do not add anything to scientific explanation. As such, any model based on primary and secondary

---

[173] Stenger, *Failed Hypothesis*, 13.   [174] Dawkins, *God Delusion*, 70, 72–3.

causation is rejected. Instead, the activity in question is one that must disrupt or replace natural causation with supernatural causes and supernatural effects. If such activity is not currently detectable, the only remaining place where it may be discovered is in scientific lacunae. Yet in the absence of sufficient scientific lacunae that could accommodate the activity of such a Being, it is highly unlikely that an eternal, omniscient and omnibenevolent God exists, for we have no experience of such a God, while everything we *do* experience is finite and temporal.[175] If science cannot detect any evidence of God's activity, it is only reasonable to conclude that there is no God.[176] The only God capable of existing for new atheists, then, is a 'god of the gaps', whose potential realm of physical activity recedes with every new scientific discovery. For as long as no such gaps exist, however, claims for the existence of God have the same epistemological status as the claim that there exists a species of invisible unicorns.[177]

A conception of God's activity as that which disrupts and replaces natural causation is also found within Protestant fundamentalist thought. The significance of the divine agency recorded in Genesis, in both its creative and diluvian aspects, is that God exercises direct providential control over nature and human society. As such, the historicity of the Genesis flood, and the special creation of human beings, demonstrate that *God is in the world*, bringing about physical changes by his immediate action, and that our scientific understanding of nature is therefore incomplete without him. As Whitcomb and Morris put it in *The Genesis Flood*:

For that universal catastrophe [The Flood] speaks plainly and eloquently concerning the sovereignty of God ... it warns prophetically of a judgment yet to come, when the sovereign God shall again intervene in terrestrial events, putting down all human sin and rebellion ... The second purpose [of this work] is to examine the anthropological, geological, hydrological and other scientific implications of the Biblical record of the Flood, seeking if possible to orient the data of these sciences within this Biblical framework.[178]

The aim of the creation science movement is to discover evidence of the effects of the sovereign God's direct activity in nature, evidence that will complete our scientific understanding of the earth and the universe, while also serving as a salutary warning to atheists and sceptics of his power, dominion and righteousness. The new atheist belief that the Christian God, if he exists, is a corporeal deity evolved by natural selection, would,

---

[175] Loftus, *Why I Became*, 98.   [176] Cf. Stenger, *Failed Hypothesis*, 94–102.
[177] Dawkins, *God Delusion*, 70–7.   [178] Whitcomb and Morris, *Genesis Flood*, xix–xx.

prima facie, appear to be very different from this bibliocentric worldview, which rejects much of contemporary scientific methodology. Yet while the new atheist conception of God is clearly incompatible with fundamentalist piety, we nevertheless see in Protestant fundamentalist understandings of divine activity a correlate with new atheist conceptions of God's materiality. For fundamentalists, the primary mode of God's activity within nature is not taken to be his creation of natural laws, or his general concurrence with natural processes, nor his non-invasive providential ordering of objects and events, but his disruptive or substitutionary interposition within creation. In such a conception of divine activity, a phenomenon is either 'natural' or 'supernatural', either explained by reference to natural causes, or explained by reference to God. Like new atheists, then, Protestant fundamentalists frequently reject the distinction between primary and secondary causation. For God to truly be said to act within the world, his activity must immediately disrupt or replace natural processes. Otherwise, he is not the Christian God. According to Kelly, it is only in this way that God's existence can be shown to have any real effect on human existence.[179] This being so, evolution, which promises a closed and internally coherent causal explanation for life, does not simply refute a literal interpretation of Genesis, but destroys the primary evidence for God's existence, and the ordained moral order of reality. Indeed, Sarfati goes further: 'A God who "created" by evolution is, for all practical purposes, indistinguishable from no God at all.'[180]

The conception of divine activity held by both groups is the source of their belief that creation and evolution are incompatible, and that the existence of one precludes the other. Either God acts directly and immediately in creation and preservation, taking the place of natural causation, or he does not. Either the universe is the direct work of immediate divine activity, or it is purely natural. These presuppositions and beliefs therefore exclude the possibility of theistic evolution, the belief that God's creative agency is mediated in some way through variation and natural selection. For new atheists, there is no need to refer to God if natural processes can account for the origin and development of life. According to Dawkins, the attempt to reconcile creation with evolution and scientific cosmology is redundant and irrelevant, and perhaps even contradictory.[181] This is because, as Stenger reminds us, 'creation' implies the immediate action of God to disrupt or substitute for natural law. Following from the logic

---

[179] Kelly, *Creation*, 17.   [180] Sarfati, *Refuting Evolution*, 22.
[181] Dawkins, *Blind Watchmaker*, 316; Dawkins, *God Delusion*, 143–4.

they share with new atheists, Protestant fundamentalists believe that there is no difference between God working through evolution or being unrelated to it, as in deism. If God's activity in creation does not subvert or substitute for natural causes, it is irrelevant.[182] For Johnson, given that evolution is inherently naturalistic and exclusive of design, theistic evolution is only an option if theologians and other appeasers are purposefully vague.[183]

The rejection of theistic evolution, however, produces a zero-sum game, in which the question of origins brings with it the promise of ruin should the truth of evolution or a six-day creation be undermined. For fundamentalists, evolution signifies the collapse of biblical authority and the absence of God from the world, and, with these, the collapse of meaning, salvation, morality and science itself.[184] For Beeke, if the plain sense of Genesis 1–3 is shown to be errant, and alternative readings become necessary, this will result in the collapse of the fundamentalist framework of meaning, generating hermeneutical anarchy: 'If plain words can take on allegorical or alternative meanings so easily that they do not mean what they plainly state, how do we know what anything means?'[185] If Genesis can be made into poetry or allegory, asks Anderson, then why not the Gospels?[186] As Ginger reminds us, the consequences for soteriology are catastrophic: 'No Adam, no fall; no fall, no atonement; no atonement, no Saviour. Accepting evolution, how can we believe in the fall?'[187] Without a historical Adam and Eve, and a historical Fall, there is no need for Christ's atoning sacrifice, and no need for faith. As Ham argues 'Every single biblical doctrine of theology, directly or indirectly, ultimately has its basis in the Book of Genesis.'[188] It is not only soteriology that is threatened by evolution, however, but morality. For Strassner, a literal reading of Genesis preserves the 'Four Ds': human *dignity*, God's *dominion*, *distinction* between men and women and *duty* to God and neighbour.[189] Without Genesis, there is no reason to uphold a distinction between humans and animals, to fear God's governance and judgment upon sin, to refrain from homosexual behaviour, or from every form of blasphemy and immorality. With salvation and morality goes all meaning, and any form of certainty:

[182] Stenger, *New Atheism*, 76, 166–7.   [183] Johnson, *Darwin on Trial*, 114–19, 168.
[184] Patterson, *Evolution Exposed*, 126.   [185] Beeke, *What Did the Reformers*, 12.
[186] Anderson, *Why We Must*, 92.
[187] Ray Ginger, *Six Days or Forever?* (Boston: Beacon Press, 1958), 63.
[188] Ham, *The Lie*, 82. Cf. Kelly, *Creation*, 17.
[189] Kurt Strassner, *Opening Up Genesis* (Leominster: Day One Publications, 2009), 24–5.

Evolution is as irrational as it is amoral. In place of God as Creator, the evolutionist has substituted chance – sheer fortune, accident, happenstance, serendipity, coincidence, random events, and blind luck.[190]

If Darwinism is true, 'the Bible's story unravels' and the only legitimate alternative is nihilism or atheism, 'a belief system about what we supposedly come from (nothing), what our purpose is in life (nothing), and what happens when we die (which again is nothing)'.[191]

The consequences of creation and design for new atheism are equally significant. For new atheists, God makes science impossible, or, at least, seriously threatened.[192] If God's creative agency and continuing providential oversight is admitted, the integrity and coherence of naturalistic descriptions of reality are endangered, as scientists must admit that there are divine causes of which they can say nothing. Allowing a 'divine foot' in the door would throw all knowledge into doubt, and would represent the overturning of the existing sciences and humanities.[193] As Dawkins writes 'a supernatural explanation of something is not to explain it at all and, even worse, to rule out any possibility of its ever being explained. Why do I say that? Because anything "supernatural" must be definitely be beyond the reach of a natural explanation'.[194] In order to prevent this, God and design must be rejected.

These attitudes are expressions of what Haught has called 'explanatory monism', a univocal conception of reality that rejects alternative forms of description.[195] The rejection by new atheists and Protestant fundamentalists of each other's core narrative is not a simple one, however, but is accomplished through a process of narrative reduction, where each group re-narrates the other in terms of its own worldview, thereby denying its integrity and independence.

For fundamentalists, Genesis provides the foundation 'of all true history as well as of true science and true philosophy'.[196] Unlike science, which depends on direct sense experience, and can therefore tell us nothing regarding origins, the Bible reveals to us the source of life, and

---

[190] MacArthur, *Battle*, 32.

[191] Stephen Lloyd, 'Christian Theology and Neo-Darwinism Are Incompatible', in *Debating Darwin*, ed. Graeme Finlay (Milton Keynes: Paternoster, 2009), 24–5; MacArthur, *Battle*, 37; Ken Ham, introduction to *A Pocket Guide to Atheism*, ed. Ken Ham (Petersburg: Answers in Genesis, 2014), 8.

[192] Johnson, *Darwin on Trial*, 164.

[193] Johnson, *Wedge of Truth*, 139–140. Cf. Whitcomb and Morris, *Genesis Flood*, xix.

[194] Dawkins, *Magic*, 23. [195] See Haught, *Atheism*, 84–91.

[196] Morris, *Genesis Record*, 18–21.

therefore completes our scientific understanding of reality. As the conception of evolution held by new atheists is shown by Scripture to be false, fundamentalism re-narrates the beliefs of non-religion in terms of its own worldview. There are two strategies used in this process of narrative reduction. The first strategy is to reduce the contemporary scientific worldview to the biblical. As we have seen, a disruptive and substitutionary conception of divine activity, a literal interpretation of Genesis, and the supposed evidence for the historicity of a six-day special creation are mutually reinforcing. These presuppositions and beliefs integrate science and physical reality into the biblical narrative, producing a single biblical-scientific description of reality as the locus of God's creative and punitive activity. Because of this connexion of scientific and biblical description, and the normative status of the latter, fundamentalists interpret science in light of Scripture, negating its independence and integrity, and reducing it to the worldview of the Bible. This process of interpretation and reduction is fully conscious. As Morris writes, 'Call it naïve literalism if you will. I call it simply taking God at His Word, and then seeking to explain all scientific data in that context.'[197] The second strategy is to re-narrate evolution and non-religion in religious terms, casting evolution not as a science, but as a religious philosophy. As Ham writes 'The controversy is not religion versus science, as the evolutionists try to make out. It is religion versus religion, the science of one religion versus the science of the other – God's word versus man's word.'[198] According to Morris, a spiritual war has raged between theism and evolution since the dawn of time, an eternal rebellion against the Word of God, of which the present controversy is only the latest instalment.[199] Evolution is not science, but a 'total philosophy', a 'pseudo-scientific rationale' for sin and rebellion against God.[200] It is to evade the judgement of God upon their sin and pride that atheists reject the historicity of Genesis, for God's curse after the Fall, and the judgement of the deluge, show that God is active in the world and will punish sinners.[201] In re-narrating evolution and atheism in religious terms, fundamentalists reduce it to their own worldview, and use it as further proof of human disobedience and the depravity of all those

[197] Morris, *Defending*, 90.
[198] Ham, *The Lie*, 40. Also see Ham's interpretation of the 2010 *Copenhagen Declaration on Religion in Public Life*, which he brands as an atheist confession of faith. Ken Ham, 'Atheists Outline Their Global Religious Agenda', in *A Pocket Guide to Atheism*, ed. Ken Ham (Petersburg: Answers in Genesis, 2014), 11–17.
[199] Morris, *Long War*, 151.   [200] Morris, *Long War*, 18.
[201] Whitcomb and Morris, *Genesis Flood*, xxii.

that challenge God's Word. In this way, evolution and the nonreligious worldview is reduced to the biblical.

New atheist descriptions of reality are, however, equally exclusive and reductionist. As we have seen, the prize of evolution for new atheists is a form of description that explains 'the whole of life', and produces an internally coherent and exhaustive account of reality, encompassing material, personal and social worlds.[202] As Midgely argues, this is not merely a desire for natural explanations of phenomena, but the construction of a habitable scientific ideology, with social, moral and political consequences. Central to this ideology is the universal jurisdiction of science to answer and exhaust all questions.[203] It is the common new atheist belief in the universal competency of science – explored further in Chapter 5 – that ensures that the presuppositions of a literal, univocal and perspicuous Scripture and the disruptive and substitutionary quality of divine activity have an atheistic, as opposed to fundamentalist, outcome. It ensures that there are not *three* sources of authority – Scripture, sense experience and deduction – but only *two*: sense experience and deduction. For this reason, the metaphysical position of new atheism is scientific realism, naturalism and eliminative materialism: the only things in existence are physical, and the physical world is all that there is. As sense experience and deduction are the sole sources of authority for new atheists, the only possible evidence for God's existence comes from these two authorities. In practice, however, the conclusions that new atheists would be most prepared to admit are those derived from empirical evidence, such as direct apprehension of God's body, or, more commonly, the discovery of God's activity in the disruption or substitution of natural causes.[204] For these reasons, the only conception of divinity and divine activity that is readily considered by new atheists is, as we saw earlier, the 'god of the gaps', a god whose activity substitutes for and usurps the place of natural causes and produces inexplicable, supernatural effects detectable by science. As it is only this god that is capable of yielding the empirical evidence necessary to disrupt metaphysical naturalism and materialism, if no lacunae in scientific description remain after thorough

---

[202] Dawkins, *God Delusion*, 141; Dennett, *Dangerous Idea*, 25.

[203] See, e.g., Mary Midgeley, *Evolution as a Religion* (London and New York: Methuen, 1985), 1–2, 15–16, 31.

[204] Although new atheists occasionally engage in philosophical critiques of proofs for the existence of God, due to their reliance upon patterns of thought they share with fundamentalists, they more commonly engage in scientific and theological critiques. These matters will be explored further in the next chapter.

investigation of all known phenomena, the rational conclusion is that God does not exist.

That this conception of God and divine activity bears little relation to that of the majority of Christians is unimportant to new atheists for three reasons. First, given their metaphysical commitments, new atheists find it difficult to interpret Christian beliefs and practices as anything else than supernatural explanations for phenomena. In doing so, atheists such as Dawkins believe they are showing religion respect by treating them as they would treat any other scientific claim about reality.[205] Yet if beliefs such as the soul, and practices such as prayer, are interpreted as offering supernatural explanations for consciousness and unexpected healings, then, when alternative natural explanations are proposed, these beliefs and practices lose their explanatory value for new atheists, and have no residual, rational content.[206] As Hitchens summarises, 'Religion has run out of justifications. Thanks to the telescope and the microscope, it no longer offers an explanation of anything important.'[207] This means that, second, the only remaining meaning that these beliefs and practices can have are as expressions of irrationality and mental illness, or, more positively, as irrational epiphenomena of underlying biological and chemical processes.[208] The first option gives rise to the belief of writers like Dawkins and Boghossian that religion is a 'virus of the mind', an 'unclassified cognitive illness disguised as a moral virtue'.[209] Boghossian therefore considers it to be a public health crisis, one that should be 'contained and eradicated', its destruction an achievement comparable to the elimination of smallpox.[210] The second approach attempts to find the underlying objective basis for these subjective irrationalities, spurring the scientist to provide natural accounts of religion through the use of evolutionary biology and psychology, and integrating them into a single scientific-materialist worldview.[211] This naturalistic account of doctrine and practice is supplemented, as we have seen, by patterns of biblical and theological interpretation that arise from presuppositions shared with fundamentalists. This allows atheists to rule out alternative conceptions of God and divine activity that can be held concurrently with scientific description, thereby precluding any resolution to the exclusivity of

[205] Dawkins, *God Delusion*, 51–99.
[206] Cf. Stenger, *Failed Hypothesis*, 77–85, 105–6, 94–102.
[207] Hitchens, *God Is Not Great*, 282.   [208] Cf. LeDrew, *Evolution of Atheism*, 70.
[209] Dawkins, *Devil's Chaplain*, 159–64; Boghossian, *Manual*, 208.
[210] Boghossian, *Manual*, 217–22, 232.
[211] E.g. Dennett, *Breaking the Spell*, 97–199; Dawkins, *God Delusion*, 190–240.

evolution and design. In this way, theological description is reduced to the scientific.

It is useful at this stage of the argument to pause and summarise what has been disclosed by our investigation of the intellectual structure of new atheist and fundamentalist texts. Initially, it appeared that any commonality between the two groups was tenuous at best. Yet analysis revealed that atheists and fundamentalists share two presuppositions: that Scripture's sense is literal, univocal and perspicuous, and that God's activity disrupts and substitutes for natural causation. The first presupposition gave rise to a range of supporting beliefs, chief among them that the literal sense of Genesis is normative, that biblical studies and academic theology are redundant and sophistical, that fundamentalism is the only true form of Christianity, and that Genesis should be interpreted literally. The second presupposition supports yet more shared beliefs, such as the incompatibility of creation and evolution, the ability of science to detect or to fail to detect divine activity and the rejection of theistic evolution. Together, these two presuppositions give rise to the belief of each group that its worldview is exhaustive of reality, with a corresponding reduction of other forms of description and narrative into their own. These shared presuppositions, and their accompanying beliefs have arisen from the common Protestant heritage of fundamentalism and atheism in Britain and America, one based upon a literal reading of Genesis, the use of science for apologetic purposes, and the harmonisation of Scripture and nature into a single system of description. It is this heritage that is now in collapse, and has become polarised into two caricatured positions: one that reads science in light of Scripture, and the other that reads Scripture in the light of science. One affirms and one denies, yet both share the same religious consciousness, agree fully on the terms of their debate, and mutually sustain each other's intellectual structure.

Both new atheists and Protestant fundamentalists, then, presuppose that Scripture's sense is literal, univocal and perspicuous, and that God's activity in nature is disruptive and substitutionary. These two presuppositions support, in turn, a range of auxiliary beliefs that strengthen these presuppositions, and cement the secret sympathy between new atheists and Protestant fundamentalists. This shared intellectual structure is largely inexplicable, however, without the social and political configurations that preserve and accentuate it. It is the social instantiation of this intellectual structure, and its place within a secularised and pluralistic society, that we must now examine.

OPPOSITES ATTRACT

This section will examine the shared social and political orientation of new atheism and Protestant fundamentalism, which grounds, and finds expression in, the intellectual structure we have just examined. New atheists and Protestant fundamentalists do not only share a common intellectual structure, but are complicit in maintaining each other's social identity and core narratives, in an age where pluralism and secularism risk relativizing their exclusive and univocal descriptions of reality. Although opposed, they both play a role in preserving and replicating fundamentalist conceptions of Christianity, and modern understandings of reason, within British and American culture. This line of analysis is broadly similar to that put forward by Cimino and Smith and LeDrew, but differs from it in viewing the intellectual dimension of both groups to be as important as their social and political impetus.[212]

The first stage in this symbiotic relationship is the erection and preservation of social boundaries that police the identities of each. It is a popular stereotype of fundamentalists that they posit a strict distinction between themselves and other groups. In Barr's classic study, this feature of fundamentalist practice is taken as foundational to its worldview, a feature present even in countries such as America, where conservative evangelicalism has traditionally held great cultural influence.[213] Separatism, and a desire for doctrinal and moral purity, is certainly a feature of fundamentalist thought. As Morris and Clark argue, human beings are not united by any spiritual bond whatsoever, for the salvation achieved by Christ 'clearly divided men'.[214] This separation between elect and reprobate extends to the Church itself, which is not the universal spiritual communion of those united in Christ, but simply a local group of committed Christians seeking to follow Scripture, and keep themselves pure from the world.[215] Following their recognition of fundamentalism as religiously normative, new atheists view this dualistic and exclusionary worldview as intrinsic to religion. According to Harris, by rendering it easier to label others, and providing illusory reasons for killing them, almost all sources of division come from religion. Faith destroys natural

---

[212] See Richard Cimino and Christopher Smith, *Atheist Awakening* (Oxford: Oxford University Press, 2014), particularly 30–37; LeDrew, *Evolution of Atheism*.
[213] Barr, *Fundamentalism*, 11–12, 104, 314–15.
[214] Morris and Clark, *Bible Has the Answer*, 161–2.
[215] Morris and Clark, *Bible Has the Answer*, 163–5.

human community, and replaces it with a community based on lies.[216] In the case of Christianity, its dependence upon the denigration of Jews is foundational, so that 'Anti-Semitism is as integral to church doctrine as the flying buttress is to a Gothic cathedral.'[217] For this reason, Hitchens argues that religion is akin to racism.[218] Even here, however, in one of the most common tropes of new atheism, the social reality betrays the rhetoric. As Smith has shown, atheists offer a particularly strong example of a community that is constituted by a strong in-group/out-group mentality.[219] The atheist identity is constituted by objectifying a religious other that is rejected and denigrated, thereby strengthening group solidarity and maintaining rigid social boundaries.[220] Conflict with religion, and social separation from religious believers, is not merely incidental to atheist identity, then, but is constitutive of it, the dualism of rational and irrational, atheist and religious being as important as saved and unsaved, elect and reprobate.[221] As Smith argues:

> to a significant degree, it [atheism] is an identity that provides meaning for the self – and indeed is constituted – by making statements of what is *not* me ... replete with discussion of the beliefs they do *not* possess.[222]

While it is wrong to suppose that this dependence means that atheists have a religion, it is certainly true that, as Farias argues, these anti-religious movements serve a similar social function to religion, providing meaning and a sense of community.[223] As atheist identity is vulnerable – and even dangerous – within communities with high levels of religiosity, the internet has been instrumental in the creation of plausibility structures that support and engender it.[224] Through the internet, individual atheists become part of a community of non-believers in diaspora, where personal and social experiences of perceived marginalisation and victimisation by Christians legitimises the core narratives of new atheism.[225] Yet the

[216] Harris, *End of Faith*, 12, 79–83, 176.   [217] Harris, *End of Faith*, 92.
[218] Hitchens, *God Is Not Great*, 35–6.
[219] Jess M. Smith, 'Becoming an Atheist in America', *Sociology of Religion* 72, no. 2 (2011): 228–9.
[220] Katja M. Guenther, Kerry Mulligan, and Cameron Papp, 'From the Outside In', *Social Problems* 60, no. 4 (2013): 457–75; Cimino and Smith, *Atheist Awakening*, 22.
[221] McGrath, *Why God Won't*, 64–6.   [222] Smith, 'Becoming an Atheist', 228.
[223] Miguel Farias, 'The Psychology of Atheism', in *The Oxford Handbook of Atheism*, ed. Stephen Bullivant and Michael Ruse (Oxford: Oxford University Press, 2013), 468–82.
[224] See Dawkins, *God Delusion*, 26–7, 65–7 for examples of the dangers facing atheists.
[225] Guenther, Mulligan, and Papp, 'From the Outside In', 457–475; Smith, 'Becoming an Atheist', 230–1; Cimino and Smith, *Atheist Awakening*, 85–117.

consequence of this is that any intra-atheist deviation from the core narrative of atheist supremacy and religious delusion is met with intense anger, and even respected atheists such as Julian Baggini have been victimised by these online communities for their failure to conform.[226] Indeed, one data analysis has suggested that online atheist communities are among the most aggressive on the internet, coming behind only 'shock-jock' radio presenters and 'men's rights' organisations in terms of their intolerance.[227] When atheists do gather to meet in physical space, their organisations are often small, poorly attended and given to infighting. In this way, they may have a similar sociology to the small fundamentalist sects that they differentiate themselves from.[228]

The second stage in this symbiotic social relationship is the recognition by both atheists and Protestant fundamentalists that the other represents its social and intellectual opposite. This mutual recognition has been recognised by McGrath, who notes that each considers the other at its most extreme.[229] As Armstrong argues, this mutual picturing of the other serves a symbolic and symbiotic function, each group constructing its identity in relation to the other, in a complex network of affirmation and negation.[230] Accordingly, Harris, Dawkins, Dennett and Loftus all explicitly address their arguments to conservative evangelicals and creationists, and view these Christians as their antithesis and chief enemy.[231] Likewise, fundamentalists are united against what they term 'secular humanism' and its chief weapon of evolution, viewing it as the denial of God's sovereignty, and part of the age-long rebellion of man's word against God's Word, atheism against Christianity.[232]

As Protestant fundamentalists and new atheists view each other as the antithesis of their own worldview, and define their identities in relation to

---

[226] McGrath, *God Won't Go*, 30–1.
[227] 'Reddit's Biggest Atheism Hangout Scores Sky-High for Toxic Content and Bigotry', last modified 16 March 2015, accessed 30 November 2015, www.patheos.com/blogs/friendlyatheist/2015/03/16/reddits-biggest-atheism-hangout-scores-sky-high-for-toxic-content-and-bigotry-data-analysts-say/.
[228] McGrath, *God Delusion*, 254.
[229] McGrath, *God Delusion*, xii. Cf. Alister McGrath, *The Twilight of Atheism* (London: Rider, 2004), 256, 274.
[230] Armstrong, *Case for God*, 7.
[231] Harris, *Letter*, xii, 68; Dawkins, *God Delusion*, xiv-xv; Dennett, *Breaking the Spell*, xi; Loftus, *Why I Became*, 12.
[232] E.g. Morris, *Long War*, 15, 23; Bodie Hodge, 'Evolutionary Humanism: The Bloodiest Religion Ever', in *A Pocket Guide to Atheism*, ed. Ken Ham (Petersburg: Answers in Genesis, 2014), 19–20; Loftus, *Why I Became*, 164–5.

one another, each views the other as the greatest present threat to humanity. This moral and political concern contextualises atheist and fundamentalist beliefs and lends them an urgency that they would otherwise lack. The moral and political impetus behind what might appear to be a purely intellectual debate has been noted by, *inter alia*, Spencer, McGrath, Fuller, Eldridge, and Gould, and is admitted by atheists and fundamentalists themselves.[233] For Protestant fundamentalists, the political and social importance of the debate is clear. As Vaterlai puts it, 'Our society is engaged in a culture war: the Left versus the Right, pro-choice versus pro-life, etc.... . But what is the foundational issue behind all of these battles?' The answer, of course, is evolution.[234] For Ham, all law and morality depend upon the truth of God's sovereign will revealed in Scripture, and it is the challenge to this morality that provokes fundamentalist alarm. 'This really is what the creation/evolution/millions of years conflict is all about. Does God the Creator have the right to tell a person what he must do with his life?'[235] The fundamentalist concern with the moral, social and political consequences of evolution must be seen against the historical context outlined in Chapter 3. Conservative evangelicalism once formed an 'informal establishment' in America, and continues to do so in many communities. Evangelical Protestantism shaped all aspects of life, including, importantly, law and social norms. All of America's major educational institutions were founded upon Scripture, and were explicitly Christian in their teaching.[236] Though offering legal protection to religious minorities, fundamentalists believe that America was founded upon the Protestant faith, so that the Constitution and Bill of Rights should only be interpreted in light of a six-day creation, and the authority of inerrant Scripture.[237] As we saw, this informal establishment began to erode under the pressure of pluralisation and secularisation, to the point where public schools became 'temples of atheism' teaching the 'religion of

---

[233] E.g. Spencer, *Origin of the Species*, xiv–xvi; McGrath, *Why God Won't*, vii–viii; Steve Fuller, 'What Has Atheism Ever Done for Science?', in *Religion and the New Atheism: A Critical Appraisal*, ed. Amarnath Amarasingam (Leiden: Brill, 2010), 60; Niles Eldridge, *The Triumph of Evolution and the Failure of Creationism* (New York: W. H. Freeman, 2000), 10–1; Stephen Jay Gould, 'Evolution as Fact and Theory' in *Science and Creationism*, ed. Asheley Montagu (Oxford: Oxford University Press, 117.
[234] Carl Kerby and Ken Ham, 'The "Evolutionising" of a Culture', in *War of the Worldviews*, ed. Gary Vaterlaus, (Hebron: Answers in Genesis, 2005), 7.
[235] Ham, *The Lie*, 108.
[236] Ken Ham and Greg Hall, *Already Compromised* (Green Forest: Master Books, 2011), 7–14.
[237] Morris, *Long War*, 42, 306–9.

secular humanism'.[238] The rejection of God in contemporary society has three inter-related outcomes for Protestant fundamentalists. First, it results in the devaluation of the most vulnerable in society, such as foetuses, the disabled and the elderly, who are treated as relative to the desires and wishes of the strong.[239] The rejection of Christianity entails the rejection of human dignity, for the *imago dei* – instrumental in the development of individual rights – requires a transcendent referent to maintain its integrity. Second, viewing morality as a product of evolution, culture, or personal choice means that moral values are relative, and lacking in substance.[240] This has the result, third, that there is a wholesale decline in social and personal morality:

With God relegated to the status of a Disney character, we grabbed for all the gifts we could. And what we got in return was adultery, abortion, and AIDS.[241]

For Patterson, evolution leads directly to racism, abortion, business mal-practice and sexism.[242] In the absence of God, there is no basis for personal responsibility, and the outcome of evolution is that, rather than evolving, humanity will devolve into barbarity, creation's material decline since the Fall being matched by the moral decline of the human heart.[243] The logical outcome of the rejection of fundamentalist Protestantism and the adoption of evolution is slavery, Adolf Hitler, and the holocaust. The denigration of non-white peoples was supported by Darwin and his allies, and Hitler himself was 'Evolution in Full Flower', an ardent disciple of Charles Darwin, who sought to implement his programme of the survival of the fittest by killing all non-Arians.[244] In a particularly graphic example of this line of argument, above a picture of decomposing corpses at a Nazi death camp, Hanegraaff places a quotation from Darwin's *Descent of Man*, apparently approving of the extermination of 'savage races'.[245] This historic genocide is mirrored in the ongoing murder of unborn children, on a scale surpassing even the terrors of the Holocaust. For Hodge, Darwinism is directly responsible for hundreds of millions of murders,

---

[238] Ham, *The Lie*, 70–1.   [239] Morris, *Long War*, 137–43.

[240] Paul Copan, 'Does the Moral Argument Show There Is a God?', in *The Apologetics Study Bible*, ed. Ted Cabal (Nashville: Holman Bible Publishers, 2007), 1687.

[241] Hanegraaff, *Farce*, 22.   [242] Patterson, *Evolution Exposed*, 141–9.

[243] Morris, *Long War*, 144–9; Ham, *The Lie*, 112; Whitcomb, *Early Earth*, 12–15.

[244] Ken Ham and A. Charles Ware, *Darwin's Plantation* (Green Forest: Master Books, 2007); Morris, *Long War*, 75; Jerry Bergman, *Hitler and the Nazi Darwinian Worldview* (Kitchener: Joshua Press, 2013).

[245] Hanegraaff, *Farce*, 26.

with the total number of children aborted during the twentieth century running as high as 778,000,000.[246] Because of the dire social and political consequences of inaction, Christians must rally to deny evolution a place in public schools and universities, pushing for alternative syllabuses, and cutting off research funding for scientists that promote an evolutionary worldview.[247]

The political and social consequences of fundamentalism are equally clear to atheists. As Stenger notes, if the issues surrounding the God debate were primarily intellectual, they would be of little relevance.[248] Yet, as Hitchens argues, religion has massive social and political consequences:

violent, irrational, intolerant, allied to racism, tribalism and bigotry, invested in ignorance and hostile to inquiry, contemptuous of women and coercive toward children: organised religion ought to have a great deal on its conscience.[249]

Atheists reverse the accusation levelled by fundamentalists, and accuse Christianity, with its inherent intolerance and bigotry, of causing the Holocaust. German soldiers marched with *Gott mit uns* upon their belts, and as it was Christianity that inspired Hitler to destroy the Jews, Onfray claims that the gas chambers were operated in the name of St John himself.[250] It is this faith, which 'looks forward to the destruction of the world', that has come to influence the domestic and international policy of the United States.[251] For Stenger, a secular, non-religious America is therefore pivotal for the preservation and protection of a world that is on the brink of disaster.[252] Harris fears that fundamentalism could lead to nuclear war, and Dennett believes religion could destroy the world.[253] In contrast to Protestant fundamentalists, new atheists believe that America was founded upon secular principles, and that these secular principles are now being threatened by the doleful effects of religion.[254] Religion suppresses personal freedom and criminalises victimless lifestyle choices such homosexuality, pornography and the smoking of marijuana.[255] It seeks to

[246] Hodge, 'Evolutionary Humanism', 21, 29–30.
[247] Jonathan Wells, *Icons of Evolution* (Washington DC: Regency Publishing, 2000), 240–5.
[248] Stenger, *Folly of Faith*, 301–22. [249] Hitchens, *God Is Not Great*, 56.
[250] Michel Onfray, *In Defence of Atheism* (London: Serpent's Tail, 2007), 164, 187.
[251] Hitchens, *God Is Not Great*, 56; Boghossian, *Manual*, 31–2.
[252] Stenger, *New Atheism*, 47.
[253] Harris, *End of Faith*, 47–8; Dennett, *Breaking the Spell*, 310.
[254] Darwin, *God Delusion*, 60–8.
[255] Harris, *End of Faith*, 153–69; Dawkins, *God Delusion*, 326–9.

control the natural desire for sexual intercourse and influenced the George W. Bush administration to divert millions of dollars from birth control and sex education classes into abstinence programmes that are ineffective and dangerous.[256] It is not only these religiously influenced policies that are to be condemned, however, but Christian morality itself. For Hitchens and Barker, the Christian belief in the divine mandate of morality, and the requirement to love others unconditionally, is unrealistic, impractical and even immoral.[257] In place of such fatuous conceptions, atheists believe morality is the product of evolution, and innate to all.[258] For Harris, reason and science alone are the guarantors of human love and goodness, and the true foundation of each is hedonic utilitarianism, the only objective basis for morality.[259] Rather than denying women their rights, and restricting access to abortion, reason tells us that the value of a foetus is equivalent to that of a rabbit, or, at least, a cow, possessing, as it does, the same capacity for pleasure and pain as these animals do.[260] The struggle, then, is between one worldview that allows us to lead decent and rational lives, and another, which leads into every absurdity and evil. As Stenger summarises the two positions, 'Science flies us to the moon. Religion flies us into buildings.'[261]

As Stahl notes, the objectification of the other as the epitome of all social and political evil means that atheists and fundamentalist view themselves as the sole defenders of Western civilisation, and see each other as representing a subversion of the values that founded America.[262] For this reason, they regard each other as little better than traitors.[263] Yet while the social and political agendas of both groups may appear to be utterly opposed, in reality, they form a symbiotic social relationship. This is the third stage in their social and political dialectic, with each group supporting the social position of the other, and conspiring to preserve the universality of reason, the normativity of fundamentalist Christianity and suspicion over the value of tolerance.

---

[256] Hitchens, *God Is Not Great*, 283–4, 48–55; Stenger, *New Atheism*, 48–53.
[257] Hitchens, *God Is Not Great*, 211–15; Barker, *Godless*, 196.
[258] Harris, *End of Faith*, 175; Stenger, *Folly of Faith*, 249–60.
[259] Harris, *End of Faith*, 190; Harris, *Letter*, 7–8.
[260] Harris, *End of Faith*, 177–8; Dawkins, *God Delusion*, 329–36.
[261] Stenger, *New Atheism*, 59.   [262] Stahl, 'One-Dimensional Rage', 106.
[263] Ronald A. Kuipers, 'The New Atheism and the Spiritual Landscape of the West', in *'God Is Dead' and I Don't Feel So Good Myself*, ed. Andrew David (Eugene: Cascade Books, 2010), 127–8.

Atheists and fundamentalists mutually support each other's social position in three ways. First, the beliefs, practices and public agitation of one group increases both the popularity and extremism of the other. This social dialectic has become increasingly apparent since the 1960s, when the unprecedented moral changes of that time provoked fundamentalists to gradually abandon separatism and return to public life.[264] This led to the political and legal struggle to establish creationist teaching in public schools, and to promote a pro-life and anti-homosexual agenda through state legislatures. The influence of conservative evangelicals upon successive republican administrations has, for the first time in American history, created a political context in which there are intermittent periods of what is a *de facto* religious establishment.[265] Just like the historical British situation, these periods of *de facto* establishment – and their perceived threat to individual freedom – have produced a contrary reaction among the religiously unaffiliated, whose identities have became increasingly anti-religious in the face of fundamentalist agitation. In Pasquale's study, respondents claimed to have become more anti-religious in light of fundamentalist lobbying, while Beit-Hallahmi and Schutzke have noted a growing coalescence between atheism and liberalism, with a marked association between atheistic beliefs and support for the Democratic Party.[266] Fuller, Hauerwas and Beattie have noted how this polarisation of political and religious identities has only increased after the new atheist breakthrough that followed the attacks of September 11th.[267] Yet as Armstrong and McGrath argue, the burgeoning public profile of new atheism, taken with its aggressive rhetoric, only furthers the cause of fundamentalist Christianity.[268] This is celebrated by one of its chief

[264] Inchausti, 'Thomas Merton's Apologies', 3–4.

[265] Cf. Victor J. Stenger, 'What's New About the New Atheism?', *Philosophy Now* April/ May 2010: 13; Cimino and Smith, *Atheist Awakening*, 35.

[266] Frank L. Pasquale, 'A Portrait of Secular Group Affiliates', in *Atheism and Secularity*, vol. I, ed. Phil Zuckerman (Santa Barbara: Praeger, 2010), 69–70; Benjamin Beit-Hallahmi, 'Morality and Immorality among the Irreligious', in *Atheism and Secularity*, vol. I, ed. Phil Zuckerman (Santa Barbara: Praeger, 2010), 132–35: 301–5; Marcus Schulzke, 'The Politics of New Atheism', *Politics and Religion* 6 (2013): 778–9.

[267] Fuller, 'What Has Atheism Done', 58–9; Stanley Hauerwas and Stanley Fish, 'Miltonian Rebukes in an Age of Reason', in *'God Is Dead' and I Don't Feel So Good Myself*, ed. Andrew David (Eugene: Cascade Books, 2010), 111; Beattie, *New Atheists*, 1, 35–6. Also see Stephen Bullivant, 'The New Atheism and Sociology', in *Religion and the New Atheism: A Critical Appraisal*, ed. Amarnath Amarasingam (Leiden: Brill, 2010), 120–4; Dennett, *Breaking the Spell*, 319; Stenger, *Folly of Faith*, 306–9; Smith, 'Becoming an Atheist', 215–6.

[268] Armstrong, *Case for God*, 295; McGrath and McGrath, *Dawkins Delusion?*, 25–7.

proponents Henry Morris, who notes that the attacks of atheists have led to a massive upturn in creationist ministries.[269] The possibility that new atheism will only engender more fundamentalism is explicitly considered by Stenger, who believes that this is, nevertheless, a small price to pay for speaking the truth regarding the falsehoods of religion.[270] The result of the activities of fundamentalists and atheists is that Britain and – in particular – America will become increasingly polarised between religious believers and atheists.

Second, in addition to fostering greater social support and extremism, the symbiotic relationship of new atheism and Protestant fundamentalism serves the additional function of maintaining the relevancy of religion, the normative standing of fundamentalist Christianity and the supposed incompatibility of science and the Christian faith in the contemporary West. Atheists and fundamentalists agree that the question of the truth of religion is fundamental to every other question, and are therefore committed to addressing this question to a Western society that – particularly in Britain – is largely indifferent to matters of religion.[271] This has resulted in the importation of the evolution and design controversy to contexts that have little or no history of such debate, as in Australia, where American-inspired atheist and creationist 'ministries' have been instrumental in raising this debate to a national profile.[272]

Atheists and fundamentalists are not neutral in advancing the relevancy of such questions, however, but do so, as we have seen, with predetermined assumptions regarding the Bible, hermeneutics, theology and the incompatibility of evolution and Christianity. The third aspect of their symbiotic social relation, then, is their mutual assertion of a univocal, modern understanding of reason, in the face of a society that is pluralistic, suspicious of absolute claims to truth, and largely committed to the political and social value of tolerance.

Despite claims by each group that the other is driven by sub-rational motivations, both atheism and fundamentalism are structured upon a shared understanding of reason as largely ahistorical and decontextualised. As truth transcends context, and is stable and univocal, both groups accord primary importance to the propositional and cognitive aspects of

---

[269] Morris, *Long War*, 321–2.   [270] Stenger, *Folly of Faith*, 298–9.

[271] Cf. Hitchens, *God Is Not Great*, 12; Mitchell, 'What Are the Tactics', 44; Samuel Bagg and David Voas, 'The Triumph of Indifference', in *Atheism and Secularity*, vol. II, ed. Phil Zuckerman (Santa Barbara: Praeger, 2010), 91–112.

[272] Ronald L. Numbers, 'Creationists and Their Critics in Australia', in *The Cultures of Creationism*, ed. Simon Coleman and Leslie Carlin (Aldershot: Ashgate, 2004), 117–8.

knowledge – whether religious or otherwise – and do not view these as subsisting within traditions or communities, or requiring any special personal or spiritual discipline on the part of individuals. Indeed, they are suspicious of tradition, community, and spiritual experience, viewing these as irrelevant, or as dangerous deviations from objectivity.[273] These beliefs arise, as we have seen, from each group's inheritance of a Western Protestant worldview that is critical of tradition, ritual, and the role of community in the practice of interpretation.[274] For Protestant fundamentalists, Scripture and the world form a coherent and closed system of truth, the words and verses of the former referring to the historical and physical elements of the latter in a stable and univocal way. Scripture's meaning and teaching is not considered to be contingent upon a specialised tradition of interpretation or a particular community of faith, and, for this reason, its truth is independent of time, place and readership.[275] Christianity, then, is not primarily a personal and contextualised response of trust towards Jesus Christ, but the apprehension and cognitive assent to the perspicuous and timeless teaching of Scripture.[276] As was discussed earlier, new atheists share a similar biblical hermeneutic, yet approach it negatively. Scripture and the world *should* form a closed and coherent system of truth independent of time, place and readership, yet, largely because of Genesis, it fails to do so, and should therefore be rejected. Once again, faith is not primarily an act of trust towards Jesus Christ encompassing intellectual, emotional and volitional elements, but is considered to be purely cognitive, fully separable from the personal and communal elements that surround it.[277] It is precisely because new atheists view truth and reason as being independent of context that Hitchens and Grayling can parallel the ahistorical and decontextualised understanding of fundamentalists by arguing that atheism is not dependent

---

[273] Boghossian, *Manual*, 135; Michael Shermer, 'The Skeptic's Chaplain', in *Richard Dawkins: How a Scientist Changed the Way We Think*, ed. Allan Grafen and Mark Ridley (Oxford: Oxford University Press, 2007), 233; Stahl, 'One-Dimensional Rage', 100; Dawkins, *Devil's Chaplain*, 284–5; Dennett, *Breaking the Spell*, 224–6; Harris, *Fundamentalism and Evangelicals*, 151–5.

[274] Stahl, 'One-Dimensional Rage', 102.

[275] Vf. David K. Clark, 'Is Logic Arbitrary?', in *The Apologetics Study Bible*, ed. Ted Cabal (Nashville: Holman Bible Publishers, 2007), 930–1; Barr, *Fundamentalism*, 310–3; Simon Coleman and Leslie Carlin, introduction to *The Cultures of Creationism*, ed. Simon Coleman and Leslie Carlin (Aldershot: Ashgate, 2004), 6; Harris, *Fundamentalism and Evangelicals*, 151–5.

[276] Barr, *Fundamentalism*, 213–34.

[277] Haught, *Atheism* 5, 12–13. Cf. Boghossian, *Manual*, 29, 64–5.

upon religion for the categories and structure of its thought, but, being the simple absence of belief, is held absolutely and identically throughout time and space.[278] The correlate to this decontextualised understanding of atheism is the decontextualised language of science, which alone is capable of uniting the warring chaos of competing cultures and perspectives around a stable, universal language of scientific description.[279]

An understanding of knowledge as univocal and universal, and a suspicion of the contextualised nature of reason, marks new atheists and Protestant fundamentalists out as holding to a thoroughly *modern* worldview, an aspect of their thought and practice highlighted by Hyman and LeDrew.[280] This modern rationality leads both groups to decry what they perceive as the pervasive relativism of contemporary Western society, a relativism, so they believe, that renders it impossible to advance their aims, and demonstrate the error of their adversaries. This critique has two aspects, one directed against the humanities and social sciences, and the second directed against the principle of political and social tolerance. Dawkins is scathing of the argument that scientific truths might be relative to particular cultures, while Boghossian expresses hatred for what he calls 'epistemic relativism', and the decline of the universality of reason and science.[281] Boghossian and Dennett associate the supposed poverty of existing critiques of religion with the popularity of cultural-anthropological approaches, which seek to investigate the lived systems of meaning held by believers.[282] This is because:

Meaning is subjective – it's a turning away from the world and turning toward our experience in the world, and to the language we use to describe that experience.[283]

If reference is made only to meaning, without reference to physical phenomena, almost anything could be true, and challenging faith and its pernicious morality becomes impossible.[284] This turn-to-meaning is particularly noticeable in the humanities and social sciences. According to Boghossian, 'Cognitive, epistemological, and moral relativism are toxins

---

[278] Hitchens, *God Is Not Great*, 255; Grayling, *Against*, 29–31.
[279] Steve Jones, *The Serpent's Promise* (London: Little, Brown, 2013), 418; Boghossian, *Manual*, 45.
[280] Hyman, *Short History*, 125–53; LeDrew, *Evolution of Atheism*, 7 and 9.
[281] Dawkins, *Devil's Chaplain*, 17–22; Boghossian, *Manual*, 179–81.
[282] Dennett, *Breaking*, 261–3.   [283] Boghossian, *Manual*, 203–4n3.
[284] Boghossian, *Manual*, 190–1. See also Harris, *End of Faith*, 178–82.

that students trained in the humanities regularly consume in large doses.'[285] This critique of the humanities and social sciences is matched by a critique of the political and social virtue of tolerance that supposedly sustains it.[286] Boghossain therefore rejects what he calls 'social liberalism', as well as

the parasitic ideologies that have given that skeleton its corrupted form: relativism, subjectivity, tolerance, diversity, multiculturalism, and respect for difference and inclusion.[287]

The seriousness of the threat posed by religion means that religious belief should be added to the *Diagnostic and Statistical Manual of Mental Disorders*, which would allow the 'removal of existing ethical barriers', and would permit 'special education programs in schools, helping children who have been indoctrinated into a faith tradition, and legitimating interventions designed to rid subjects of the faith affliction'.[288] 'Respect' is the 'weasel word' of our time, according to Dawkins, and has given rise to both creationism and the appeasement strategy of NOMA.[289] Tolerance for the absurdities of religion is not only cowardly and foolish but deadly, for it furthers the cause of terrorism. As Harris argues, 'Some propositions are so dangerous that it may even be ethical to kill people for believing them', and Onfray suggests that atheism must be purged of its association with the Judaeo-Christian virtue of tolerance if Western society is to survive.[290]

Fundamentalists also reject postmodernity, relativism and the neutrality of the state on religious questions. In considering contemporary interpretations of Scripture and other texts, Ham and Hodge echo the concerns of Boghossian over the prominence given to personal and cultural meanings:

In this postmodern age, bizarre interpretations are accepted because people believe they have the right to decide for themselves what a passage means. In other words, meaning is in the eye of the beholder, so you can decide the truth for yourself.[291]

---

[285] Boghossian, *Manual*, 190. See also Dawkins, *Devil's Chaplain*, 35–62.
[286] See LeDrew, *Evolution of Atheism*, 74–88 for an amplification of this argument.
[287] Boghossian, *Manual*, 178–9.   [288] Boghossian, *Manual*, 221–2.
[289] Dawkins, *Unweaving*, 19–21; Dawkins, *Greatest Show*, 4; Dawkins, *God Delusion*, 91, 94.
[290] Harris, *End of Faith*, 52–3; Onfray, *Defence*, 216–17.
[291] Chaffrey, 'How Should We Interpret?', 122.

While this postmodern attitude has the effect of relativizing evolutionary biology and the metanarrative of Darwinism, it must ultimately be rejected, argues Groothuis, as it also relativizes biblical authority and Christian doctrine.[292] Truth belongs not to interpretations but to the text and to the external world, both of which are objective. 'Despite our limitations,' claims Copen, 'we still cannot escape objectivity. To deny its possibility is to affirm its actuality'.[293] This intellectual critique is mirrored by a political one. Echoing the argument of new atheists that the tolerance of the state towards pluralism and multiculturalism furthers extremism, Ham argues that the supposed neutrality of the state furthers secularism and atheism, particularly when this neutrality governs the provision of education in schools.[294]

In rejecting the relevance of culture and context for the construction and interpretation of truth, and favouring a univocal and decontextual-ised understanding of reason, atheists and fundamentalists affirm a modern rationality in the face of intellectual, social and political plural-ism. While fundamentalists are commonly considered to be defending a *pre*-modern conception of religion, Chapters 1–3 have shown that, in its current form, Protestant fundamentalism can only be traced to the late nineteenth or even early twentieth century, when evangelical Protestant-ism assumed a new identity and *modus operandi* in the face of evolution, biblical criticism and social change. As such, fundamentalism is not a pre-modern reaction to modernity, but, as a number of commentators have noted, a development *within* modernity itself, and one that has become increasingly necessary for its self-understanding.[295] While intransigence and intolerance were latterly believed to be the preserve of fundamental-ists only, as Kuipers notes, postmodernism, the threat of terrorism, the failure of classic theories of secularisation and the resurgence of global Christianity have frustrated the core narrative of atheists, who believed

---

[292] Douglas R. Groothuis, 'How Should a Christian Understand Postmodernism?', in *The Apologetics Study Bible*, ed. Ted Cabal (Nashville: Holman Bible Publishers, 2007), 1385–6.

[293] Paul Copen, 'Isn't That Just Your Interpretation?', in *The Apologetics Study Bible*, ed. Ted Cabal (Nashville: Holman Bible Publishers, 2007), 1858.

[294] Ham, *The Lie*, 30–32; Ham, 'Atheists Outline', 11–17.

[295] Cf. Savage, 'A Psychology of Fundamentalism', 31; Harriet A. Harris 'Fundamentalism in a Protestant Context', in *Fundamentalism: Church and Society*, ed. Martyn Percy and Ian Jones (London: SPCK, 2002), 12; Coleman and Carlin, introduction, 24–5; Martin E. Marty and R. Scott Appleby, *The Power and the Glory* (Boston: Beacon Press, 1992), 16–17.

that modernity would result in the demise of religion.[296] The rejection of political and social tolerance towards religion by new atheists is an expression of the fear that the exclusivity of its core narratives and descriptions of reality are partial, incomplete and under threat.[297] Modern and enlightenment reason has failed to bring religious, social and moral unity to the West, and, due to this failure, atheists must now reject the enlightenment value of tolerance in order to preserve enlightenment.[298] New atheism, then, like Protestant fundamentalism, is a product of late modernity, and it is as products of late modernity that both groups must be considered. In defending the universality and univocity of reason, and the shared understanding of Christianity that accompanies it, both groups are complicit in the maintenance of modern understandings of religion and science, understandings which promise certainty and authoritative pronouncements on religious and moral questions.[299] New atheists and Protestant fundamentalists represent the culture of late-modern British and American Protestantism in both its Christian and anti-Christian expressions. Each is a pole in a dialectic of Protestant modernity, struggling to survive, adapt and understand itself in the wake of unprecedented social and intellectual change. In this endeavour, they are parasitic upon one another, each requiring the counter-narrative of the other to differentiate and identify its own.[300] Each unintentionally works with the other to maintain its social position, and, in doing so, the normative status of conservative evangelicalism, and the exclusivity of evolution and design.[301]

It is this symbiotic social and intellectual relationship that results in the conversion and re-conversion of fundamentalists to atheists and *vice versa*. While there is debate as to what proportion of converts to atheism come from conservative evangelical and fundamentalist backgrounds, the evidence seems to point to at least a disproportionate intake from this constituency.[302] As we have seen, this form of Christianity is structured

[296] Kuipers, 'Spiritual Landscape', 127–8. Also see LeDrew, *Evolution of Atheism*, 55.
[297] Cf. Lash, *Pilgrims*, 31.
[298] Stahl, 'One-Dimensional Rage', 107–8; Christopher R. Cotter, 'Consciousness Raising', *International Journal for the Study of New Religions* 2, no. 1 (2011): 77–103.
[299] Stahl, 'One-Dimensional Rage', 97–8. [300] Harding, *Falwell*, 264, 268–9.
[301] Cf. Martin and Appleby, *Power and Glory*, 194.
[302] Cf. Smith, 'Becoming an Atheist', 220, Pasquale, 'A Portrait', 46, 61; Bob Allemayer, 'Atheism and Secularity in North America', in *Atheism and Secularity*, vol. II, ed. Phil Zuckerman (Santa Barbara: Praeger, 2010), 1–22; Ralph W. Hood and Zhuo Chen, 'Conversion and Deconversion', in *The Oxford Handbook of Atheism*, ed. Stephen Bullivant and Michael Ruse (Oxford: Oxford University Press, 2013), 538–9.

by oppositions between the inerrancy and falsehood of Scripture, true Christianity versus liberalism, Church versus world, objectivity versus subjectivity and evolution versus design. The outcome of this intellectual structure is that if Scripture can be shown to contain errors or contradictions, or if science can provide a coherent account of origins, then Christianity is very likely to be false. As summed up by Morris:

> If Genesis were not historically trustworthy, then simple logic showed that neither was the rest of the Bible, including its testimony about Christ.[303]

In Babinski's anthology of those that have abandoned fundamentalism for atheism, loss of faith arising from the inaccuracy of Genesis is a recurring theme.[304] The other recurring theme in these loss of faith narratives is the discovery of error or contradiction in Scripture, which, according to one fundamentalist survey, is even more important for loss of faith than the problem of suffering.[305] Given the intellectual structure of fundamentalism, which locates the authority of Scripture in its inerrancy and internal harmony, if Genesis or any part of the Bible is considered to be at variance with known fact, or contradicts another passage, it is not only the passage in question that should be rejected, but all of Scripture, along with the core Christian doctrines that are based on it.[306] This is confirmed by sociological studies, which reveal that many conservative Christians feel compelled to adopt atheism due to their failure to reach the high standards of biblical certainty expected by their communities.[307] Yet as we saw in relation to the in-group/out-group mentality of certain atheist groups, the identities of those that reject Christianity are closely connected to the Christianity they reject, and atheists often continue to hold similar conceptions of Christianity to the Protestant evangelicalism they leave behind. Because of this, they congratulate themselves in having understood Scripture better than believers themselves, and credit this as the cause of their unbelief:

---

[303] Morris, *Genesis Record*, xii.

[304] E.g. Edward T. Babinski, *Leaving the Fold* (Amherst: Prometheus Books, 1995), 321–7, 360.

[305] E.g. Babinski, *Leaving the Fold*, 325, 343; Terry Mortenson, 'Did Bible Authors Believe in a Literal Genesis?', in *The New Answers Book 3*, ed. Ken Ham (Green Forest: Master Books, 2010), 81–9.

[306] Cf. Graeme Finlay and Stephen Pattermore, 'Christian Theology and Neo-Darwinism Are Compatible' in *Debating Darwin*, ed. Graeme Finlay (Milton Keynes: Paternoster, 2009), 32.

[307] Smith, 'Becoming an Atheist', 216; Pasquale, 'A Portrait', 61.

in trying to be even more biblical, we all discovered what the Bible actually says and as a result lost our faith. Taking the Bible seriously does that. If you read the Scriptures and are not shocked out of all your religious beliefs, you have not understood them.[308]

This reliance upon Protestant categories also structures the narratives atheists use when describing their loss of faith. These are couched in terms of spiritual darkness leading to spiritual light, of moving from childhood to adulthood, and are usually explicitly referred to as 'conversions'.[309] The website of Richard Dawkins contains a section entitled 'Converts Corner', in which former Christians – very often conservative evangelicals – credit Dawkins with saving them from the superstition of faith and liberating them to live happier and more virtuous lives.[310] In Babinski's anthology, the word 'testimony' is even used, explicitly mimicking evangelical conversion narratives.[311] The reason for such conversions is not hard to understand. Atheism preserves the core narratives and beliefs of fundamentalist Christianity while inverting them. It preserves the *content* of fundamentalist Christianity while altering its *form*, inverting it into a negative relationship with these beliefs and narratives, a relationship compatible with the pervasive scepticism of contemporary Western thought. It is successful because, in challenging fundamentalism, it does not confront fundamentalism as something alien, but confronts it as one that shares its consciousness of Christianity and the nature of reason. In attacking fundamentalism, atheism presents fundamentalism with itself.

This chapter has sought to determine whether comparisons between new atheists and Protestant fundamentalists are well founded or spurious. Apart from certain psychological similarities, both groups appear, *prima facie*, to be distinct and unrelated. Analysis revealed, however, that they share a similar intellectual and social structure. This structure is built upon the presuppositions whose genealogy was traced in Chapters 1–3: that Scripture's sense is literal, univocal and perspicuous and that God's activity in nature disrupts and substitutes for natural causation. These presuppositions support, in turn, a range of shared beliefs, chief among

[308] Gericke, 'Can God Exist', 137. See also Barker, *Godless*, xiv, 222; Stenger, *Folly of Faith*, 119.
[309] Richard Cimino and Christopher Smith, 'The New Atheism and the Empowerment of American Freethinkers', in *Religion and the New Atheism: A Critical Appraisal*, ed. Amarnath Amarasingam (Leiden: Brill, 2010), 154; Barker, *Godless*, 42.
[310] 'Convert's Corner', Richard Dawkins Foundation, last modified 4 September 2015, last accessed 2 December 2015, https://richarddawkins.net/community/convertscorner/.
[311] Babinski, *Leaving the Fold*, 15.

them that non-fundamentalist Christians are not truly Christians and that evolution and design are exclusive of one another. New atheists and Protestant fundamentalists, then, share a number of beliefs that have been inherited from a common Protestant culture, a culture now in the process of disintegration. British and American atheism is fundamentalist Protestantism negating itself, the sympathetic antipathy that arises only from grudging admiration.

If this work ended here, however, the true significance of the secret sympathy between Protestant fundamentalist and new atheists would be lost. The concluding chapter will therefore recapitulate the genealogy charted in Chapters 1–3, and integrate it with the discussion undertaken in this present chapter. This will reveal that the foundational presuppositions shared by new atheists and Protestant fundamentalists are, as they have always been, highly unstable, and require additional beliefs and practices to support them. Yet these auxiliary beliefs and practices contradict the presuppositions they are charged with protecting, rendering both new atheist and Protestant fundamentalist thought contradictory, unstable and untenable. This poses questions not only for new atheism and Protestant fundamentalism, however, but also for mainstream Protestant theology, for the presuppositions that ground new atheist and Protestant fundamentalist thought are not *external* to Protestant theology, confronting it as an alien other, but have their genesis, and have long been found within, the theologies of Britain and America.

5

A House Divided

This chapter builds upon the analysis of atheist and fundamentalist thought undertaken in the previous chapter. That analysis revealed how new atheists and Protestant fundamentalists share a range of beliefs and attitudes towards the interpretation of Scripture, the nature of knowledge and the significance of modern science for the truth of the Christian faith. These beliefs are supported by two shared presuppositions: that Scripture's sense is literal, univocal and perspicuous and that divine activity in nature is disruptive or substitutionary. This chapter presents two arguments in light of the preceding analysis. First, that the opposing positions of atheists and fundamentalists are unstable and require additional strategies to stabilise them. Yet these strategies fail, and conflict with their foundational presuppositions and supporting beliefs, rendering each form of thought self-contradictory. Second, through a recapitulation of the genealogy of Chapters 1–3, and its integration with the analysis of Chapter 4, it will be argued that the Reformation in England inadvertently gave rise to presuppositions whose ambiguity and instability have generated two contradictory positions in atheism and fundamentalism. These conclusions pose serious questions not only for our understanding of new atheist and Protestant fundamentalist thought but to historic and contemporary forms of Protestant theology as well. This brings the question of new atheism and Protestant fundamentalism from the margins of academic theological enquiry to the centre and raises the prospect of a new field of diagnostic and reparative enquiry for both ecclesiastical historians and theologians.

NEW ATHEISTS

The analysis undertaken in the previous chapter revealed that new atheists view their position as being founded upon the natural sciences. Science is the means by which we see the universe for what it is, and what science cannot discover almost certainly does not exist. Science offers a universal and irrefutable basis for knowledge, and a sure foundation for our moral and political thinking. The belief that science can answer all types of question, and exhausts all that there is to know – sometimes described as *scientism* – is a central stabilising and exclusionary strategy employed by new atheists. It is the primary means by which the presuppositions that new atheists share with fundamentalists remain atheistic and anti-religious. If scientism were questioned, or shown to be false, the outright rejection of the spiritual realities described in Scripture would not be possible, nor would the rejection of alternative models of divine activity that do not entail the disruption or substitution of natural causation. Scientism is particularly important in relation to the latter, for, without it, new atheists would be forced to admit that there may be forms of divine activity that are undetectable by science, and that theological enquiry may be necessary to describe their nature and operation.

Central to the stabilising strategy of scientism are three beliefs: that science entails no metaphysical assumptions, that its universal scope is demonstrated by its success and that its universal jurisdiction is confirmed by the failure of religion. The first two beliefs are found within the following quotation from Loftus:

With modern science, we simply don't need metaphysical assumptions ... The bottom line, if nothing else, is that science justifies itself pragmatically.[1]

The pragmatic justification of science does not simply prove its reliability, however, but forms the basis for much stronger claims regarding the capacity of scientific description to exhaust reality, and, *a fortiori*, disprove religious claims. According to Stenger, the proposition 'it is wrong to accept any claims that cannot be verified in principle by science' is proved by science's practical success, and does not need to be demonstrated by any further philosophical argument.[2] This is contrasted with religion, whose repeated failure confirms the universal jurisdiction of science. While science earns our trust through its success, religion has

---

[1] Loftus, *Why I Became*, 115.   [2] Stenger, *New Atheism*, 61–2.

destroyed our trust by its repeated failure.[3] For Dawkins, the success of science disproves all religious claims, and the falsehood of religion is further demonstrated by the way in which traditional cultures will quickly abandon their beliefs when presented with it.[4] Materialism, then, is understood not as a philosophical position but a scientific one, and one that is 'eminently testable and falsifiable'.[5]

Four moves bring these beliefs into relation with each other. First, it is argued that science has beneficial practical effects. Second, that the practical success of science means that its methods and conclusions are true. Third, that its practical success and resulting trustworthiness mean that we have no reason to think that there are any questions or problems that science cannot answer. This third move is guaranteed by a fourth, holding up religion as a rival worldview whose failures only confirm the success of science. What is interesting about these moves is that, from the perspective of many leading new atheists, they require no philosophical or metaphysical beliefs at all, but are simply self-evident, and follow naturally from the existence of science as a discipline. There are, however, a number of very large assumptions in this position. First, it presumes that utility entails truth. Second – and following from the explanatory monism recounted in the previous chapter – it presumes that scientific description is exhaustive. Third, and most curiously of all, it presumes that these two assumptions are not philosophical, but that, nevertheless, they compel assent to certain metaphysical truths.

While there are a number of difficulties with these assumptions, we will confine our attention to only two. The first is with the pragmatic argument that the success of science proves the truth of its universal competency. This argument proves too much, however, for the practical success of religion in encouraging happiness, altruism and community may then be taken as proof of its truth also. While new atheists may question these benefits, this questioning is made problematic by the undisputed evolutionary benefits that religion has brought to humanity. If religious beliefs did not accrue benefits, they would not have enjoined the universal success they have. As Fiala suggests then, at the very least, a pragmatist philosophical approach must take a far more conciliatory approach towards religion than most new atheist writers would be

---

[3] Stenger, *Folly of Faith*, 25.
[4] Dawkins, *Magic of Reality*, 23; Dawkins, *Devil's Chaplain*, 17–22.
[5] Stenger, *New Atheism*, 161.

willing to countenance.[6] The second difficulty with these assumptions is the naivety of believing that science, and the anti-religious position of new atheism, require no metaphysical assumptions. A number of commentators have expressed serious doubt regarding this belief. Ward sees Dawkins's *The God Delusion* as a primarily philosophical work, utilising the natural sciences to draw metaphysical conclusions.[7] Cunningham views *The God Delusion* as an extra-scientific work, designed to strengthen a materialist interpretation of Darwinism, at a time when this interpretation is under strain from within science itself.[8] Murphy also argues that writers like Dawkins drift from science to philosophy, yet believes that this is largely unconscious, due to the tendency of naturalism to overlook its own philosophical commitments.[9] The critique of new atheism as philosophy masquerading as science is one shared not only by academic commentators but also fundamentalists, who have long denounced Darwinism as materialism masquerading as science. Johnson, for example, argues that the philosophical framework in which data is analysed and interpreted by scientists is eliminative materialism.[10] These critiques are related to those of Pigliucci, who, though an atheist himself, is scathing about the philosophical naivety of new atheist writers. To argue that all non-theological disciplines are 'science', argues Pigliucci, is to ignore the disciplinary boundaries and methodological differences between natural science, the social sciences, the humanities and the discipline of philosophy. This 'disciplinary imperialism' not only leads to confusions and category errors, but actually issues in a form of anti-intellectualism that harms the cause of atheism. Pigliucci's critique, however, has been rejected by Stenger, who continues to affirm his belief in the universal jurisdiction of natural science, and its primacy over philosophy.[11]

While many new atheist authors claim that their scientific worldview requires no philosophical assumptions, others, however, are open to

---

[6] Andrew Fiala, 'Militant Atheism, Pragmatism, and the God-Shaped Hole', *International Journal for Philosophy of Religion* 65 (2009): 139–51.

[7] Keith Ward, *God, Chance and Necessity* (Oxford: Oneworld Publications, 1996), 11.

[8] Cunningham, *Pious Idea*, 266–7, 320–32; see also Alvin Plantinga, 'The Dawkins Confusion: Naturalism "Ad Absurdam",' in *God Is Great, God Is Good*, eds. William Lane Craig and Chad Meister (Downers Grove: Inter-Varsity Press, 2009), 248.

[9] Nancey Murphy, 'Engaging Robert J. Russell's Alpha and Omega', *Zygon* 45, no. 1 (2010): 197–201.

[10] E.g. Johnson, *Darwin on Trial*, 106.

[11] Massimo Pigliucci, 'New Atheism and the Scientistic Turn in the Atheism Movement', *Midwest Studies in Philosophy* 38 (2013): 152–3.

celebrating the philosophical debt of science in general, and new atheist writings in particular. Dennett, for example, praises Dawkins' works not only as examples of scientific research, but also as works of *philosophy*.[12] Moreover, Dennett is suspicious of scientists who believe that fact can be isolated from philosophical assumptions, for 'there is no such thing as philosophy-free science; there is only science whose philosophical baggage is taken on board without examination'.[13] What Dennett does not address, however, is the difficulties that remain even *after* such philosophical assumptions are admitted, for it is these that render the scientism of new atheists unstable and self-contradictory. Consider the following the quotation from Park, which vocalises the implicit assumption of much new atheist literature:

Science is the only way of knowing – everything else is just superstition.[14]

The philosophical claim advanced by this statement is that the only knowledge we have is scientific knowledge. As Stenmark argues, however, the proposition 'the only knowledge we have is scientific knowledge' is self-refuting, for it is not a scientific proposition at all but a philosophical one. It has not – nor could be – disclosed by empirical investigation. Indeed, it is not even an essential component of methodological naturalism.[15] As Ruse argues, methodological naturalism does not rule out the existence of God or the spiritual realities taught by religion. Rather, it simply does not ask the kinds of question that would take God, spiritual realities and divine activity into account.[16] The error of many new atheists is to take the absence of scientific questions implicating God to mean that God does not or cannot exist, as science, in their thinking, exhausts all the questions that can be asked. As Turner has argued, however, the idea that one discipline could exhaust all questions, or would prohibit the asking of certain questions, is, echoing Pigliucci, irrational and anti-intellectual.[17] While Stenmark accuses Dawkins, *inter*

---

[12] Daniel C. Dennett, '*The Selfish Gene* as a Philosophical Essay', in *Richard Dawkins: How a Scientist Changed the Way We Think*, ed. Allan Grafen and Mark Ridley (Oxford: Oxford University Press, 2007), 101–15.

[13] Dennett, *Dangerous Idea*, 21.

[14] Robert L. Park, *Superstition: Belief in an Age of Science* (Princeton: Princeton University Press, 2010), 215.

[15] Mikael Stenmark, *Scientism* (Aldershot: Ashgate, 2001), 21–2, 32–3.

[16] Michael Ruse, 'Naturalism and the Scientific Method', in *The Oxford Handbook of Atheism*, ed. Stephen Bullivant and Michael Ruse (Oxford: Oxford University Press, 2013), 383–97.

[17] Denys Turner, *How to Be an Atheist* (Cambridge: Cambridge University Press, 2002).

alia, of consciously using philosophy to create an atheist-scientific ideology, this credits new atheist writings with a level of self-consciousness they lack. On the contrary, the univocal and exclusive nature of the new atheist narrative presumes the universality and self-evident nature of the scientific ideology they hold, and views the presumptions that ground this rationality *not* as foundational metaphysical or philosophical presuppositions but integral and constituent parts of reason itself, without which its exercise is impossible. This belief is both true and false. Its truth lies in the fact that, without it, the distinct form of *new atheist* rationality is impossible, for the realisation that its scientific ideology is dependent on philosophical presuppositions that are typically unexamined, unjustified and even self-contradictory would destabilise its core narrative. Its falsehood lies, of course, in the fact that the new atheist narrative simply presupposes the capacity of science to exhaust reality, and that this presumption is philosophical, not scientific.

New atheists are therefore caught in a double bind. If they refrain from consideration of philosophical issues, preferring instead to cite the utilitarian value of science as proof of its universal jurisdiction and exhaustive nature, they are vulnerable to analogous pragmatic arguments for the moral, hedonistic and evolutionary benefits of religious faith. If, however, they admit their philosophical assumptions, and attempt to argue for them, they make two fatal concessions. First, they admit that new atheism is as dependent on metaphysical assumptions and philosophical argumentation as the religious beliefs they attack. Second, they must jettison their principal narrative that the only knowledge is scientific knowledge, for this narrative is secured by a philosophical, not scientific, proposition, and one that is self-refuting. Without justification and repair, the philosophical superstructure that supports the belief that God's activity can only be disruptive and substitutionary, and that if science cannot detect such activity it does not exist, will remain self-contradictory and unstable.

Yet just as new atheists are dependent upon philosophical presuppositions that are undisclosed and unjustified, so too are they dependent upon theological beliefs that are unconscious, naïve and incompatible with their irreligious stance. Given that new atheism's sole intention is the eradication of religion, this is a surprising claim. Yet, as Chapters 1–4 have demonstrated, new atheists in Britain and America are historically, intellectually and socially dependent upon Protestantism, and, since the late nineteenth century, increasingly dependent upon Protestantism in its most reactionary aspect. New atheists are intellectually dependent upon Protestant Christianity in four ways. First, they are unaware that, in order to disprove the existence of God, divine creation and the errancy of the Scriptures, they must assume – and sometimes defend – a large number of theological beliefs, and engage in the task of theology. As discussed earlier, new atheist texts are replete with arguments concerning the nature of God. One of the best examples comes from Dan Barker's *Godless*, where the author engages in a sustained theological exploration whose intent is to show that God's attributes are impossible or self-contradictory. Barker argues, for example, that God cannot know every-thing, for this would create an infinite loop of knowing that, as modern computers show, would be physically impossible, and could even result in the destruction of God's mind.[18] On the subject of divine eternity, Barker has these insights:

If God is outside of time, then is time outside of God? If so, there is something else besides God in the cosmos. To say that God does not exist within space-time is to say God does not exist.[19]

These explorations terminate in the argument that God cannot love us, as love requires vulnerability, which an omnipotent God lacks. This diffi-culty is increased by the qualitative difference between Creator and creature, for '[y]ou can't have a love relationship with someone who is not your equal'.[20] Another example comes from Long, who ponders whether God is powerful enough to make a burrito that is so hot that he is incapable of eating it:

If he can eat any burrito he makes, he can't make one hot enough; thus, he's not omnipotent. If he makes one too hot to eat, he can't bear the product of his own creation; thus, he's not omnipotent. As I hope you realize from this illustration, an omnipotent being cannot exist.[21]

The crucial point to draw from Barker and Long's arguments is not their lack of sophistication but their *theological* form, that in order to disprove God's existence atheists must adopt, defend and utilise a particular doc-trine of God. The god of Barker, for example, is a being who is incapable of transcendence, while Long's god has a material form, and is capable of eating. The deductions made by new atheist writers are therefore directly analogous to the reflection of Christian theologians, yet are undertaken with a negative, anti-Christian intent. The same dependence is shown in new atheist attitudes towards the supposed falsehood of Scripture.

---

[18] Barker, *Godless*, 121–4.   [19] Barker *Godless*, 139.   [20] Barker, *Godless*, 150–1.
[21] Long, *Biblical Nonsense*, 145.

In order to prove the falsehood of Scripture, new atheists, as we have seen, must assume that the Bible is a harmonious whole, without contradiction, teaching both spiritual and scientific truth. This belief is strengthened by the literal and univocal hermeneutic they adopt, which they are swift to defend against alternatives. Without such beliefs, it is not possible to disprove the truth of Scripture by giving examples of supposed internal contradiction, or variance with known fact. An analogous reliance is demonstrated in new atheist arguments against design. As Sarfati, Anderson, Stenmark and Fuller argue, when new atheists cite examples of supposedly poor design, or the existence of suffering, as proofs of the absence of design, providence and even the existence of God, they fail to see that these are not scientific arguments but theological ones. They imply the normative status of certain beliefs regarding creation and its creator, and to launch them is to engage in the task of theology.[22] There is not, of course, anything wrong with new atheists engaging in such theological argumentation. Yet it is naïve of new atheists to believe that their investigations are narrowly scientific, or could only have an irreligious outcome. As Hauerwas and Fish remind us, there is nothing in the arguments of the new atheists that has not been raised, many times before, by Christian theology. The only difference, of course, is that Christian theologians typically handle such questions with more competence.[23] Properly speaking, then, much of new atheism is not atheism at all, if by that word is meant – as its proponents conventionally argue – the simple absence of a belief in God. Rather, what new atheists are engaged in is atheology, the utilisation and re-narration of theological categories to establish and perpetuate an anti-Christian worldview.[24]

This is nowhere clearer than in the second form of new atheist dependence on theology: its dependence on fundamentalist Protestantism for the specific content of its thought. As Chapter 4 showed, at both the intellectual and social level, new atheist thought possesses very little specific content of its own, gaining its subject matter almost entirely from Protestant fundamentalism. As the present chapter has outlined, where it *does* possess specific content – such as the exhaustive capacity of science to describe reality – it is naïve and self-contradictory. This brings us to the third aspect of new atheist dependence, that the plausibility of its thought

---

[22] Sarfati, *By Design*, 191; Anderson, *Why We Must*, 55; Stenmark, *Scientism*, 109–15; Fuller, 'What Has Atheism Done', 63–5.
[23] Hauerwas and Fish, 'Miltonian Rebukes', 118–19.
[24] Cf. Robertson, *Dawkins Letters*, 125–6.

is largely negative in form. If, in itself, new atheist thought is contradict-ory and unfounded, it acquires logical coherence and psychological satis-faction from its unremitting engagement with fundamentalist religion. In its rejection of six-day creationism, an inerrant, self-authenticating Bible and the castigation of the social and political errors of fundamentalism, it is plausible and even impressive. Yet this is a *negative* plausibility, one whose success masks new atheism's errors, and exaggerates the coherence of its epistemological and metaphysical claims.

This sleight of hand is displayed in new atheism's fourth form of dependence upon theological categories, the use of quasi-theological lan-guage to describe the natural world and our place within it. Consider the following quotation from Carl Sagan, which often features in new atheist publications:

The cosmos is all that is or was or ever will be. Our feeblest contemplations of the cosmos stir us – there is a tingling in the spine, a catch in the voice, a faint sensation, as if a distant memory, of falling from a height. We know we are approaching the greatest of mysteries.[25]

This quotation has a number of interesting features. First is the eternity and limitlessness of the cosmos: it is all that there will ever be, and we are only small and insignificant parts of it. Second is the effect that the cosmos has upon human beings. It makes the spine tingle and the voice catch in wonder, while the contemplation of its great immensity leads to disorien-tation and a sense of floating through the air. Third, and perhaps most telling, is the unfathomable mysteriousness of the cosmos, which, as 'the greatest of mysteries' is like approaching the holy of holies. As Ross argues, in rhetoric of this kind, nature has become a god, who is the originator and sustainer of all that is, was, and ever will be.[26] No one could object to writers like Sagan engaging in occasional poetic excur-sions to illustrate scientific findings. Yet when such imagery assumes a theological form, and is advanced as an alternative to religion, it becomes clear that these are not merely artistic renderings of scientific discoveries but expressions of a rival worldview, one that deploys a range of rhet-orical weaponry to champion its worldview over others.[27] When this

---

[25] 'The Shores of the Cosmic Ocean', *Cosmos – Carl Sagan Episode Scripts*, last modified 14 September 2012, accessed 5 December 2015, www.springfieldspringfield.co.uk/view_ episode_scripts.php?tv-show=cosmos-carl-sagan&episode=s01e01.

[26] T. M. Ross, 'The Implicit Theology of Carl Sagan', *Pacific Theological Review* 18, no. 2 (1985): 30–1.

[27] Ross, 'Implicit Theology', 30.

happens, Ross argues, science and nature have become the functional equivalents of a religion, yet one that continues to unconsciously utilise theological language and categories. It is not only a functional equivalence between the universe and God that Ross notices, however, but the existence of *duties* in relation to the mystery of nature.[28] This can be detected in statements by Dawkins. The great mystery of the universe is not only to be marvelled at, but demands certain actions and attitudes from us:

An astronomically overwhelming majority of the people who could be born never will be. You are one of the tiny minority whose number came up. Be thankful that you have a life ... [29]

We should be grateful to the mystery of the universe for the great improbability of our birth, for we, a small remnant, have been given life from the great mass of those who were never born. This gratitude, however, does not carry with it the expectation of one to be grateful to, nor the prospect that the gift received should extend past death. To complete the quotation:

Be thankful that you have a life, and forsake your vain and presumptuous desire for a second one.

Here the improbability of our birth makes the hope of eternal life presumptuous and vain. Our duty is not one of hope, but of gratitude and submission: gratitude for the gift of life, and submission to the scientific fact that there is no afterlife, and no alternative spiritual reality. A scientific attitude towards nature, for writers like Dawkins, gives rise in an unproblematic way to such existential duties.[30]

The frequent use of quasi-religious language to describe the universe and our place within it by atheist and non-religious writers is – perhaps surprisingly – admitted by the leading atheist and sceptic Michael Shermer, and has also been noted by Vernon, MacArthur and Johnson.[31] The significance of such language is twofold. First, it demonstrates the perseverance of traditional theological categories and forms of expression

---

[28] Ross, 'Implicit Theology', 27–8.
[29] Richard Dawkins, 'The Atheist', Salon.com, last modified 30 April 2005, last accessed 5 December 2015, www.salon.com/2005/04/30/dawkins/.
[30] For a similar interpretation see Patterson, *Territories*, 179–80.
[31] Michael Shermer, *Why Darwin Matters* (New York: Henry Holt and Company, 2006), 159, 184n3; Vernon, *After Atheism*, 66–8; MacArthur, *Battle*, 11–14; Johnson, *Darwin on Trial*, 82–5.

in new atheist texts, and their use by atheists to construct a worldview that is psychologically satisfying and socially habitable. This is important given the absence of any positive content to atheism, its intrinsic negativity, and its overly cognitive form. Second, such quasi-religious language provides atheists with the means to conceal the non-exhaustive character of science. As a discipline whose sole purpose is to gain knowledge of the universe by means of testable explanations and predictions, scientific description lacks the vocabulary and grammar to express personal experiences of wonder or spirituality. The use of such language in ostensibly scientific discourse gives *the impression* that science itself generates and supports such poetic, emotionally charged descriptions, creating the illusion that it can offer a form of description that encompasses both the material and personal worlds. Yet this is false, as this language is not derived from the methods or conclusions of science at all, but is, instead, drawn from literature and the arts. This feature of new atheist thought is explicitly considered – and rejected – in another example from Richard Dawkins:

It is raining DNA outside. On the bank of the Oxford canal at the bottom of my garden is a large willow tree, and it is pumping downy seeds into the air ... [Spreading] DNA whose coded characters spell out specific instructions for building willow trees that will shed a new generation of downy seeds ... It is raining instructions out there; it's raining programs; it's raining tree-growing, fluff-spreading, algorithms. That is not a metaphor, it is the plain truth. It couldn't be any plainer if it were raining floppy discs.[32]

What is curious about this passage is the explicit statement that the poetic imagery Dawkins uses is *not* metaphorical, but is 'plain truth'. Such imagery is not an interpretation or artistic rendering of certain phenomena for Dawkins, but is *scientific fact*. As Midgely notes, such language is not mere 'flannel' to sell popular science, but is often something far more serious: a manifestation of the attempt to raise science – and, in particular, evolution – into an ideology and surrogate religion, one which absorbs all existing disciplines and modes of description into itself. Descriptions of natural phenomena like the foregoing passage mask the inability of science to provide meaning-rich descriptions of reality by claiming that such descriptions are actually scientific. Insofar as such claims are hollow, they are disingenuous and misleading.[33]

---

[32] Dawkins, *Blind Watchmaker*, 111.   [33] Midgely, *Evolution as a Religion*, 67.

As we have seen, new atheist dependence upon theological categories, like its indebtedness to philosophy, is typically undisclosed and unconscious. The naivety of British and American new atheist engagements with theology is highlighted when we contrast their self-understanding to that of French atheism. There is a realisation among contemporary French atheists that atheism has, and is, heavily dependent upon the Christian theology it rejects, and that sustained reflection is required if it is to be rid of religion, and produce a genuinely godless philosophy.[34] This realisation is prevalent even among popular French atheists such as Michel Onfray, who most resemble the new atheists of Britain and America. Onfray laments Christianity's continuing influence upon atheism, and he argues for the ejection of Christian morality from its ethics, especially the virtue of tolerance and respect for difference, which, he believes, fuels relativism and social and political quietism.[35]

A critical awareness of the dependence of atheism on Christianity is difficult for new atheists, however, due to their heavy dependence upon Protestant fundamentalism. Writing in a Roman Catholic context, Onfray's primary critique of Christianity is not intellectual but political, social and moral, launching attacks upon the power of the Church, and the life-denying morality it teaches. Yet new atheists in Britain and America are doubly barred from attaining consciousness of the theological nature of their beliefs. First, because they share the same content and attitudes as Protestant fundamentalists, they typically reject all non-fundamentalist Christianity as heterodox. This means that new atheists generally understand Christianity to be stable and unambiguous, and do not, therefore, consider their commitment to fundamentalist theology to be in any way significant or problematic. Second, as it possesses an intellectual dependence upon Protestant fundamentalism, the realisation that it was parasitic upon an unrepresentative – and perhaps heterodox[36] – strain of Christianity would entail new atheism's collapse, for it is sustained by the belief that it is intellectually independent of Christianity, and that it has accurately understood what it rejects. This provides new atheists with strong reasons for not investigating their dependence upon theology.

---

[34] Christopher Watkin, *Difficult Atheism* (Edinburgh: Edinburgh University Press, 2011), 1–16.

[35] Onfray, *Defense*, 47, 55–8, 213–17.

[36] See Jack B. Rogers and Donald K. McKim, *The Authority and Interpretation of the Bible* (San Francisco: Harper & Row, 1979).

This lack of self-understanding culminates with the claim rehearsed in Chapter 4, that atheism is not a belief, and has no dependence upon the religion it rejects. In *Letter to a Christian Nation*, Harris makes the following pronouncement:

Atheism is not a philosophy; it is not even a view of the world; it is simply an admission of the obvious. [37]

While Grayling argues that:

atheism is to theism as not collecting stamps is to stamp-collecting ... To think of non-stamp-collectors as theists think of atheists, stamp-collectors would have to that non-stamp-collectors have stamp interests of (so to speak) a *positively* negative kind; that they share their own obsessions and interests about stamps *but in reverse*, for example in the form of hating stamps, deliberately doing stamp-related non-stamp-collecting things, and the like.[38]

In light of the preceding analysis carried out in this work, such claims are implausible, as both historic and contemporary forms of atheism in Britain and America have been shown to be wholly dependent on Protestantism for their motivation and intellectual structure. Grayling's argument concerning non-stamp-collecting is particularly ironic, given that it is made in one of his many polemical works seeking to prove the hatefulness and irrationality of a phenomenon he claims to take no real interest in. His conduct betrays his argument. The naivety of otherwise intelligent men like Grayling arises from the tradition in which they have been educated. As Murphy notes, atheists have their own historically situated tradition of naturalism, which, paradoxically, teaches them that they have no tradition, and therefore no historical and social dependence upon the religion they reject.[39] It should not be thought, however, that such critiques come only from Christians. An atheist commentator such as Eller, for example, has advanced the following critique of new atheism:

The new atheism, and all past argumentative atheism, is as much in the theist universe as theism is: in fact, so far all atheism that argues against Christianity has been as much in the Christian universe as Christianity is ... the new atheism is trapped in the gravitational pull of theism generally and Christianity specifically as surely as any Christian congregation. If recent psycholinguistics is right, then arguing against god(s) is just as effective at perpetuating god-concepts as arguing

---

[37] Harris, *Letter*, 51.   [38] Grayling, *God Argument*, 133.
[39] Murphy, 'Alpha and Omega', 197–201, 203.

for god(s). No doubt this is why theists love to debate atheists: they can get atheists publically talking about their god(s)![40]

As Antony notes, the only way in which new atheists could have no dependence upon theism is if they had no knowledge of it. Yet as new atheists come from a British and American culture indebted to Protestant Christianity, no such possibility exists.[41] As Eller concludes, in such a context, the only way to be free from a dependence on Christianity is to stop all reference to, and engagement with, religious questions, something that, as Grayling illustrates, shows no signs of occurring.[42]

The unconscious dependence of new atheist thought upon fundamentalism means, moreover, that it ignores mainstream Christian beliefs and practices, leaving its rejection of Christianity empirically uninformed and unsubstantiated. As Vernon notes, the fundamentalist caricature that new atheists present bears no relation to the average churchgoer in Britain and America.[43] While McGrath overstates the marginalisation and eccentricity of fundamentalists, there is nevertheless truth in his statement that atheists like Dawkins present 'the pathological as if it were the normal, the fringe as it were the centre, crackpots as if they were mainstream'.[44] To read the works of new atheists is to enter into a closed canon, where atheists acquire the majority of their information regarding religion from other atheist works. As Robertson argues, this is akin to Christians learning about evolution from six-day creationist texts.[45] There is no sustained interest in testing what is read. Having reached the conclusion that all religions are the same, and that all are false, Dawkins, Grayling and Stenger argue that the actual beliefs and practices of Christians are irrelevant, and beneath their attention.[46] While this situation arises largely from the normative status of fundamentalist thought for atheists, it also arises due to the historic Protestant principle of the perspicuity of Scripture, and the rejection of specialism in theology. As we noted earlier, for new atheists like Barker, '[w]hat the Bible means in plain English is what most people read. If it embarrasses itself in plain English, then it fails to make its point'.[47] Because of this attitude, new atheist texts often read

---

[40] Jack David Eller, 'What Is Atheism?', in *Atheism and Secularism*, ed. Phil Zuckerman (Santa Barbara: Praeger, 2010), 15.

[41] Michael Antony, 'Where's the Evidence?', *Philosophy Now* April/May 2010: 18–19.

[42] Eller, 'What Is Atheism?', 16–17.   [43] Vernon, *After Atheism*, 89.

[44] McGrath and McGrath, *Dawkins Delusion?*, 5.   [45] Robertson, *Dawkins Letters*, 57.

[46] Eagleton, *God, Faith, and Revolution*, 51. Cf. Dawkins, *God Delusion*, 14–15; Grayling, *God Argument*, 41; Stenger, *New Atheism*, 12.

[47] Barker, *Godless*, 185.

like the work of autodidacts, righting the perceived obfuscation of reli-gious elites, who have rejected the plain meaning of Scripture to conceal its error.[48] Yet, as Lash argues, new atheists are wrong to suppose that the views of an untrained, non-academic atheist are as valuable as a specialist Christian theologian. While many practices of the Christian life – such as prayer and worship – are accessible to all, theology is a 'vast body of texts and arguments', and *is* specialist.[49] New atheist rejection of specialism in theology and biblical interpretation leads to the strange yet not uncom-mon belief that atheists understand canonical texts better than Christians, a belief which further encourages the neglect of actual Christian beliefs and hermeneutical methods.[50] This is an important factor in the new atheist belief that non-literal interpretations of biblical texts are recent innovations, a view that, as Lash reminds us, is almost the opposite of the truth.[51] The injustice of these representations is made greater by the occasional admission from new atheists that faith is more complex and nuanced than their critiques would suggest. Dennett can admit that the category of 'religion' should be applied loosely, and should be attentive to diverse practices and beliefs. Likewise, Dawkins can admit at times that faith does not provide the motivation for most violence considered 'reli-gious', and that it was secular philosophy, not Christianity, that halted the discovery and eventual acceptance of evolution.[52] Yet these occa-sional admissions are not accorded a functional role within new atheist thought, and serve no real purpose. The neglect of actual Christian beliefs and practices, the perceived normative standing of fundamentalism, and the belief that atheists understand Scripture better than Christians, largely confirm Hart's thesis that new atheism consists of 'attitudes masquerad-ing as ideas, emotional commitments disguised as intellectual honesty'.[53] For this reason, as Eagleton and McGrath argue, new atheist texts end up replicating the worst features of the irrational forms of faith that they reject.[54]

If new atheist narratives concerning the universality and exhaustive capacity of scientific description require additional philosophical and theological presuppositions that lead to self-contradiction, further

---

[48] Cf. Lash, *Pilgrims*, 3.   [49] Lash, *Pilgrims*, 5n9.

[50] E.g. Gericke, 'Can God Exist', 137. Cf. Onfray, *Defense*, xii.   [51] Lash, *Pilgrims*, 9.

[52] Dennett, *Breaking the Spell*, 7; Dawkins, *Devil's Chaplain*, 186–9; Dawkins, *Greatest Show*, 22–7.

[53] Hart, *Atheist Delusions*, 19.

[54] Eagleton, *God, Faith, and Revolution*, 52; McGrath and McGrath, *Dawkins Delusion?*, 25.

difficulties attend these narratives in their own right, difficulties that, once again, render new atheism self-contradictory. We considered Dennett's conception of Darwinism as a 'universal acid' in Chapter 4. The evolution of life and human rationality through variation and natural selection is viewed by all new atheist writers as undermining religion. By offering a natural explanation for life, evolution also produces a natural explanation for the existence of religious belief. Religion is therefore shown not to be the result of divine revelation, but to be a stage in the evolutionary development of our species, which, with the advent of modern science, can now be left behind. As religion is the product of variation and natural selection, it can be subjected to evolutionary analysis. The unit of this evolutionary analysis is the *meme*. A meme is any cultural idea or practice considered from an evolutionary perspective. The meme first made an appearance in Richard Dawkins' *The Selfish Gene*, before being taken up by a number of new atheist writers. Memes develop and adapt through variation and natural selection, and have their ultimate basis in the chemical processes and biological structures of the human brain.[55] Memetics is used to undermine the doctrines of the Church, by arguing that these are the not the product of revelation but of natural social and biological processes governed by natural selection.

A number of commentators have questioned, however, whether this evolutionary analysis does not prove too much. As Cunningham, McGrath, Stenmark and Ward argue, if human beliefs and practices are reducible to biological processes, and have come into existence only because they aid fitness and survivability, then memetics, scientism, evolutionary critiques of religion and perhaps natural science itself are dangerously undermined. They are relativised to the same level of the religion they attack, and cannot claim to accurately represent reality, but only contribute to fitness and survivability.[56] The remaining option would be to argue that new atheism and scientism are somehow exempt from their own evolutionary critique, or are more successful at aiding fitness and survivability than other beliefs and practices, especially religious ones. Dawkins, for example, uses the analogy of computer software and viruses to differentiate between non-religious reason and religion. Science is akin to beneficial computer software that is evaluated and passed on willingly

---

[55] Dawkins, *Selfish Gene*, 192–201, 322–31.
[56] Cunningham, *Pious Idea*, 262–3; McGrath, *Why God Won't*, 66–71; Stenmark, *Scientism*, 86; Ward, *God, Chance, Necessity*, 167–89. See also Stephen Bullivant, *Faith and Unbelief* (Norwich: Canterbury Press, 2013), 26–7.

due to its usefulness, while religion is like a computer virus that is passed on unwittingly, and is damaging and destructive.[57]

The difficulty with this analogy is twofold. First, it is contradicted by the uncontested role religion plays in the construction and maintenance of human communities, even communities possessing high levels of reflexivity and self-awareness. Second, the analogy is contradicted by the evolutionary analysis it is based on, which can only account for religion by emphasising the *benefit* it has brought to fitness and survivability over millennia of human history.[58] There is a deeper sense, moreover, in which an evolutionary critique of religion has consequences so damaging to new atheism that they call into question its very coherence. In advancing an evolutionary critique of religion, new atheists argue that beliefs and practices develop and subsist not through their intrinsic rationality, but by adaptation to their environment, and the social power that supports and transmits them.[59] Whatever rationality they possess is secondary to a range of sub-rational social and psychological factors. This undermines the universal, univocal and exhaustive capacity of reason, and renders it relative, contextualised and polyvocal.

While memetics begins as a natural explanation for faith, then it ends with an almost postmodern mistrust for the hidden social and political structures that legitimise and enforce it. There is thus a cleft between new atheism's conception of itself as the embodiment of universal reason, and its own evolutionary and memetic analysis. The only substantial difference between new atheism and the postmodernity it anathematises is that it insulates itself from its own critiques. If it ceased to do so, it would cease to exist, for it would recognise that it is as much a product of sub-rational causes as the religion it attacks. Once again, new atheist strategies for defending its core presuppositions prove too much, and end up contradicting its foundational beliefs, while, in so doing, endangering the validity of all human knowledge. As Cunningham sums up this predicament 'it is not heaven that is under threat but Earth, the common sense world, the world of nature and of the natural. This is the abolition of the human – not God.'[60]

[57] Dawkins, *Devil's Chaplain*, 171, 140–50.
[58] This is countenanced even by Daniel Dennett and Richard Dawkins. See Dennett, *Breaking the Spell*, 153–99; Dawkins, *God Delusion*, 190–240.
[59] See Dawkins, *Devil's Chaplain*, 140–50 for a particularly postmodern understanding of cultural beliefs and practices.
[60] Cunningham, *Pious Idea*, 320–32.

In this section we have examined how the foundational presuppositions of new atheist thought require additional strategies to maintain their plausibility, but that such strategies render new atheist thought self-contradictory. As we have seen, this self-contradiction is not accidental, but integral. In order to preserve the hegemony and exhaustive capacity of scientific description, new atheists turn to the extra-scientific discipline of philosophy; in rejecting the claims of Christianity, they accept and defend the beliefs and practices of fundamentalist Protestantism; in seeking to preserve the capacity of evolutionary theory to explain faith, their own beliefs are shown to be false; and in order to preserve rationality, they must practice irrationality.

PROTESTANT FUNDAMENTALISTS

The analysis given in Chapter 4 revealed the importance of two presuppositions for Protestant fundamentalist thought: a literal, univocal and perspicuous understanding of Scripture, and a disruptive and substitutionary understanding of divine activity in nature. These presuppositions give rise to a number of beliefs, such as the rejection of evolution, biblical criticism and the authority of specialist interpreters. While these beliefs may appear unambiguous – if naïve – they are also highly unstable, and require a range of additional strategies and beliefs to stabilise them, strategies and beliefs that inadvertently contradict the foundational presuppositions that structure Protestant fundamentalist thought.

The fundamentalist belief in scriptural inerrancy, and the self-authenticating nature of the Bible, lead to the adoption of strategies to overcome apparent contradictions and errors within the biblical text. These strategies for preserving the inerrancy and authority of Scripture have two outcomes. First, they subvert the literal sense, and substitute it with extra-textual speculations. Second, they can, surprisingly, result in the use of methods not unlike modern biblical criticism, which cast doubt on the inerrancy they are intended to protect. The subversion of the literal sense takes two forms. The first way in which fundamentalists subvert the literal sense is by duplicating events or altering textual chronologies to harmonise conflicting passages. In order to make sense of the Gospel of John's placement of the cleansing of the Temple at the beginning of Jesus' ministry, contrary to the testimony of the synoptic Gospels, fundamentalists have to posit the existence of *two* cleansings. Likewise, in order to make sense of the discrepant accounts given of Peter's betrayal, Peter is held to have betrayed Christ *six* times, while the cock is supposed to have crowed *three* times on *two* occasions, including one that Peter missed.[61] This trend is seen in another example of fundamentalist harmonisation, one concerning Genesis 6:4:

The Nephilim were on the earth in those days – and also afterward – when the sons of God went in to the daughters of humans, who bore children to them. These were the heroes that were of old, warriors of renown.

The difficulty faced by fundamentalists is that the meaning of Nephilim in Hebrew is 'fallen ones', while the Septuagint translates it as *gigantes*, or giants, a translation followed in the King James Version. In order to make sense of this discrepancy, Morris adopts the conjecture that the children of these fallen angels possessed demonic powers, powers that allowed them to grow to gigantic proportions. In this way, both the Nephilim and the *gigantes* are accommodated. In saving the text from errancy, however, Morris inadvertently alters its meaning, 'clarifying' what is thought to be God's inerrant Word.[62] The second way in which the literal sense is subverted is through non-literal interpretations designed to safeguard the credibility of Scripture, and protect it from mockery. Take the following text from Revelation 9:17–19:

The horses and riders I saw in my vision looked like this: Their breastplates were fiery red, dark blue, and yellow as sulphur. The heads of the horses resembled the heads of lions, and out of their mouths came fire, smoke and sulphur. A third of mankind was killed by the three plagues of fire, smoke and sulphur that came out of their mouths. The power of the horses was in their mouths and in their tails; for their tails were like snakes, having heads with which they inflict injury.

Fundamentalist preference for the literal sense renders passages such as this problematic, as a literal interpretation of 'horses' given in this passage would render the text implausible, as no known horses have these characteristics. Because the Book of Revelation cannot be considered to be allegorical in its entirety without subverting all of fundamentalist hermeneutics, fundamentalist interpreters must therefore adopt isolated non-literal interpretation to preserve the credibility of the text. This results in the interpretation that the horses in question are not horses at all, but perhaps modern-day tanks or military rockets. The literal sense is

---

[61] E.g. Bodie Hodge, 'Cock-a-Doodle One or Two?', in *Demolishing Supposed Bible Contradictions*, ed. Ken Ham, Bodie Hodge and Ted Chaffey (Green Forest: Master Books, 2012), 123–8; Boone, *Bible Tells Them*, 63–4.

[62] Morris, *Biblical Creationism*, 32.

therefore rejected, and substituted by an extra-biblical gloss completely alien to the intention of the biblical author.[63]

The need to preserve the credibility of Scripture goes much further, however, and issues in the adoption of a form of biblical criticism, and– remarkably – even the rejection of inerrancy itself. In an attempt to explain certain repetitions and *non sequiturs* in the text of Genesis, Morris argues that breaks in the narrative arise from where Shem, Ham and Japheth continued the narrative of Noah after his death.[64] This approach is found also in Morris and Morris' explanation for the textual differences between excerpts from Isaiah used in Jeremiah and 2 Kings and the text of Isaiah itself. They argue that:

Rather than rewrite these histories, he [the biblical author] simply incorporates them as appropriate in his own book, with such modification and additions as was necessary for his own purposes.[65]

This approach, which can also admit that differences between the Gospels have arisen due to different authorial intentions, replicates, in fundamentalist form, many of the assumptions of modern biblical criticism: that biblical texts have been edited, that texts are produced according to the intentions of their authors, and that discrepancies and *non sequiturs* are the outcome of editing, collation and redaction.[66] This inadvertent acceptance of a form of biblical criticism goes much further, however, and even impinges upon inerrancy itself. For example, Morris and Morris – perhaps in tacit admission of the difficulties of reconciling the disparate texts of Scripture – admit that apparent contradictions have been providentially placed by God within Scripture for the following reasons: to eliminate suspicion of collusion between scriptural authors, to stimulate Bible study, and to provide reasons for unbelievers to scoff, thereby revealing their wicked hearts.[67] Here, in a final, paradoxical attempt to preserve the doctrine of inerrancy, the inerrant Scriptures are re-conceptualised to include within themselves divinely-ordained apparent contradictions, whose purpose is to generate fundamentalist harmonisations and apologetics, and to further secure the division between the elect and the reprobate. The difficulties are sometimes too great, however, and inerrancy itself must be questioned. While attempting to explain the

---

[63] Boone, *Bible Tells Them*, 41–4.

[64] Morris, *Biblical Creationism*, 36; cf. Morris, *Genesis Record*, 28–30.

[65] Henry M. Morris and Henry M. Morris III, *Many Infallible Proofs* (Green Forest: Master Books, 1996), 187.

[66] Morris and Morris, *Infallible*, 186.   [67] Morris and Morris, *Infallible*, 221–3.

difficulties of Genesis 6:4, Morris ultimately concludes that Noah was *wrong* to call the fallen angels in that text 'Sons of God', for this gives the impression that they are somehow holy, or accomplishing God's work.[68] This is a remarkable admission for two reasons. First, it appears to suggest that the text of Genesis in question was uniquely *Noah's* rather than God's, and that, second, it is errant. The reason why fundamentalists can, on occasion, admit that scriptural texts have been re-worked according to need, and that their authors committed errors, is that these criticisms are voiced from *within* the fundamentalist community, and are not intended to question the authority of Scripture but to strengthen it, even if the former consequence is the one most evident to outsiders.

The malleability of fundamentalist interpretations of Scripture, and the ease by which contradictions and errors are written off as inconsequential, reveals something far more damaging, however: that the plain sense of Scripture can be sacrificed to preserve inerrancy, and that inerrancy is not the quality of a fixed text with a univocal meaning, but of whatever interpretation fundamentalists put upon the biblical text. In other words, it is the interpretive narrative of *fundamentalists*, and not the biblical text itself, that is, in practice, inerrant, something noted by Barr many decades ago.[69] This situation arises because of the scriptural discrepancies and errors just described, yet also because of the doctrine of perspicuity and private interpretation. In order to balance perspicuity and private interpretation against fundamentalist orthodoxy, strong ecclesial and hermeneutical controls are necessary. At the end of her study of Jerry Falwell's Thomas Street Church, Harding reached the following conclusion regarding Protestant fundamentalist hermeneutics:

The interpretive tradition is literalist in the sense that it presumes the Bible to be true and literally God's Word, but the interpretive practices themselves are not simply literalist. The biblical text is considered fixed and inerrant, and it means what God intended it to mean, but discovering that meaning is not simple or sure or constant. The Bible is read within a complex, multidimensional, shifting field of fundamental Baptist (becoming evangelical) folk-narrative practices, and so are the lives of the preachers and their peoples. The Bible is at once a closed canon and an open book, still alive, a living Word. Preachers and their peoples are third testaments, the authors of always unfolding chapters and verses.[70]

Between the Bible and its literal sense always stands the preacher, Bible commentator or apologist. In discerning its meaning for Christians today,

[68] Morris, *Biblical Creationism*, 32.   [69] Cf. Barr, *Fundamentalism*, 34.
[70] Harding, *Falwell*, 28.

they mediate, amend and transform its sense, albeit in ways that, as Boone reminds us, are not always intentional or conscious. This unconscious element makes it possible for fundamentalists to disavow the very real institutional and ecclesial influence upon exegesis. Such control is necessary for two reasons. First, given its basis in Calvinism and Scottish Common Sense Realism, fundamentalist Protestantism has no rational way to account for disagreements of interpretation, leaving it vulnerable to schism. Disagreement is a sign of personal sinfulness, or an unwillingness to receive the teaching of the Holy Spirit. The implicit mediation of ecclesial control between the Bible and the individual interpreter makes it possible to preserve the narrative of perspicuity and private interpretation, while tacitly policing and undermining it.[71] Second, the mediation of preacher, Bible commentator and apologist is necessary to preserve the inerrancy of Scripture. As we have seen, fundamentalists can admit that Scripture contains many *apparent* contradictions. These contradictions, left unexplained, naturally tend towards the rejection of inerrancy, and, given the conservative evangelical logic discussed in Chapter 4, the rejection of Scripture itself.

The commentary of pastors and apologists is inevitable given the exalted and infallible status of the scriptural text and the need to defend it, yet it is highly problematic. As Boone notes 'It is ironic that commentary has become so influential in a movement purposefully devoted to the sole authority of the text.'[72] Nowhere is this seen more clearly than in the phenomenon of apologetic Bibles in conservative evangelical circles. In these, the biblical text – in a manner directly analogous to medieval glosses – is surrounded and interweaved by commentary designed to harmonise contradictions, and preserve the credibility of Scripture in the face of contemporary criticism.[73] In this way, Morris' belief – examined earlier – that Scripture does not need to be interpreted, is directly contradicted by his own voluminous oeuvre, whose sole purpose is to interpret and defend Scripture in the face of geology, evolutionary theory and biblical criticism. This situation has led commentators such as Marsden to suggest that the key to challenging fundamentalism is not to attack inerrancy, but to point out that fundamentalist hermeneutics are not derived from Scripture at all, but are extra-biblical and plastic, bending

---

[71] Boone, *Bible Tells Them*, 15–18, 72.   [72] Boone, *Bible Tells Them*, 78–81.
[73] See, e.g., Ray Comfort, ed., *The New Defender's Study Bible* (Nashville: World Publishing, 2006); Ted Cabal, ed., *The Apologetics Study Bible* (Nashville: Holman Bible Publishers, 2007).

to the exigencies of the times.[74] Yet while, to non-fundamentalists, such hermeneutical glosses directly contradict the authority and perspicuity of Scripture, this realisation is hidden from fundamentalists themselves. This is because Protestant fundamentalist thought, drawing upon the Reformed tradition, and strengthened by Scottish Common Sense Realism, does not view interpretation as a socially situated and conditioned practice, but as the direct apprehension of the Spirit's teaching. Commentary is simply a helpful guide that points out what is timeless and uncontested, and performs no other function. The narrative of Protestant fundamentalist thought thus has the effect of masking its own presuppositions, and strengthening the univocal conception of reason that animates it.

The importance of extra-biblical presuppositions and the ecclesial control of Scripture's meaning is most clearly seen in fundamentalist critiques of evolution. These critiques begin by undermining evolution, but they end with undermining Protestant fundamentalist thought itself. This takes four forms. First is the ubiquitous use of extra-biblical sources when dealing with Genesis 1–3. A wide range of evidence is used to protect the literal sense and to undermine evolution, making use of evidence drawn from palaeontology, biology, geology and carbon dating, among many other disciplines. In this way, religious truth, and scriptural authority itself, comes to depend on extra-biblical evidence, undermining the principle of *sola scriptura*. As Young notes, while modern scholarship attempts to understand the text of Genesis in its own right, no other group – apart, importantly, from atheists – has made more appeal to extra-biblical evidence than Protestant fundamentalists. This is in contrast to non-fundamentalist theologians and biblical scholars, who arguably stand more firmly within the tradition of Reformed theology by not searching beyond the text to discern its meaning.[75] While the use of extra-biblical evidence is an attempt to support literal interpretations of Genesis 1–3, the use of such evidence, second, actually undermines the literal sense. As Harris argues, in defending a literal six-day creation, and the scientific cogency of the Noahic flood, fundamentalists such as Whitcomb and Morris posit a geological and meteorological upheaval that is nowhere mentioned in the text. Their attempts only result in additions to, or even corruptions of, God's inerrant Word.[76] Third, the use of extra-

---

[74] Marsden, 'Views of Science', 110–2.
[75] Davis A. Young, *The Biblical Flood* (Grand Rapids: Eerdmans, 1995), 245, 264, 277–9, 304.
[76] Marl Harris, *The Nature of Creation* (Durham: Acumen, 2013), 43–4.

biblical evidence to defend inerrancy and the literal sense also endangers the perspicuity of Scripture, for it hands authority to specialist interpreters, causing six-day creationism to fall foul of its own critique against the supposedly undemocratic nature of Roman Catholic exegesis, and the counter-intuitive nature of evolutionary theory. Many individuals reading Genesis 1–3 today, without the guidance of Church teaching and theological tradition, would either presume that it contradicts current understandings of cosmology and biology, or else read it as a poetic representation. Very few outwith the fundamentalist community would read it as being literally, historically and scientifically true. In order to forestall these common sense conclusions, fundamentalists must gloss the text with a range of extra-biblical evidences, woven into a biblical-scientific account that subverts evolution and preserves the literal sense. The difficulty with this is that the reader must learn to understand and accept this extra-biblical, specialist and often highly technical gloss in order to accept the plausibility of a recent six-day creation. The result is that Scripture loses its perspicuity, and its sense and authority come to depend not upon its divine author but a host of interpreters and apologists. These strategies raise a fourth problem. The use of extra-biblical evidence and specialist commentary leads fundamentalists to contradict their own injunction against looking behind the facts of nature and Scripture, an injunction that, as we saw in Chapter 4, underlies their rejection of both biblical criticism and evolution. As they attempt to describe geological and cosmological events that occurred long in the past, and are no longer accessible to sense experience, the quasi-scientific explanations of fundamentalists are as speculative as the theory of evolution they are designed to refute. Both attempt to explain what they take as fact through the construction of models and theories. If it were to be objected that there is nothing speculative for fundamentalists about the literal sense of Genesis itself, the reply would come that this is quite so – but without the quasi-scientific speculations of creationist apologetics, there is no way to reconcile it with known fact, and it must be admitted to be false.

Fundamentalists, however, are aware of such issues, and attempt to forestall them by relativising both six-day creationism and evolution, arguing that the interpretation of each is based on presuppositions that cannot be proven. *Prima facie*, this confession might appear to bring a level of self-awareness to fundamentalist thought that is surprising, and even refreshing. Yet, whatever its candour, it is severely problematic to both the specific content of fundamentalist thought, and its basis in a rationality that is supposedly universal and univocal. As mentioned in Chapter 4, fundamentalists argue that six-day creationism and evolution are two contradictory conclusions that are reached because of differing presuppositions and interpretive frameworks. In the following text, we see this same argument, yet also indications of something far more radical. According to Sarfati:

It is a fallacy to believe that facts speak for themselves – they are always interpreted according to a framework ... so it's not a question of biased religious creationists versus objective scientific evolutionists; rather, it is the biases of the Christian religion versus the biases of the religion of secular humanism resulting in different interpretations of the same scientific data.[77]

The first part of this text repeats the presupposition-based argument recounted in Chapter 4. Yet the latter part of Sarfati's text strays into far stranger territory, and seems to suggest that reason is, ultimately, impotent to settle the controversy between fundamentalist Christianity and irreligion, as both arise from biases that are non-rational. This surprising view is echoed in other creationist writings. According to Johnson, reason does not supply its own premises, except those derived from sense experience, and the majority of premises are simply inherited. As the premises of reason are largely assumed, reason can be used to justify almost anything.[78] For this reason, fundamentalists such as Anderson argue that neither creationism nor Darwinism can claim to represent the outworking of neutral reason.[79] For Ham, both atheists and fundamentalists are biased, yet fundamentalist six-day creationism is still superior, because 'It is not a matter whether one is biased or not. It is really a question of which bias is the best biased with which to be biased', a sentiment echoed almost word by word by Sarfati.[80] As Barr notes, these concessions regarding the presuppositional nature of reason and fundamentalist thought are extremely problematic, as they suggest that fundamentalist Protestantism is dependent upon extra-biblical, tradition-dependent assumptions, and therefore fails to conform to its own norm of *sola scriptura*.[81] The fundamentalist conception of reason as universal and univocal is therefore substituted for a relative, pluralist conception. This has consequences not only for science and reason, but also for perspicuity, univocity and perhaps even scriptural authority itself.

[77] Sarfati, *Refuting Evolution*, 15–16.   [78] Johnson, *Wedge of Truth*, 36, 176.
[79] Anderson, *Why We Must*, 22–5.
[80] Ham, *The Lie*, 36–7; Sarfati, *Refuting Evolution*, 17.
[81] Barr, *Fundamentalism*, xvii–xviii.

As with new atheist thought, then, Protestant fundamentalist thought is rendered self-contradictory. Its attempt to stabilise difficulties in its thought inadvertently contradicts the presuppositions that structure it. As such, fundamentalists find themselves in a 'performative contradiction', acting against their own foundational presuppositions while attempting to defend them.[82] In order to preserve the inerrancy of Scripture, they must substitute or ignore Scripture; in order to preserve the supreme authority of Scripture's text and the right of private interpretation, they must control Scripture's meaning through the mediation of preacher and apologist; in order to preserve the perspicuity and literal truth of Genesis, they must impose a speculative and specialist gloss; and in order to preserve the rationality of the Protestant fundamentalist worldview, they must defend bias, and relativise reason itself.

DIALECTIC OF PROTESTANTISM

The preceding analysis of new atheist and Protestant fundamentalist thought completes the diagnostic and critical component of this work. It is now possible to integrate this discussion with the argument of Chapters 1–4, and present the conclusions of this work.

Chapter 1 charted the genesis of the presuppositions that would later come to structure both new atheist and Protestant fundamentalist thought. In order to undermine the authority of the Roman Catholic Church, the Reformers deployed three inter-related strategies. First, against the witness of the Church, they advanced the independent authority of Scripture, an authority that was authenticated first by the Holy Spirit, but also be the internal harmony of its contents, the fulfilment of prophecy and the miracles accompanying the teaching of Christ and the apostles. Second, against the tradition and teaching office of the Church, the Reformers taught that Scripture's sense was literal and perspicuous, and accessible to the lay faithful. Third, against the penitential cycle of the Church, the Reformers taught that salvation was not dependent on the sacramental machinery of the Church, but through faith in the saving Person of Jesus Christ. These strategies, which came to coalesce around the principles of *sola scriptura* and *sola fide*, helped to undermine the authority of the Roman Catholic Church in England, and bring about a Protestant settlement.

---

[82] Stahl, 'One-Dimensional Rage', 105.

Yet the oppositions established by these strategies accomplished too much, and began a crisis of authority that came to undermine the authority of the Church of England itself. The principle of *sola scriptura*, which legitimated the Reformation of the English Church, undermined episcopacy and the Prayer Book, as readers, earnestly searching the Scriptures, failed to find biblical authorisation for many features of the Church's doctrine and practice. In addition, the principle of *sola fide* weakened the role of the Church in the order of salvation, and led to the formation of conventicles, many of whom held heterodox views. These instabilities erupted during the English Civil War, as the principles of *sola scriptura* and *sola fide* led to a profusion of competing sects, the most extreme of which rejected Christianity altogether in favour of pantheism and even materialism. The haemorrhaging of views and sects permitted by the breakdown of political and ecclesiastical authority made it imperative to find new bases for stabilising the oppositions created by Protestantism, and achieving religious certainty. On the level of polity, this was achieved through the force of the Clarendon Code, and the ejection of many hundreds of dissenting clergy. On the intellectual level, in order to forestall radical interpretations by Protestant enthusiasts, and thwart the pretensions of Roman Catholics and High Churchmen, the self-authentication of Scripture – and its literal and perspicuous sense – was strengthened, with an increasing emphasis upon univocity. Instrumental in this process was the philosophy of John Locke, which systematised many of the assumptions of the age. Locke blamed confessions and systems of doctrine for obscuring the true meaning of Scripture, an obfuscation that lay behind religious division. The rejection of these credenda, and the adoption of a strengthened literal hermeneutic would, so he believed, stabilise and secure a rational Protestant settlement.

Yet this strategy for stabilising the literal sense gave rise, almost immediately, to the first sustained flowering of anti-Christian freethought. The mysteries of the faith were denounced as intellectually vacuous and politically dangerous, the chief means by which superstition flourished, and the machinations of priestcraft were preserved. Scripture's words, now considered to be narrowly literal and univocal, could no longer support internal proofs for the authority of Scripture based on the fulfilment of Old Testament prophecy in Christ. This had two effects. First, Christ could no longer be shown to be the long-expected Messiah, and he and his disciples' use of Scripture was either fraudulent or deluded. Second, the unity of the Old and New Testaments disintegrated,

imperilling revelation and calling into doubt the episcopacy, which drew
its legitimacy by analogy to the Aaronic priesthood.

The progress of freethought was checked, however, by the use of
natural theological arguments. The methods and discoveries of the burgeoning sciences were used to provide an objective basis for Protestant
unity, through the demonstration of God's existence, power, benevolence
and providential oversight. These fundamental truths, written in the book
of nature, would provide an indubitable basis for religion, and help to
secure the divine right of the restored monarchy and Church. Yet this
natural theological strategy was based on the presupposition that God's
activity disrupted natural causation, and that his activity could be incorporated within natural philosophical descriptions of reality. This led to a
growing opposition between divine and natural causation, and the decline
of the traditional distinction between primary and secondary causation. It
also created a hermeneutical and natural theological synthesis, in which a
literal reading of Genesis 1–3 guided natural philosophy, and natural
philosophy justified a literal reading of Genesis 1–3. In seeking to unify
science and Christianity, and achieve new unity among theological adversaries, the natural philosophers and divines of the Restoration left the
faith dangerously dependent on science, and on the ability of divine
activity to perform explanatory functions within scientific description.

Chapter 2 examined how the synthesis of a literal, univocal and
perspicuous Scripture, and a disruptive and substitutionary understanding of divine activity fell apart in the wake of scientific advances and
social upheaval. The biblical hermeneutic established in the wake of the
Restoration, influenced all sections of the English Church, yet was particularly strong among dissenters. This hermeneutic led to the abandonment of previously accepted creeds and confessions as guides to
interpretation. These hermeneutical practices, however, soon gave rise
to heterodoxy, and the Presbyterians – who had most fully embraced
them – went into decline. The fortunes of a literal, univocal and perspicuous reading of Scripture were reversed, however, by the evangelical
revival, which saw unprecedented numbers of working people encouraged to read Scripture for themselves, and adopt new positions of leader-
ship and teaching within nonconformity, and especially Methodism.
Given the growing isolation of Scripture from a confessional superstructure, however, Scripture's authority came to rely more heavily upon the
internal harmony of its contents, and its agreement with known fact. This
left its authority vulnerable to unsympathetic readings. In a newly indus-
trialised and urbanised society, accompanied by poverty and the

breakdown of traditional social bonds, the same groups recruited to nonconformity and Methodism were also the most likely to be politically radical. At this time, however, the close connection between Church and state meant that an attack upon the authority of the state necessitated an attack upon the Church, which legitimised the prevailing order. This unique nexus of biblical hermeneutics and political radicalism created the conditions for the first popular atheist movements in British history, where a section of radicalised working people, unsympathetic to the establishment, and noting apparent contradictions and errors within Scripture, rejected the faith.

Plebeian agitation against the Church-State establishment was checked once again, however, by the use of natural theology, which purported to demonstrate the top-down creation and direct providential governance of the world by God and his appointed leaders. This natural theological conception of nature and society was opposed by working class atheists, who, drawing upon Lamarckian science and advances in geology, proposed a range of alternative proto-evolutionary theories, where order was not imposed from above but arose spontaneously from below. The use of evolution by plebeian radicals long made evolutionary theory suspect, however, and it would take its acceptance by a member of the establishment to begin the process by which evolution was shorn of its radical overtones, and made respectable. This was achieved with Darwin's *On the Origins of Species*. Darwin had three important influences on the course of biblical hermeneutics and natural theology in Britain and America. First, Darwin's theory demonstrated that a literal reading of Scripture, so vital for Protestant hermeneutics, could not be applied to Genesis 1–3 without contradicting known fact. Second, the theory of evolution did irreparable damage to the design argument, which had justified both political authority and the unity of science and Christian faith. These effects led, third, to the possibility of real conflict between Christianity and science, as evolution had disproved traditional understandings of a special creation, and had destroyed the natural theological framework that united biblical hermeneutics and theology to the discoveries of science. While the more bibliocentric churches warred against Darwin for a time, it would be among scientists that the conflict was most keenly felt. These possibilities for conflict were exploited by Thomas Huxley and others, who used the recent discoveries of science to attack the influence of the clergy in the practice and patronage of science, and to increase the professionalisation and public esteem of scientists. Importantly, however, this group maintained many of the presumptions of the Protestant Christianity they rejected, such as a preference for literal readings of Genesis, and the belief that God's activity in nature was disruptive, substitutionary, and incompatible with natural processes. The only major difference was that these presumptions were now held negatively, so that Christianity was rejected. By the early twentieth century, this group was well-established, particularly within the universities, and communicated the biblical and natural theological views we have been examining to a wider audience.

Chapter 3 examined how the presupposition of a literal, univocal and perspicuous Scripture, and a disruptive and substitutionary conception of divine activity gave rise, under the unique social and political conditions of America, to Protestant fundamentalism. As a colony for much of the seventeenth and eighteenth centuries, American Protestantism inherited the same biblical hermeneutic and natural theological presuppositions as Britain. What differed, however, was the Scottish Common Sense philosophy that came to shape these presuppositions. This philosophy, which grew in reaction against perceived irreligious tendencies in Locke's thought and their exploitation by Hume, argued for the mind's ability to directly intuit objects of knowledge, without the mediation of ideas. By stressing the credibility and certainty of sense experience, and severely limiting the role of theories and deduction in scientific and philosophical investigation, it was believed that biblical, natural theological and scientific truth could be placed on a more certain footing. Its influence gave rise to a widespread admiration for 'Baconianism', a narrow, inductive method that became popular in a range of disciplines. Among the most important was the Protestant theology of the Princeton School, which applied Baconianism to biblical hermeneutics, and argued that there was a single method for the discernment of truth, which should be applied equally to both science and Scripture. An important part of the application of this method to Scripture was a drastic reduction in the importance of hermeneutics, which was held to be the simple apprehension of the clear teaching of Scripture.

The influence of Baconianism in theology remained dominant until after the Civil War, before beginning to decline. The influence of idealism, evolution and biblical criticism gave rise to new trends of theological liberalism, which directly challenged the presuppositions of a literal, univocal and perspicuous Scripture and the disruptive and substitutionary nature of divine activity. These challenges led to new accounts of inerrancy, and a growing defensiveness among conservative evangelicals, who, by the 1920s, had adopted the title *fundamentalist*.

In spite of these challenges, the majority of conservative evangelical theologians had, within a few years of *On the Origins of Species*, come to terms with evolution, and it would be social and political factors such as immigration, the secularisation of the education system, and the First World War that would volatise conservative evangelical thought, and raised to new importance the direct, disruptive agency of God in creation. Instrumental in this process was William Jennings Bryan, who, through his popularity and great rhetorical skills, successfully directed fundamentalist opinion against evolution, equating it with every form of religious, social and moral evil. The anti-evolutionary strain in fundamentalist thought grew as the twentieth century progressed, and, with the cultural upheavals of the 1960s, fundamentalism returned to public life to challenge evolution.

By the early twentieth century, therefore, the presupposition that Scripture's sense is literal, univocal and perspicuous, and that divine activity disrupts and substitutes for natural causation, had come to structure both Protestant fundamentalist and new atheist forms of thought. Chapter 4 analysed the structure of new atheist and Protestant fundamentalist forms of thought, noting that, despite superficial differences, their shared presuppositions give rise to a number of common beliefs. New atheists and Protestant fundamentalists both believe that Scripture should be inerrant, and fully coherent in all its parts. Against non-fundamentalist Christians and academic theologians, both groups affirm that the only legitimate reading of Scripture is a literal one. This literal reading affirms that the words of Scripture should be taken in their plain or natural sense without the guidance of theological tradition, and that each verse can be treated in a propositional manner, so that proof texting is possible and appropriate. These scriptural and hermeneutical beliefs give rise to the further belief that only fundamentalist religion is true religion. Further, the literal reading of Scripture supports the view – prevalent within new atheist writings – that, if God does exist, he is in some sense corporeal, and lacks true transcendence. The presupposition of a literal, univocal and perspicuous Scripture also gives rise to the belief of both groups that Genesis 1–3 can only be interpreted literally. This belief is closely related to the second presupposition of new atheist and Protestant fundamentalist thought, that God's activity disrupts, and substitutes, for natural causation. Together, these two presuppositions give rise to a belief in the mutual exclusivity of divine activity and natural processes, the incompatibility of design and evolution, the ability of science to detect, or fail to detect, divine activity, and explanatory monism, where each group delegitimises the other through a process of narrative reduction.

The shared intellectual structure of new atheists and Protestant fundamentalists is instantiated in, and supported by, their social and political orientation. Each group practices strong in-group preferences, and ostracises the other as the source of almost every moral and social evil. Yet the shared intellectual structure of both groups, and their objectification of each other as morally repugnant, leads to a symbiotic social relationship, in which each group supports and aids the other. This has three consequences. First, the growth in numbers of one increases popularity and extremism of the other. Second, their symbiotic social relationship means that both are committed to the preservation and normative standing of fundamentalist Protestantism, and those presuppositions that have been the focus of this study. Third, they defend and advance a universal and decontextualised understanding of reason and religion in the face of a society that is increasingly tolerant of polyvocal and contextual understandings of reason.

The presuppositions they advance, however, are unstable, and, as this chapter has shown, require additional philosophical, hermeneutical and theological strategies if they are to remain intellectually stable. Unfortunately, these additional strategies contradict the foundational presuppositions of new atheist and Protestant fundamentalist thought, and end in self-contradiction for both.

This instability is not distinctive to Protestant fundamentalist or new atheist thought, however, but is a product of the presuppositions that ground them, presuppositions that have been inherited from the Protestant culture of Britain and America. The notion of a self-authenticating Scripture, whose authority rested on its internal harmony, the fulfilment of prophecy, its verification by miracles, or its agreement with scientific fact, was, as we have seen, undermined by a literal, univocal and perspicuous understanding of its text. To argue that Scripture's sense is clear and open to all, and that theological tradition and Church teaching should be rejected, is, as has been shown, intellectually problematic and even destructive. Intellectually, it is naïve, for ecclesiastical and social control is necessary to stabilise and police the meaning of Scripture, and even the most fundamentalist of Protestants utilise elaborate exegetical and apologetic strategies to maintain the credibility and integrity of their interpretations. More damaging, however, is the repeated capacity of this presupposition to negate itself. Time and again, literal readings, without the guidance of tradition and Church teaching, have given rise to the conclusion that Scripture is contradictory, fallible and very different from the Church's understanding of it. Positively, these conclusions gave rise to biblical criticism, and the scientific study of Scripture. Yet, negatively, they gave rise to the loss of faith, and a damaging polemic against Christianity. As Ruthven and Cunningham note, these outcomes would have been less likely to occur in social and interpretive contexts that permitted varied, non-literal readings drawn from tradition.[83] *Sola scriptura* set in train an intellectual crisis of authority that could only be stemmed with political force, or through the imposition of hermeneutical controls in a tacit and even dishonest way. In either case, the attempt to derive all doctrine from Scripture alone failed.

A similar picture emerges from the second presupposition we have examined, that God's activity in nature is disruptive or substitutionary, so that it is mutually exclusive of natural processes. The natural theological arguments based on this presupposition made God's direct, immediate activity a vital constituent of scientific knowledge, without which science was incomplete. These arguments were useful in the effort to unite Protestants and answer the criticisms of freethinkers after the Civil War, and were, for a time, successful. Yet utilising God's direct, immediate activity as a constituent part of scientific description and natural theological reasoning endangered the independence and integrity of theology, and when science discovered natural causes to replace divine action, God's presence and activity in the universe came to look ever smaller, or even non-existent. The collapse of natural theology was not total, however, for what remained in atheist and Protestant fundamentalist thought was the presupposition that God's activity in nature was disruptive, substitutionary and exclusive of natural causation, establishing the conditions for the perceived conflict between science and religion, and evolution and design.

New atheist and Protestant fundamentalist thought, then, represent the historical outworking of the hermeneutical and natural theological synthesis initiated by the Reformation and solidified at the Restoration. This synthesis was necessary to secure the stability of the oppositions between Church and Scripture, literal and non-literal, and personal and institutional faith ushered in by the Reformers, and used to undermine the Roman Catholic Church. It is this Protestant heritage that sets the terms of their debate, the categories they employ, the methods they use and the

---

[83] Ruthven, *Search for Meaning*, 63; Cunningham, *Pious Idea*, 294.

238 Atheism, Fundamentalism and the Protestant Reformation

areas of agreement they share. The separation of these two forms of thought into opposing worldviews can therefore be seen as part of a dialectic within Protestantism in Britain and America. This dialectic has been present since the Reformation itself, but has increased in volatility in the wake of scientific advances, and the move from modernity to postmodernity. It must be stressed, however, that this dialectic is *historical,* and not logical or necessary. In and of themselves, the presuppositions of a literal, univocal and perspicuous Scripture, and the belief that divine activity in nature is disruptive or substitutionary, do not logically entail atheism or fundamentalism. Yet due to a range of contingent social, political, economic and scientific factors, these presuppositions, and their accompanying oppositions, became instrumental in the historical genesis of both forms of thought. Fundamentalist and atheist thought are two manifestations or poles of the traditional Protestant culture of Britain and America, a culture that is now in disintegration. Fundamentalist thought can be understood as positive Protestantism, possessing a distinct content, while atheist thought, in its negation of this content, can be seen as negative Protestantism. One holds the presuppositions of Protestant thought in a positive way, the other holds them in a negative way. One affirms and one denies, yet both are manifestations of the same underlying theology. Yet because they share the same presuppositions and intellectual structure, they remain locked in a symbiotic intellectual and social relationship, each working with the other to maintain their core presuppositions in the wake of postmodern scepticism and religious indifference. Protestant fundamentalists give new atheists a content for their thought, and, in their negation of it, atheists present fundamentalists with the logical outworking of that thought in the modern world. In short, the secret of atheism is fundamentalism, and the secret of fundamentalism is atheism.

Given that new atheist and Protestant fundamentalist thought have both arisen from the same presuppositions, and that these presuppositions are unstable and – in practice – self-contradictory, it would be reasonable to conclude that the solution to fundamentalism and atheism would be to reject a literal, univocal and perspicuous understanding of Scripture, and a disruptive and substitutionary conception of divine activity in nature. Why pretend, in this day and age, that the Bible should be taken 'literally'? Why not accept that it has a multiplicity of reader and context-dependent senses? Or, if it does have a single sense, why not admit that it is one that is only accessible to biblical scholars, and available to the lay faithful only with great difficulty? Why continue to believe that God disrupts natural, immanent processes? Why not accept that God's activity in nature is limited to the act of creation, or some minimal act of conservation, and that the laws of the universe work out their purpose without his interference? Why lie to ourselves and others that God directly answers prayer, and admit instead that our prayers are answered only tangentially through the spiritual and moral renewal of the individual? Why countenance these troublesome presuppositions?

These are the conclusions that have been reached by a large number of Christians in Britain and America. Chapters 2 and 3 briefly discussed the way in which non-fundamentalist Protestants attempted to move away from traditional understandings of Scripture, creation and divine activity in the wake of biblical criticism and evolution. These re-conceptualisations of Protestant tradition were successful in accommodating theology to contemporary knowledge, and were accepted within a relatively short period. Yet in rejecting biblical inerrancy, reading Scripture as a primarily human text, and casting doubt on the miraculous events recounted in its pages, these theologies – which came to be known by the epithet 'liberal' – were, consciously or unconsciously, dissociating themselves from many of the foundational presuppositions of Reformed and Anglican theology, and, by extension, the traditional Protestant culture of Britain and America.[84]

This accommodation remained successful as long as Britain and America remained culturally Christian, and the liberal Church retained a position of political and social influence. Yet the unprecedented social changes of the 1960s, taken with increasing immigration and pluralisation, began to seriously challenge this cultural dominance, and the traditional denominations of Britain and America – Presbyterians, Anglicans, Methodists – which had performed important functions as arbiters of public morality and respectability began a precipitous decline. This severely weakened the ability of the once dominant non-fundamentalist denominations to affect public opinion, and to maintain their moderate and liberal Christianity as the normative expression of the faith. While popular stereotypes of the Church had – for much of the twentieth century – pictured fashionable, liberal clergy ranged against outmoded conservatives, public understanding slowly shifted from this intra-

---

[84] While no two liberalisms are the same, Lindbeck's 'experiential-expressive' model still captures the essence of much contemporary Church theology in Britain and America. See especially George A. Lindbeck, *The Nature of Doctrine* (Louisville: Westminster John Knox, 2009), 16–31.

ecclesial contrast to a contrast between outmoded Christianity – or religion in general – and progressive unbelief.[85]

The growing eclipse of liberal Christianity within the Church, the academy and wider society is acknowledged by a number of its supporters.[86] As Chapman notes, liberal theology has been linked with everything from Nazisim and Stalinism to rampant capitalism and selfish individualism.[87] Yet liberals consider their theology as a vital 'mediating matrix' between the binary of fundamentalism and atheism, and the only remedy for restoring Christianity to a position of cultural relevance. As Hodgson argues, the disappearance of liberal Christianity

> would have tragic consequences both politically and religiously. We would be left with the alternatives of fundamentalism and neoconservativsim on the one hand, and atheism and secularism on the other – the reigning dogmatisms of our time.[88]

Bradley champions liberal theology as a means to combat 'the prevailing and growing conservative fundamentalism of out times' as well as the 'secular militants, militant atheists' who would welcome the end of religion.[89] In arguing against fundamentalism, Bradley believes that it is liberalism that stands in line with the Reformers, while '[i]t is narrow conservatism that represents innovation and departure from tradition'.[90] This belief is linked with a genealogy of liberalism and fundamentalism that is outlined in more detail by Keith Ward. Ward locates the origins of liberalism in the same event that we have identified as instrumental to the genesis of Protestant fundamentalism and atheism: the Reformation. The changes in practice and hermeneutics that occurred at that time had momentous consequences for the nature of religious authority, for 'the individual was given the power of judging the institution by reference to a publicly accessible text'.[91] As Ward argues, 'to put the Bible directly into

---

[85] Ben Suriano, 'Three Questions on Modern Atheism: An Interview with John Milbank', in *'God Is Dead' and I Don't Feel So Good Myself*, ed. Andrew David (Eugene: Cascade Books, 2010), 59.

[86] Peter C. Hodgson, *Liberal Theology: A Radical Vision* (Minneapolis: Fortress Press, 2007), 3; Ian Bradley, *Grace, Order, Openness and Diversity* (London: Continuum, 2010), 16–19.

[87] Mark D. Chapman, introduction to *The Future of Liberal Theology*, ed. Mark D. Chapman (Aldershot: Ashgate, 2002), 6–17.

[88] Hodgson, *Liberal Theology*, ix.

[89] Bradley, *Grace, Order, Openness and Diversity*, xii, xiii.

[90] Bradley, *Grace, Order, Openness and Diversity*, xii.

[91] Keith Ward, 'The Importance of Liberal Theology', in *The Future of Liberal Theology*, ed. Mark D. Chapman (Aldershot: Ashgate, 2002), 41.

the hands of the populace, and tell them that they must decide for themselves who has erred in interpreting it, is to shatter the authority of any church forever'.[92] The shattering of authority could not be contained to the Church alone, however, but soon impacted Scripture itself. As Bradley relates:

> The Reformation had a double-edged effect on the development of liberal theology, sowing the seeds of modern fundamentalism as well as modern liberalism. The principle of *Sola Scriptura* championed by the Reformers led directly to the doctrines of literalism and inerrancy at the heart of Christian fundamentalism ... However, the Reformers also encouraged the development of liberal thought through their attacks on priestly authority and tradition and their emphasis on the exercise of individual judgement and conscience.[93]

For Ward, the attack on religious authority begun at Reformation led to the present-day liberal belief that the Bible is not 'the last divine word' on things, but is only 'a collection of documents which was often mistaken in its understanding of the physical cosmos, which rationally incorporated legend and mythology into its accounts of historical fact, and which often expressed the rather limited moral outlook of the culture in which it was promulgated'.[94] For this reason, it is difficult to say which Christian beliefs are true or not, with the result that faith becomes less about doctrine and more about 'the passionate commitment to a symbolically expressed discernment of supreme value'.[95]

In this way, liberal theologians such as Ward, Bradley and Hodgson reject the biblical and theological presuppositions that structure new atheist and Protestant fundamentalist thought. In their place, they teach the ambiguity and doubtfulness of faith, and a corresponding doctrinal pluralism. Yet, in spite of his confidence in the rejection of much of traditional Protestantism, Ward nevertheless expresses some doubts about 'how one can treat as authoritative a text which is subject to continual critical scrutiny'.[96] These doubts are shared by Hardy, who wonders whether liberalism's attempt to straddle Christianity and contemporary forms of thought is not the theological equivalent of the emperor's new clothes, persuading no one save liberals themselves:

[92] Ward, 'Importance of Liberal Theology', 42.
[93] Bradley, *Grace, Order, Openness and Diversity*, 8–9.
[94] Ward, 'Importance of Liberal Theology', 46.
[95] Ward, 'Importance of Liberal Theology', 50–1.
[96] Ward, 'Importance of Liberal Theology', 50.

it is at least possible that deeper engagement with aspects of modernity ...
may produce a lesser form of Christian faith while at the same time inflating
Christians with their own importance while not enhancing the credibility of the
Christian faith.[97]

It is this critical ambivalence – and liberalism's intention to occupy a
mediating position between fundamentalism and atheism – that Cupitt
views as its greatest weakness, and the means by which liberal theology
will negate itself. While happy to use secular understandings of reason to
question biblical literalism and the miraculous events recounted in Scripture, this form of 'Old-style liberal religion' was 'reluctant to let go
completely. It clung to at least semi-realism about God, the objective
world and moral value'.[98] Yet reason does not only lead to the negation
of fundamentalism but to liberalism's own negation. This occurs in two
stages. First, the consistent use of secular forms of reason reveals that
Scripture and Christian tradition can be accounted for in purely natural
terms, and unmasks the Church's authority as only a concealed will-to-
power. Second, reason eventually comes to negate itself, as advances in
anthropology, sociology, and philosophy reveal that there is no tradition-
independent reason nor unmediated spiritual experience capable of providing the basis for neutral religious judgements. The disappearance of its
epistemological and theological foundations means that 'Liberalism is
being squeezed out, in society, in the Church, and in the intellectual
world'.[99] The result of this is that the choice is no longer between liberal
and conservative forms of Christianity, but only between postmodernity
and different species of fundamentalism.[100]

The intellectual self-negation of liberalism, and what Cupitt views as
its role in the growth of fundamentalism, is matched by the assessment of
Steve Bruce concerning liberalism's *social* self-negation. In a cutting
analysis, Bruce argues that theological liberalism – as it is instantiated
and promoted within many of the traditional denominations – is both
'symptom and cause' of secularisation, prompting as it does individual
autonomy and cultural pluralism.[101] According to Bruce, liberalism has
no way to preserve and grow its theological culture, possessing a 'number

---

[97] Daniel W. Hardy, 'Epilogue: The Structures of Liberalism', in *The Weight of Glory*, ed.
Daniel W. Hardy and Peter H. Sedgwick (Edinburgh: T&T Clark, 1991), 300.
[98] Don Cupitt, 'After Liberalism', in *The Weight of Glory*, eds. Daniel W. Hardy and Peter
H. Sedgwick (Edinburgh: T&T Clark, 1991), 255.
[99] Cupitt, 'After Liberalism', 255.   [100] Cupitt, 'After Liberalism', 252–4.
[101] Steve Bruce, 'The Problems of a Liberal Religion', in *The Future of Liberal Theology*, ed.
Mark D. Chapman (Aldershot: Ashgate, 2002), 232.

of organisationally deleterious features' that make social success almost impossible:

Liberal religion is weak because epistemological individualism makes it hard to develop consensus; reduces individual commitment; makes it hard to preserve the belief system from mutation; and weakens the will to reproduce the belief system.[102]

Lacking the features of a robust religious culture, for liberal Christians:

The purpose of church-going is to make us happy and comfortable and give our consciences a little jolt so that we buy ethically-traded coffee.[103]

While the tone of Bruce's argument is unkind, its analysis is supported by the great numerical decline of traditional – largely liberal – denominations. Liberalism attempted to deal with the challenge of modern thought and scepticism by undertaking critiques of traditional Christian doctrine, in particular, by largely rejecting the presuppositions that we have been examining. Yet the liberal critique of traditional doctrine is increasingly viewed as piecemeal, arbitrary, and self-negating, and its social structure incapable of presenting and sustaining a plausible expression of the Christian faith in today's society. While liberal Christians may wish to dissociate themselves from their past, they cannot dissociate themselves from the widespread public perception that they are guilty of self-contradiction: confessing creeds that are acceptable only as poetry, and preaching from Scriptures they believe to be full of errors. It is this perception that leads to a corresponding increase in the plausibility of fundamentalism, and the atheism that feeds off it. Whatever may be said regarding the orthodoxy of Protestant fundamentalist thought, there is cogency to the argument that it replicates more of traditional Protestantism than contemporary liberalism.[104] In a media age where, if one is explaining, one is losing, fundamentalists and atheists offer clarity, comprehensibility and the social demarcations necessary to survive and prosper in a sceptical, pluralist age.[105] While Cunningham has bemoaned the 'vulgar' aspect of new atheism, and Inchausti has blamed new atheism upon the theological poverty of Western societies, Hauerwas and Fish are

---

[102] Bruce, 'Problems of a Liberal Religion', 236.
[103] Bruce, 'Problems of a Liberal Religion', 236.
[104] See Rogers and McKim, *Authority and Interpretation of the Bible*; cf. John. D. Woodridge, *Biblical Authority: A Critique of the Rogers/McKim Proposal* (Grand Rapids: Zondervan, 1982).
[105] Boone, *Bible Tells Them*, 107; Stahl, 'One-Dimension Rage', 97–8.

perhaps closer to the truth, then, in their accusation that it is *liberal theology* that is at least partly responsible for new atheism, for liberalism has failed to advance a plausible alternative to fundamentalism, reverting instead to nebulous platitudes and religious universalism.[106] In this respect, the arguments of new atheists and Protestant fundamentalists are of value, for they locate errors and missteps in liberal and moderate forms of Christianity that are often hidden from their champions. In considering their arguments, and the growing social implausibility of non-fundamentalist forms of Christianity, the traditional Protestant denominations should perhaps consider whether more of their heritage might be retained or repaired, and whether they, in their judgement upon traditional Protestantism, may not have unwittingly condemned themselves.

This chapter has analysed the self-contradiction that new atheists and Protestant fundamentalists are led into by the attempt to stabilise their thought. This analysis was then integrated with the argument of Chapters 1–4. It was shown how new atheist and Protestant fundamentalist thought are both products of a common Protestant heritage, one that has now broken apart into conflicting poles, which, in their antipathy towards each other, share a secret sympathy. While the intolerant, specious and caricatured arguments of new atheists and Protestant fundamentalists are easy to scorn, non-fundamentalists dismiss them at their peril, for in their dependence upon the Protestant heritage of Britain and America, they at times represent that heritage more faithfully than the theologies that govern the major denominations. For this reason, we must not reject the presuppositions that ground and structure their thought out of hand, but seek to understand and, if possible, repair them.

---

[106] Cunningham, *Pious Idea*, xvii; Inchausti, 'Thomas Merton's Apologies', 4; Hauerwas and Fish, 'Miltonian Rebukes', 112.

Conclusion

This work has sought to answer two questions: first, what common historical and theological root does new atheist and Protestant fundamentalist thought come from, and, second, how does this common root, and the presuppositions that arise from it, structure their thought? In answering these questions, it has sought to defend the proposal that new atheism and Protestant fundamentalism share a common historical root in the English Reformation and its aftermath, and that this heritage has given rise to two presuppositions that play an important structural role in their thought: that Scripture's sense is literal, univocal and perspicuous and that divine activity in nature is disruptive or substitutionary.

In the course of advancing its primary argument, this work has reached a number of original conclusions regarding atheism, fundamentalism and the structure of Protestant thought in Britain and America. First, it has been demonstrated that, while lacking detail, popular comparisons between new atheists and Protestant fundamentalists are cogent. Second, it has been shown that atheism in Britain and America grew out of problems within Protestantism. This discovery undermines a range of academic and popular works that see no such connection, or which vehemently deny any historical dependence of atheism upon Christianity. Third, it has been shown that Protestant fundamentalism was a response to the same sequence of problems that gave rise to atheism and anti-Christian thought. Fourth, it has been demonstrated that theology is vital for the methodology and conclusions of new atheism, and that, in order to reject the Christian faith, atheists must engage in the task of theology, albeit negatively. Fifth, doubt has been cast on the self-understanding of both Protestant fundamentalism and new atheism, showing that

Protestant fundamentalism is not properly biblical, nor new atheism scientific. Instead, each are heavily indebted to presuppositions that neither can properly justify, utilising stabilising strategies that render both self-contradictory.

Whatever the substantive conclusions of this study, however, there are two more general outcomes that may be of use to the Western Church as it struggles to adapt to a post-Christian society as well as the intra-ecclesial and secular conflicts that accompany this development. The first possible use of this work is – to coin a phrase favoured by new atheists – as an aid to 'consciousness-raising' among Christians and atheists of all stripes. If the discoveries of this work are heeded, they can help to overcome the sterile public debate over religion in Britain and America, the foundation of which is the groundless belief that the religious and the non-religious have little in common. On the contrary, they share a great deal. Fundamentalism, atheism and liberal Christianity have all grown out of Protestant Christianity, and each represents divergent – yet related – responses to a shared set of historic problems. Awareness of this heritage, and the commonalities that come arise from it, can help to move us away from an understandable – if futile – preoccupation with the rationality of faith and towards a greater appreciation of the biblical, hermeneutical and theological assumptions that we bring to such questions. If groups as opposed as new atheists and Protestant fundamentalists share as much as this study suggests, there is hope that even greater commonalities can be found among those of a less extreme temperament.

The second possible significance of this study is as a spur to better theology among both atheists and Christians. As this study has shown, atheists are heavily engaged in the task of theology and advance arguments that are analogous to those that have been used by Christian theologians. Instead of treating atheists as immoral nihilists, or as ignorant interlocutors who do not deserve a hearing, this study suggests that they are often individuals who, given an imperfect understanding of the ground and grammar of Christian theology, have reached atheistic conclusions they need not have, conclusions that have serious consequences for both them and their readers. Given the theological presuppositions of new atheism identified by this study, Christian theologians should not treat this phenomenon as an existential threat but as an opportunity for service, friendly debate and love. Theologians can help clarify the biblical, hermeneutical and theological assumptions that atheists have, and – by reference to the rich tradition of the Church – introduce them to alternative intellectual paths. If nothing else, such efforts will improve the

atheism that atheists espouse, and make possible a more fruitful theological dialogue with unbelief, such has been seen in relation to classic
atheists such as Marx and Nietzsche. Rather than hurtful polemic, which
only confirms atheists in their hostility to the faith, seeing their efforts as
legitimate – if flawed – attempts to undertake the task of theology will
make the relationship between theology and atheism productive and
positive, rather than destructive, futile and fractious.

Yet this potential relationship also has consequences for Christian
theologians. As this study has suggested, it is not only new atheism that
stands in need of repair but certain core assumptions of British and
American Protestant theology. For ecclesiastical historians, this study
has highlighted a number of historical periods that stand in need of
further exploration, so that the complex constellation of intellectual,
social and political factors that precipitated atheism can be better understood. For systematic theologians, this study has identified two crucial
presuppositions for the genesis of new atheism. Constructive ways should
be found to repair these deficient beliefs, which are not only things of the
past but continue to inform much of contemporary Protestantism in
Britain and America. If the presuppositions that this work has examined
can be repaired in these ways, they can continue to inform Protestant
thought, without giving rise to atheism or fundamentalism.

It is this last need that is perhaps the most pressing, and it is in this
effort of repair that the arguments of new atheists and Protestant fundamentalists can act as spurs to better Christian theology and better Christian witness. Theologians must be shaken from the misapprehension that
what is popular is unimportant, and realise that it is atheists and fundamentalists – and not academic theologians – who have succeeded in
making their conception of the Christian faith normative within much
of the public consciousness of Britain and America. Rather than dismissing their criticisms as the fulminations of extremists, the Church – if it is to
fashion a vision of Christianity that can speak to the age – must listen to
the barbs of its uncultured despisers, for it is not through contemptuous
neglect of its theological adversaries but by patient and innovative study
that it will meet their criticisms and advance the cause for which it stands.

Bibliography

Abrams, Douglas Carl. *Selling the Old-Time Religion*. Atlanta and London: University of Georgia Press, 1998.
Addinall, Peter. *Philosophy and Biblical Interpretation*. Cambridge: Cambridge University Press, 1991.
Alexander, Denis. *Creation and Evolution: Do We Have to Choose?* Oxford: Monarch Books, 2008.
Allemayer, Bob. 'Atheism and Secularity in North America'. In *Atheism and Secularity*, vol. II, edited by Phil Zuckerman, 1–22. Santa Barbara: Praeger, 2010.
Anderson, David. *Creation or Evolution: Why We Must Choose*. Littlethorpe: J6D Publishers, 2009.
Answers in Genesis. *Journey through the Creation Museum*. Green Forest: Master Books, 2008.
Antony, Michael. 'Where's the Evidence?' *Philosophy Now*, April/May (2010): 18–21.
Aquinas, Thomas. *Summa Theologiae*, vol. I. California: NovAntiqua, 2008.
Summa Theologiae, vol. II. California: NovAntiqua, 2010.
Armstrong, Karen. *The Case for God*. London: Vintage Books, 2010.
Arnold, John. *Belief and Unbelief in Medieval Europe*. London: Hodder Arnold, 2005.
Astore, William J. *Observing God*. Aldershot: Ashgate, 2001.
Avalos, Hector. 'Why Biblical Studies Must End'. In *The End of Christianity*, edited by John W. Loftus, 107–29. Amherst: Prometheus Books, 2011.
Babinski, Edward T. *Leaving the Fold*. Amherst: Prometheus Books, 1995.
Bacon, Francis. *The New Organon*. Translated by Lisa Jardine and Michael Silverthorne. Cambridge: Cambridge University Press, 2000.
Bagg, Samuel, and David Voas. 'The Triumph of Indifference'. In *Atheism and Secularity*, vol. II, edited by Phil Zuckerman, 91–112. Santa Barbara: Praeger, 2010.
Baggini, Julian. *Atheism: A Very Short Introduction*. Oxford: Oxford University Press, 2003.

Barker, Dan. *Godless*. Berkeley: Ulysses Press, 2008.

Barr, James. *Fundamentalism*. London: SCM Press, 1977.

Bayer, Oswald. 'Martin Luther'. In *The Reformation Theologians*, edited by Carter Lindberg, 51–66. Oxford: Blackwell, 2002.

Beattie, James. *An Essay in the Nature and Immutability of Truth*. Bristol: Thoemmes Press, 2000.

Beattie, Tina. *The New Atheists*. London: Darton, Longman and Todd, 2007.

Bebbington, David W. *Evangelicalism in Modern Britain*. London and New York: Routledge, 2005.

Beeke, Joel R. *What did the Reformers Believe about the Age of the Earth?* Petersburg: Answers in Genesis, 2014.

Beit-Hallahmi, Benjamin. 'Morality and Immorality among the Irreligious'. In *Atheism and Secularity*, vol. I, edited by Phil Zuckerman, 113–48. Santa Barbara: Praeger, 2010.

Bentley, Richard. *Eight Sermons Preach'd at the Honourable Robert Boyle's Lecture*. Cambridge: Cornelius Crownfield, 1724.

Bergman, Jerry. *Hitler and the Nazi Darwinian Worldview*. Kitchener: Joshua Press, 2013.

Berman, David. *A History of Atheism in Britain*. London: Crook Helm, 1988.

Boghossian, Peter. *A Manual for Creating Atheists*. Durham, NC: Pitchstone Publishing, 2013.

Boone, Kathleen C. *The Bible Tells Them So*. Albany: State University of New York, 1989.

Bozeman, Theodore Dwight. *Protestants in an Age of Science*. Chapel Hill: University of North Carolina Press, 1977.

Bradlaugh, Charles. *The Bible: What It Is!*. London: 1857.

Bradley, Ian. *Grace, Order, Openness and Diversity*. London: Continuum, 2010.

Brooke, John Hedley. *Science and Religion: Some Historical Perspectives*. Cambridge: Cambridge University Press, 1991.

Brooke, John Hedley, and Geoffrey Cantor. *Reconstructing Nature: The Engagement of Science and Religion*. Edinburgh: T&T Clark, 1998.

Brown, Callum G. '"The Unholy Mrs Knight" and the BBC'. *English Historical Review* 128 (2012): 345–76.

Brown, Robert E. 'Edwards, Locke and the Bible'. *Journal of Religion* 79, no. 3 (1999): 361–84.

Bruce, Steve. 'The Problems of a Liberal Religion'. In *The Future of Liberal Theology*, edited by Mark D. Chapman, 221–41. Aldershot: Ashgate, 2002.

Buckley, Michael J. *At the Origins of Modern Atheism*. New Haven: Yale University Press, 1987.

Budd, Susan. 'The Loss of Faith: Reasons for Unbelief among Members of the Secular Movement in England 1850–1950'. *Past and Present* 36 (1967): 106–25.

Varieties of Unbelief. London: Heinemann, 1977.

Bullivant, Stephen. 'The New Atheism and Sociology'. In *Religion and the New Atheism: A Critical Appraisal*, edited by Amarnath Amarasingam, 109–24. Leiden: Brill, 2010.

'Defining "Atheism"'. In *The Oxford Handbook of Atheism*, edited by Stephen Bullivant and Michael Ruse, 11–21. Oxford: Oxford University Press, 2013.

Faith and Unbelief. Norwich: Canterbury Press, 2013.

Burnet, Gilbert. *Rational Method for Proving the Truth of the Christian Faith*. London, 1875.

Cabal, Ted, ed. *The Apologetics Study Bible*. Nashville: Holman Bible Publishers, 2007.

Calhoun, David B. *Princeton Seminary*, vol. I. United States: Banner of Truth Trust, 1994.

Calvin, John. *Institutes of the Christian Religion*. Translated by Henry Beveridge. Peabody: Hendrickson, 2008.

Cameron, Euan K. *The European Reformation*. Oxford: Clarendon Press, 1991.

Carpenter, Joel A. *Revive Us Again*. New York and Oxford: Oxford University Press, 1997.

Chadwick, Owen. *The Victorian Church, Part I*. London: A&C Black, 1966.

'The Established Church Under Attack'. In *The Victorian Crisis of Faith*, edited by Anthony Symondson, 91–105. London: SPCK, 1970.

The Victorian Church, Part II. London: SCM Press, 1972.

Chaffey, Tim. 'How Should We Interpret the Bible?' In *How Do We Know the Bible Is True?*, edited by Ken Ham and Bodie Hodge, 121–37. Green Forest: Master Books, 2011.

Chambers, Robert. *Vestiges of Natural Creation*. London: John Churchill, 1844.

Champion, J. A. I. *The Pillars of Priestcraft Shaken*. Cambridge: Cambridge University Press, 1992.

Chandler, Edward. *A Defence of Christianity from the Prophecies of the Old Testament*. London: James Knapton, 1725.

Chapman, Mark D. Introduction to *The Future of Liberal Theology*, edited by Mark D. Chapman, 3–17. Aldershot: Ashgate, 2002.

Cheyne, A. C. *Studies in Scottish Church History*. Edinburgh: T&T Clark, 1999.

Chillingworth, William. *The Religion of Protestants a Sure Way to Salvation*. London: Henry G. Bohn, 1846.

Cimino, Richard, and Christopher Smith. 'The New Atheism and the Empowerment of American Freethinkers'. In *Religion and the New Atheism: A Critical Appraisal*, edited by Amarnath Amarasingam, 139–56. Leiden: Brill, 2010.

Atheist Awakening. Oxford: Oxford University Press, 2014.

Clark, David K. 'Is Logic Arbitrary?' In *The Apologetics Study Bible*, edited by Ted Cabal, 930–1. Nashville: Holman Bible Publishers, 2007.

Clark, J. C. D. *English Society 1688–1832*. Cambridge: Cambridge University Press, 1985.

'Religion and Origins of Radicalism in Nineteenth-Century Britain'. In *English Radicalism 1550–1850*, edited by Glenn Burgess and Matthew Festenstein, 241–84. Cambridge: Cambridge University Press, 2007.

Clarke, Samuel. *A Demonstration of the Being and Attributes of God*. Cambridge: Cambridge University Press, 1998.

Cole, Stewart G. *The History of Fundamentalism*. London: Archon Books, 1963.

Coleman, Simon, and Leslie Carlin. Introduction to *The Cultures of Creationism*, edited by Simon Coleman and Leslie Carlin, 1–28. Aldershot: Ashgate, 2004.

Collingwood, Robert G. *An Essay on Metaphysics*. Oxford: Clarendon Press, 1969.

Collins, Anthony. *A Discourse of Free-Thinking*. London, 1713.

Grounds and Reasons of the Christian Religion. London, 1737.

Priestcraft in Perfection. London: B. Bragg, 1770.

Collinson, Peter. *The Religion of Protestants*. Oxford: Clarendon Press, 1982.

Comfort, Ray, ed. *The New Defender's Study Bible*. Nashville: World Publishing, 2006.

Cooke, Bill. *The Gathering of Infidels*. Amherst: Prometheus Books, 2004.

Copan, Paul. 'Does the Moral Argument Show There Is a God?' In *The Apologetics Study Bible*, ed. Ted Cabal, 1687. Nashville: Holman Bible Publishers, 2007.

'Isn't That Just Your Interpretation?' In *The Apologetics Study Bible*, edited by Ted Cabal, 1858. Nashville: Holman Bible Publishers, 2007.

Cotter, Christopher R. 'Consciousness Raising'. *International Journal for the Study of New Religions* 2, no. 1 (2011): 77–103.

Cunningham, Conor. *Darwin's Pious Idea*. Grand Rapids: William B. Eerdmans, 2010.

Cupitt, Don. 'After Liberalism'. In *The Weight of Glory*, edited by Daniel W. Hardy and Peter H. Sedgwick, 251–6. Edinburgh: T&T Clark, 1991.

Currid, John D. *A Study Commentary on Genesis*, vol. I. Darlington: Evangelical Press, 2003.

Currie, Robert. *Methodism Divided*. London: Faber & Faber, 1968.

Daniels, George H. *American Science in the Age of Jackson*. New York: Columbia University Press, 1968.

Darwin, Charles. *The Descent of Man*. London: John Murray, 1901.

Davie, Donald. *Dissentient Voice*. Notre Dame: University of Notre Dame Press, 1982.

Davie, George. *The Scotch Metaphysics*. London & New York: Routledge 2001.

Dawkins, Richard. *A Devil's Chaplain*. London: Phoenix, 2003.

An Appetite for Wonder. London: Black Swan, 2014.

'Convert's Corner'. Richard Dawkins Foundation. Last modified 4 September 2015. Accessed 2 December 2015. https://richarddawkins.net/community/convertscorner/.

'The Atheist'. Salon.com. Last modified 30 April 30 2005. Accessed 5 December 2015. www.salon.com/2005/04/30/dawkins/.

The Blind Watchmaker. London: Penguin Books, 2006.

The God Delusion. London: Black Swan, 2006.

The Selfish Gene. Oxford: Oxford University Press, 2006.

Unweaving the Rainbow. London: Penguin Books, 2006.

The Greatest Show on Earth. London: Black Swan, 2010.

The Magic of Reality. London: Bantam Press, 2011.

De Botton, Alain. *Religion for Atheists*. London: Hamish Hamilton, 2012.

Dennett, Daniel C. *Darwin's Dangerous Idea*. London: Allen Lane, 1995.

Breaking the Spell. London: Penguin Books, 2007.

'*The Selfish Gene* as a Philosophical Essay'. In *Richard Dawkins: How a Scientist Changed the Way We Think*, edited by Allan Grafen and Mark Ridley, 101–15. Oxford: Oxford University Press, 2007.

Desmond, Adrian. 'Artisan Resistance and Evolution in Britain, 1819–1848'. *Osiris* 3 (1987): 77–110.

 Huxley: The Devil's Disciple. London: Michael Joseph, 1994.

 Huxley: Evolution's High Priest. London: Michael Joseph, 1997.

DeWitt, David A. *Unravelling the Origins Controversy*. Lynchburg: Creation Curriculum, 2007.

Ditchfield, George M. *The Evangelical Revival*. London: University College London Press, 1998.

Donne, John. *Essayes in Divinity*. Oxford: Clarendon Press, 1952.

Dorrien, Gary. *The Making of American Liberal Theology: Imagining Progressive Religion 1805–1900*. Louisville: Westminster John Knox Press, 2001.

Draper, John W. *History of the Conflict between Religion and Science*. London: Kegan Paul, Trench & Co, 1887.

Drummond, Andrew L., and James Bulloch. *The Church in Victorian Scotland*, vol. II. Edinburgh: Saint Andrew Press, 1975.

 The Church in Late Victorian Scotland, vol. III. Edinburgh: Saint Andrew Press, 1978.

Dupree, A. Hunter. 'Christianity and the Scientific Community in the Age of Darwin'. In *God and Nature*, edited by David C. Lindberg and Ronald L. Numbers, 351–68. Berkeley: University of California Press, 1986.

Eagleton, Terry. *God, Faith, and Revolution*. New Haven: Yale University Press, 2009.

Eldridge, Niles. *The Triumph of Evolution and the Failure of Creationism*. New York: W. H. Freeman, 2000.

Ellegård, Alvar. *Darwin and the General Reader*. Göteborg: Göteborgs Universitet, 1958.

Eller, David. 'Christianity Evolving'. In *The End of Christianity*, edited by John W. Loftus, 23–51. Amherst: Prometheus Books, 2011.

Eller, Jack David. 'What Is Atheism?' In *Atheism and Secularism*, edited by Phil Zuckerman, 1–18. Santa Barbara: Praeger, 2010.

Emsley, Clive. *British Society and the French Wars 1793–1815*. London: Macmillan, 1979.

Endersby, Jim. Introduction to *On the Origin of Species, by Charles Darwin*, ix–lxv. Cambridge: Cambridge University Press, 2009.

Erdozain, Dominic. *The Soul of Doubt*. Oxford: Oxford University Press, 2015.

Evans, Gillian R. *Problems of Authority in the Reformation Debates*. Cambridge: Cambridge University Press, 1992.

Falcioni, Ryan C. 'Is God a Hypothesis? The New Atheism and the Philosophy of Religion'. In *Religion and the New Atheism: A Critical Appraisal*, edited by Amarnath Amarasingam, 203–24. Leiden: Brill, 2010.

Farias, Miguel. 'The Psychology of Atheism'. In *The Oxford Handbook of Atheism*, edited by Stephen Bullivant and Michael Ruse, Oxford, 468–82. Oxford University Press, 2013.

Ferreira, M. Jamie. 'Locke's 'Constructive Skepticism' – A Reappraisal'. *Journal of the History of Philosophy* 24, no. 2 (1986): 211–22.

Feyerabend, Paul K. 'Classical Empiricism'. In *The Methodological Heritage of Newton*, edited by Robert E. Butts and John W. Davis, 150–70. Oxford: Basil Blackwell, 1970.

Fiala, Andrew. 'Militant Atheism, Pragmatism, and the God-Shaped Hole'. *International Journal for Philosophy of Religion* 65 (2009): 139–51.

Finlay, Graeme, and Stephen Pattermore. 'Christian Theology and Neo-Darwinism Are Compatible'. In *Debating Darwin*, edited by Graeme Finlay, 31–67. Milton Keynes: Paternoster, 2009.

Firma, Terry. 'Reddit's Biggest Atheism Hangout Scores Sky-High for Toxic Content and Bigotry'. Last modified 16 March 2015. Accessed 30 November 2015. www.patheos.com/blogs/friendlyatheist/2015/03/16/reddits-biggest-atheism-hangout-scores-sky-high-for-toxic-content-and-bigotry-data-analysts-say/.

Foote, F. W., and W. P. Ball. *The Bible Handbook*. London: Progressive Publishing, 1888.

Frei, Hans. *The Eclipse of Biblical Narrative*. New Haven and London: Yale University Press, 1974.

Fuller, Steve. 'What Has Atheism Ever Done for Science?' In *Religion and the New Atheism: A Critical Appraisal*, edited by Amarnath Amarasingam, 57–77. Leiden: Brill, 2010.

Funkenstein, Amos. *Theology and the Scientific Imagination*. Princeton: Princeton University Press, 1986.

Fyfe, Aileen. 'William Paley's Natural Theology in the University of Cambridge'. *British Journal for the History of Science* 30 (1997): 321–35.

Garner, Paul. *The New Creationism*. Darlington: Evangelical Press, 2009.

Gericke, Jaco. 'Can God Exist if Yahweh Doesn't?' In *The End of Christianity*, edited by John W. Loftus, 131–54. Amherst: Prometheus Books, 2011.

Gillispie, Charles C. *Genesis and Geology*. Cambridge, Mass.: Harvard University Press, 1951.

Gillespie, Michael Allen. *The Theological Origins of Modernity*. Chicago: University of Chicago Press, 2008.

Ginger, Ray. *Six Days or Forever?* Boston: Beacon Press, 1958.

Gish, Duane T. *Evolution? The Fossils Say No!* San Diego: Creation-Life Publishers, 1973.

Evolution: The Fossils Still Say No! El Cajon: Institute for Creation Research, 1995.

Glover, Willis B. *Evangelical Nonconformists and Higher Criticism in the Nineteenth Century*. London: Independent Press, 1954.

Goodwin, Charles W. 'On the Mosaic Cosmogony'. In *Essays and Reviews*, 206–53. London: J. W. Parker & Son, 1860.

Gould, Stephen Jay. 'Evolution as Fact and Theory'. In *Science and Creationism*, edited by Ashley Montagu, 117–25. Oxford: Oxford University Press, 1984.

Goring, Jeremy. Introduction to *The English Presbyterians*, edited by C. Gordon Bolam, 17–28. London: George Allan and Unwin, 1968.

'The Break-Up of the Old Dissent'. In *The English Presbyterians*, edited by C. Gordon Bolam, 175–218. London: George Allan and Unwin, 1968.

Grayling, A. C. *Against all Gods*. London: Oberon Books, 2007.

    The God Argument. London: Bloomsbury, 2013.

Gregory, Brad S. *The Unintended Reformation*. Cambridge: Belknap Press of Harvard University Press, 2012.

Grislis, Egil. 'The Hermeneutical Problem in Hooker'. In *Studies in Richard Hooker*, edited by W. Speed Hill, 159–206. Cleveland: Case Western Reserve University, 1971.

Groothuis, Douglas R. 'How Should a Christian Understand Postmodernism'. In *The Apologetics Study Bible*, edited by Ted Cabal, 1385–6. Nashville: Holman Bible Publishers, 2007.

Guenther, Katja M., Kerry Mulligan and Cameron Papp. 'From the Outside In'. *Social Problems* 60, no. 4 (2013): 457–75.

Gunton, Colin. *The Triune Creator*. Edinburgh: Edinburgh University Press, 1998.

Ham, Ken. *The Lie*. Green Forest: Master Books, 2012.

    Six Days. Green Forest: Master Books, 2013.

    'Atheists Outline Their Global Religious Agenda'. In *A Pocket Guide to Atheism*, edited by Ken Ham, 11–17. Petersburg: Answers in Genesis, 2014.

    Introduction to A Pocket Guide to Atheism, edited by Ken Ham, 7–10. Petersburg: Answers in Genesis, 2014.

Ham, Ken, and A. Charles Ware. *Darwin's Plantation*. Green Forest: Master Books, 2007.

Ham, Ken, and Greg Hall. *Already Compromised*. Green Forest: Master Books, 2011.

Hanegraaff, Hank. *The Farce of Evolution*. Nashville: Word Publishing, 1998.

Harding, Susan Friend. *The Book of Jerry Falwell*. Princeton: Princeton University Press, 2000.

Hardy, Daniel W. 'Epilogue: The Strategy of Liberalism'. In *The Future of Liberal Theology*, edited by Mark D. Chapman, 299–304. Aldershot: Ashgate, 2002.

    'Epilogue: The Structures of Liberalism'. In *The Weight of Glory*, edited by Daniel W. Hardy and Peter H. Sedgwick. Edinburgh: T&T Clark, 1991.

Harold, Francis, Raymond Eve, and John Taylor. 'Creationism: American-Style'. In *The Cultures of Creationism*, edited by Simon Coleman and Leslie Carlin, 67–84. Aldershot: Ashgate, 2004.

Harris, Harriet A. *Fundamentalism and Evangelicals*. Oxford: Clarendon, 1998.

    'How Helpful Is the Term "Fundamentalist?"' In *Fundamentalisms*, edited by Christopher H. Partridge, 3–18. Carlisle: Paternoster, 2001.

    'Fundamentalism in a Protestant Context'. In *Fundamentalism: Church and Society*, edited by Martyn Percy and Ian Jones, 7–24. London: SPCK, 2002.

Harris, Mark. *The Nature of Creation*. Durham: Acumen, 2013.

Harris, Sam. *The End of Faith*. London: The Free Press, 2006.

    Letter to a Christian Nation. London: Bantam Press, 2007.

Harrison, Peter. *The Bible, Protestantism, and the Rise of Natural Science*. Cambridge: Cambridge University Press, 1998.

    The Fall of Man and the Foundations of Science. Cambridge: Cambridge University Press, 2007.

The Territories of Science and Religion. Chicago and London: Chicago University Press, 2015.

Hart, David Bentley. *Atheist Delusions*. New Haven: Yale University Press, 2009.

Hauerwas, Stanley, and Stanley Fish. 'Miltonian Rebukes in an Age of Reason'. In *'God Is Dead' and I Don't Feel So Good Myself*, edited by Andrew Davis, 108–19. Eugene: Cascade Books, 2010.

Haughen, Kristine L. *Richard Bentley: Poetry and Enlightenment*. Cambridge, Mass.: Harvard University Press, 2011.

Haught, John F. *God and the New Atheism*. Louisville: Westminster John Knox Press, 2008.

Herrick, Jim. *Vision and Realism: A Hundred Years of the Freethinker*. London: G. W. Foote & Co, 1982.

Hitchens, Christopher. *God Is Not Great*. London: Atlantic Books, 2008.

Higgens-Biddle, John C. Introduction to *The Reasonableness of Christianity, by John Locke, xv-cxv*. Oxford: Clarendon Press, 1999.

Hill, Christopher. *Some Intellectual Consequences of the English Revolution*. London: Weidenfeld & Nicholson, 1980.

'Irreligion in the "Puritan" Revolution'. In *Radical Religion in the English Revolution*, edited by J. F. McGregor and B. Reay, 191–211. Oxford: Oxford University Press, 1984.

The English Bible and the Seventeenth-Century Revolution. London: Allen Lane, 1993.

'Freethinking and Libertinism: The Legacy of the English Revolution'. In *The Margins of Orthodoxy*, edited by Roger D. Lund, 54–70. Cambridge: Cambridge University Press, 1993.

Hobsbawn, Edward. 'Methodism and Revolution'. In *Religion and Revolution in Early-Industrial England*, edited by Gerald W. Olsen, 145–51. Lanham: University Press of America, 1990.

Hodge, A. A., and B. B. Warfield. 'Inspiration'. *The Presbyterian Review* 6 (1881): 225–60.

Hodge, Bodie. 'Cock-a-Doodle One or Two?' In *Demolishing Supposed Bible Contradictions*, edited by Ken Ham, Bodie Hodge, and Ted Chaffey, 123–8. Green Forest: Master Books, 2012.

'Evolutionary Humanism: The Bloodiest Religion Ever'. In *A Pocket Guide to Atheism*, edited by Ken Ham, 19–33. Petersburg: Answers in Genesis, 2014.

Hodge, Charles. *Systematic Theology*, vol. I. London and Edinburgh: Thomas Nelson & Sons, 1880.

'What Is Darwinism?' and Other Writings on Science and Religion, edited by Mark A. Noll and David N. Livingstone. Grand Rapids: Baker Books, 1994.

Hodgson, Peter C. *Liberal Theology: A Radical Vision*. Minneapolis: Fortress Press, 2007.

Holder, R. Ward. *John Calvin and the Grounding of Interpretation*. Leiden: Brill, 2006.

Holyoake, G. J. *Paley Refuted in His Own Words*. London: J. Watson, 1851.

Hood, Ralph W., and Zhuo Chen. 'Conversion and Deconversion'. In *The Oxford Handbook of Atheism*, edited by Stephen Bullivant and Michael Ruse, 537–52. Oxford: Oxford University Press, 2013.

Hovenkamp, Herbert. *Science and Religion in America*. Philadelphia: University of Philadelphia Press, 1978.

Hughes, John, ed. *The Unknown God*. Eugene: Cascade Books, 2013.

Hunter, G. W. *Civic Biology*. New York: American Book Company, 1914.

Hunter, Michael. 'The Problem of 'Atheism' in Early Modern England'. *Transactions of the Royal Historical Society* 35 (1985): 125–57.

Huxley, Thomas H. *Collected Essays*, vol. II. Cambridge: Cambridge University Press, 2011.

   Collected Essays, vol. IV. Cambridge: Cambridge University Press, 2011.

   Collected Essays, vol. V. Cambridge: Cambridge University Press, 2011.

   Lay Sermons, Addresses and Reviews. Cambridge: Cambridge University Press, 2009.

Hyman, Gavin. 'Postmodern Theology: The Apotheosis or Scourge of Liberalism?' In *The Future of Liberal Theology*, edited by Mark D. Chapman, 191–207. Aldershot: Ashgate, 2002.

   A Short History of Atheism. London: I. B. Tauris, 2010.

Inchausti, Robert. 'Thomas Merton's Apologies to an Unbeliever'. In *'God Is Dead' and I Don't Feel So Good Myself*, edited by Andrew David, 2–8. Eugene: Cascade Books, 2010.

Jacobs, Margaret C. *The Newtonians and the English Revolution 1689–1720*. Hassocks: Harvester Press, 1976.

Jacoby, Susan. *Freethinkers: A History of American Secularism*. New York: Henry Holt and Company, 2004.

Johnson, Philip E. *Darwin on Trial*. Downer's Grove: Inter-Varsity Press, 1993.

   The Wedge of Truth. Downer's Grove: Inter-Varsity Press, 2000.

Jones, Julie S. *Being the Chosen*. Farnton: Ashgate, 2010.

Jones, Steve. *The Serpent's Promise*. London: Little, Brown, 2013.

Jowett, Benjamin. 'On the Interpretation of Scripture'. In *Essays and Reviews*, 330–433. London: J. W. Parker, 1860.

Juergensmeyer, Mark. 'The Debate over Hindutva'. *Religion* 26 (1996): 129–35.

Katz, David S. *God's Last Words*. New Haven and London: Yale University Press, 2004.

Kelly, Douglas F. *Creation and Change*. Ross-shire: Mentor Books, 2010.

Kennedy, Ludovic. *All in the Mind*. London: Hodder and Stoughton, 1999.

Kerby, Carl, and Ken Ham. 'The 'Evolutionising' of a Culture'. In *War of the Worldviews*, edited by Gary Vaterlaus, 7–14. Hebron: Answers in Genesis, 2005.

Knott, Edward. *Mercy and Truth, or Charity Mayntayned*. Saint-Omer, 1634.

Kors, Alan C. *Atheism in France 1650–1729*. Princeton: Princeton University Press, 1990.

Kuipers, Ronald A. 'The New Atheism and the Spiritual Landscape of the West'. In *'God Is Dead' and I Don't Feel So Good Myself*, edited by Andrew David, 120–8. Eugene: Cascade Books, 2010.

Kuklick, Bruce. *A History of Philosophy in America 1720–2000*. Oxford: Clarendon Press, 2001.

Lardas, John. *Secularism in Antebellum America*. Chicago: University of Chicago Press, 2011.

Larson, Edward J. *Trial and Error*. Oxford: Oxford University Press, 2003.

Larsen, Timothy. *Crisis of Doubt*. Oxford: Oxford University Press, 2006.

A People of One Book. Oxford: Oxford University Press, 2011.

Lash, Nicholas. *Theology for Pilgrims*. Notre Dame: University of Notre Dame Press, 2008.

Leask, Ian. 'Personation and Immanent Undermining: On Toland's Appearing Lockean'. *British Journal for the History of Philosophy* 18, no. 2 (2010): 231–56.

LeDrew, Stephen. *The Evolution of Atheism*. Oxford: Oxford University Press, 2016.

Lienesch, Michael. *In the Beginning*. Chapel Hill: University of North Carolina Press, 2007.

Lindbeck, George A. *The Nature of Doctrine*. Louisville, Ken.: Westminster John Knox, 2009.

Lloyd, Stephen. 'Christian Theology and Neo-Darwinism Are Incompatible'. In *Debating Darwin*, edited by Graeme Finlay, 1–29. Milton Keynes: Paternoster, 2009.

Locke, John. *An Essay Concerning Human Understanding*. Edited by Peter H. Nidditch. Oxford: Clarendon Press, 1979.

Loftus, John W. *Why I Became an Atheist*. Amherst: Prometheus Books, 2008.

Introduction to *The End of Christianity*, edited by John W. Loftus, 9–20. Amherst: Prometheus Books, 2011.

Long, Jason. *Biblical Nonsense*. New York: iUniverse, 2005.

Longfield, Bradley J. *The Presbyterian Controversy*. New York and Oxford: Oxford University Press, 1991.

Lubac, Henri de. *Medieval Exegesis*, vol. I. Translated by M. Sebanc. Grand Rapids: William B. Eerdmans, 1998.

Medieval Exegesis, vol. III. Translated by E. M. Macierowski. Grand Rapids: William B. Eerdmans, 1999.

Luther, Martin. 'How Christians Should Regard Moses'. In *Martin Luther's Basic Theological Writings*, edited by Timothy F. Lull, 135–48. Minneapolis: Fortress Press, 1989.

'The Freedom of a Christian'. In *Martin Luther's Basic Theological Writings*, edited by Timothy F. Lull, 585–629. Minneapolis: Fortress Press, 1989.

'Preface to the Old Testament'. In *Martin Luther's Basic Theological Writings*, edited by Timothy F. Lull, 118–34. Minneapolis: Fortress Press, 1989.

MacArthur, John. *Battle for the Beginning*. United States: W Publishing Group, 2001.

MacCulloch, Diarmaid. *Thomas Cranmer*. New Haven: Yale University Press, 1996.

Machen, J. Gresham. *Christianity and Liberalism*. Grand Rapids: William B. Eerdmans, 2009.

Mack, Phyllis. *Heart Religion in the British Enlightenment*. Cambridge: Cambridge University Press, 2008.

Mahieu, D. L. Le. *The Mind of William Paley*. Lincoln, Neb.: University of Nebraska Press, 1976.

Martin, A. L. *The World of the Ranters*. London: Lawrence & Wishart, 1970.

Martin, Joseph W. *Religious Radicals in Tudor England*. London: Hambleden Press, 1989.

Martin, T. T. *Hell and the High Schools*. Kansas City: Western Baptist Publishing, 1923.

Marty, Martin E. *The Infidel*. Cleveland: Meridian Books, 1961.

Marty, Martin E., and R. Scott Appleby. *The Power and the Glory*. Boston: Beacon Press, 1992.

Marty, Martin E., and R. Scott Appleby, eds. *The Fundamentalism Project*. Chicago: Chicago University Press, 1993–1995.

Marsden, George M. *Fundamentalism and American Culture*. Oxford: Oxford University Press, 1980.

'Understanding Fundamentalist Views of Science'. In *Science and Creationism*, edited by Ashley Montagu, 95–116. Oxford: Oxford University Press, 1984.

Understanding Fundamentalism and Evangelicalism. Grand Rapids: Eerdmans, 1991.

Marsh, Joss L. '"Bibliolatry" and "Bible-Smashing": G. W. Foote, George Meredith, and the Heretic Trope of the Book'. *Victorian Studies* 34 (1991): 315–36.

May, Henry F. *The Enlightenment in America*. New York: Oxford University Press, 1976.

McCalman, Iain. *Radical Underworld*. Oxford: Clarendon Press, 1993.

McCosh, James. *The Scottish Philosophy*. London: Macmillan & Co, 1875.

McGrath, Alister. *The Intellectual Origins of the European Reformation*. London: Blackwell, 2004.

The Twilight of Atheism. London: Rider, 2004.

Why Faith Won't Go Away. London: SPCK, 2011.

McGrath, Alister, and Joanna Collicutt McGrath. *The Dawkins Delusion?*. London: SPCK, 2007.

McGregor, J. F. 'Seekers and Ranters'. In *Radical Religion in the English Revolution*, edited by J. F. McGregor and Barry Reay, 129–34. Oxford: Oxford University Press, 1984.

McNaughton, Ian, and Paul Taylor. *Darwin and Darwinism 150 Years Later*. Leominster: Day One, 2009.

Midgeley, Mary. *Evolution as a Religion*. London and New York: Methuem, 1985.

Miller, Hugh. *The Testimony of the Rocks*. Boston: Gould and Lincoln, 1857.

Mitchell, Elizabeth. 'What Are the Tactics of the New Atheists?' In *A Pocket Guide to Atheism*, edited by Ken Ham, 35–50. Petersburg: Answers in Genesis, 2014.

Moffat, Russel. *Atheists Can Be W***ers Too*. Milton Keynes: AuthorHouse, 2009.

Moore, J. T. 'Locke's Analysis of Language'. *Journal of the History of Ideas* 37 (1976): 707–14.

Moore, James R. *The Post-Darwinian Controversies*. Cambridge: Cambridge University Press, 1979.

Moorhead, James H. *Princeton Seminary in American Religion and Culture*. Grand Rapids: Eerdmans Publishing Co., 2012.

More, Thomas. *Complete Works of St Thomas More*, vol. VIII. Edited by Louis A. Schister, Richard Marius, James P. Lusardi. New Haven: Yale University Press, 1973.

Complete Works of St Thomas More, vol. VI. Edited by Thomas M. C. Lawler, Germain Marc'hadour and Richard Marius. New Haven: Yale University Press, 1981.

Morris, Henry M. *Men of Science – Men of God*. San Diego: Master Books, 1988.

Science and the Bible. Chicago: Moody Press, 1995.

The Genesis Record. Grand Rapids: Baker Book House, 1998.

The Beginning of the World. Green Forest: Master Books, 1999.

Defending the Faith. Green Forest: Master Books, 2000.

The Long War Against God. Green Forest: Master Books, 2000.

Biblical Creationism. Green Forest: Master Books, 2013.

Morris, Henry M., and John D. Morris. *The Modern Creation Trilogy*, vol. I. Green Forest: Master Books, 1996.

The Modern Creation Trilogy, Vol III. Green Forest: Master Books, 1996.

Morris, Henry M., and Henry M. Morris III. *Many Infallible Proofs*. Green Forest: Master Books, 1996.

Morris Henry M., and Martin E. Clark. *The Bible Has the Answer*. Green Forest: Master Books, 1999.

Mortenson, Terry. 'Did Bible Authors Believe in a Literal Genesis?' In *The New Answers Book 3*, edited by Ken Ham, 81–9. Green Forest: Master Books, 2010.

Murphy, Nancey. 'Engaging Robert J. Russell's Alpha and Omega'. *Zygon* 45, no. 1 (2010): 193–212.

Nesbitt, G. L. *Benthamite Reviewing: the First Twelve Years of the Westminster Review*. New York: Columbia University Press, 1934.

Newton, Isaac. *Opticks*. 2nd ed. London, 1718.

Philosophiae Naturalis Principia Mathematica. Translated by I. Bernard Cohen and Anne Whitman. Berkeley: University of California Press, 1999.

Noll, Mark A. 'Common Sense Tradition and American Evangelical Thought'. *American Quarterly* 37, no. 2 (1985): 212–38.

'The Irony of the Enlightenment for Presbyterians in the Early Republic'. *Jounral of the Early Republic*, 5, no. 2 (1985): 149–75.

Between Faith and Criticism. Vancouver: Regent College Publishing, 1998.

Numbers, Ronald L. 'Creationists and Their Critics in Australia'. In *The Cultures of Creationism*, edited by Simon Coleman and Leslie Carlin, 109–23. Aldershot: Ashgate, 2004.

The Creationists. Cambridge, Mass.: Harvard University Press, 2006.

Nuovo, Victor. Introduction to *Vindications of the Reasonableness of Christianity*, by John Locke, xvii–cxi. Oxford: Clarendon Press, 2012.

Oberman, Heiko A. *Luther: Man between God and the Devil*. New Haven and London: Yale University Press, 1988.

Ocker, Christopher. 'Scholastic Interpretation of the Bible'. In *A History of Biblical Interpretation*, vol. II, edited by Alan J. Hauser and Duane Frederick Watson, 254–79. Grand Rapids: William B. Eerdmans, 2009.

O'Higgins, James. *Anthony Collins: the Man and His Work*. The Hague: Martinus Nijhoff, 1970.

Oliver, Simon. *Philosophy, God and Motion*. London and New York: Routledge, 2005.

Olsen, Gerald W., ed. *Religion and Revolution in Early-Industrial England*. Lanham: University Press of America, 1990.

Onfray, Michel. *In Defence of Atheism*. London: Serpent's Tail, 2007.

Ozment, Steven E. *Mysticism and Dissent*. New Haven: Yale University Press, 1973.

   The Age of Reform 1250–1550. New Haven and London: Yale University Press, 1980.

Paine, Thomas. *Rights of Man*. London: J. S. Jordan, 1791.

   Age of Reason, Part I. Paris: 1794.

   Age of Reason, Part II. London, 1799.

Paley, William. *Collected Works*, vol. IV. London: Thomas Davison, 1825.

   Natural Theology. Oxford: Oxford University Press, 2006.

Park, Robert L. *Superstition: Belief in an Age of Science*. Princeton: Princeton University Press, 2010.

Parker, Henry W. *The Agnostic Gospel*. New York: John B. Alden, 1896.

Partridge, Christopher H. Introduction to *Fundamentalisms*, edited by Christopher H. Partridge, 1–16. Carlisle: Paternoster, 2001.

Pasquale, Frank L. 'A Portrait of Secular Group Affiliates.' In *Atheism and Secularity*, vol. I, edited by Phil Zuckerman, 43–87. Santa Barbara: Praeger, 2010.

Patrick, Simon. *A Brief Account of the New Sect of Latitude-Men*. London, 1662.

Patterson, Roger. *Evolution Exposed*. Hebron: Answers in Genesis, 2007.

   'Self-Refuting Skepticism'. In *A Pocket Guide to Atheism*, edited by Ken Ham, 67–73. Petersburg: Answers in Genesis, 2014.

Perkin, Harold. *The Origins of Modern English Society 1780–1880*. London: Routledge, 1969.

Pigliucci, Massimo. 'New Atheism and the Scientistic Turn in the Atheism Movement'. *Midwest Studies in Philosophy* 38 (2013): 142–53.

Pitkin, Barbara. 'John Calvin and the Interpretation of the Bible'. In *A History of Biblical Interpretation*, vol. II, edited by Allen J. Hauser and Duane Frederick Watson, 341–71. Grand Rapids: William B. Eerdmans, 2009.

Pius IX, Pope. 'The Syllabus of Errors Condemned by Pius IX'. Last modified 2002. Accessed 15 September 2015. www.papalencyclicals.net/Pius09/p9syll.htm.

Plantinga, Alvin. 'The Dawkins Confusion: Naturalism "Ad Absurdam"'. In *God Is Great, God Is Good*, edited by William Lane Craig and Chad Meister, 247–58. Downers Grove: Inter-Varsity Press, 2009.

Pocock, J. G. A. 'Within the Margins: the Definition of Orthodoxy'. In *The Margins of Orthodoxy*, edited by Roger D. Lund, 33–53. Cambridge: Cambridge University Press, 1995.

Popkin, Richard H. *The History of Scepticism from Erasmus to Spinoza*. Berkeley: University of California Press, 1979.
Porterfield, Amanda. *Conceived in Doubt*. Chicago: Chicago University Press, 2012.
Pyle, Andrew. *Agnosticism*. Bristol: Thoemmes Press, 1995.
Reardon, Bernard M. G. *Religious Thought in the Reformation*. London: Longman, 1995.
Rectenwald, Michael. 'Secularism and the Cultures of Nineteenth-century Scientific Naturalism'. *The British Journal for the History of Science* 46, no. 2 (2013): 231–54.
Reid, Thomas. *Essays on the Intellectual Powers of Man*. Indianapolis: Hackett Publishing Company, 1983.
Enquiry into the Human Mind. Edinburgh: Edinburgh University Press, 1997.
Reid, William H. *The Rise and Dissolution of the Infidel Societies of the Metropolis*. London, 1800.
Reventlow, Henning Graf. *The Authority of the Bible and the Rise of the Modern World*. Translated by. J. Bowden. London: SCM Press, 1984.
Rhodes, Ron. 'Has the Bible's Text Been Changed over the Years?' In *How Do We Know the Bible Is True?*, edited by Ken Ham and Bodie Hodge, 265–74. Green Forest: Master Books, 2011.
Riesen, Richard A. ''Higher Criticism' in the Free Church Fathers'. *Records of the Scottish Church History Society* 20 (1980): 119–42.
Roberts, Jon H. *Darwinism and the Divine in America*. Madison: University of Wisconsin Press, 1988.
Robertson, David. *The Dawkins Letters*. Ross-shire: Christian Focus, 2010.
Rogers, Jack B., and Donald K. McKim. *The Authority and Interpretation of the Bible*. San Francisco: Harper & Row, 1979.
Ross, T. M. 'The Implicit Theology of Carl Sagan'. *Pacific Theological Review* 18, no. 2 (1985): 24–32.
Royle, Edward. *Victorian Infidels*. Manchester: Manchester University Press, 1974.
Radicals, Secularists and Republicans. Manchester: Manchester University Press, 1980.
Royle, Edward, and James Walvin. *English Radicals and Reformers 1760–1848*. Brighton: Harvester Press, 1982.
Rummel, Erika. 'The Renaissance Humanists'. In *A History of Biblical Interpretation*, vol. II, edited by Allen J. Hauser and Duane Frederick Watson, 280–98. Grand Rapids: William B. Eerdmans, 2009.
Rupp, E. Gordon. *Religion in England 1688–1791*. Oxford: Clarendon Press, 1986.
Ruse, Michael. 'Naturalism and the Scientific Method'. In *The Oxford Handbook of Atheism*, edited by Stephen Bullivant and Michael Ruse, 383–97. Oxford: Oxford University Press, 2013.
Russell, Bertrand. *Religion and Science*. London: Oxford University Press, 1960.
Why I am Not a Christian and Other Essays. London: Unwin Books, 1967.
Ruthven, Malise. *Fundamentalism: The Search for Meaning*. Oxford: Oxford University Press, 2004.

Sagan, Carl. 'The Shores of the Cosmic Ocean'. Cosmos: Carl Sagan Episode Scripts. Last modified 14 September 2012. Accessed 5 December2015. www .springfieldspringfield.co.uk/view_episode_scripts.php?tv-show=cosmos-carl-sagan&episode=s01e01.

Sandeen, Ernest R. *The Roots of Fundamentalism*. Chicago: Chicago University Press, 1970.

Sarfati, Jonathan. *Refuting Evolution*. Brisbane: Answers in Genesis, 2002.

Savage, Sara. 'A Psychology of Fundamentalism'. In *Fundamentalism: Church and Society*, edited by Martyn Percy and Ian Jones, 25–52. London: SPCK, 2002.

Schaefer, Donovan O. 'Blessed, Precious Mistakes: Deconstruction, Evolution, and New Atheism in America'. *International Journal for Philosophy of Religion* 76 (2014): 75–94.

Schreiner, S. E. *The Theater of His Glory*. Durham: Labyrinth Press, 1991.

Schulzke, Marcus. 'The Politics of New Atheism'. *Politics and Religion* 6 (2013): 778–99.

Secord, James A. *Victorian Sensation*. Chicago: Chicago University Press, 2000.

Sell, Allan P. F. *John Locke and the Eighteenth-Century Divines*. Cardiff: University of Wales Press, 1997.

Sellers, Ian. *Nineteenth-Century Nonconformity*. London: E. Arnold, 1977.

Shapiro, Barbara J. *A Culture of Fact*. Ithaca: Cornell University Press, 2000.

Shermer, Michael. *Why Darwin Matters*. New York: Henry Holt and Company, 2006.

   'The Skeptic's Chaplain'. In *Richard Dawkins: How a Scientist Changed the Way We Think*, edited by Allan Grafen and Mark Ridley, 227–35. Oxford: Oxford University Press, 2007.

Smith, Jess M. 'Becoming an Atheist in America'. *Sociology of Religion* 72, no. 2 (2011): 215–37.

Spencer, Nick. *Atheists: The Origin of the Species*. London: Bloomsbury Continuum, 2014.

Sprat, Thomas. *The History of the Royal Society of London*. London, 1667.

Stahl, William A. 'One-Dimensional Rage'. In *Religion and the New Atheism: A Critical Appraisal*, edited by Amarnath Amarasingam, 97–108. Leiden: Brill, 2010.

Statham, Dominic. *Evolution: Good Science?* Leominster: Day One, 2009.

Steinmetz, David C. 'John Calvin as an Interpreter of the Bible'. In *Calvin and the Bible*, edited by Donald K. McKim, 282–91. Cambridge: Cambridge University Press, 2006.

Stenger, Victor J. *God: The Failed Hypothesis*. Amherst: Prometheus Books, 2007.
   The New Atheism. Amherst: Prometheus Books, 2009.
   'What's New About the New Atheism?' *Philosophy Now* April/May 2010: 16–17.
   God and the Folly of Faith. Amherst: Prometheus Books, 2012.

Stenmark, Mikael. *Scientism*. Aldershot: Ashgate, 2001.

Stent, Gunther S. 'Scientific Creationism: Nemesis of Sociobiology'. In *Science and Creationism*, edited by Ashley Montagu, 136–41. Oxford: Oxford University Press, 1984.

Stephen, Leslie. *History of English Thought in the Eighteenth Century*, vol. I. London: Harbinger, 1962.

Stewart, M. A. 'Rational Religion and Common Sense'. In *Thomas Reid: Context, Influence and Significance*, edited by Joseph Houston, 123–60. Edinburgh: Dunedin Academic Press, 2004.

Stillingfleet, Edward. *Origines Sacrae*. Oxford: 1815.

Strassner, Kurt. *Opening Up Genesis*. Leominster: Day One Publications, 2009.

Suderman, Jeffrey M. 'Religion and Philosophy'. In *Scottish Philosophy in the Eighteenth Century*, edited by Aaran Garrett and James A. Harris, 196–238. Oxford: Oxford University Press, 2015.

Sullivan, Robert E. *John Toland and the Deist Controversy*. Cambridge, Mass.: Harvard University Press, 1982.

Suriano, Ben. 'Three Questions on Modern Atheism: An Interview with John Milbank'. In *'God Is Dead' and I Don't Feel So Good Myself*, edited by Andrew David, 58–66. Eugene: Cascade Books, 2010.

Taylor, Charles. *A Secular Age*. Cambridge, Mass., and London: Belknap Press, 2007.

Taylor, Paul F. *The Six Days of Genesis*. Green Forest: Master Books, 2007.

Temple, Frederick. 'The Relations between Science and Religion'. In *Science and Religion in the Nineteenth Century*, edited by Tess Cosslett, 190–216. Cambridge: Cambridge University Press, 1984.

Thomas, Roger. 'Presbyterians in Transition'. In *The English Presbyterians*, edited by C. Gordon Bolam, 113–174. London: George Allan and Unwin, 1968.

Thompson, E. P. *The Making of the English Working Class*. Harmondsworth: Penguin, 1980.

Thompson, Mark D. 'Biblical Interpretation in the Works of Martin Luther'. In *A History of Biblical Interpretation*, vol. II, edited by Allen J. Hauser and Duane Frederick Watson, 299–318. Grand Rapids: William B. Eerdmans, 2009.

Thrower, James. *Western Atheism*. Amherst: Prometheus Books, 2000.

Tillotson, John. *The Rule of Faith*. London, 1666.
  A Sermon Preached at White-Hall. London, 1679.
  A Sermon Concerning the Unity of the Divine Nature and the Blessed Trinity. London, 1693.

Tindal, Matthew. *Christianity as Old as the Creation*. London, 1730.

Toland, John. *Letters to Serena*. London: Bernard Lintot, 1704.
  Christianity not Mysterious. Dublin: Lilliput Press, 1997.

Torrey, Reuben A. *Difficulties in the Bible*. London: James Nisbet, 1900.
  What the Bible Teaches. London: James Nisbet, 1902.

Torrey, Reuben A., and Andrew C. Dixon, eds. *The Fundamentals: A Testimony to the Truth*. Grand Rapids, Baker Books, 1917.

Turner, Denys. *How to Be an Atheist*. Cambridge: Cambridge University Press, 2002.

Turner, James. *Without God, Without Creed*. Baltimore: Johns Hopkins University Press, 1985.

Turner, William. *The Huntyng and Fyndyng Out of the Romish Foxe*. Bonn, 1843.

Tyndale, William. *The Obediéce of a Christen Man*. Norwood: Walter J. Johnson, 1977.

An Answere Vnto Sir Thomas Mores Dialoge. Edited by Anne M. O'Donnell and Jared Wicks. Washington, DC: Catholic University of America Press, 2000.

Upchurch, John. 'Confessions of a Former Atheist'. In *A Pocket Guide to Atheism*, edited by Ken Ham, 83–91. Petersburg: Answers in Genesis, 2014.

Varghese, Roy A., Preface to Anthony Flew, *There Is a God*, vii–xxiv. New York: HarperOne, 2008.

Vernon, Mark. *After Atheism*. London: Palgrave Macmillan, 2007.

Waligore, Joseph. 'The Piety of the English Deists'. *Intellectual History Review* 22, no. 2 (2012): 181–97.

Walsh, John. 'Methodism at the End of the Eighteenth Century'. In *A History of the Methodist Church in Great Britain*, vol. I, edited by Rupert E. Davies and E. Gordon Rupp, 277–315. London: Epworth Press, 1965.

Ward, Keith. *God, Chance and Necessity*. Oxford: Oneworld Publications, 1996.

'The Importance of Liberal Theology'. In *The Future of Liberal Theology*, edited by Mark D. Chapman, 39–53. Aldershot: Ashgate, 2002.

Why There Almost Certainly Is a God. Oxford: Lion Books, 2008.

Warren, Sidney. *American Freethought 1860–1914*. New York: Columbia University Press, 1943.

Waterman, A. M. C. 'The Nexus between Theology and Political Doctrine'. In *Enlightenment and Religion*, edited Knud Haakonssen, 193–218. Cambridge: Cambridge University Press, 1996.

Watkin, Christopher. *Difficult Atheism*. Edinburgh: Edinburgh University Press, 2011.

Watts, Michael R. *The Dissenters*. 3 vols. Oxford: Clarendon Press, 1985–2015.

Webb, R. K. 'The Emergence of Rational Dissent'. In *Enlightenment and Religion*, edited by Knud Haakonssen, 12–41. Cambridge: Cambridge University Press, 1996.

Wells, Jonathan. *Icons of Evolution*. Washington, DC: Regency Publishing, 2000.

Whiston, William. *Essay Towards Restoring the True Text of the Old Testament*. London, 1772.

Whitcomb, John C. *The Early Earth*. Grand Rapids: Baker Book House, 1997.

Whitcomb, John C., and Henry M. Morris. *The Genesis Flood*. Phillipsburg: P&R Publishing, 1961.

White, Andrew D. *A History of the Warfare of Science and Theology*. New York: Dover Publications, 1960.

White, Paul. *Thomas Huxley: Making the 'Man of Science'*. Cambridge: Cambridge University Press, 2007.

White, Peter. 'The Via Media in the Early Stuart Church'. In *Reformation to Revolution*, edited by Margo Todd, 78–94. London: Routledge, 1995.

Wigelsworth, Jeffrey R. *Deism in Enlightenment England*. Manchester: Manchester University Press, 2009.

Wise, Kurt. *Faith, Form and Time*. Nashville: Broadman & Holman, 2002.

Witherspoon, John. *Ecclesiastical Characteristics*. Glasgow, 1753.

Wood, Paul. Introduction to *Thomas Reid on the Animate Creation*, by Thomas Reid, 3–78 Edinburgh: Edinburgh University Press, 1995.

Woodridge, John D. *Biblical Authority: A Critique of the Rogers/McKim Proposal*. Grand Rapids: Zondervan, 1982.

Woolhouse, Roger. 'Locke's Theory of Knowledge'. In *The Cambridge Companion to Locke*, edited by V. C. Chappell, 147–71. Cambridge: Cambridge University Press, 1994.

Young, B. W. *Religion and Enlightenment in Eighteenth-Century England*. Oxford: Clarendon Press, 1998

Young, Davis A. *The Biblical Flood*. Grand Rapids: Eerdmans, 1995.

Young, Don de. *Thousands ... Not Billions*. Green Forest: Master Books, 2006.

Young, Edward J. *In the Beginning*. Edinburgh: Banner of Truth Trust, 1976.

Zenk, Thomas. 'New Atheism'. In *The Oxford Handbook of Atheism*, edited by Stephen Bullivant and Michael Ruse, 245–60. Oxford: Oxford University Press, 2013.

Index